ASIAN MARITIME STRATEGIES

Navigating Troubled Waters

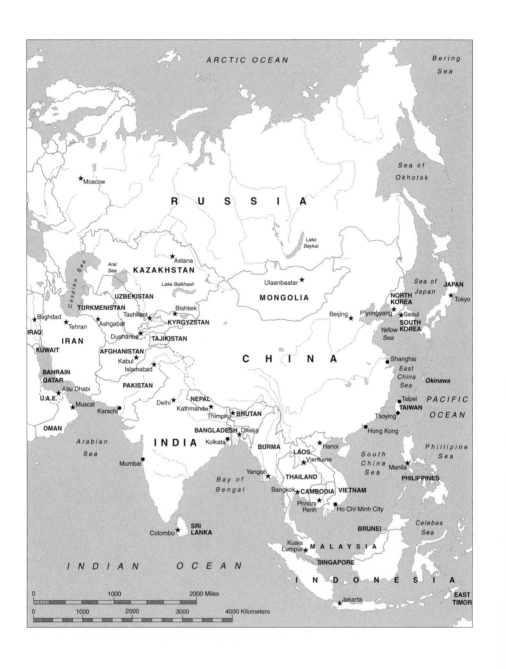

ASIAN MARITIME STRATEGIES

Navigating Troubled Waters

BERNARD D. COLE

NAVAL INSTITUTE PRESS
ANNAPOLIS, MARYLAND

Naval Institute Press
291 Wood Road
Annapolis, MD 21402

Library of Congress Cataloging-in-Publication Data
Cole, Bernard D., 1943-
  Asian maritime strategies : navigating troubled waters / Bernard D. Cole.
    1 online resource.
  Summary: "Asian Maritime Strategies explores one of the world's most complex
and dangerous maritime arenas. Asia, stretching from the Aleutian Islands to
the Persian Gulf, contains the world's busiest trade routes. It is also the scene of
numerous maritime territorial disputes, pirate attacks, and terrorist threats. In
response, the nations of the region are engaged in a nascent naval arms race. In
this new work, Bernard Cole, author of the acclaimed The Great Wall At Sea,
examines the maritime strategies and naval forces of the region's nations, as well
as evaluating the threats and opportunities for cooperation at sea. The United
States Navy is intimately involved in these disputes and opportunities, which
threaten vital American economic, political, and security interests"— Provided by
publisher.
  Includes bibliographical references and index.
  Description based on print version record and CIP data provided by publisher;
resource not viewed.
  ISBN 978-1-61251-313-3 (epub) — ISBN 978-1-61251-313-3 (mobi) — ISBN
978-1-59114-162-4 (hardback) 1. Sea-power—Pacific Area. 2. Sea-power—
Pacific Area—History. 3. Pacific Area—Strategic aspects. 4. Navies—Pacific
Area. 5. Navies—Asia. I. Title.
  VA620
  359'.03095—dc23
                              2013022614

∞Print editions meet the requirements of ANSI/NISO z39.48-1992
(Permanence of Paper).
Printed in the United States of America.

21 20 19 18 17 16 15 14 13   9 8 7 6 5 4 3 2 1
First printing

Contents

Acknowledgments

I researched and wrote this book during a teaching sabbatical granted by the U.S. National Defense University for the 2011–12 academic year; I am grateful to the university president, Vice Adm. Ann Rondeau, USN, and to my commandant at the National War College, Rear Adm. Douglas McAneny, USN, for allowing me that privilege. At the college, Ms. Susan Schindler, Mr. David Pearson, and Ms. JoAnn Monroe were generous with their administrative support. The NDU Library, under the direction of Dr. Meg Tulloch, offered the hospitality of a temporary office and provided its usual superb research support; it remains the finest library with which I have ever worked, staffed with wonderful professionals.

Many U.S. and foreign naval officers and security analysts contributed information and opinions but must remain nameless. I was privileged to serve as a visiting senior scholar during the year at the Center for Naval Analyses, in Arlington, Virginia, where Dr. David Finkelstein welcomed me to his team of China experts. Among them I especially thank Dr. Thomas Bickford, Ms. Maryann Kivlehan, Dr. Scot Tanner, Dr. Albert Willner, Ms. Tamara Hemphill, and Ms. Rebecca Martin. Rear Adm. Michael McDevitt, USN (Ret.), also welcomed me to his delegation to India and continues to inspire as a sailor-scholar.

Several colleagues read parts or all of the manuscript and were generous with suggestions and corrections. These included Maj. Kenneth Allen, USAF (Ret.); Lt. Col. Dennis Blasko, USA (Ret.); Dr. Andrew Erickson; Cdr. Peter Dutton, USN (Ret.); Dr. Paul Godwin; Lt. Col. Roy

Kamphausen, USA (Ret.); Capt. David Mayo, USN; Rear Adm. Eric McVadon, USN (Ret); Dr. Douglas Paal; Col. Susan Puska, USA (Ret.); Capt. Peter Swartz, USN (Ret.); Dr. Cynthia Watson; and Dr. Christopher Yung. I received my usual expert advice and assistance from the staff of the U.S. Naval Institute Press, especially Ms. Susan Brook and freelancer Mr. Pelham Boyer. Of course, all errors or omissions are my responsibility alone. The views in this book are my own and do not represent those of the Center for Naval Analyses, the National Defense University, or any other agency of the U.S. government.

Dr. Paul Godwin, senior member of the U.S. community of People's Liberation Army watchers, continues to serve as mentor and example of what a scholar should be. My biggest debt is to my companion and inspiration, Dr. Cynthia Watson, to whom this book is dedicated.

Acronyms and Abbreviations

A2/AD	anti-access/area denial
AAW	antiair warfare
ACD	Asia Cooperation Dialogue
ADB	Asia Development Bank
ADIZ	air defense identification zone
ADMM	ASEAN Defense Ministers' Meeting
ADMM+	ASEAN Defense Ministers' Meeting Plus
AH	hospital ship
AIP	air-independent propulsion
AIS	automatic identification system
ALB	Air-Land Battle
AMF	ASEAN Maritime Forum
AMS	Academy of Military Science
AMW	amphibious warfare
ANZUS	Australia–New Zealand–United States
AO	oiler
AOR	oiler and ordnance resupply ship; area of responsibility
APEC	Asia-Pacific Economic Cooperation
ARF	ASEAN Regional Forum
ASB	Air-Sea Battle

ASBM	antiship ballistic missile
ASCM	antiship cruise missile
ASEAN	Association of Southeast Asian Nations
ASEAN+3	ASEAN Plus Three
ASEM	Asia-Europe Meeting
ASUW	antisurface warfare
ASW	antisubmarine warfare
AUSCANNZUKUS	Australia–Canada–New Zealand–United Kingdom–United States
BBLS	barrels
BIMSTEC	Bay of Bengal Initiative for Multisectoral Technical and Economic Cooperation
BN	Bangladesh navy
C4ISR	command, control, communications, computers, intelligence, surveillance, and reconnaissance
CARAT	Cooperation Afloat Readiness and Training
CCP	Chinese Communist Party
CEC	cooperative engagement capability
CFC	Combined Forces Command
CLCS	Commission on the Limits of the Continental Shelf
CMC	Central Military Commission
CMS	China Maritime Surveillance
CNO	Chief of Naval Operations
COLREGS	International Regulations for Preventing Collisions at Sea
COTS	commercial off-the-shelf
CS	continental shelf
CS-21	*Cooperative Strategy for 21st Century Seapower*
CSI	Container Security Initiative
CTF	Combined Task Force
C-TPAT	Customs-Trade Partnership against Terrorism
CVN	nuclear-powered aircraft carrier
CZ	contiguous zone
DDG	guided-missile destroyer
DOD	Department of Defense

DOS	Department of State
DPG	Defense Program Guidelines
DPP	Democratic Progressive Party
DPRK	Democratic People's Republic of [North] Korea
DRP	Defense Reform 307 Plan
EALAF	East Asia–Latin America Forum
EAS	East Asia Summit
EEZ	exclusive economic zone
EU	European Union
EW	electronic warfare
FBM	fleet ballistic missile
FFG	guided-missile frigate
FLEC	Fisheries Law Enforcement Command
FPDA	Five-Power Defense Agreement
GCC	Gulf Cooperation Council (Cooperation Council for the Arab States of the Gulf)
GDP	gross domestic product
GFS	Global Fleet Station
GOA	Gulf of Aden
HA/DR	humanitarian assistance and disaster relief
HNS	host-nation support
HUK	Hukbalahap
ICBM	intercontinental ballistic missile
ICG	Indian Coast Guard
IJN	Imperial Japanese Navy
IMB	International Maritime Bureau
IMF	International Money Fund
IMO	International Maritime Organization
IN	Indian navy
INS	Indian Naval Service
IO	information operations
IONS	Indian Ocean Naval Symposium
IOR	Indian Ocean region
IOR-ARC	Indian Ocean Rim Association for Regional Cooperation

IOZP	Indian Ocean Zone of Peace Declaration
IPCL	International Peace Cooperation Law
IRGCN	Islamic Revolutionary Guard Corps Navy
IRIN	Islamic Republic of Iran Navy
ISA	International Seabed Authority
ISC	Information Sharing Center
ISO	International Shipping Organization
ISPS	International Ship and Port Security
IT	information technology
ITLOS	International Tribunal for the Law of the Sea
IW	information warfare
JASDF	Japan Air Self-Defense Force
JCG	Japan Coast Guard
JDF	Japan Defense Force
JMSDF	Japan Maritime Self-Defense Force
JOAC	Joint Operational Access Concept
JSDF	Japan Self-Defense Force
KMT	Kuomintang
KTS	knots
LDP	Liberal Democratic Party
LHD	landing helicopter dock
LIMO	low-intensity maritime operations
LPD	landing platform dock
LROD	long-range overseas deployment
LSCI	Liner Shipping Connectivity Index
LSD	landing ship dock
LST	landing ship tank
LTTE	Liberation Tigers of Tamil Eelam
LY	Taiwan Legislative Yuan
MAD	mutually assured destruction
MALSINDO	Malaysia-Singapore-Indonesia
MARPOL	International Convention for the Prevention of Pollution from Ships
MCG	Maldives Coast Guard
MDA	maritime domain awareness

MGOS	maintaining good order at sea
MGP	Mekong Ganga Project
MMCA	Military Maritime Consultative Agreement
MNDF	Maldives National Defense Force
MOFA	Ministry of Foreign Affairs
MOOTW	military operations other than war
MTSA	Maritime Transportation Security Act
NATO	North Atlantic Treaty Organization
NDPO	National Defense Program Outline
NEO	noncombatant evacuation operations
NFU	no first use
NIDS	National Institute of Defense Studies
nm	nautical mile
NOC	*Naval Operational Concept*
NPA	New People's Army
NPAP	Northwest Pacific Action Plan
OPV	offshore patrol vessel
OSD	Office of the Secretary of Defense
PACOM	U.S. Pacific Command
PBSC	Politburo Standing Committee
PEMSEA	Partnership in Environmental Management for the Seas of East Asia
PLA	People's Liberation Army
PLAAF	People's Liberation Army Air Force
PLAN	People's Liberation Army Navy
PN	Pakistan navy
PRC	People's Republic of China
PSB	Public Security Bureau
PSI	Proliferation Security Initiative
RAN	Royal Australian Navy
RAS	replenishment at sea
ReCAAP	Regional Cooperation Agreement on Combating Piracy and Armed Robbery against Ships
RHIB	rigid-hull inflatable boat
RNZN	Royal New Zealand Navy

ROE	rules of engagement
ROK	Republic of South Korea
ROKN	Republic of South Korea Navy
RP	Republic of the Philippines
SAARC	South Asian Association for Regional Cooperation
SAR	search and rescue
SCG	Seychelles Coast Guard
SCO	Shanghai Cooperation Organization
SLOC	sea line of communication
SOA	State Oceanic Administration
SOLAS	Safety of Life at Sea
SOP	standard operating procedure
SS	submarine
SSBN	ballistic-missile nuclear-powered submarine
SSN	nuclear-powered attack submarine
SUA	Convention for the Suppression of Unlawful Acts against the Safety of Maritime Navigation
TEU	twenty-foot-equivalent unit
TN	Taiwan navy
TPP	Trans-Pacific Partnership
TRA	Taiwan Relations Act
UAV	unmanned aerial vehicle
UN	United Nations
UNCLOS	United Nations Convention on the Law of the Sea
UNODC	United Nations Office on Drugs and Crime
UNPKO	United Nations peacekeeping operation
USCG	U.S. Coast Guard
USN	U.S. Navy
USSR	Union of Soviet Socialist Republics
VLS	vertical-launch system
WIO	western Indian Ocean
WMD	weapons of mass destruction
WTO	World Trade Organization

INTRODUCTION

The sea is a boundless expanse whereon great ships look like tiny specks; naught but the heavens above and the waters beneath; . . . [t]rust it little. Fear it much. Man at sea is but a worm on a bit of wood, now engulfed, now scared to death.

AMRU BIN AL-'AS

T his book is concerned with both the national security concerns of Asian maritime nations and the security of the Asian maritime commons.[1] These "commons" are defined as the Pacific and Indian Oceans and associated seas, bays, and gulfs, with their included sea lines of communication (SLOCs).[2] The most useful geographical designation for maritime Asia is the "Indo-Pacific." Myanmar perhaps symbolizes this duality: a member of the Association of Southeast Asian Nations (ASEAN) but otherwise considered a South Asian state.

Asia's maritime commons form the background for examining the maritime strategies, strengths, and weaknesses of the states bordering on Asia's littoral. We will focus on the United States, China, Japan, and India; our assessment will also deal with regional navies in North, Southeast, and South Asia. These tableaux will then frame discussion of potential incidents of conflict and cooperation on Asia's seas.

The maritime strategies of the Asian powers are designed primarily to defend their homelands and associated vital national security interests on the oceans and seas. Ensuring a nation's ability to use the maritime commons is a standard secondary priority.

Discussions among many strategists, especially in the United States, have focused on the concept of the "global commons." That phrase usually is divided into maritime, space, and cyber spheres. While a characteristic of the post–Cold War period—an era of peace among the world's major powers—defense of the global commons will always be secondary, for any state, to that of the homeland. That said, maritime security issues in Asia are consistently rising in national importance; furthermore, national maritime awareness and claimed jurisdictions are extending seaward.

These issues include nontraditional naval missions, which address maintaining the security of the commons against threats such as the proliferation of weapons of mass destruction (WMD), piracy and international criminal activity, and terrorism, as well as the performance of humanitarian assistance and disaster relief ashore. They require the efforts of both navies and littoral maritime forces—usually called coast guards.

East Asia since the 1960s has been the scene of remarkable economic growth. Japan led the way, followed during the next decades by South Korea, Taiwan, Indonesia, Singapore, Malaysia, and Thailand. China has set the standard for the past thirty years.

Disruptions have occurred, such as Japan's two decades of economic problems, the early 1990s slowdown, the 1997 Asian economic crisis, and the 2008 global recession. China's remarkable economic growth did not begin until the early 1980s. Overall, however, the growth of most Asian economies during the past forty years has been remarkable. This phenomenon has included efforts to modernize the maritime forces necessary to safeguard the increased economic stakes in the maritime arena.

This period has also seen the rapid development of naval technology, which has required increasing investment in the modernization of seagoing forces, especially for the important missions of surveillance, search, and localization. This means gaining awareness of activities in a specific ocean area; searching that area to detect unidentified aircraft, ships, or submarines; and then being able to pinpoint them to the degree necessary for targeting with weapons.

Finally, the recent major environmental disasters that have struck Asian nations—Bangladesh in 1991, Southeast and South Asia in 2004–5, Japan in 2011, and the frequent typhoons that strike the Philippines, Taiwan, China, and other nations—have increased the profile and importance of possessing maritime forces capable of supporting humanitarian relief efforts ashore.

This book also addresses an aspect of the larger geopolitical issue described by Niall Ferguson as "the end of 500 years of western ascendancy."[3] This in turn assumes that Asia will continue rapidly to gain geopolitical and economic influence in the future. This is a problematic assumption—one must remember the mid-1980s prognostications for Japan—but in 2013 Asia's progress and promise are undeniable, as is the essentially maritime character of that region.

THE MARITIME SCENE

The fact that the earth's surface is mostly water is not as important as the way in which that water continues to dominate relations among people, nations, and the international organizations they have formed over the millennia. The oceans provide the most important medium for both peacetime and wartime activities, from trade to existential national conflict.

In the Asian maritime theater, encompassing the Pacific and Indian Oceans, maritime conflict has been highlighted in modern times by several seminal events. One is the massive Mongol attempt in the thirteenth century to invade Japan; its failure, due primarily to environmental disruption, attests to the power of nature in the maritime arena.[4]

Second is the early fifteenth-century voyages of Zheng He, the great Chinese Muslim explorer; his fall from favor in the Ming court and China's voluntary ceding of world maritime leadership are unique in history and certainly contributed to the eventual downfall of imperial China.[5] Zheng He's downfall evidences the power of domestic political will on maritime usage. Third is the Western subjugation of most of maritime Asia by virtue of European maritime power. European navies dominated the Indo-Pacific from as early as the late eighteenth century and were not displaced until the Japanese naval onslaught of 1941 and 1942.

Fourth is the world's greatest war, which for eastern Asia lasted fifteen years, from 1931 to 1945. The most intense phase of this conflict was the largely maritime struggle from 1941 to 1945 between the great Japanese and U.S. navies. Fifth, and most enduring, is the ocean's foundational role in sustaining the commercial and economic life of the nations of East and South Asia, a role that continues.

History's great wars end; man's economic dependence on the oceans does not. Today's Asia features the world's top three economies (the United States, China, and Japan); the world's largest democracy (India, also an economic power); the oft-described "tigers" (including South Korea and Singapore); and the modern if flawed economies of Indonesia, Vietnam, Taiwan, Malaysia, and Thailand. The United States, still the world's largest economic power, exerts massive influence throughout Asia, while the European Union, Australia, Canada, and Russia are also significant players in Asia's economic life. All of these economies, independently and complementarily, depend on the sea-lanes for their well-being.

ASIA DEFINED

Asia is the major part of the Eurasian landmass, the largest "island" on a globe that is more than 70 percent "maritime"—covered by water. Eurasia was a focus of Halford Mackinder, a British geographer who in 1904 wrote *Democratic Ideals and Reality*, a seminal work in which he described the Eurasian supercontinent as the "World-Island." It contained the world's "Heartland" and the "pivot" of global power. Mackinder offered the following syllogism in 1919: "Who rules Eastern Europe commands the Heartland; who rules the Heartland commands the World-Island; who rules the World-Island commands the world." He averred that the world had evolved into a closed system, interpreting history as largely a contest between continental and maritime powers; he further argued that the advent of railroads (and presumably airplanes) had irrevocably shifted the strategic balance in favor of the continental nations.

An American geostrategist, Nicholas Spykman, further developed Mackinder's ideas but arrived at a dissimilar conclusion. Writing during World War II, he speculated about power projection into and out of the heartland. Whereas Mackinder assumed that geographical formations made access easiest from the center, Spykman argued that the littoral areas of the heartland, or what he called the "rimland," were key to controlling the world. He updated Mackinder, positing, "Who controls the Rimland rules Eurasia; who rules Eurasia controls the destinies of the world."

The Crimean War and the lesser wars of the second half of the nineteenth century, which were relatively localized conflicts, influenced

Mackinder, while Spykman lived from 1893 to 1943 and witnessed global war. Both, however, were focused on control of the Eurasian supercontinent, home to many of the world's leading industrial and energy-consuming countries during the nineteenth and much of the twentieth centuries.

Spykman was a political scientist by training but believed geography was "the most fundamentally conditioning factor because of its relative permanence" and should be considered a prime motivator of a nation's national security strategy.[6] During the Cold War (1947–90), the United States led an anticommunist strategy of containment focused on the Soviet Union; that campaign may fairly be described as a Western attempt to use the oceanic rimlands to control the continental heartland, which was dominated by Russia and China.

This Cold War construct may accurately be rephrased for the twenty-first century as using sea power to control land power. The Eurasian supercontinent today remains dominated by Russia and China, with India a rapidly rising force on that same landmass.

Japan is the Asian nation most dependent on the maritime commons, followed by the insular countries of Southeast Asia: Taiwan, the Philippines, Indonesia, Brunei, Singapore, Malaysia, Australia, New Zealand, and the small island states of the South and Southwest Pacific. The Indian Ocean maritime states of Bangladesh, Sri Lanka, India, and Pakistan abut the Persian Gulf states, led by Iran. Perhaps most important from an Asian perspective is that the United States, although not geographically an Asian nation, is so powerful a maritime power that it dominates the rimlands.

This position as the dominant power is neither limitless nor timeless. China's rise as a naval and commercial sea power is a fact of the twenty-first century; in India, similar modernization and potential for expansion of maritime presence may finally be reaching maturity. Japan is already a sea power, while Russia retains the resources to reemerge as an Asian maritime power should Moscow decide seriously to pursue that path. Meanwhile, U.S. preoccupation with the so-called global war on terror and economic perturbations, along with shrinkage of its naval and merchant fleets, all indicate the limits and even vulnerability of American power.

The United States made economic forays into Asian waters in the late eighteenth century, deployed its first warships to the region in the

1830s, and debuted as an Asian and world power as the twentieth century dawned, with the vanquishing of Spain. The century ended with the United States established as a superpower stronger than any other in the history of the world.

The twenty-first century has begun with a revitalized and prospering Asia; the economic "tigers" that developed during the later part of the previous century were severely damaged by the vicissitudes of the 1990s but remain important economic and political actors. They have been overshadowed, however, by China's unprecedented economic growth during the past quarter century. Only Japan (and possibly India) among Asian nations has the potential to match China in economic and military terms. Both Japan and India are crucial participants in the Asian energy calculus of availability, affordability, and security.

China and Russia alone among the Northeast Asian states possess significant indigenous supplies of oil, natural gas, and coal; both have been developing their huge energy reserves. Japan, South and North Korea, and Taiwan possess very limited energy resources, even as their need for energy increases dramatically. India's accelerating economic development increasingly positions it with Japan and China among the world's most voracious energy consumers. All are located in a region usefully described as a continental "heartland" bordered by a maritime "rimland."

GEOGRAPHY

Asia is delineated by a series of geographic features, beginning in the northeast with Russia's Kamchatka Peninsula and the Kurile Islands extending to the south; next, beyond the Soya, or La Perouse, Strait lie Japan's four large main islands and the Ryukyu Islands, extending southward beyond the Tsushima Strait.

The Ryukyus point south-southwest to the disputed Senkaku Islands (Diaoyutais, to the Chinese) and then to Taiwan. The Taipei government, whose territorial claims conform to those of Beijing's, claims and occupies the islands of Mazu and Jinmen, as well as the Penghus, all lying between Taiwan and China.

Sea of Okhotsk and Southward

The Sea of Okhotsk is bounded almost entirely by Russian territory: the Kamchatka Peninsula to the north and northeast, the Siberian coast to the west, and the Kurile Islands to the east. The northernmost Japanese home island, Hokkaido, forms the sea's southern boundary. Okhotsk's most significant feature is the large island of Sakhalin, with its huge off-shore natural-gas fields.

This sea is relatively deep, reaching nearly two thousand fathoms, often icebound during the winter; during the Cold War it served Moscow as a haven in which fleet ballistic-missile submarines operated as the sea-borne leg of the Soviet nuclear deterrent triad. This capability remains a strategic factor, as does the Russo-Japanese sovereignty dispute over the southern Kurile Islands: Iturup, Kunashir, and Shikotan, and the Habomai islets. Tokyo calls these islands the Northern Territories; they were never permanently inhabited, but they embody Japanese national pride. Moscow places a more strategic value on the islands, since with the rest of the Kuriles chain they protect the Sea of Okhotsk and turn it almost into a Russian lake.

Immediately to the south-southwest, the Soya (La Perouse) Strait lies between Hokkaido and the Russian island of Sakhalin, marking the northern boundary of the second major Asian maritime basin, the Sea of Japan, called the East Sea by Korea. This strait will increase in importance as the natural-gas fields in the waters around southern Sakhalin Island become increasingly productive, with Japan as the future primary customer. The Sakhalin project is planned to comprise six phases of development, with Korea, possibly China, and other nations eventually sharing in the vast natural-gas reserves that lie in the waters off the long island. Some energy is already being produced in Phase One of the project, but major benefits to Japan are unlikely to be realized before 2015.[7]

South of, and dividing Hokkaido from, the Japanese main island of Honshu is the Tsugaru Strait, connecting the Sea of Japan and the North Pacific Ocean. The Tsugaru is a primary SLOC for merchant shipping following the great-circle route from the west coasts of the United States and Canada to Korean and Russian ports, as well as to ports on Japan's west coast. It is a sensitive military choke point from Tokyo's perspective, guarding the country's northern islands and the Sea of Japan.

The Ryukyus are Japan's southernmost island group, stretching southwest to within a hundred nautical miles of Taiwan. Their area of 2,200 square miles is largely accounted for by Okinawa, Miyako, and Ishigaki, as is the population of approximately one million. The Ryukyu Kingdom was a Chinese tributary state from 1372 to 1609, when it was seized by Japan; in 1869 it was annexed by Tokyo. The Ryukyus' Japanese sovereignty is not formally challenged, despite this history and the (unlikely) possibility of a Chinese claim.

The Tsushima Strait, lying between the southern Japanese island of Kyushu and the Korean Peninsula, pierces the Sea of Japan's southern boundary. It is divided by Tsushima Island, as well as by a very small group of land features. This bit of disputed territory—little more than a collection of rocks—is called Dokdo by Korea and Takeshima by Japan and lies just north of Tsushima. Korea, as noted previously, disputes the very name of this sea, insisting on calling it the East Sea. From South Korea's perspective the Tsushima Strait also serves as a reminder of the deeply despised Japanese aggression and colonization early in the twentieth century.

The Yellow Sea, called the West Sea by Korea, forms the ocean basin across the Korean Peninsula from the Sea of Japan. It lies northwest of Tsushima and is bounded by the Korean Peninsula and China. Although the sea is claimed in its entirety by Beijing, both North and South Korea dispute exact maritime boundaries with China. This relatively shallow sea, with an average depth of just twenty-four fathoms, has important economic and military value for China; hence, any maritime disputes involving lines of demarcation or resources there draw Beijing's immediate attention.

The Yellow Sea also continues to be the scene of significant disputes between North Korea and South Korea. These involve nationalboundary, fishery, and defense concerns that occasionally degenerate into naval clashes, with death and destruction inflicted on both sides. Seoul and Pyongyang disagree on this sea border, and armed clashes continue between the two navies; the most serious occurred in 2010, when a North Korean torpedo sank a South Korean corvette, *Cheonan*.[8]

The East China Sea is the maritime basin lying south of Korea, southwest of Japan, and west of the Ryukyus, between the Yellow and the Philippine Seas. The East China Sea stretches south from Tsushima to Taiwan, which is separated from China by the Taiwan Strait. The legal status of this channel, no more than 105 nautical miles (nm) at its widest point, is part and parcel of the Taiwan issue. The strait is marked by shallows and shipwrecks, and notoriously susceptible to unpredictable weather changes.

The North Pacific Ocean is the name given to the swath of the Pacific lying to the east of Japan and the Kurile Islands and extending northward to the Kamchatka Peninsula and the Aleutian Islands chain. These northern waters are renowned for fog and rough seas, especially during the winter months. The western Pacific Ocean south and east of the Ryukyus and Taiwan is the Philippine Sea. It stretches eastward to a line approximately two thousand nautical miles from the Asian mainland and its important archipelagos. This sea thus includes the U.S. Marianas Islands and the semi-independent island states of Micronesia. The Philippine Sea is notoriously susceptible to powerful typhoons, which cause devastating flooding throughout the region's nations.

The Philippine archipelago lies south of Taiwan, beyond the Luzon Strait. This strait extends two hundred nautical miles from the southernmost tip of Taiwan to the main Philippine island of Luzon; the Batanes and Babuyan island groups divide it into a series of channels. The main channels are the Bashi in the north of the strait, Balintang in the center, and Babuyan in the south. The Republic of the Philippines includes over seven thousand islands extending 1,200 nm to the south, ending in the disputed state of Sabah on the island of Borneo, which is also claimed by Malaysia.

The Philippines form the eastern boundary of the South China Sea, which it calls the West Sea, separating it from the Philippine Sea and the vast expanses of the Pacific Ocean. Deep waters and plentiful fisheries mark the South China Sea.

Several important straits link this sea with the Philippine Sea; the most notable of these, from north to south, and running west to east, are first the San Bernardino Strait, opening to the Pacific between Luzon to the north and Samar to the south, reached after first circumnavigating Mindoro to gain access to the heart of the archipelago. Second is the Surigao Strait, running between the islands of Leyte to the north and Mindanao to the south to reach the Pacific after first transiting the Bohol Sea south of the islands of Negros, Cebu, and Bohol. The third main transit route through the Philippines runs through the Sulu and Celebes

Seas, south of Mindanao through the Sarangani Strait or farther offshore to reach the Pacific.

The Philippine Islands lead directly to the Indonesian archipelago, which is marked at its eastern extremity by the many islands of the Moluccas group and then stretches westward across the important Makassar Strait to the large island of Borneo. Approximately two-thirds of this island is sovereign Indonesian territory, but Borneo also hosts the large eastern part of Malaysia and the small sultanate of Brunei. Indonesia itself is the world's largest island nation, with an archipelago of more than 14,000 islands, of which between six and seven thousand are inhabited. The great island chain extends approximately three thousand nautical miles east to west across the southern end of the South China Sea.

Several important straits running north–south mark the Indonesian archipelago. From east to west, these are, first, the Flores Strait, through the Lesser Sunda Islands, with the islands of Sumbawa to the west and Flores and Sumba to the east; second, the Lombok Strait, between Bali and Lombok; and third, the Sunda Strait, between the islands of Sumatra and Java. Other SLOCs are available just east of Indonesia, between Timor and New Guinea, running north–south through the Timor, Banda, and Molucca Seas.

The waters lying between Indonesia, Singapore, and Malaysia are commonly referred to as the Malacca Strait but actually include both Malacca and Singapore Straits. They form the most sensitive choke point in maritime Asia. The Malacca Strait, more than four hundred nautical miles long, narrows to 1.5 nm near Singapore, where it also shoals to a depth of sixty-two feet, thus limiting the passage of supertankers.

Approximately 40 percent of total world trade, including a good deal of the petroleum imported by Japan, South Korea, China, and Taiwan, passes through these narrows. Malacca is the most important shipping lane in the world, more important than either the Suez or Panama Canal in terms of geopolitical significance, as well as the number of ship and amount of tonnage it supports.

It is the main ship route between the Pacific and Indian Oceans, directly linking Southwest, South, and Southeast Asia with Northeast Asia. It is actively threatened by piracy and terrorism; its geopolitical importance means that it is potentially at risk in the event of major military conflict anywhere along the Asian rimland. This choke point lies on the direct trade routes on which India, China, Japan, South Korea, and the other Indo-Pacific nations depend for their international economic livelihoods.

Seventy-five thousand transits by 8,678 seagoing vessels were made through Malacca in 2006, carrying 3 billion metric tons of cargo, which equated to almost 25 percent of the world's maritime trade and had a value of US$390 billion. This includes more than 25 percent of the world's shipborne oil, approximately 12 million barrels daily in 2006, an amount that is increasing in direct proportion to Asian energy consumption.[9]

Such narrow straits obviously increase the risk of ship collisions and groundings; forty-four of the former and fifteen of the latter occurred between 1995 and 2005, with one observer estimating that this number will "increase dramatically" as transit passages of the Malacca and Singapore Straits increase over the 94,000 recorded in 2004. The trend—that traffic increased by 61 percent between 1999 and 2007—may lead to the volume of cargo growing to 6.4 billion tonnes carried by 141,000 ships in 2020. Such startling figures underline the straits' importance as security, economic, and environmental issues.

Indian Ocean

West of the Malacca Strait lies the Indian Ocean, the third-largest body of water in the world, after the Atlantic and Pacific Oceans. It is bounded on the east by Thailand, Malaysia, Indonesia, and Australia; on the north by the Indian subcontinent and other South Asian nations; on the west by the Arabian Peninsula and Africa; and on the south by Antarctica and its associated ocean. The Indian Ocean's littoral is divided into the Andaman Sea, Bay of Bengal, Arabian Sea, the Gulfs of Aden and Oman, the Red Sea and the Persian (or Arabian) Gulf, and smaller associated bodies of water. The Indian Ocean's weather cycle is marked from approximately May to October by the Southwest Monsoon, which brings with it high winds, rain, and seas ten feet or higher on a daily basis.

The Malacca Strait empties to the west into the Andaman Sea, bounded by Thailand and Malaysia to the east and Burma to the north. It contains the Andaman and the Nicobar Islands, two small Indian archipelagos that provide New Delhi with naval outposts close to the Malacca Strait.

The Andaman Sea serves as entry to the easternmost of the two great basins into which the northern Indian Ocean is divided. This is the Bay of Bengal, lying north and west of the Andaman Sea and framed by India to the west, Bangladesh to the north, and Burma to the east. This is a tragic body of water, heavily trafficked by small merchant and fishing vessels and all too often the scene of piracy and massive, devastating cyclones.

Lying directly south of India is the Chagos Archipelago, with Diego Garcia the group's major atoll. Although claimed by both Seychelles and Mauritius, these small islands are administered by Great Britain, which has, de facto, ceded Diego Garcia to the United States as a naval facility, logistics hub, and strategic air base. Their value to the American employment of military force in Southwest Asia cannot be overestimated.

The Indian Ocean contains several insular nations. Sri Lanka lies less than thirty nautical miles off India's southeast coast; it is still recovering from the effects of a vicious, decades-long civil war that ended in 2009, a conflict that even direct Indian political and military intervention was unable to resolve. The island nation of Maldives lies 348 nm southwest of Sri Lanka. Seychelles, Mauritius, the Comoros, and Madagascar are other Indian Ocean island states. The former two are in the central Indian Ocean, while the latter pair lie just off the East African coast. None of these island states possesses significant economic potential or military strength, but all have energy-security concerns and play roles in Indian Ocean geopolitics.

The Indian Ocean's other major basin is the northern Arabian Sea, which lies to the west of the subcontinent. This sea leads to the Persian Gulf through the Strait of Hormuz and to the Red Sea (and the Suez Canal) through the Bab el-Mandeb Strait.

The Strait of Hormuz narrows at one point to less than eighteen nautical miles and is bounded on the north by Iran, with Oman and the United Arab Emirates (UAE) to the south. Hormuz is the only route for seaborne oil transport from the rich oil fields of the Persian Gulf nations, including Iraq and Kuwait. Saudi Arabia ships most of its oil from its Persian Gulf ports but also borders the eastern side of the thousand-nautical-mile-long Red Sea, which the fourteen-nautical-mile-wide Bab el-Mandeb connects to the Arabian Sea, between the Arabian Peninsula and the African continent. Although the major Saudi Arabian oil port of Yanbu is located on it, the Red Sea is chiefly important as the waterway that connects Asia to Europe, through the Suez Canal and the Mediterranean Sea.

Small islands in their channels further constrict the Hormuz and Bab el-Mandeb. These islands both complicate sovereignty disputes in the area and provide potential military bases for organized militaries and nonstate groups seeking to disrupt the flow of oil to East Asia. Over 90 percent of Persian Gulf oil exports pass through Hormuz. The Gulf region suffers from very high heat and severe sandstorms, both of which can deleteriously affect ship operations.

Choke Points

As noted for these two straits, threats to Asian's maritime nations are focused on "choke points," where the seas narrow to such a degree as to be amenable to blockade or the interception of transiting vessels by naval forces. The great maritime expanse from the northeastern to the southwestern extremities of the Asian continent is marked by many of the world's most important navigational choke points: the straits of the Kuriles, Soya (La Perouse), Tsugaru, Korea (Tsushima), those through the Ryukyus, Taiwan, Luzon, San Bernardino, Surigao, Torres (between Australia and New Guinea, east of Indonesia), Sunda, Lombok, and Malacca, in addition to Hormuz and Bab el-Mandeb. Less obvious but on this list are the Six and Nine Degree Channels in the Indian Ocean.

All are heavily traveled by seaborne traffic; most of them are vital to the flow of petroleum from the world's center for those energy reserves in southwestern Asia to the South and Northeast Asian economic giants of India, China, Japan, and Korea. Southwest Asia remains the world's petroleum "breadbasket," a situation unlikely to change before the mid-century (at the earliest) realization of the potential contained in Russian Siberia and the multinational Caspian Basin in Central Asia. Southwest Asian energy supplies, in turn, depend on seaborne transport to reach their global markets. The same dependence applies to African, Canadian, and Latin American oil; Southeast Asian natural gas; and Australian and North American coal.

This great Asian maritime sweep from the far northwestern Pacific Ocean to the Red Sea includes more than half of the earth's surface. Seaborne commerce dominates its international economic life, both in the bulk cargo now largely carried in containers and in the Southeast and Southwest Asian energy supplies so increasingly crucial to the economic powers of East Asia. The distances of the SLOCs that cross these seas are impressive—up to five thousand nautical miles between Shanghai and the Persian Gulf, for instance.[10]

In addition to their length, the Asian SLOCs traverse a very complex geographical environment. Despite the great distances involved, few areas of the Asian seas are remote from continental or insular landmasses.

The length and geographical complexity of these SLOCs pose severe challenges to both their defense and attempts to intercept their merchant traffic. The sensitivity of the navigational choke points is due not solely to their width—although all are much narrower than the seas or other bodies of water they connect—but also to their location on major SLOCs. For example, in 2011 approximately 88 million barrels of oil were produced globally each day. Seventeen million of those barrels transited the Strait of Hormuz, while approximately 14 million were carried through the Malacca and Singapore Straits.[11]

Commercial sea power is even more important at the beginning of the twenty-first century than it was at the end of the nineteenth, when petroleum began to gain world prominence. The United States uses approximately one-quarter of daily global petroleum production, but the rapid rise of China, as a global economic power surpassing Japan, has already constrained U.S. influence over the price and supply of oil.

Thousands of islands, some of them nation-states but many under clouds of disputed sovereignty, mark Asia's maritime rimland. These disputes include Russia and Japan over the southern Kuriles; Korea and Japan over Dokdo-Takeshima; China and Japan over Daoyutai-Senkaku Shoto; China and Taiwan; China, Vietnam, the Philippines, Indonesia, Brunei, and Malaysia over South China Sea land features, primarily the Paracels and Spratlys; the Philippines and Malaysia over Sabah; Indonesia and Malaysia over Ambalat Island; Great Britain, Mauritius, and Seychelles over the Chagos Archipelago; Iran and the UAE over Abu Musa and Tomb Islands.

Geography rarely changes. The geopolitical importance of energy-resource locations, fisheries, SLOCs and the straits, distances and depths, coastal contours, and ocean-bottom gradients are all factors that contribute to defining Asia's maritime arena—and its political and military fate. In 1941 the American publisher Henry Luce declared the world's first "American century."[12] As the son of missionaries in China, Luce likely would have agreed with current descriptions of the twenty-first century as "Asia's." While the center of global economic gravity may be described as now residing in East Asia, the analogy fails on comparison of the still-powerful United States, a single nation, with the disparate countries that make up the Indo-Pacific.

MARITIME STRATEGY DEFINED:
MAHAN, CORBETT, AUBE

Formalized, modern maritime strategy began in the mid to late nineteenth century, as Great Britain's century of dominance at sea was challenged first by France, then by the United States and Germany. Three main schools of maritime strategic thought were represented by the writings of an American, Adm. Alfred Thayer Mahan; a British strategist, Sir Julian S. Corbett; and a French naval officer, Adm. Theophile Aube. These strategic concepts proved effective in the Pacific and Indian Oceans during the twentieth century.

Mahan and Corbett both wrote of "command of the sea." The former approached that condition more as an absolute, tied to the ability of a nation's navy to triumph in battle against an opponent's fleet. Corbett treated command of the sea as an equally valuable, but possibly transitory, limited condition to be achieved as "control of passage and communication"—or in the more modern term, "sea control."

In either's view, command of the sea was perhaps most usefully defined as a nation's ability to use the sea as it wishes while denying that use to its enemy, without stipulating geographic or temporal scope of "command." Aube believed France's most effective use of its navy was in attacking the commerce of an imperial enemy. Submarines most effectively demonstrated this theory during World Wars I and II.

Mahan was a career naval officer and a founding professor at the new U.S. Naval War College in the 1880s. His magnum opus was published in 1890; *The Influence of Sea Power upon History, 1660–1783* was a discourse on Great Britain's preeminence as the world's leading sea power, from which the author derived strategic principles. He addressed politics, economics, and naval power in arguing that sea power is essential to national greatness. Mahan wrote eighteen books over a two-decade period, and his thoughts did not remain static; his development of maritime strategic thought is more complex than popularly thought.

Furthermore, "Mahan is, and will always remain, the point of reference and departure for any work upon 'sea power.'"[13]

He theorized that sea power played and would continue to play a decisive role in international relations. Mahan's economic argument was that a nation's prosperity depends on international trade, including secure sea lines of communication. This security, he believed, requires a powerful navy, which a nation could afford only if its economy prospered—and vice versa.

As a strategist, Mahan presented principles he believed immutable. He is sometimes classified as a follower of Antoine de Jomini, who analyzed and wrote about land warfare strategy in the Napoleonic era—and who was deeply studied by Mahan's father, Dennis Hart Mahan, a professor at the U.S. Military Academy at West Point. But the younger Mahan did not agree with Jomini's formulism when it came to command, believing that wartime command of the sea could not be prescribed by a system of rules.

Mahan differentiated between naval power and maritime power. In his view, the former—nationally organized warships—was a subset of the latter, to which he ascribed three factors. First, strong maritime economic factors—production, shipping, colonies—were "key to national prosperity." Second, history demonstrated that these factors required "naval supremacy" for their defense. Third, a nation's ability to develop strong maritime power rested on six requirements: geographical position, physical conformation, extent of territory, population size, national culture, and political structure.[14]

Mahan emphasized the principle of concentrating a navy's strength, of never dividing the fleet in the face of an enemy. This would facilitate victory in the climactic battle with the enemy fleet envisioned by Mahan. He did not favor either commerce raiding or amphibious warfare, because he thought that neither could be decisive. Mahan did believe, however, that a navy's role was to defend its own commerce at sea while denying the sea to enemy commerce, an end best achieved by a blockade, not commerce raiding. Mahan's most important lesson in the application of naval strategy is not often quoted: "Good men in poor ships," he wrote, "are better than poor men with good ships."[15]

Julian S. Corbett was a British naval historian and professor. He was Mahan's contemporary but differed in important ways from his American counterpart. Corbett agreed with Mahan on the importance of maritime strength to a nation, with naval power a subset of that strength. He also agreed with Mahan on the vital importance of maintaining the security of communication at sea, of keeping the SLOCs open. While not downplaying the importance of a strong battle fleet, Corbett pointed out how Britain's historical naval record illustrated the value of detached squadrons, insisting that climactic battle with an enemy fleet was not necessarily the key to achieving victory in war.

Corbett's strategic thought is more applicable in today's operational and budget spheres than is Mahan's. Of particular note is his emphasis on the limited use of naval power, similar to Clausewitz's argument that limited objectives may be achieved with limited military—that is, naval—force. Corbett's emphasis was on safeguarding one's lines of communication at sea; destroying the enemy's fleet was one way to accomplish that goal, but so was blockade.

Corbett's relevance to twenty-first-century maritime concerns in Asia is buttressed by his emphasis on the navy's duty to project power ashore. No major war in history has been decided by a single maritime battle.[16] The "actual functions of the fleet," Corbett wrote, are "the furtherance or hindrance of military operations ashore[,] . . . [t]he protection or destruction of commerce[,] . . . [and the] prevention or securing of alliances."[17] He emphasized that the importance of "combined operations" required the fleet not only to safeguard the troops during transit to the objective area but also to support their operations ashore.

He described the "moral" of one of his early works as "the powerlessness of a Navy without an Army equally well organized to act where the power of the fleet ends."[18] To Corbett, amphibious operations were an important naval mission, but to Mahan they were not. This thought was echoed by a twentieth-century U.S. strategist, Adm. J. C. Wylie, who stated that while maritime strategy aims to make use of maritime communications "to establish control over one's enemies," its final "phase" is "the exploitation of that control by projection of power [onto] the land."[19]

The third major theoretician of modern maritime strategy, the French admiral Theophile Aube, advocated a campaign focused almost solely on destroying the enemy's seaborne commerce, as a guerre de course. As envisioned in the nineteenth century, this method would rely on surface ships to raid the SLOCs, intercepting and destroying or seizing enemy merchant ships. As practiced in the nineteenth and earlier centuries by cruisers and privateers, which often were privately financed and crewed, this policy was more bothersome than effective, although the Confederate raiders of the American Civil War did do significant damage.

More effective was the guerre de course of the twentieth century, executed largely by submarines.[20] German U-boat efforts in the two world wars were devastating but eventually were defeated by a combination of convoy, airpower, and signals intelligence. U.S. submarines carried out the most effective guerre de course in history against Japan's merchant fleet between 1942 and 1945. By the end of the war, the Japanese merchant fleet had shrunk from 6.4 million tons to 1.5 million tons, much of it locked in port.[21] Even this campaign, however, was part of a larger effort by U.S. forces, especially Army Air Forces and naval aviation.

Guerre de course remains a viable campaign element in Asian waters, for specific scenarios. Submarine warfare poses a serious threat to a nation's SLOCs, especially if combined with blockade and an air campaign.

To sum up this discussion, Mahan and Corbett differed on the decisiveness of sea power. To the former, sea power was essential to national greatness, with strong fleets needed to protect a nation's international trade. Thus, Mahan believed that maritime nations needed fleets of capital ships (battleships in his day, replaced by aircraft carriers during World War II) capable of fighting and winning decisive battles to gain command of the sea.

Corbett thought sea power was important but not determinant in warfare. He disagreed with Mahan's premise that the enemy fleet was always the center of gravity, and he did not advocate the "big battle" approach. The two also differed on the concentration of forces. Mahan thought that the fleet must remain unified, while to Corbett concentration was a more flexible concept.

Corbett was a student of Karl von Clausewitz, the German master of strategic thought, and believed that "war is a form of political intercourse, a continuation of foreign politics which begins when force is introduced to our ends."[22] Furthermore, while Clausewitz ignored maritime strategy, Corbett disparaged the idea of a separate naval strategy, noting that "naval strategy . . . does not exist" other than as part of maritime strategy, which in turn is part of military strategy, of "the art of war" involving both army and navy.[23]

From this belief, Corbett classified as "minor strategy" the operational employment of navies, while "major strategy," which is what concerns us here, was concerned with "passage and communication." This latter point meant for him being able to use the sea for commercial and military purposes as desired, while denying the same to an opponent.

This book follows a Corbettian definition of maritime strategy as "the principles which govern a war in which the sea is a substantial factor." This includes the operations of navies and their associated armies ashore. Effective maritime strategy requires the close coordination of the two services to protect vital national political and economic security interests at sea. In modern terms, then, to be effective a maritime strategy must be both joint and politically determined by national policy makers. This in turn requires, first, the most careful delineation of the political aims of the employment of maritime power and, second, the necessary presence of commercial and naval resources to accomplish those aims.

This paradigm must include a degree of flexibility, however, in view of changing political objectives and of what Mahan referred to as "the uncertainties peculiar to the sea"—weather and the unmarked vastness of the oceans.[24] That vastness is characteristic of Asia, which is increasingly dependent on international maritime trade that contributed to 87 percent of the region's gross domestic product (GDP) in 2006. Increased economic reliance on the sea historically has engendered increased attention to deploying modern navies, a factor as true for today's Asia as it was for eighteenth- and nineteenth-century Europe.

Maritime strategy is not simply a matter of naval forces and national security objectives; a nation's domestic political priorities and economic demands are major, indeed vital, influences on the development and execution of a maritime strategy. A further blurring has occurred between "foreign" and "domestic" security regimes; between missions assigned to the police and to the military; between navies and coast guards; and between intelligence agencies with domestic or foreign assignments. All these distinctions have become less clear as a result of the rise of nonstate actors and other nontraditional security threats.

Furthermore, developing strategy is a complex process, even if defined simply as a plan of action to achieve a desired end. The U.S. maritime strategy that emerged in the 1980s was in a major way the result of a dedicated effort by naval officers and civilian officials, but this was a rare example of straightforward development. More commonly, as described by Adm. Arleigh Burke, a major influence on post–World War II U.S. national security policy and strategy, "Naval philosophy and maritime strategy are not spectacular. They offer no panaceas. Their success depends upon long, dull hours of hard work in which no one action is clearly decisive by itself. Its success depends upon a series of small successes."

In other words, effective naval strategy does not result primarily from the composition of "overarching, erudite strategic theories [but from] day by day policy and program choices, backed up by thorough training and experience . . . and by a modern, multi-faceted fleet capable of swift deployment and effective employment" of naval forces.[25]

Expenditures on naval armaments are expected to grow with Asia's economy in future decades; the major French naval armaments firm DCNS has predicted that "the defense market in the Asia-Pacific should be, in approximately 2016, a major market—even above the U.S."[26] Furthermore, naval modernization among Asian nations is aiming at larger, more advanced surface, subsurface, and aviation platforms.

China and India lead the region in naval modernization, including aircraft carriers, nuclear-powered submarines, and at least fourth-generation tactical aircraft.[27] Japan and South Korea already deploy Aegis-armed surface combatants, modern conventionally powered submarines, and fourth-generation tactical aircraft. Russia's latest attempt to modernize its Pacific Fleet, however, promises to be no more successful than previous efforts of the past quarter century—an assessment that perhaps reflects the Eurocentric nature and concerns of all Russian regimes, from that of Ivan I to Vladimir Putin.

Even lesser Asian powers—Pakistan, Thailand, Malaysia, Singapore, Vietnam, Indonesia, Australia—are acquiring modern submarines, some with air-independent propulsion (AIP); large surface combatants; and fourth- or fifth-generation aircraft. Practically all the region's states are equipping their navies with state-of-the-art cruise missiles and improved information-warfare capabilities.

This naval modernization brings concerns for the security of the Asian maritime commons. The navies and associated maritime forces of the region's nations are focused primarily on these waters, as described below.

CHAPTERS TO FOLLOW

Chapter 1, "Setting the Scene," begins with discussion of some historical case studies of maritime strategy in Asia. These include aspects of Japan's wars with China and Russia, in 1895 and 1905, respectively. The development and application of the U.S. World War II strategy against Japan, culminating in the latter's 1945 surrender aboard a U.S. battleship, will be the primary case study in this chapter, which then offers a section on Asian maritime geopolitics.

This includes the current bilateral and multilateral treaty structure in the Pacific–Indian Ocean area, as well as the multilateral organizations that affect the maritime arena. The chapter then discusses conventional and nonconventional threats on the seas and concludes with reference to the trade that makes the region's SLOCs so important. Finally, a discussion of the United Nations Convention on the Law of the Sea (UNCLOS) will view that treaty's provisions, with a focus on current disputes in the Asian region.

The book then embarks on a series of chapters that address the region's major nations and groups of smaller maritime states. First, the United States is discussed in chapter 2. Its interests are addressed, to include threats to those interests, followed by a brief discussion of available maritime forces. U.S. maritime strategy, both published and apparent, is discussed in depth.

This chapter on the United States sets the pattern for chapters 3, 5, and 7, which address Japan, China, and India, respectively. Chapter 4 considers the maritime importance of North Asia, focusing on Canada, Russia, and the Koreas. Chapter 6 takes a similar look at Southeast Asia, including Australia, Taiwan, the Philippines, Vietnam, Indonesia, Singapore, Malaysia, and Thailand. Chapter 8 then examines the South Asia nations of Myanmar, Bangladesh, Sri Lanka, Pakistan, and the Persian Gulf states, particularly Iran.

Following this geographically focused series of discussions, chapter 9 surveys current and potential conflict and cooperation scenarios in maritime Asia. The former are Korea, the East China Sea, Taiwan, South China Sea, and the western Indian Ocean, including the Gulf of Aden. Points of possible cooperation focus on stability, security, training, and reconstruction operations. SLOC security is surveyed, with consideration of counterpiracy and counterterrorism.

The book's conclusion sums up the preceding chapters and offers the reader the opportunity to judge whether the work's goals, elucidated in the introduction, have been met. Despite the risks inherent in forecasting the future, the conclusion attempts to do just that, with an eye toward developments that are likely to affect maritime strategic thought in Asia in 2050.

one

SETTING THE SCENE

INTRODUCTION

T he most useful definition of strategy is simply a national plan for achieving security objectives with the most effective employment of available resources. A subset is maritime strategy, which for our discussion of Asia will be dated in modern application to 1368, when Han Chinese forces overturned the Mongols' Yuan Dynasty and established the Ming Dynasty, at a time when China was the world's leading economic and military power. The new rulers won the military contest for many reasons, not the least of which was the breakdown of the Yuan hierarchy and loss of control over its civil society. Maritime power played a significant role, albeit on China's inland waters.[1]

The Ming court later dispatched seven extraregional exploratory voyages commanded by the famous eunuch admiral Zheng He. These expeditions were conducted between 1405 and 1433, reaching as far as Mombasa, Mogadishu, and Mecca. They demonstrated China's world-leading status in shipbuilding, maritime technology, and logistics. They also demonstrated Beijing's willingness to use naval power to punish and overawe lesser states and their rulers.[2]

The Ming ended these voyages, likely for several reasons. One was Zheng He's death, apparently at the end of or shortly following his seventh voyage. A second was domestic priorities; the court considered explorations an expensive luxury, especially in the face of continental threats to the regime from the north and west. Third was the need to conserve governmental revenue and reduce spending, overtaxed by ambitious efforts on land and at sea.

Zheng He's voyages began and ended for reasons summed up by the American scholar, Edward Dreyer: "Zheng He's first six voyages took place because Emperor Yongle wanted to force the countries of the Western Ocean into tributary relations with China. Zheng He's seventh voyage took place because Emperor Xuande was concerned that tribute missions from these countries had ceased to arrive." Dreyer also noted that "none of the eleven Ming emperors who succeeded Xuande cared about the Western Ocean and its countries."[3] In other words, maritime power projection and strategy lost its standing in China's national priorities.

Maritime strategy continued to matter in Asia, however, especially during the commercial intrusions by European nations, joined in the eighteenth and nineteenth centuries by the United States and Japan. China's lack of an effective navy or maritime strategy was a significant factor in reducing its status to, in the words of Mao Zedong, that of a "semi-colony and colony," foreigners having "carved up the whole country into imperialist spheres of influence."[4] Similar situations developed in Korea, in Japan, and throughout colonized Southeast and South Asia. Only Thailand (Siam) avoided colonization.

Chinese reformers attempted to build a modern navy in the middle and late nineteenth century, but their efforts foundered on failure or inability to organize the new naval forces, divided into four geographic fleets, on a national basis and with either coherent administration or unified strategy. Also unfortunately for Beijing, its ships' crews were inadequately trained and poorly commanded.

This resulted in near-total naval defeats in two wars. The first, against the French in 1884, was anomalous, since the sinking of China's new southern fleet was just one campaign in a war during which the Chinese army fought effectively against French ground forces. The second and even more dramatic defeat, in 1894–95, was inflicted on China's northern fleet by Japan's navy, itself newly developed and considered by Western observers inferior to China's.[5]

Japan's victory over China signaled its arrival as an Asian military power and was the first in a remarkable string of maritime successes that included dramatic sea victories over Russia in 1904 and 1905. Japanese naval success reached its peak in February 1942 during the violent confrontations that constituted the battle of the Java Sea, when the Imperial Japanese Navy (IJN) totally defeated an Allied fleet composed of ships from Australia, the Netherlands, the United Kingdom, and the United States.

Japan decisively won this and other naval battles between 1894 and 1942 because of several factors. These included technological advances, especially in torpedoes, optics, aircraft-carrier operations, tactical aircraft, personnel training, and most important, advances in maritime tactics and operational art. All of these vital elements of naval warfare were subsumed within a national maritime strategy that was coherent and carefully thought out, but devastatingly irrelevant to Japan's strategic circumstances.

Between 1906 and 1941 the Japanese navy was focused on preparing to fight the U.S. Navy. Its planners thought in terms not of strategy but of becoming ready for battle—the grand climactic battle they mistakenly thought the center of Mahanian strategy. In effect, the IJN mistook "tactics for strategy and strategy for the conduct of war."[6] Japanese officers themselves later concluded that the navy planned only for a short war and failed to develop realistic war aims.[7]

The IJN's efforts to destroy opposing naval forces were planned and carried out—no matter how effectively early in the war—without regard for strategic goals and without effective attention to joint efforts with the army. Even its perceived goals, perhaps best stated as achieving Japanese economic independence and political domination in East Asia, were neither clearly thought out nor balanced against national resources.

This failure did not result from lack of appreciation of Japan's economic or political situation in the world in general, or in Asia in particular. Nor did it represent a failure to understand the maritime strategy being developed by its obvious major opponent in the twentieth century, the United States. Rather, Japan's failure to carry out a workable maritime strategy resulted from its navy's failure to understand one of the most basic requirements for developing such a strategy: Are the necessary material and personnel resources available to achieve the desired and planned strategic goals?

A series of diplomatic agreements between the United States and Japan, including the 1905 Root-Takihara and 1908 Taft-Katsura pacts, aimed to establish a de facto "deal" with Japan. That is, Washington would allow Tokyo a favored position on the Asian mainland, while the latter would not threaten the new American colony in the Philippines. This unsavory bit of realpolitik finally failed, of course, when President Franklin D. Roosevelt refused in the late 1930s to countenance Japan's attempt to colonize large portions of East Asia, especially China, and as Japan launched its own flawed maritime strategy, which began with the surprise attacks on U.S. forces in Hawaii and the Philippines, on 7 and 8 December 1941, respectively.

Ironically, the most capable officer in the prewar IJN, Adm. Isoroku Yamamoto, had spent several years in the United States, at Harvard University and as Japan's naval attaché in Washington, and had a clear-eyed view of Japan's inadequacies compared to the industrial and resource might of the United States. Nonetheless, because of intense loyalty to country and emperor, and perhaps relying on hope rather than his own estimates, Yamamoto planned the 7 December 1941 attack on Pearl Harbor and commanded the IJN until his death in 1943, when his plane was intercepted and shot down by American fighter aircraft.

Underlying Japan's maritime plan when it attacked Pearl Harbor was an assumption that the United States would require two years to recover from such a devastating surprise attack. This period would enable Japan to build a defensive perimeter so formidable that Washington would be daunted and so negotiate rather than fight. This in turn would leave Japan in possession of the Southeast Asian resources it required.

The fatal weakness in Tokyo's plan, at least partially understood by Yamamoto, was that American industrial capacity was in fact so massive that the two-year period required for Japan to establish its defensive perimeter was unattainable. Indeed, in less than half a year the U.S. naval victory at Midway in May 1942 had doomed the IJN and Japan to defeat.

By contrast, the United States entered World War II in 1941 with a maritime strategy long in the making and thoroughly tested in fleet-sized exercises that proved prescient. This plan for possible war with Japan, which was designated as country "Orange," was long in development in the Navy staff's planning organization in Washington but also, and primarily, beginning as early as 1906, at the Naval War College, in Newport, Rhode Island. In fact, this planning continued to evolve, as part of the "Rainbow Plans" series for a two-ocean war, up to and arguably during the first year of the great maritime war with Japan, from 1941 to 1945.[8]

Several generations of U.S. naval officers, including most who were to serve as admirals during World War II, attended the Naval War College, conducting more than three hundred various war games during the decades preceding 1941, with a scenario against Japan predominating.[9] The plan's basic premise was Mahanian—the war would be decided by a single, climactic battle between the U.S. and Japanese battle fleets. Having gained command of the sea, the United States would lay siege to Japan until Tokyo surrendered.

An important subset of Plan Orange was the acknowledged need for supply bases to support the American fleet as it sortied from its West Coast bases en route to engaging the IJN, perhaps in the vicinity of the Marianas Islands. The need to seize and defend islands for these "advanced bases" as the fleet crossed the Pacific was embraced in the 1920s by the U.S. Marine Corps, under the leadership of Maj. Gen. John A. Lejeune, and under succeeding commandants as well.[10]

War Plan Orange's background included dissension between the Army and Navy over defending the Philippines. This argument dated almost to the 1898 acquisition of that American colony and the realization that such possessions needed to be defended, especially in the environment of newly risen Japanese military power. Effective defense of the islands was impractical, because of the weak peacetime strength of the services, particularly the Army, and the vast Pacific distances. Neither Army nor Navy wanted to admit that officially, however, and attempts at joint planning continued, even after Japan's successful invasion of the Philippines began in December 1941.[11]

World War II began very inauspiciously for the United States in the Pacific, given Japan's successes at Pearl Harbor, the Philippines, and elsewhere. Nonetheless, and despite these losses and the decision to place first priority on defeating Germany, Plan Orange proved a successful maritime strategy. Perhaps most important, its long gestation meant that most of the U.S. naval officers who commanded against Japan had participated in the plan's development and were surprised by few wartime events. In fact, the U.S. Pacific commander, Adm. Chester W. Nimitz, stated after the war that only the Japanese employment of suicidal "kamikazes" had not been foreseen in the long planning process that had produced War Plan Orange.

This does not mean that the successful American maritime strategy for the 1941–45 war in the Pacific led to an easy victory. On the contrary, by the time of Tokyo's surrender in August 1945, triggered by the revolutionary detonation of two atomic bombs, Japan, a maritime nation, had been completely isolated, its navy and merchant fleet largely on the bottom of the sea, its army isolated on the Asian mainland, and its people starving—yet resilient and seemingly determined to fight to a suicidal end.

The IJN fought courageously but suffered from several shortcomings. First, its commanders too often failed to act decisively and wisely in battle, as exemplified by Vice Adm. Takeo Kurita in the battle of Leyte Gulf. Second, the navy failed to adjust its lengthy, rigorous training regimes to wartime requirements. Third, Japan failed to appreciate and take full advantage of its submarine force's capabilities, although a few notable successes occurred. Fourth, the IJN was not part of a joint effort; the army and navy not only very rarely operated in concert but often actually lied to each other about operations and results. Finally, while both U.S. and Japanese forces were steeped in racist stereotypes about each other, the Japanese military, including the navy, fought the war with a cruelty and racial disdain for its opponents that continue to shadow Japan's relations with its Asian neighbors nearly three-quarters of a century after the war's end.

The fact that in August 1945 the Japanese army still mustered more than 2 million troops in organized units was irrelevant to the war's outcome. Japan, a maritime nation without a successful maritime strategy, lost to the United States, a maritime nation that exercised a successful maritime strategy.[12]

World War II was followed by the Cold War, a global contest between international communism led by the Soviet Union (USSR) and Western-style democratic capitalism under the aegis of the United States. The military challenge was focused on Western Europe, despite the fact that actual warfare broke out only in Asia, most notably in Korea and Indochina. This changed to a degree with the 1962 Cuban missile crisis, which spurred Moscow to launch a maritime challenge against the United States and its North Atlantic Treaty Organization (NATO) allies.

U.S. naval efforts at containing the USSR threat gave priority to Europe; successive Pacific commanders frequently tried, with very little success, to increase understanding of their theater's strategic importance. Hence, U.S. maritime strategy during the Cold War reached its apogee in the 1980s with a pointed focus on supporting NATO campaign plans to succor Western Europe in the event of a Soviet-bloc attack.

In the East Asian waters that were the focus of the Pacific commander's maritime strategy, the Soviet Pacific Fleet posed a significant threat, particularly with respect to a possible invasion of Japan's northernmost island of Hokkaido, but hardly at the level of those represented by the three other Soviet fleets—the Northern, Baltic, and Black Sea Fleets—confronting the European theater.

UNITED NATIONS CONVENTION ON THE LAW OF THE SEA

Asia's maritime picture is clouded by many disputes over sovereignty delimitation, seabed resources, environmental concerns, and fisheries. Although the United States has not ratified it, almost all regional nations are parties to the United Nations Convention on the Law of the Sea (UNCLOS), which provides avenues for resolving most such disputes.

The third United Nations Conference on the Law of the Sea (UNCLOS III) drew up the UNCLOS during a ten-year process ending in 1982. The UNCLOS replaced four 1958 treaties and defines nations' rights and responsibilities in using the world's oceans. It includes rules for safeguarding the environment and the management of marine natural resources, especially fisheries. The UNCLOS came into effect in 1994; 162 countries had signed and ratified it as of 2012. Seventeen countries have signed but not ratified the treaty, including Cambodia, Iran, the Democratic People's Republic of Korea (North Korea), and as mentioned, the United States. Another seventeen countries, none of them Asian, have neither signed nor ratified the UNCLOS.

Background

The UNCLOS replaced the seventeenth-century definition of national sovereignty as extending to a specified distance from a nation's coastline, typically three nautical miles, which was then accepted cannon-shot range. The sea beyond that distance from shore was considered international waters (or the "high seas," a vernacular term apparently without standing in law), free to be used by all nations. This concept was subjected to challenge in the early twentieth century, when weapon ranges increased significantly and nations wanted to extend sovereignty over coastal mineral resources and fish stocks and to protect the environment.

A 1930 League of Nations conference on this subject failed to produce meaningful results, but President Harry S Truman in 1945 extended U.S. control over natural resources on its continental shelf (CS). Other nations soon followed; between 1946 and 1950, Argentina, Chile, Peru, and Ecuador claimed ownership of economic resources out to a distance of two hundred nautical miles, to include Humboldt Current fisheries. Other nations extended their territorial seas to twelve nautical miles.

By 1967 sixty-six nations had adopted twelve-nautical-mile territorial limits, while eight had set two-hundred-nautical-mile limits. The first UNCLOS conference was convened in 1956; when it concluded two years later, it had produced four conventions: Territorial Sea and Contiguous Zone (although neither area's breadth was specified), Continental Shelf, High Seas, and Fishing and Conservation of Living Resources.

A second UN conference on the law of the sea was convened in 1960 but after six weeks had not produced any new agreements, probably as a result of the zero-sum Cold War attitude then in full bloom. A third conference met in 1973 and lasted for ten years, with more than 160 nations participating. The conference produced the current UNCLOS, which entered into force in 1994.

The Treaty

The UNCLOS is intended as a cooperative arrangement among its signatories and is not managed by the United Nations (UN). In addition to UN bodies, such as the International Seabed Authority (ISA) and the currently sitting Commission on the Limits of the Continental Shelf (CLCS), other international organizations play roles. These include the International Maritime Organization (IMO) and the International Whaling Commission.

The UNCLOS addresses sovereignty limits, exclusive economic zones, continental shelf limits, navigation standards, archipelagic status, and transit regimes. More specific issues include seabed mining and exploitation, environmental protection, scientific research, military operations, and settlement of disputes.

The distances to the UNCLOS zones' limits are measured from a nation's coastal baseline. This line normally follows the low-water mark; a "straight baseline" may be drawn between the headlands along a deeply indented coast, but the parameters for doing so are strongly debated among claimants. The UNCLOS zones are as follows:

- *Internal waters*, which include all water and waterways on the landward side of the baseline. The coastal state is free to set laws, regulate use, and use any resources in these waters, while foreign vessels have no right of passage.
- *Territorial waters* extend from the coastal baseline out to twelve nautical miles. The coastal state is free to set laws, regulate use, and use any resources in this zone, while foreign vessels have the right of innocent passage.

In *strategic straits,* such as the Sunda or Lombok Straits through the Indonesian archipelago, the passage of military vessels must be allowed, because naval vessels are allowed to maintain an operational status not permissible in territorial waters. *Innocent passage* is defined as passing in an expeditious, continuous manner not "prejudicial to the peace, good order or the security" of the coastal state.

Examples of non-innocent activities include fishing, environmental damage, weapons practice, and military surveillance. Submarines are required to navigate on the surface and to show their flags. A nation has the authority temporarily to suspend innocent passage in specific areas of its territorial seas to protect its security interests. An example is declaring an "exclusion zone" for waters in which weapons firings are scheduled.

- *Archipelagic waters* have the same rights as internal waters for the claimant nation, but foreign vessels have the right of innocent passage (like territorial waters); they are defined by a baseline drawn between the outermost islands of an archipelagic nation. Indonesia and the Philippines are obvious examples, but the definition is easily subject to questionable application.
- The *contiguous zone* (CZ) extends twelve nautical miles beyond the twelve-nautical-mile-wide *territorial sea,* within which the claiming state can enforce its customs, taxation, immigration, and pollution laws. If violations of these laws occur within a nation's territorial sea, it may pursue the offender throughout the CZ.

It is empowered to (a) prevent infringement of customs, fiscal, immigration, or sanitary laws within its territory or territorial seas; and (b) punish infringement of the above laws and regulations committed within its territory or territorial sea.

- The *exclusive economic zone* (EEZ) is the UNCLOS zone that most often appears in the media. It extends out to a maximum distance of two hundred nautical miles from a nation's baseline. The EEZ is an area in which the state has "sovereign rights for the purpose of exploring and exploiting, conserving and managing the natural resources, whether living or non-living." The nation's EEZ also includes jurisdiction over artificial islands, installations, and structures; marine research; and protection and preservation of the environment. These rights do not, however, apply to the airspace over the EEZ.

- The *continental shelf* may extend as far as 350 nm from a nation's coastal baseline, although since it is defined by the sea-bottom gradient, a mathematical computation, the CS in some circumstances extends no more than two hundred nautical miles. The claiming state has the exclusive right to subsoil minerals and other nonliving material in the CS subsoil, as well as to living resources on the seabed. The state has sovereign rights throughout the continental shelf "for the purpose of exploring it and exploiting its natural resources," both living and nonliving. The state does not, however, have any legal rights on the water surface or in the airspace above the continental shelf.

The UNCLOS also addresses safeguarding the environment and the freedom of scientific research; the UN created the International Seabed Authority to control recovery of mineral resources from the seabed outside the CS. Finally, the UNCLOS stipulates that landlocked states have the right of untaxed access to the sea.

Two other UNCLOS provisions are particularly important to national maritime claims. First, the UNCLOS defines an "island" as "a naturally formed area of land, surrounded by water, which is above water at high tide." An island possesses the territorial sea, contiguous zone, EEZ, and continental shelf characteristics of a continental state.

Second, the UNCLOS provision for delimiting the EEZs between states less than four hundred nautical miles apart—and the CS between states less than seven hundred nautical miles apart—particularly affects China's maritime territorial claims with North Korea, South Korea, Japan, and several Southeast Asian nations. States with conflicting EEZ or CS claims are urged to "achieve an equitable solution." If they cannot agree, they are supposed to submit the dispute to UNCLOS-created adjudication bodies for resolution.

The UNCLOS raised some new problems in its effort to resolve old questions of maritime law, two of which particularly apply to China's claims in Southeast Asian waters. First is the creation of the two-hundred-nautical-mile EEZ in a region where multiple claims often overlap. One extreme example is the Gulf of Thailand, where the EEZ claims of Cambodia, Malaysia, and Vietnam theoretically leave Thailand with no EEZ at all.

Second, the UNCLOS-related right of states to impose navigation restrictions within their territorial waters allows archipelagic states to make troublesome claims. Indonesia, for instance, periodically has tried to limit the freedom of navigation of ships transiting the vital Sunda and Lombok Straits into the South China Sea.

Many states included formal "declarations and statements" when signing or ratifying the UNCLOS. EEZ parameters are often the subject of these pronouncements about specific concerns, particularly the permissibility of military operations—ranging from aircraft-carrier flight operations to surveillance missions by civilian-manned ships to fishing.

Hence, the EEZ has gained the status of a legal and economic issue, point of national hubris, national security concern for maritime powers, and military focus for the major Asian maritime powers. Japan and South Korea dispute ownership of the islands of Takeshima/Dokdo (as the two countries have respectively named them) and attendant EEZs; Japan disputes with China possible EEZs associated with sovereignty of the Diaoyu/Senkaku Islands (again, as the two countries have named them).

The vast majority of the UNCLOS signatories do not agree with a major focus of China's maritime concerns, its claims to excessive sovereignty rights within the EEZ—approximating those applicable to territorial waters. The Southeast Asian nations are concerned about that Chinese attitude but themselves dispute ownership of various land features and possible EEZs in the South China Sea. EEZ disputes also exist in the Gulf of Thailand and between India and Myanmar, while New Delhi is concerned about any Chinese sovereignty claims that might impact its security. Also, and perhaps most significant, the United States has adopted a position on freedom of navigation that challenges all recent attempts to expand concepts of sovereign territorial rights and restrictions, dating from the twentieth century and earlier, that may be imposed in claimed national waters.

Beijing is not alone in its view of national rights within the EEZ. India, for instance, also has stated claims that the United States and most UNCLOS signatories regard as excessive.

In 1996 the CLCS established a period, ending 13 May 2009, during which states could submit survey findings on the limits of their continental shelves. Several Asian nations have submitted claims to the CLCS, as will be discussed below.

SEA LINES OF COMMUNICATION

SLOCs are as vital to Asia's economic and political health as they are elsewhere in the world. More than 40 percent of all global seaborne trade occurs in Asia, which is also the location of eight of the world's busiest container ports.[13] More generally, the Liner Shipping Connectivity Index (LCSI) has increased for 75 percent of the world's nations, while international container traffic has grown from 40 million twenty-foot-equivalent units (TEUs) in 1982 to more than 500 million TEUs in 2008.[14]

The sea-lanes are especially crucial for energy flows to the region's nations. Since approximately two-thirds of the world's proven oil reserves are in the Persian Gulf and surrounding nations, and since China and Japan are two of the world's three largest petroleum importers, the importance of the SLOCs across the Indian and Pacific Oceans is self-evident. Furthermore, oil from Africa's west-coast fields also is normally transported to Asia around the Cape of Good Hope and across the Indian Ocean.

China relies on the SLOCs for more than 60 percent of its imported oil, while Japan relies entirely on imports. Some of these oil imports come from Asian fields, such as those of Indonesia and Brunei, but the majority still come from the Persian Gulf region.

MULTILATERAL TREATIES

Multilateralism is alive in maritime Asia but is far from providing a platform with the firmness of NATO. The United Nations provides a forum for all these nations to speak and act; the Asia-Pacific Economic Cooperation (APEC) pact, the Association of Southeast Asian Nations (ASEAN), the ASEAN Regional Forum (ARF), and the Five-Power Defense Agreement (FPDA) are the most productive and promising multilateral bodies, while the Indian Ocean boasts the Indian Ocean Rim Association for Regional Cooperation (IOR-ARC), the South Asian Association for Regional Cooperation (SAARC), and the Bay of Bengal Initiative for Multisectoral Technical and Economic Cooperation (BIMSTEC), among others. The elements of the international economic infrastructure—World Trade Organization (WTO), World Bank, International Monetary Fund (IMF), and Asia Development Bank (ADB)—all play roles in the maritime economic arena.

Bilateral treaties, however, offer the most reliable platforms for cooperative security efforts. These include U.S. mutual defense treaties with South Korea, Japan, the Philippines, and Australia. A similar American agreement exists with Thailand, while significant military relations are maintained with Singapore and Taiwan. Other military relationships are those between China and North Korea and among the members of the Shanghai Cooperation Organization (China, Russia, Mongolia, Kazakhstan, Kyrgyzstan, Tajikistan, and Uzbekistan).

MARITIME THREATS

No major naval conflict has been fought in Asian waters since 1945, and the near-term risk of such a conflict is very low. The wars in Korea and Vietnam lacked almost any maritime aspect, other than carrier-launched air strikes, while lesser crises at sea have been severely constrained. These have included the 1950 and 1996 Taiwan Strait crises; the 1975 *Mayaguez* affair; the Indo-Pakistani wars in 1947, 1965, and 1971; the 1974 and 1988 Sino-Vietnamese sea battles in the South China Sea; the Sri Lankan civil war in the 1990s and early 2000s; and several naval clashes between North and South Korea.

The primary dangers to maritime security in the great Asian bight arise from threats falling under the category of "other than war." These embrace crime at sea, including piracy; terrorism at sea; environmental disaster, both man-made and arising from nature; and clashes in pursuit of economic benefit, such as over contested natural resources, from fish to petroleum.

Previous antipiracy efforts in the South China Sea were successful in reducing such incidents significantly, although the endemic nature of that crime in those waters remains. Current counterpiracy patrols in the Gulf of Aden (GOA) and surrounding waters have drawn widespread participation from navies throughout Asia, from South Korea to Pakistan, but the problem remains, as a product of the poverty of the region.

Piracy in the Indian Ocean remains a serious problem, roiling the waters in the Bay of Bengal and especially in the Gulf of Aden. Pirates operating from Somalia are the chief culprits and have attained near-corporate status in organization and technology. Piracy in this area increased during 2011 but also saw an increasing aggressive response by naval forces operating against piracy. The total cost of piracy in the GOA in 2011 is estimated to have been more than $6.5 billion.[15]

Very few terrorism incidents have occurred at sea, but the potential for a terrorist group to disrupt navigational choke points remains real. Incidents at sea simply to create terror also represent a viable tactic, perhaps by creation of deliberate environmental disasters or the widespread murder of innocents.

The most likely nontraditional mission for Asian maritime forces in the future is the maritime support of humanitarian assistance and disaster relief (HA/DR) efforts ashore. Prime examples are the U.S. relief expedition in Bangladesh following the disastrous 1991 floods in that country and the multinational efforts in Southeast and South Asia following the tsunami that struck those regions in 2004. All the major Asian navies, as well as that of the United States, already possess the large amphibious ships and aircraft carriers essential to mounting major HA/DR efforts; the United States and now China also are able to deploy large hospital ships on such missions.

CONCLUSION

Maritime Asia is the world's most dynamic economic arena, with the most heavily traveled sea-lanes. The navigational choke points in the Pacific and Indian Oceans mark the region's lifelines for trade and energy flows, while those seas provide vital food products to the center of the world's population.

The countries on the Indo-Pacific maritime commons are also following the historical model of economically modernizing nations: they are modernizing their navies. These efforts range from giant China's apparent focus on deploying a world-class maritime force, comprising both naval and coast guard fleets, to tiny Brunei's program to modernize its naval fleet of a half-dozen or so significant vessels. Particularly noteworthy is the effort to acquire submarines. China, South Korea, Japan, Indonesia, Australia, India, and Pakistan are improving their submarine fleets, while Singapore, Malaysia, and Thailand are establishing such a capability. Even the Philippine navy is discussing acquisition of submarines. Only Russia's navy remains stuck in its post–Cold War quagmire.

The United States remains maritime Asia's strongest military and economic presence, but it may be overtaken by China during this century. This power shift would pose a dilemma for the other Asian nations, none of which wish to be dominated by a rising China but all of which fear reductions and an eventual U.S. withdrawal from the region, at least in terms of naval presence. Hence, the general political atmosphere for Asia's maritime nations is one of balancing or hedging, of trying to maintain strong relations with the United States while accommodating Chinese expansion with equanimity.

The next chapter is the first of a series of detailed examinations of the maritime strategies of these various nations, beginning with the United States and then focusing on China, Japan, and India. Regional analyses will also be provided.

two

THE UNITED STATES

INTRODUCTION

T he need for a navy was specifically delineated in the 1787 constitution that formally established the United States. The Navy was tested almost immediately, in the quasi-war against France in the 1790s and as an antipiracy force in the Caribbean and Mediterranean Seas.

The new navy may have lacked a formal, written strategy, but a de facto strategy quickly emerged, which required the Navy to execute classic maritime missions in defense of the nation. These included traditional defense of the homeland, presence, defense of the sea lines of communication against piracy and other crimes at sea (to include the suppression of slavery, after 1808), and enforcement of customs requirements.

The constitutional requirement for the Congress of the United States to "provide and maintain a navy" is accompanied by several other duties pertaining directly to the maintenance and responsibilities of the Navy.[1] These include defining and punishing "piracy and felonies committed on the high seas, and offenses against the Law of Nations." Congress is also charged in the Constitution with declaring war, "grant[ing] Letters of Marque and Reprisal," making "rules concerning captures and water," and making "rules for the government and regulation of . . . naval forces." Finally, Congress has the duty of making "all laws which shall be necessary and proper for carrying into execution the foregoing powers."

No such requirements and responsibilities were levied on the Congress regarding an army.

First U.S. Maritime Strategy

The U.S. Navy (USN) was only a periodically effective force during the first seventy-five years of its existence. It recorded several successes, but the onset of the American Civil War in 1861 found the Navy ill prepared in numbers to execute the quickly designed maritime strategy designed to surround, blockade, and defeat the rebellious Southern states.

This "anaconda" strategy, elucidated in 1861 by the Army chief of staff, Gen. Winfield Scott, was successful, if not decisive, in defeating the Confederacy and maintaining the union.[2] Following victory in 1865, however, the large, modern American navy was allowed to deteriorate, to the point that by 1878 it did not even rank among the world's twelve most powerful maritime forces.

That status resulted from two factors. First, during the post–Civil War period the United States grew dramatically, geographically and economically. By the turn of the twentieth century, it was to be a world economic power. At that point it would begin to exert itself militarily as well, on the global scene, but almost all political and social energies following 1865 had been focused on carrying out the Industrial Revolution and on expanding the country to the west, beyond even the continental coast. Military concerns too during the nearly half century were focused on western expansion and were largely entrusted to the small U.S. Army.

Second, the United States during this period was confronted by no significant maritime threats. The small naval force available dealt with periodic fishing disputes and protection of American businessmen and missionaries overseas.

Maritime awareness developed with the emergence of political and societal advocacy needed to build a modern navy. Alfred Thayer Mahan's theories became popular in the 1890s, when western expansion pushed beyond the continent into the Pacific reaches. The war with Spain in 1898 cemented the view among political leaders and the populace that Mahan was right: a nation's greatness was defined by its global economic power, backed by a strong, global navy.

The new navy that began to appear in the 1880s and reached fruition of a sort in 1898 made a further mark on the world stage in 1907–8, when President Theodore Roosevelt, Mahan's most powerful acolyte, sent the U.S. battleship flotilla around the world as the "Great White Fleet." This fleet, not incidentally, made many headlines during its cruise through the Indo-Pacific oceans, notably with port calls in New Zealand, Australia, Japan, the Philippines, China (Xiamen, then known in the West as Amoy), and Sri Lanka (then known as Ceylon).

The American navy received another huge boost in strength and capability with U.S. participation in World War I. That war was followed, however, by the American-sponsored naval disarmament movement of the 1920s and 1930s, most famously marked by the 1921–22 Washington Conference treaties. These were unique in history. The world's major naval powers (the United States, Great Britain, Japan, France, and Italy) agreed to reduce their naval might—and then, remarkably, actually did so. These treaties were focused on East Asian waters, where the United States aimed at reducing Japanese naval power and maintaining American access to China.

Twentieth-century naval disarmament ended in the 1930s, not with a bang but with a whimper, as Japan and Germany began ignoring treaty limitations. The United States began expanding and modernizing its navy, with major naval construction bills in the mid-1930s. The most significant of these were passed in 1934 and 1938, nominally to rejuvenate an economy wrecked by the Great Depression.

Second Maritime Strategy

The most significant U.S. maritime development of the first half of the twentieth century had little to do with warships, however. It was instead the decades-long development, at the Naval War College, in Newport, Rhode Island, and in the Navy staff in Washington, of a maritime strategy. This process occurred largely in the seminar room and on the gaming floor, as generations of fairly junior naval officers thought about and worked through the problems of defending U.S. maritime interests, especially in the Pacific, where growing Japanese naval power was seen as a threat.[3] War Plan Orange emerged in anticipation of war with Japan.

This analytical process gave rise to the second definitive U.S. maritime strategy, but one subsumed in the "Atlantic First" policy picked from the Rainbow war plans of 1941. It must be emphasized that this selection was a political decision made by civilian leaders and was counter to the recommendations of senior U.S. naval officers.

These two strategies, the Anaconda Plan in 1861 and Plan Orange in 1941, heralded long, active wars. Both contributed mightily to victory in the two most important wars in which the United States has ever engaged.

THIRD MARITIME STRATEGY

The third definitive U.S. maritime strategy was developed during the Cold War. This period began almost simultaneously with the establishment in 1947 of the Department of Defense (DOD), which removed the secretary of the Navy from the president's cabinet. The new department was further empowered by a 1958 DOD reorganization that removed the Chief of Naval Operations (CNO) from operational control of forces at sea. It forced the Navy further into a joint paradigm, to which it has since only very slowly acclimated itself.

The Navy's mission during the Cold War was most clearly spelled out in the 1986 Maritime Strategy. This has been the only authoritative maritime strategy developed, promulgated, and exercised by the United States in the nearly three-quarters of a century since the end of World War II.

The 1986 Maritime Strategy was written and instituted in the environment of possible global nuclear assault led by the Soviet Union against the United States and allies, an attack centered on a land assault on Western Europe. The 1986 document was developed for several reasons. The first was to support U.S. and allied land forces on the European continent; the second was to recognize that the full capability of the U.S. Navy and allied maritime forces had to be brought to bear in the fight and to ensure that it would be. The third was to ensure that the Navy gained and retained significant recognition and resource prominence in the U.S. national security infrastructure.[4]

The 1986 strategy became largely outdated with the end of the Cold War and victory over the Soviet Union in 1990. Its fate was similar to that of its 1861 and 1941 antecedents—near irrelevance with the end of the wars for which they had been designed.

In a 1998 forecast of the maritime world of 2020, the *National Security Strategy for a New Century* emphasized the effects of globalization, noting that "outlaw states and ethnic conflicts" would threaten U.S. interests, as would the spread of weapons of mass destruction, terrorism, drug trafficking, and organized crime.[5]

A decade and a half later, the factors addressed—an increased reliance on maritime trade in 2020, increased threats from nonstate actors, improved space-based monitoring systems, and increased exploitation of living and nonliving maritime resources—remain valid, as do degradation of the marine environment and the rise of new maritime powers, particularly in Asia. The 2012 document *Sustaining U.S. Global Leadership* reiterates these concerns and also addresses the need to "project power despite anti-access/area denial challenges."[6] This priority applies directly to U.S. maritime power in Asia, since it names China and Iran as the primary causes of its formulation.

The latest effort to develop an effective maritime strategy has been accompanied by renewed political emphasis on Asia. Several senior U.S. officials discussed in 2011 a rebalancing of security focus to that region as the commitments in Iraq and Afghanistan wind down.

President Barack Obama noted the increasing importance of the western Pacific security environment in November 2011. National Security Advisor Thomas Donilon, Secretary of State Hillary Clinton, and other senior officials have echoed the president. All three have described this "rebalancing" as part of the U.S. role as a Pacific nation; Clinton, while emphasizing the need to work with China and the international community, particularly emphasized the historical U.S. demand for equal access to Asian economic and political venues.[7] Secretary of Defense Leon Panetta repeated the emphasis on Asia later that month.[8] Do these statements mean the United States is developing a new or updated maritime strategy to address these dangers effectively in the new century's second decade?

This modern era of maritime strategic thinking may be dated to the end of World War II, when, not surprisingly, the U.S. Navy found itself at strategic loose ends. It would do so again in the second half of the twentieth century, when the nation, having "fought" a Cold War in which the Navy's role had not been preeminent, emerged victorious. The result for the Navy was a continuing search for a strategy that would enhance its prominence in the nation's defense.

Writing in the U.S. Naval Institute *Proceedings* in 1947, Samuel P. Huntington suggested a maritime strategy for a "transoceanic navy," in recognition of the vastly reduced maritime assets at Washington's command in the face of the expanding global commitments of the dawning Cold War. The key passage in his prescient article was a caution: "If a service does not possess a well-defined strategic concept, the public and political leaders will be confused as to the role of the service . . . and apathetic or hostile to the claims made by the service on the resources of society."[9]

The ensuing Korean War allowed the Navy to operate from an oceanic sanctuary, and indeed the Cold War gained a maritime focus only after 1962. The Cuban missile crisis of that year taught the Soviet Union a renewed lesson of the value of naval power; the next quarter century witnessed development by Moscow and its European allies of a strategy of global naval power that directly challenged the North Atlantic Treaty Organization navies.

In the 1970s, under the presidency of Vice Adm. Stansfield Turner, the Naval War College tried to resume its position as the leader of maritime strategy development. Turner described the U.S. Navy's missions in a classic paradigm, listing them as strategic deterrence, naval presence, sea control, and power projection.[10] Turner outlined a path leading to the U.S. Navy's most coherent strategic response to this Cold War challenge, a project that began in the early 1980s, under the aegis of Secretary of the Navy John Lehman.

Lehman was almost unquestionably the most strategically minded secretary of the Navy in U.S. history. He gathered on his staff a coterie of talented junior and midgrade officers who thought widely but purposefully as participants in the most productive maritime strategic development since War Plan Orange, three-quarters of a century earlier. As War Plan Orange had had an obvious opponent, Japan, the U.S. maritime strategy that emerged in 1986 had an obvious opponent, the Soviet Union. Both opponents had formidable navies, and both posed access problems for the United States in bringing its combat power to bear, but the threats they offered were very different.

In Japan, the United States confronted a powerful navy able to execute across the warfare spectrum, particularly with surface combatants and airpower. The Soviet navy, however, offered primarily an airpower threat, in the form of missiles and long-range bomber aircraft. Another important difference was that the threat posed by Japan was largely maritime, while in a war with the Soviet Union the maritime campaign would have been peripheral to the primary, land-based threat posed against Western Europe by the Warsaw Pact armies and air forces.

That said, the Lehman era produced a viable, carefully thought out, well-resourced strategy. This 1986 strategy was a living document designed to maximize the Navy's effective role in defending the United States against the Soviet bloc's maritime threat. Of enduring utility was its "curve of conflict," which begins with "Peacetime Presence" and proceeds through the escalatory phases of "Surveillance," "Show of Force," "Use of Force," "Limited War," "Global Conventional War," and "Theater Nuclear War" to "Strategic Nuclear War."[11]

The end of the Cold War in 1990 eliminated the Soviet threat, and the Navy faced an international situation even more challenging than it had confronted in the late 1940s, when Huntington wrote his important article. U.S. Navy planners since then have promulgated maritime strategies on a routine, if sporadic, basis.

First came *From the Sea . . .,* in 1992.[12] This document "defined the strategic concept intended to carry the Naval Service—the Navy and Marine Corps—beyond the Cold War and into the twenty-first century." It aimed to change the focus and the priorities of the Navy and Marine Corps away from operations on the open sea "toward power projection and the employment of naval forces from the sea to influence events in the littoral regions of the world."

Developing an idea elucidated by the late nineteenth-century British strategist Julian Corbett, the U.S. Navy defined the littoral as "those areas adjacent to the oceans and seas that are within direct control of and vulnerable to the striking power of sea-based forces." The emphasis on littoral rather than open-ocean waters perhaps was intended to emphasize naval missions other than war. However, virtually every major naval battle in history has been fought within two hundred nautical miles of a coast, in "littoral" waters.

Forward . . . from the Sea succeeded this document in 1994, with a self-description as the "Navy Operational Concept," driving the "process of innovation that is rapidly transforming the Navy into a twenty-first century force."[13] It further defined the Corbettian *From the Sea . . .*, describing forward U.S. naval operations "to ensure unimpeded use of the seas and to project American influence and power into the littoral areas of the world." "Expeditionary operations" by "forward based forces" would continue to "ensure unimpeded use of the seas and to project American influence and power into the littoral areas of the world."

As was the case with the "transoceanic navy" concept, these post–Cold War strategies, perhaps better described as "operational concepts," sought to justify a strong, large navy and explain its vitality as a core element in safeguarding the United States and its global interests. They lacked the gravitas of War Plan Orange or the 1986 Maritime Strategy but served a purpose within the Navy, if not in the national command structure as a whole, during the decade of post–Cold War reductions in the defense budget and relative drift in U.S. national security policies.

That seeming malaise changed with the terrorist attacks of 11 September 2001. President George W. Bush's decision to declare "war" on terrorism, globally, rather than follow the examples of other nations that had suffered similar attacks by seeking policing solutions, opened a strategic window for the armed forces, especially the army and Marine Corps. The United States almost immediately invaded Afghanistan to flush out the 9/11 attackers, and in 2003 it invaded Iraq in pursuit of far less substantive goals that—as many observers insistently warned the White House, only to be ignored—eventually proved to be false.

The Navy responded in 2002 with *Sea Power 21,* a strategy seeking to employ the "tremendous increases in naval precision, reach, and connectivity," employing "innovative concepts and technologies [to] integrate sea, land, air, space, and cyberspace to a greater extent than ever before." The sea, in the words of the CNO, Adm. Vernon Clark, would "provide a vast maneuver area from which to project direct and decisive power around the globe."

Clark emphasized utilizing technological advances to ensure "information dominance," leading to effective

- Sea Strike: expanded power projection;
- Sea Shield: global defensive assurance, including "extended" homeland defense, access to littorals, and projection of power deep overland; and

- Sea Basing: provided by networked, mobile, and secure sovereign platforms operating at sea.[14]

Adm. Michael Mullen succeeded Clark as Chief of Naval Operations. Mullen's most important contribution to developing maritime strategic thought following the end of the Cold War was, first, to recognize the declining global capacity of the U.S. Navy, as a result of the decreasing number of its assets—especially ships, submarines, and aircraft—and of the problematic commitments of military force made by the administration following the September 2001 terrorist attacks. Second, Mullen advocated a "thousand-ship navy," or "Global Maritime Partnership," which he explained as "a fleet-in-being of nations willing to participate in global maritime partnerships: 'To face the challenges we do today, nobody can do it alone. Many countries are looking for ways to help create security through an international navy. The barriers to entry here are very low. You don't have to join; you don't have to sign a treaty.'"[15] Mullen's proposal was visionary, to bring together "a network of international navies, coast guards, maritime forces, port operators, commercial shippers and local law enforcement—all working" to secure the seas against piracy and crime, terrorism, and other threats to the global SLOCs.[16]

Mullen was also building on the maritime strategy addressed in the *National Strategy for Maritime Security,* issued by the White House in September 2005. This document began with the near truism that "the safety and economic security of the United States depends upon the secure use of the world's oceans."[17]

The 2005 document included eight supporting plans for coping with the maritime environment:

- National Plan to Achieve Domain Awareness
- Global Maritime Intelligence Integration Plan
- Interim Maritime Operational Threat Response Plan
- Maritime Infrastructure Recovery Plan
- Maritime Transportation System Security Plan
- Maritime Commerce Security Plan
- Domestic Outreach Plan

The plan identified five specific threats to maritime security: terrorism, transnational crime, transnational piracy, environmental destruction, and illegal seaborne immigration. Maintaining freedom of the seas was noted as the most effective way to ensure that these threats were contained, as was the government's responsibility to "facilitate and defend commerce" and to "facilitate the movement of desirable goods and people across our borders, while screening out dangerous people and material."

The steps to achieve these three goals were as follows:

- Enhance international cooperation
- Maximize domain awareness
- Embed security into commercial practices
- Deploy layered security
- Ensure continuity of the marine transportation system

This strategy was described as integrating sea power "with other elements of national power, as well as those of our friends and allies." It described its aims as "security, stability and sea power," the last defined as "the unifying force and common denominator that enables global security stability and prosperity." The mobility and rapid-response capability of naval forces were emphasized, as was building international trust and confidence; "the prevention of war" was held to be "equal to the conduct of war."

The 2005 document meant that *Seapower 21* had a short life and was in turn superseded, by the *Cooperative Strategy for 21st Century Seapower* (CS-21), in 2007. Claiming to be "an historical first," CS-21 was described as the first maritime strategy to be proclaimed by the United States as a "joint effort by the Navy, Marine Corps, and Coast Guard."[18] This strategy unsurprisingly emphasized securing "the United States from direct attack," to include ensuring "secure strategic access and [retaining] global freedom of action." It is notable also because it named no enemies but emphasized navy roles of ensuring the safety of shipping at sea and preventing unlawful and terrorist activities.[19]

CS-21 remained the Navy's most authoritative strategic instrument as of mid-2012, augmented by several subsidiary documents. These include *Naval Operations Concept 2010, Naval Doctrine Publication 1: Naval Warfare* (March 2010), *US Navy Vision for Confronting Irregular Challenges* (2010), *Irregular Warfare: Counter Irregular Threats Joint Operating Concept,* and *Marine Corps Operating Concepts,* third edition.[20]

In 2010 the Chief of Naval Operations, Adm. Gary Roughead, essentially reiterated the *Cooperative Strategy for 21st Century Seapower* as his *CNO Guidance for 2011*. He began by highlighting the ongoing conflicts in Iraq and Afghanistan, where the Navy had "more than 14,500 Sailors on the ground and another 12,000 offshore," a surprising balance for the most powerful navy in the world.[21] The *2010 Naval Operations Concept* (NOC) superseded the 2006 NOC, which had been the first such strategic document jointly issued by the Navy, Marine Corps, and Coast Guard.

The 2006 iteration was notable also because of its proposed Global Fleet Station (GFS) concept. This concept represents a peacetime version of the 1969 Nixon Doctrine—that the United States would provide maritime training and support to nations around the world, by means of a nearly constant naval presence, albeit more often by single ships than by the traditional task groups.[22]

The 2010 NOC recognized the continuing burden posed by the wars in Iraq and Afghanistan and aimed to "describe when, where, and how U.S. naval forces will contribute to enhancing security, preventing conflict and prevailing in war."

The NOC is described specifically as a strategy, not a body of tactics or doctrine. It lists two "strategic imperatives":

- Regionally concentrated, credible combat power to:
  - Limit regional conflict with deployed, decisive maritime power
  - Deter major power war
  - Win our nation's wars.
- Globally distributed, mission-tailored maritime forces to:
  - Contribute to homeland defense in depth
  - Foster and sustain cooperative relationships with more international partners
  - Prevent or contain local disruptions before they impact the global system.

The 2010 NOC retains the skeleton of naval missions delineated by Stansfield Turner in 1974: presence, deterrence, power projection, and sea control. The NOC emphasizes the ubiquity of the sea, where a force may operate "free from reliance on local ports and airfields," a value that at least by implication attests to the U.S. ability to function as a hegemon: to intervene in crises with or without allies. Sea basing is offered as a means for executing far-flung missions. United States–only capabilities are qualified by recognition of the need for "global awareness," the need to collect and use information, a task greatly facilitated by allying with partners and global information networks.

Irregular challenges are recognized by the NOC, which identifies "criminal, insurgent, and terrorist" threats, in addition to humanitarian assistance and disaster assistance operations. Two interesting examples of the emphasis on such missions are a "fisheries patrol" through Pacific island exclusive economic zones by one of the Navy's newest *Arleigh Burke*–class destroyers and the embarkation of a destroyer-squadron commander in one of the Navy's two hospital ships for a five-month deployment to six Southeast Asian and Oceania nations.[23]

The focus of this strategy remains, however, on the requirement for the sea services—Navy, Marine Corps, Coast Guard—to guarantee the maritime security of the United States, to protect the sovereignty and maritime resources of the nation, to support free and open sea lines of communication, and to counter maritime terrorism, weapons proliferation, transnational crime and piracy, environmental damage, and illegal immigration. Of note is the NOC's support for "homeland defense in depth," defined as "globally-distributed naval forces conducting maritime security operations."

The 2010 NOC is an inherently joint and combined strategy, dependent for success on cooperation with all concerned U.S. government agencies and foreign partners. Sea-power challenges are identified as arising from "increasingly capable blue water adversaries," a phrase obviously denoting China, particularly since the next item on this list is "theater anti-access weapons," followed by "area denial weapons," and then "technologies that disrupt space and cyberspace capabilities."

The mission of deterrence is logically categorized as both nuclear and conventional, with the former carried out in the maritime realm by a new fleet of ballistic-missile submarines. Conventional deterrence includes ballistic-missile defense as a mission for Aegis-armed ships but includes "preventive deterrence" through U.S. cooperation with friends and allies possessing capable naval forces.

The NOC's success depends, of course, on the United States being able to deploy the naval force structure required to carry it out. Despite the fact that the Navy in 2009 deployed total tonnage equal to that of the seventeen next-largest navies combined, this construct, focused on nuclear-powered aircraft carriers (CVNs) and their embarked air wings, rests in 2012 on a foundation less assured than at any time since the end of the Cold War in 1990.[24]

CVNs are moving toward prohibitive cost, with the next class, the first of which will be USS *Gerald R. Ford,* currently estimated to cost at least \$13.1 billion apiece, not including the air wing.[25] That air wing, featuring F/A-18 and F/A-35 aircraft, will face range and payload limitations that will force truly innovative air mission planning. Another problem for future U.S. airpower, both Air Force and Navy, is that upon completion of the F/A-35 aircraft, unless currently unannounced programs emerge, the United States will for the first time since 1903 not have a tactical aircraft in development.

The numbers of warships, submarines, and supporting logistics vessels required to execute NOC 2010 also face uncertain futures. The Navy's stated goal of 313 ships is derived from anticipated missions in a maritime world dominated by nontraditional threats and is a significant increase over the 2012 strength of 288 ships. With the dramatically increased cost of the advanced technologies and the need for the maximum capabilities in these ships, that number of ships currently appears out of reach, especially in view of post-Iraq/Afghanistan defense-budget reductions.[26]

The U.S. Navy's *Program Guide for 2012* highlights increased investment in unmanned systems and increased use of advanced bases—Djibouti, the Philippines, and Diego Garcia are mentioned—to maximize "the most forward presence possible" to be extracted from a fleet reduced in numbers.[27] This heavy commitment ashore both represents the Navy's ability to support divergent national security policies and reflects a wider interpretation of "power projection," in this case extending naval power overland and, often, supplementing nominal Army and Marine Corps warfare missions.

The lessening mission ashore in Southwest Asian waters will not, however, reduce the role played by the U.S. Navy in carrying out the dictates of national security priorities laid out in the 2007 maritime strategy. At sea, on any given day an average of more than 44,000 sailors are deployed, and almost half of the fleet's 288 ships are under way somewhere on the world's oceans. Many of these at-sea commitments concern training and exercises, but a major portion of the ship days under way are spent in Asian waters, in support of bilateral and multilateral commitments in the Pacific and Indian Oceans.

In support of these goals, Roughead listed five priorities for the Navy:

- Continue to be the dominant, ready naval force across all maritime missions
- Build a Navy with appropriate force structure and strategic laydown
- Maintain decision superiority
- Align the requirements, resources, and acquisition processes
- Evolve and establish international relationships.

He then provided eighteen intentions that would "guide our actions and communications":

- Continue to be the most dominant, ready and influential naval force, globally and across all naval missions
- Build a Navy with appropriate force structure and strategic lay down necessary to implement the Maritime Strategy
- Achieve Decision Superiority
- Align the requirements, resources, and acquisition processes to achieve accountability and deliver the right capability and capacity on time and at the optimum cost throughout the lifecycle
- We will evolve and establish international relationships to increase security and achieve common interests in the maritime domain
- Integrate war-fighting capabilities with the Marine Corps to meet objectives of the Maritime Strategy and Naval Operations Concept
- Anticipate changes in joint force posture and operational demands in the middle East, determine how those changes will affect Navy posture, positioning, and operational tempo and adjust accordingly
- Anticipate changes in global military (especially naval) forces, discern changes in operational and strategic patterns, and adjust Navy posture, positioning, and operational tempo accordingly
- Optimize Navy staffs to efficiently and effectively support the Fleet and external constituencies
- Instill in our uniformed and civilian force a focus on mission and individual readiness that is underpinned by our Navy ethos

- Attract, recruit, develop, assign, and retain a diverse, high-performing, competency-based and mission-focused force and ensure the welfare of our Sailors, Navy civilians, and their families
- Develop preeminent expertise and proficiency in planning, organizing and commanding at the operational level
- Define the roles and responsibilities of each element within the Enterprise and determine how the Enterprise construct should be most effectively integrated into headquarters processes
- Leverage Science and Technology (S&T) initiatives to ensure warfighting benefits accrue to future Sailors
- Assess the return on investment (ROI) in all we do, appreciating that our people, time and money are finite; and we must manage initiatives to guarantee the appropriate balance of efficiency and risk
- Define and articulate how we win
- Complement key actions and initiatives with effective communication methods and messages to maximize our effectiveness and return on investment
- Move forward with the Coast Guard to ensure security in the maritime domain.

Close Navy–Coast Guard cooperation is particularly important for homeland defense. Measures implemented since the 9/11 attacks include the Maritime Transportation Security Act (MTSA) of 2002, which requires merchant ships bound for U.S. ports to provide notice from twenty-four to ninety-six hours in advance of their arrival and to install automatic identification systems (AISs). The United States also led a campaign to add an International Ship and Port Security (ISPS) Code to the Safety of Life at Sea (SOLAS) Convention.[28]

These programs represent positive steps in U.S. presentation of a maritime strategy involving both Navy and Coast Guard. Their success, however, depends on the cooperation of the international maritime community. The continued U.S. failure to ratify the UNCLOS is not a step forward in engaging that community.

FUTURE COURSE

U.S. maritime power faces the most complex—although, as a consequence of its superior capabilities, notably not the most dangerous—mission set of any nation. U.S. combatants today are certainly more capable and numerous than those of any other navy; in fact, the nation's 203 warships nearly match the combined Chinese and Russian navies of 205 in numbers and in capabilities, based on technological, equipment, and personnel factors.

The United States shows very little sign of ceding its place as the world's most powerful naval power—its $700 billion 2009 defense budget almost matched the rest of the world's defense spending put together. But it confronts many improving navies in an increasingly challenging world. The 113th Congress surprisingly agreed with significant defense cuts proposed by the executive branch as part of the sequester, but the increasing cost of ships, aircraft, and weapon systems is likely to impose reductions in any event.

The Navy and Air Force have joined to develop a new strand of operational art, known as "Air-Sea Battle" (ASB). ASB remained in 2013 very much a concept, with no written doctrine, proven technology, or demonstrated operational feasibility.[29] It originated as a means, during the defense budgetary battles following the drawdown of U.S. forces from Iraq and Afghanistan, for the Navy and the Air Force to maximize the synergistic effect of increased operational jointness. ASB's similarity to the U.S. Army's "Air-Land Battle" (ALB) of the 1970s and 1980s lies in their respective abbreviations, not their operational concepts.

ALB was developed to confront a Soviet land invasion on the central European front. ASB has no such specificity but reflects U.S. concern with any restricted maritime area, especially with the Strait of Hormuz under the gun of a belligerent Iran or a Taiwan scenario involving Chinese forces.[30] Since its inception in 2009, ASB has been subsumed within the Joint Operational Access Concept (JOAC), an all-service formulation described by the chairman of the Joint Chiefs of Staff, Gen. Martin E. Dempsey, as a "framework [that] describes how we will gain entry and maintain access anywhere and in any domain: land, air, space, sea, and cyber."[31]

Thus, both ASB and the JOAC are in keeping with the nearly two-century-old, basic U.S. maritime strategic consideration of maintaining access to the world's maritime arenas. The Pacific commander, Adm. Samuel J. Locklear, has outlined five priorities for his huge command:

- Strengthen and advance alliances and partnerships
- Mature the U.S.-China military-to-military relationship
- Develop the U.S.-India strategic partnership
- Remain prepared to respond to a Korean Peninsula contingency
- Counter transnational threats[32]

These follow recent U.S. security policy dictates and reflect the maritime nature of the Pacific Command, stretching from the U.S. West Coast to the northern Arabian Sea. The five priorities recognize the need for more extensive participation by allied and friendly navies to respond to reduced U.S. Navy numbers, the increasingly transnational nature of such threats as piracy and terrorism, and the continuing dangers posed by North Korea. The second and third points recognize the increasing maritime presence of China and India and the vital necessity of cooperating with both, while being prepared to counter threats not perceived as such by one or the other.

The Navy's task is not eased by the refusal of Congress to ratify the UNCLOS treaty. Every president since Ronald Reagan has urged ratification and has stated that pending ratification the United States would abide by the treaty's stipulations.[33] Despite this decades-old bipartisan support for the treaty, the UNCLOS remains opposed by enough senators to have failed passage in 2012.[34]

U.S. Navy

The new strategy announced by the White House in early 2012 incorporated the decommissioning of several ships, including seven *Ticonderoga*-class cruisers equipped with the Aegis antiair warfare system, reducing the Navy to less than 280 ships. Speaking in late February 2012, Secretary of the Navy Ray Mabus insisted that "the fleet is not going to go down. . . . [T]he fleet of 2017 will have more capable ships equipped with state-of-the-art technology. . . . In the next five years after this FYDP—so from 2018 through 2022—we have a plan to grow our fleet. . . . [W]e're going to cross the threshold of 300 ships in our fleet by 2019."[35]

Mabus did not repeat that the Navy's goal for 2030 was 313 ships, which as noted appears to be an increasingly unattainable number, given present and likely future resources available for ship and aircraft acquisition. In fact, the almost certain permanent reduction of the fleet to below three hundred ships will place increased burdens on those ships and their sailors. Barring a major reordering of U.S. national security priorities, the Navy must be prepared to operate not just in the U.S. littoral, in defense of the homeland, but also worldwide.

Adm. Jonathan Greenert, who succeeded Roughead as CNO, issued the Navy's *2012 Program Guidance*. He lists six "Strategic Imperatives of Our Maritime Strategy":

- Deter major power war
- Win our nation's wars
- Limit regional conflict with forward-deployed decisive maritime power
- Contribute to homeland defense in depth
- Foster and sustain cooperative relationships with more international partners
- Prevent or contain local disruptions

These imperatives require:

- Actively countering violent extremists and destabilizing threats
- Rebalancing our focus toward the Asia-Pacific
- Sustaining our presence in the Middle East and South Asia
- Evolving our posture in Europe and pursuing new partnerships in Africa and Latin America
- Assuring freedom of access throughout the global commons
- Countering the proliferation of weapons of mass destruction[36]

Core capabilities in the face of this challenge are given as forward presence, deterrence, sea control and power projection; maritime security and HA/DR are described as "expanded core capabilities."

This 2012 document provides further evidence that the 313-ship goal is not considered realistic by the Navy's senior leadership. The imperatives and supporting core capabilities are traditional naval paradigms. The "challenges and opportunities" are significant in their signaled shift

from the decade-old campaigns in Southwest Asia to the more traditional
U.S. maritime interests in Asian waters.

2012 MARITIME ISSUES

The various documents promulgated by the U.S. Navy since 2001 address
current maritime security concerns. They do so, however, without a
discrete, targeted focus, and for several reasons. First, as has been the
case since the end of the Cold War, the United States is not confronted
by a major maritime threat. No Japanese or Soviet navy is on the horizon; some analysts point to the growing Chinese navy as a threat, but
the People's Liberation Army Navy (PLAN) remains far behind the U.S.
Navy in terms of numbers and capability. Second, the past decade's wars
have been primarily ground oriented. Third, the maritime problems that
currently receive national attention are of a relatively low order—piracy,
terrorism at sea, proliferation of WMD on the sea-lanes, smuggling, and
HA/DR situations in which naval forces can play a significant role.

All of these missions are subsumed within the most basic maritime
requirement of all—defense of the homeland. This mantra comes easily
to the lips but involves a very wide range of geographic, political, social,
economic, and technological issues. The Navy also must continue striving
to maintain a force capable of classic maritime warfare; however, the lack
of a likely opponent makes it difficult to garner enthusiastic support for
that. Instead, the Navy is seizing upon those lower-order missions, all of
which are most effectively executed through multilateral cooperation.

COUNTERPIRACY AND COUNTERTERRORISM OPERATIONS

A prime example of a lower-order mission is the current campaign against
piracy in the Gulf of Aden and proximate Indian Ocean waters. Somalia
is the source of twenty-first-century piracy in Southwest Asian waters,
a phenomenon resulting in large part from the political, economic, and
social strife that has marked the Horn of Africa for at least the past twenty

years. The lack of stable government and the absence of the rule of law ashore have led directly to the rise of piracy at sea. Fighting piracy is more a law-enforcement mission than classic naval combat, although navies have been fighting pirates since navies were founded.

The United States has been deploying ships to this area on a dedicated antipiracy mission since 2001. Warships from at least a dozen other nations, including all the world's major maritime powers, have joined the counterpiracy campaign. This impressive multilateral effort has taken several organizational forms.

CONCLUSION

Since the late 1940s, successive generations of national leaders in Washington have pursued policies based on a U.S. role as guarantor of world peace. This mission requires the Navy to deploy fleets with global capabilities, fleets that in turn require nuclear rather than conventionally powered submarines; aircraft carriers capable of providing airpower at great distances and for extended periods of time away from the United States; large, high-endurance escort ships to defend those carriers; and a large train of support ships capable of providing fuel, stores, and repair parts over those same distances and periods. Admiral Greenert testified in February 2012 to the impressive, perhaps excessive, pace of operations maintained by the Navy, stating, "On any given day over the last year, more than 50,000 sailors were underway or deployed on 145 of the Navy's 285 ships and submarines, 100 of them deployed overseas. They were joined by more than 15 land-based patrol aircraft and helicopters, 1,000 information dominance personnel, and over 4,000 Naval Expeditionary Combat Command Sailors on the ground."[37]

This mission and force composition continues to support and to be supported by a system of treaties with foreign allies and partners. In Asia, this alliance structure features mutual defense treaties with Japan, South Korea, the Philippines, and Australia. The U.S.-Australian pact was originally the ANZUS treaty, including New Zealand. The United States has a series of defense agreements with Thailand, port and berthing arrangements with Malaysia and Singapore, and a unique defense relationship with Taiwan, spelled out in the 1979 Taiwan Relations Act (TRA).

Except for the TRA, these agreements arose out of Cold War concerns about Soviet-sponsored international communism, with its attendant insurgencies, civil wars, and nuclear tightrope walking. That they continue in effect is due in part to inertia, in part to loyalty to long-standing allies, in part to concern for regional stability, and in part to concern about current Chinese military modernization and future challenges to U.S. interests in Asia.

One response to that latter concern has been the U.S. Navy's long campaign to draw closer to the Indian navy. This campaign has borne fruit, as the two forces now engage in major exercises, in coordinated operations to ameliorate the effects of the tsunami that struck South Asia in 2004, and in cooperative efforts to counter piracy in the northwestern Indian Ocean.

The U.S.-Indian navy relationship is still very much a work in progress, however, since the Indian government remains leery about forming alliances. Additionally, New Delhi's strategic concerns are largely limited to the Indian Ocean region (IOR), although recent moves toward the South China Sea and the Pacific Ocean indicate a broadening of that strategic focus. More specifically, New Delhi does not share Washington's depth of feeling about Iran's putative nuclear weapons program, and it views U.S. support for Pakistan with misgivings.

A closer relationship with the Indian navy also will require changes by the United States. First, the current division by the Departments of Defense and State between East and South Asia will have to be modified in administrative and operational realms to yield a more logical "Indo-Pacific" focus. Second, the 2011 rebalancing from Southwest Asia to East Asia must be managed in such a way as to retain some effort in the Indian Ocean, from Malacca to Hormuz.

The shift in U.S. policy toward East and South Asia will require a reorientation of naval deployments in this intensely maritime region. As first steps, the United States has already announced the homeporting of at least one, and possibly four, warships in Singapore and the creation of a training facility for Marines in northwestern Australia. U.S. Navy ship deployments have already begun reflecting the rebalancing.[38] Forward homeporting has long proven viable in Japan; in addition to Singapore, the United States is considering the forward basing of warships in the Persian Gulf.[39]

Despite post-2008 economic concerns, there seems little possibility in 2013 that the United States will relinquish its "world police" role, although the wars of this century's first decade have placed sobering constraints on an expansive definition of associated missions. Hence, an imbalance between strategic desire and capability has developed.

Key to the future ability of the U.S. Navy to successfully execute missions assigned by the national command authority are the resources on which it has to draw—namely, the ships, aircraft, and submarines that form the fleet and, especially, the men and women who form their crews. The required capabilities are increasingly expensive, as technological complexity grows and advanced technology becomes more commonly available to maritime forces around the world.

There is little indication that the Navy intends to deviate from its reliance on very large aircraft carriers as the centerpiece of its fleet. This commitment to large carriers flies in the face of several naval developments, including increasing numbers and capabilities of conventionally powered submarines, the advent of effective cyber warfare, increasing presence of (but also doubts about the inviolability of) crucial space-based assets for communication and surveillance, increasingly sophisticated antiship cruise and ballistic missiles, and the huge cost of the behemoth carriers. Furthermore, as a result of globalization, several nations are fielding systems that threaten carriers or arguably make them less cost-effective than alternatives.

At the other end of the ship-procurement spectrum is the U.S. Army and Marine Corps acquisition of high-speed ferries for the Pacific theater. These are essentially unarmed vessels capable of carrying more than nine hundred troops at thirty-six knots, a capability that provides a rapid seaborne response for civil disturbances, disaster relief, and other contingencies best relieved by low-level military operations.

U.S. maritime strategy in the twenty-first century, as periodically and repetitively promulgated since the end of the Cold War, would seem to require forces and resources that are not likely to be available. A strategy less ambitious than continued hegemonism (global command of the sea) is required. That more realistic maritime strategy might be called "selective engagement," or "offshore balancing"—implying increased reliance on multilateralism.

Continued U.S. hegemony at sea will require "full spectrum dominance," by a navy omnipotent and omniscient in specific theaters and scenarios. Selective engagement implies a dramatic change in ship deployment patterns, from a regularly scheduled model to one of on-call assignments. Offshore balancing implies a multilateral approach, with greatly increased reliance on both friends and allies—and on nations not fitting either category but having interests in particular maritime situations in line with that of the United States.

This last concept would offer policy makers more limited maritime power but might force a more intelligent employment of it. As the navy grows smaller and Asian nations prosper economically and modernize militarily, Washington will be obliged to reassess its three-quarters of a century as *the* global power, turning to an alternative strategy, perhaps offshore balancing, that will offer a menu of selective engagement options. These will perforce be limited to the securing of vital national security objectives.

Any U.S. naval analyst is concerned with actual and potential competition. Shipbuilding plans must be substantiated; the end of the Cold War deprived naval planners of that necessary target against which to plan. The temptation, of course, is to put China in that position, but it must be emphasized that the Cold War is over and that China is not the Soviet Union. Clearly, however, Beijing's increasing defense spending, with pride of place going to the air force and navy, naturally draws the attention of U.S. naval planners and strategists.

Friends and allies are crucial in the Asian maritime balance of power in the twenty-first century. The United States is fortunate in having a substantial list of maritime nations with which it shares political objectives and with whose navies it frequently operates. This list is headed by Japan, to which we turn next.

three

JAPAN

INTRODUCTION

No Asian nation is more dependent on the sea than Japan; whether with respect to its primary source of food, the arteries vital to its economic survival, or the essential medium for its national security, Japan is the maritime nation without compare.[1] Furthermore, the country has significant maritime disputes over islands and fisheries with all its immediate neighbors: Russia, both Koreas, and China.

One result of this dependence is a navy that ranks near or at the top of indigenous Asian maritime forces, in terms of personnel competence and technical sophistication, if not in numbers of ships. The Japan Coast Guard (JCG) ranks similarly high among its Asian counterparts. Other signs of Japan's maritime orientation are its merchant fleet and its shipbuilding industry, the latter ranking among the world's top three.[2]

STRATEGIC VIEW FROM TOKYO

Japan's modern navy, the Japan Maritime Self-Defense Force (JMSDF), emerged when Tokyo began rearming within a few years of its devastating defeat in World War II. The new forces were strictly defensive in purpose and character. Today, however, Japan's self-defense forces have shifted from a strictly minimalist defense of Japanese territory to missions with a global focus. This change has to a degree been a gradual process over the past sixty years, but it has been driven by several factors.

These have occurred under Japan's overarching strategic situation of near-total reliance on global supply lines for food, energy, and foreign trade. This reliance has been shadowed by pressure from the United States to play a greater, more wide-ranging role in security affairs, pressure from domestic political elements for the nation to act more as a "normal" country, and by the changing character of the East Asian security environment, marked by sometimes belligerent actions by China and North Korea. Other, more generic, post–Cold War factors that have influenced the shift of Japan's defense focus include the advent of fourth-generation war, the rise of nonstate actors as security threats, and the emergence of space and cyber as two new theaters of warfare.[3]

Japan's first significant post-1945 strategy document was the 1957 Basic Policy on National Defense.[4] It addressed defense of Japanese territory, which includes the home islands and Ryukyu island chain, in close coordination with the United States.[5] This approach to defense of the homeland, with reliance on U.S. assistance, was repeated in the 1976 National Defense Program Outline (NDPO).

The 1969 Nixon Doctrine apparently influenced the thinking of Japanese strategists, but it did not result in significant changes to Tokyo's defensive strategy. The doctrine, announced by President Richard M. Nixon in Guam as he returned from what must have been a depressing visit to South Vietnam, emphasized the responsibility of U.S. allies to increase their contributions to the worldwide fight against communism. This doctrine was reflected in a communiqué between Nixon and Prime Minister Sato Eisaku that was signed in November 1969. The communiqué extended Japan's security concerns from the home islands to include Korea and Taiwan.[6]

Japan's Diet passed the International Peace Cooperation Law (IPCL) in 1992, authorizing the Japanese Defense Force (JDF), which included naval, air, and land forces, to participate in United Nation peacekeeping operations (UNPKOs). None of the UNPKOs in which the JDF has since participated have directly threatened Japan's security; hence, these operations have supported global concerns, not homeland defense.

The 1993–94 North Korean nuclear crisis and the 1996 Taiwan Strait crisis both emphasized the regional nature of possible threats to Japan's security. These fit the pattern addressed in the 1995 iteration of the NDPO for situations in areas surrounding Japan "which have important influence on national peace and stability." This phrase was repeated at the 1996 summit meeting in Tokyo between President William J. Clinton and Prime Minister Hashimoto Ryutaro; their joint statement noted "situations that may emerge in the areas surrounding Japan and which will have an important influence on the peace and stability of Japan." This geographic description—"areas surrounding Japan"—obviously applies to a maritime area but has never been precisely described by Tokyo, a factor that lends it strength, although causing much concern on the part of Beijing, which fears that it includes Taiwan.[7]

The phrase achieved the status of gospel when it was repeated in the 1999 Law Concerning Measures to Enhance Peace and Security of Japan in Situations in Areas Surrounding Japan. Beijing again expressed unease with the phrase, asking whether Taiwan was included, but did not receive a definitive answer.[8]

The trend toward greater international commitment by the JMSDF and other military services reached a threshold in Afghanistan and Iraq following the terrorist attacks of 11 September 2001. Tokyo authorized deployment to the northern Arabian Sea to support U.S. operations against Afghanistan. The Ministry of Foreign Affairs justified JMSDF efforts in the Indian Ocean in 2004 with the statement, "Japan is vigorously tackling the Iraq issue, understanding that it is a critical issue directly related to Japan's national interests."[9]

Despite the fact that regular JMSDF oiler deployments to support U.S. operations in the Indian Ocean ended in 2010, the period from 1957 to 2012 has seen as both an expansion of JMSDF operations and a broadening of Japan's maritime strategy from a narrowly focused defense of the home islands to a global focus. Today, Japan's naval strategy, although not formally promulgated, aims at controlling the waters surrounding the Japanese archipelago—essentially, an anti-access/area-denial (A2/AD) strategy.

In support of this strategy, the JMSDF evolved into a navy capable of twenty-first-century warfare. It is especially proficient in antisubmarine warfare (ASW), with the capability of operating effectively, and the intention to do so, throughout the western Pacific Ocean, between Japan and the South China Sea. Indeed, there is evidence that the JMSDF has plans to operate in that sea.[10] The JCG and JMSDF are also expanding their efforts to help smaller nations develop more capable maritime forces.[11]

JAPAN MARITIME SELF-DEFENSE FORCE

The capability of the JMSDF in 2012 represents a remarkable growth from the abolishment of Japan's armed forces following the country's complete defeat in World War II. The force's avowed defense-only role quickly grew obsolete during the Cold War. Some JMSDF forces, particularly minesweepers, participated in the Korean War; the JMSDF de facto area of operations was significantly extended in 1978 by an agreement with the U.S. Navy's Pacific Fleet. The accord was formalized in 1982, when the two national governments agreed to its thrust, which was to commit Japan to protect the SLOCs out to a distance of a thousand nautical miles from the home islands.[12]

The JMSDF's scope of operations widened more significantly in 1991, when it deployed several minesweepers to the Persian Gulf to locate and destroy mines sown by Iraq. This mission demonstrated both the JMSDF's impressive professional competence and its ability to operate far from home. Another significant step in loosening restrictions on Tokyo's exercise of naval force occurred in December 2001, following the terrorist attacks of 9/11, when Japan amended its IPCL to allow its military to participate in "the core operations of peacekeeping forces," without specific geographic restrictions.[13]

These Indian Ocean deployments were not without political cost to Japan's government. Restrictions emerged from the Diet limiting refueling operations to those U.S. ships engaged in operations in Afghanistan; supporting U.S. ships engaged in Iraqi operations was forbidden. When the realities of Indian Ocean operations came to the attention of some legislators—that limiting refueling to ships engaged in support of the Afghanistan incursion was extremely difficult, if not impossible—investigation into JMSDF practices occurred. Tokyo finally ended these refueling deployments in 2010, after several earlier attempts in the Diet to do so failed.[14]

This far-station competence has been repeated throughout Japan's participation in counterpiracy operations in the Gulf of Aden, ongoing since 2009. The operations by Japanese forces on scene, two destroyers and two P-3C patrol aircraft based at the Republic of Djibouti, were in July 2012 extended for another year.[15]

As for threats to its vital national security concerns, Tokyo is seriously concerned about Beijing's expanding maritime power, both commercial and naval. In its 2011 *China Security Report*, the National Institute of Defense Studies (NIDS), the Japanese Ministry of Defense's think tank, concluded that "China is rigorously exploring maritime resources and security sea lanes of communication," while its coast-guard forces—including the China Maritime Surveillance (CMS) and Fisheries Law Enforcement Command (FLEC)—were strengthening their capabilities, especially in the East and South China Seas. Regarding the People's Liberation Army Navy, NIDS concluded that China's navy "aims to extend its 'near seas' operational capabilities to cover the area as far as the so-called 'Second Island Chain'" to enforce an A2/AD strategy.[16]

Furthermore, NIDS opined, the PLAN was striving to become a blue-water navy to oppose "an enhancement of U.S. military presence in the Asia-Pacific region." This represented an expansion of Chinese foreign policy making, resulting in "China's increasing assertiveness," which has negatively affected East Asia's "maritime security environment." More immediately, it advised, Tokyo must be alert to Beijing's extending its "assertive attitude" from the South China Sea to the East China Sea and "the waters surrounding Japan."[17]

JAPAN'S MARITIME STRATEGY

The current Japanese defense strategy is addressed in the 2005 National Defense Program Guidelines, which affirm that the country's security depends on its defense forces and its alliance with the United States.[18] Of Japan's armed services, the maritime self-defense force is the most important, because it is responsible for safeguarding the sea lines of communication upon which the nation depends for its economic well-being.

Any question about this priority was settled by the 1973 oil crisis, an event that conclusively demonstrated Japan's dependence on the SLOCs. Their defense was confirmed as a strategic priority beyond naval circles.

The mid-1970s Soviet emphasis on strengthening its Pacific Fleet emphasized this priority on a national level.

Tokyo reassessed its maritime priorities following the end of the Cold War. Both the 1995 NDPO and the 2004 Defense Program Guidelines (DPG) sought to delineate capabilities to confront a potential military problem in Northeast Asia. Of particular concern were, and remain, China's naval modernization, exacerbated by forward-leaning activities in the East China Sea, and North Korea's nuclear threats.

By the beginning of 2009, the JMSDF had reassessed its growth of the preceding two decades, as part of the drafting of a maritime strategy for the new century. Japanese maritime strategy had been understood and prominent during the Cold War. It is striking that it was only a short two decades after the Cold War's end that the situation in Northeast Asia developed to the point where Tokyo recognized a need for a new, formal maritime strategy.

The essence of the new maritime strategy is twofold. The first aspect is defense of regional SLOCs, perhaps best defined by a triangle, the points of which are Tokyo, Guam, and Taiwan. This area is not dissimilar to that for which the JMSDF took ASW responsibility during the Cold War. It is not an easily managed responsibility, because it requires proficiency across the spectrum of both coast-guard and naval missions, from surveillance to defense against ballistic missiles.

Second, the JMSDF is tasked with fulfilling responsibilities under the mutual defense treaty with the United States. This relationship continues to provide the basis for Japan's maritime defense efforts. In addition to expressing support for the U.S. policy reorientation, or "rebalancing," toward East Asia announced by Washington in 2011, Tokyo's policy is characterized by "enhancement of its defense posture in areas including the Southwestern Islands." Japan has expressed concern about the "increasingly uncertain security environment in the Asia-Pacific region," advocating strengthening "engagement with countries in the Asia-Pacific region."[19]

Tokyo's primary national security focus was directed against possible Soviet aggression during the Cold War but now is focused on North Korea and China, the most likely maritime threats to Japanese interests. Cooperation with friendly third nations is being pursued; Tokyo invited Australia and the United States to the Sixth Pacific Island Leaders Meeting in Naga, on Okinawa, in May 2012.[20] Such increased international cooperation is envisioned further in the possible defense of common interests with the Republic of South Korea (ROK) and India. Officially unspoken is the possibility of support for operations in support of Taiwan.[21]

The 2011 DPG thus has long been under development and has led to increased, more open Japanese interest in security arrangements with other Asian nations, from South Korea to India. Interacting with the Association of Southeast Asian Nations has been an objective of Tokyo since the 1977 Fukuda Initiative, whereby the then–prime minister announced a policy of increasing ties with Southeast Asia. By 2008 Japan was ASEAN's second-largest trading partner.[22]

Closer relations with India in the maritime security sphere were signaled in 2009, when an Indian navy task group conducted an exercise with the JMSDF in Japanese waters. In late 2011 the Japanese and Indian defense ministers agreed on further cooperation between their two navies.[23]

Japan is pursuing similar, closer security relationships with both Vietnam and Australia. Tokyo and Hanoi signed a Memorandum on Defense Cooperation Enhancement in 2011. This agreement is aimed specifically at keeping "in check China's growing assertiveness in the South China Sea and East China Sea."[24]

Prime Ministers John Howard of Australia and Shinzo Abe signed a Joint Declaration on Security Cooperation in March 2007; this was reinforced in 2010, when the two governments signed an Acquisition and Cross-Servicing Agreement, which pledged closer military cooperation and provided for the "reciprocal provision of supplies and services between the Self-Defense Forces of Japan (JSDF) and the Australian Defense Force (ADF)."[25] These agreements with Hanoi and Canberra demonstrate Tokyo's increasingly active foreign policy. This development reflects Japan's attempts to overcome further the still-present memories of World War II, concern about Chinese and North Korean activities, and perhaps a perceived weakening of U.S. military capability in East Asia.[26]

These foreign-policy initiatives and the new defense guidelines will become effective only if the JMSDF is funded for the modernization and expansion required if the nation is to maintain its status as a major Asian maritime power. This funding is at issue, particularly for two reasons.

First, the 2011 Fukushima disaster is leading Japan rapidly away from reliance on nuclear power, a change that will increase the nation's reliance on the seaborne import of fossil fuels from the Middle East.[27]

Second, Japan faces growing naval prowess on the part of South Korea and China, two countries with which it has sovereignty and maritime-resource disputes. A corollary to this second reason may be the shrinking U.S. fleet, with attendant major defense-budget reductions looming in Washington, a popular focus on economic problems, and the strong links between the U.S. and Chinese economies. This situation has the potential to turn American public support away from a Cold War–era defense treaty seen as no longer necessary.

Tokyo has set out in the DPG three security objectives: (1) to prevent external threats from harming Japan; (2) to contribute to improving international security so as to prevent threats from emerging; and (3) to contribute to global peace and stability and to human security.

The guidelines lay out steps to reach these objectives, including cooperation with the United States and with the international community. Defense will continue to form "the basic principles of defense policy," as will the "three non-nuclear principles." These were stated by Prime Minister Sato in 1967 and formally endorsed by the Diet in 1971; they are that Japan will neither possess nor manufacture nuclear weapons and will not permit their presence in Japanese territory. The objective of more participation in international peace cooperation activities is stated, as is an active role in nuclear disarmament and nonproliferation efforts.

The "security environment surrounding Japan" is described as comprising a "number of so-called 'gray zone' disputes," which are characterized as "confrontations over territory, sovereignty and economic interests" that do not pose a danger of escalation into wars but that are "on the increase." The security environment is further marked by a "global shift in the balance of power," as a result of "the rise of emerging powers and the relative change" of U.S. influence.

Although invasion of Japan's home islands is not considered a viable threat, the guidelines identify issues of concern.[28] These are "sustained access to cyberspace," terrorism, piracy, North Korean nuclear and missile threats, China's military modernization and lack of transparency, and increased Russian military activities.

The guidelines' section on issues of concern is followed by a discussion of four "basic policies to ensure Japan's security." First are the nation's own efforts, including improved capability "to collect and analyze information, while strengthening the information security system."

Second is the effort to enhance rapidity in decision making, to ensure a "coordinated and integrated response to contingencies."

Establishment of an organization similar to the U.S. National Security Council is a third issue; the fourth is participation in international peace-keeping activities "in a more efficient and effective manner," with "consideration of the actual situations of UN peace-keeping operations." This caveat indicates the ongoing domestic political discussion about the depth of Japan's participation in international security affairs. Most interesting of all is the shift in basic defense philosophy expressed in the resolution that Japan will build a "dynamic defense force," superseding the current "basic defense force concept." The decision means deploying military capability for purposes beyond the needs of deterrence, enabling the country to play "a more active role" in international security activities.

"Cooperation with its ally" is then emphasized, because the alliance with the United States is "indispensable in ensuring Japan's peace and security." Cooperation will include continuing strategic dialogue and collaboration, with a new emphasis on cyberspace security. Increased regional cooperation is noted, with specific mention of South Korea, Australia, India, and the ASEAN nations, as part of creating "a security network" in the Asia-Pacific region.

China, the European Union (EU), the North Atlantic Treaty Organization, and other European countries—even Russia—are mentioned as possible partners in addressing "global security issues." This broadening of intended international cooperation seems to reflect two decisions: first that a more proactive posture is required to ensure Japan's security, and second that U.S. military capabilities, especially in the maritime realm, are in decline. The first point reflects loosening of constitutional and psychological limits imposed in the post–World War II period.[29]

Domestic political concerns are again addressed, in the point that "Japan will reduce the burden on local communities where U.S. military bases are located." This step is couched in terms of maintaining the U.S. contribution to deterrence, the subject of the fourth major point. This is deterrence to ensure "security in the sea and air space surrounding Japan," to include "responding to attacks on Japan's offshore islands," while trying to increase a stable security environment in the Asia-Pacific and globally.

The guidelines discuss the Japan Self-Defense Force (JSDF), but not in detail. They note the importance of enhancing capability but acknowledge a "drastic review" of the defense budget. This has meant a continued stagnation of that budget, just as the nation is trying to improve military efficiency through increased joint capability and focusing on defense of offshore islands. A list of steps to increase efficiency—to "maximize defense capability"—is provided, but even if such general measures are taken, the thrust of Tokyo's determination to reduce military expenditures cannot be overcome by more verbiage.

In sum, Japan's 2010 DPG and 2011 DPG reflect a perception that the nuclear threat that was the focus of the Cold War has ended, replaced by conventional security threats. China is the center of this concern, with North Korea its acolyte. The latter's ballistic-missile tests in 1998, 2006, 2009, 2012, and 2013 have reinforced this perception of Pyongyang. The guidelines' emphasis on building a dynamic instead of a defensive force indicate an intention to enhance the JSDF's proactive capability, especially with respect to the Senkakus and Takeshima; this capability is also reflected in the aim to exercise a greater international role, a notable change from the 2004 DPG's focus on deterring external threats from reaching Japan.

Tokyo's concerns about China as a military threat to Japanese security interests are clear. They are most evident in the goal of increasing the ability to defend the Senkakus, but they are also notable in the complaint about Beijing's lack of transparency regarding the composition and missions of its military. Tokyo's concerns are based on experience, such as the fact that in fiscal year 2010, 80 percent of the emergent flights by the Japan Air Self-Defense Force (JASDF) were in reaction to Russian or Chinese incursions into the nation's airspace.[30]

Concerns with China's growing military strength and naval operations have increased in recent years. In mid-2011 the Japanese government expressed its unease with "China's growing assertiveness and widening naval reach in nearby waters."[31] This sentiment was repeated in Japan's 2011 defense guidelines and has been followed by direct actions.

Japan is renaming many of the privately owned and other, previously unnamed, land features in the East China Sea, sovereignty over much of which is disputed by Beijing. Also, additional monitoring facilities are reportedly planned. This move is intended to strengthen Tokyo's sovereignty claims over not just the Senkakus but also the Shirakaba/ Chunxiao gas fields in the area.[32]

North Korea's threatened development of nuclear weapons and missiles capable of reaching Japan certainly concerns Tokyo, but China's increased military capability and pugnacious attitude is viewed as even more threatening. A third, if less intense, threat is perceived from Russia, with the considerable reduction of Moscow's military forces in Asia offset by its refusal to discuss returning to Japan control of the southern Kurile Islands it occupied at the end of World War II.[33]

These various threats are not simply perceptions. North Korea in the past few years has engaged in hostile activities, including sinking the South Korean corvette *Cheonan* in March 2010 and shelling the South Korean island of Yeonpyeong six months later. Numerous incidents involving North Korean and Chinese fishing boats have also occurred, during which neither Pyongyang nor Beijing has evinced interest in compromise.

THE UNITED NATIONS CONVENTION ON THE LAW OF THE SEA

Japan has signed and ratified the United Nations Convention on the Law of the Sea, although only after much hesitation about establishing exclusive economic zones—Japan being the only maritime nation so worried. Its concerns were outweighed by its dependence on the sea; seaborne shipping carries 99.7 percent of the nation's overall trade, and as stated by one Japanese analyst, "the maritime highway along the Eurasian rim literally constitutes the lifeline of the Japanese economy."[34]

Continuing concern with the maritime legal regime addressed by the UNCLOS occupies Japanese maritime analysts, who worry about China's self-declared "legal warfare." This concept, part of China's "three warfares," with psychological and media the other two, leads Beijing to pursue interpretations of the UNCLOS provisions at variance with those of the vast majority of the other signatories.[35]

Japan's legal concerns at sea are guarded primarily not by the Maritime Self-Defense Force but by the large and capable Japanese Coast Guard. The JCG has a challenging mission in enforcing maritime law, given the nation's very extensive coastline and the fact that territorial or maritime resource disputes exist with all its neighbors—Russia, Korea, and China (including Taiwan).

The JCG has achieved new prominence in the twenty-first century. For one thing, it is nominally a civilian organization and hence not bound by article 9 of the Japanese constitution imposed by the United States following World War II, stating that "land, sea, and air forces, as well as other war potential, will never be maintained."[36] Various administrations have defined this language in increasingly restrictive ways, banning participation in "collective self-defense," defining that term as referring to "defending an ally under attack." In the 1960s Tokyo "banned the military use of space, the export of arms, and the maintenance of a nuclear arsenal."[37]

This concept of purely "defensive defense" was in place by the late 1970s. It did not directly affect the JCG, but it negatively influenced the progress of the JMSDF toward twenty-first-century naval competence. The JCG by 2012 had become the nation's first line of maritime defense for issues other than outright war.

The JCG, with 13,000 personnel, is just one-quarter the strength of the JMSDF, but it operates under more liberal rules of engagement (ROE). The 2001 revision by the Diet of the Japan Coast Guard Law in the shadow of the 9/11 events authorized "the outright use of force to prevent maritime intrusion and to protect the Japanese homeland." It also authorized firing on noncooperative, suspicious vessels, authority demonstrated in action in the sinking of a North Korean "suspicious ship" in 2001.[38]

The JCG remains a very constrained force in terms of weapons and sensor capabilities, but appreciation of the its ability to engage in defense of Japan more actively than the JMSDF is reflected in the former's continued budget increases notwithstanding JDF cuts. These increases have been justified by "mounting concerns in the East China Sea area" resulting from Chinese actions.[39]

2010 Defense Plan

This defense plan was intended to cover the next ten years. Defense spending—which arguably defines strategy, in the end—is expected to increase by only about 0.1 percent during that period. This modest estimate does not promise very significant changes in JMSDF capabilities, especially in view of the defense budget's decrease in 2009.

Japan's maritime strategy includes a strong diplomatic element. What has been called its "sea-lane diplomacy" is a direct result of Tokyo's awareness of the nation's dependence on the SLOCs. Particularly important are the straits of Malacca and Singapore, Sunda, Lombok-Makassar, and the South China Sea itself—through which in the aggregate pass more than 40 percent of Japan's trade and 90 percent of its energy imports.[40]

This concern for the sea-lanes ties directly to concerns for the security of Japan's huge merchant shipping industry, including ships, shipyards, and port facilities, all of which rank near the top in global standing. Tokyo has taken a lead in furthering the strictures of the International Maritime Organization, the industry's primary regulatory body. These measures include the International Convention for the Safety of Life at Sea, which covers ship construction and safety; the International Convention for the Prevention of Pollution from Ships (MARPOL); the International Regulations for Preventing Collisions at Sea (COLREGS); the International Ship and Port Facility Code; and the International Safety Management Code, which regulates operating licenses for shipping companies.[41]

Tokyo's efforts to play the maritime diplomacy card have been enhanced by the JCG's nonmilitary nature. They have included a five-year program of assistance to the Philippine Coast Guard, which was reorganized and reequipped in 2001. Similar assistance has been provided to Indonesia and Malaysia. Japan has also contributed to regional efforts for the security of the Malacca Strait area. Foreign cadets are welcomed at the JCG academy.

JMSDF COMPOSITION

The JMSDF remains the smallest of Japan's military services, although it is the most capable maritime force in East Asia.[42] It is not as large as China's navy but is more technology-intensive, more experienced, and more highly trained. The JMSDF includes sixteen submarines, with six more planned;[43] two small *Hyuga*-class aircraft carriers, with a third under construction; two large destroyers with multihelicopter capability;

thirty-two destroyers, four of them equipped with the Aegis system and eight more under construction; six frigates; three large amphibious warfare ships; twenty-seven mine-warfare vessels, with at least two more planned; and five oilers.

The naval air arm is also formidable, with helicopters and a very capable maritime patrol force, including eight P-3 Orions and five EP-3 electronic surveillance aircraft. Still pending is arrival of the long-delayed F-35 aircraft from the United States, which will fly from the *Hyuga*s.[44] These ships will for the first time provide the fleet with organic, independent airpower, a key ingredient of twenty-first-century naval power.

The JMSDF's capital ships are submarines, but small aircraft carriers are joining the fleet. The professionalism of the service's personnel makes it a force able to fight very well in all naval warfare areas. The addition to the fleet of Aegis-equipped destroyers has provided the JMSDF with state-of-the-art antiair-warfare capability; the new *Soryu*-class submarine is both stealthier than its predecessors and equipped with air-independent propulsion.

Conclusion

Japan's maritime defense is closely tied to the mutual defense treaty with the United States and through that instrument to the U.S. Navy. This relationship includes homeporting of significant U.S. forces in Japan, primarily naval units. A U.S. aircraft carrier and escorts are stationed in Yokosuka, just south of Tokyo, while an amphibious assault group of three large ships is based in Sasebo. Japan pays most of the costs of this presence, under the title of "host-nation support" (HNS), amounting to $2.2 billion in 2011.[45]

The 2010 DPG is primarily concerned with China and North Korea, leading to an emphasis on the southwest rather than on the northern axis of Cold War concern. While the 2010 DPG was the first time this change of threat axis was spelled out, it is not new for the JMSDF. As long ago as 1996, Japan's Diet passed bills relating to the new Guidelines for Japan-U.S. Defense Cooperation, bills that received support from all the major parties, and Tokyo and Washington adopted them in April 1996. These guidelines stated that the 1978 Guidelines for Japan-U.S. Defense

Cooperation were superseded, in view of the downfall of the Soviet Union. The new measures highlighted concern about threats to Japan's security arising in "areas surrounding Japan," which the government defined as including the Taiwan Strait, with a regional emphasis "to contribute to the security of Japan and the maintenance of international peace and security in the Far East."[46]

A navy is a national symbol; in some cases, it represents a degree of hubris that influences national policies in negative, even disastrous, directions. The Imperial Japanese Navy played a role, albeit one secondary to the army's, in the militarization that beset Japan's policies in the 1930s. These policies led directly to World War II in Asia, a war that began with Japan's aggression in China in 1931 and ended fifteen years later in the aforementioned disaster, the atomic bombing of Hiroshima and Nagasaki.

Japan's strategic concerns today may be focused on North Korea and China, but the environment within which Tokyo operates remains strongly colored by the half-century from 1895 to 1945. During that period Japan conducted in East Asia a foreign policy of imperialism and warfare. Furthermore, Japanese policies were so harsh as to be self-defeating in the long term, leaving a residue of hatred that still remains a factor in the conduct of international relations throughout East Asia.

A Japanese navy was re-created as the JMSDF in 1950 and since has served admirably in a restricted role as an instrument of Japan's national security policy. In a way, the 1991 deployment of minesweepers to the Persian Gulf and the 2001 refueling operations in the Indian Ocean signaled Tokyo's reappearance as a power ready and willing to participate in international efforts to maintain maritime security.

The Indian Ocean refueling mission ended in 2010, but JMSDF participation in antipiracy efforts in the Gulf of Aden continue; Japan's international maritime role was also manifest in the 2005 disaster-relief operations in the tsunami-ruined areas of Indonesia. The JMSDF has also assumed a more prominent role in the most basic naval mission—homeland defense, especially against North Korea, the most frequent violator of Japanese territorial sovereignty, with notable clashes occurring in 1999 and 2001.

More recently, the JCG and the JMSDF have confronted incursions into home waters by Chinese naval combatants and vessels from other Chinese government agencies. Several reasons underlie these incursions.

First is the disputed sovereignty over the Senkaku Islands, which lay less than two hundred nautical miles southwest of Okinawa. Second is the disputed line of demarcation between the continental shelves claimed by Japan and China. This is significant because of seabed energy reserves coveted by both nations. Third is the effect on seaborne trade relative to claimed territorial waters. A fourth reason is the seabed mapping being conducted by Chinese hydrographic research vessels; this mapping is of use for both seabed mineral exploration and submarine operations.

Finally, national pride forms a significant driving force in most if not all sovereignty disputes, and it is no small factor in Japan's relations with China. This in turn involves domestic political considerations in both countries. Japan's politics, long dominated by the Liberal Democratic Party (LDP), have in recent years become notoriously unstable. In China, despite the complete domination of the political scene by the Chinese Communist Party (CCP), sovereignty issues draw so much attention from a public sensitive to national status that the regime must be cautious not to be perceived as weak in dealing with them.

Japan has a relatively short but proud naval tradition. Success in wars with strong maritime elements against China and Russia at the turn of the twentieth century was followed by disastrous defeat in 1945. When successful, Japan's navy has evidenced technological acumen and innovation and personnel expertise, dedication (perhaps tending toward excess), and strong professionalism. The current navy is an extremely capable force, able to defend Japan's maritime interest in littoral and regional waters, perhaps as far as a thousand nautical miles from the home islands.

This strategic paradigm is included in the December 2011 National Defense Program Outline published by Tokyo. This document embraced naval modernization, including the new class of submarines. The JMSDF's planned responses to its correct perception of Japan's vulnerability due to its overwhelming reliance on seaborne commerce continue to fall afoul of budget limitations. Japan's defense budget has been cut in real terms since the end of the Cold War; the wonder is that the JMSDF today is such a formidable naval force.

The character of the JCG has to a degree compensated for JMSDF limitations and has led to a competitive atmosphere between the two services. That may be a positive factor, but it implies a lack of coherence in Japan's overall maritime defense.[47]

An effective navy is vital to the country's defense and continued economic well-being, since Japan remains almost completely dependent on maritime trade and energy imports. Even the national diet is essentially based on seafood. A crucial aftereffect of World War II in Asia—continuing resentment toward and even hatred of the Japan that rampaged so mercilessly from 1931 to 1945—remains a force in Japan's defense capability. Hence, the JMSDF remains dependent on maintaining the closest possible relationship with the USN.

National policy makers in Tokyo during the past decade or more have failed to acknowledge this maritime dependence; they have not adequately funded the armed service most crucial to Japan's national security. The strategy promulgated in 2010 does provide maritime guidance appropriate to Japan's dependence on the sea and direction upon which the JMSDF can rely for modernization in platforms and capabilities. It is, for the first time in post–World War II Japan, a dynamic rather than a static strategy.

In 1988 the JMSDF devised a long-range building plan for a fleet of eight flotillas, each with a large air-capable ship. It now seems on track to fulfill that vision.[48] The JMSDF faces a conundrum, however, in the gap between mission and resources. Until the national government eliminates that gap, the JMSDF will face a problematic future.

That future will be strongly influenced by the degree of confidence that Japan's leaders have in the security treaty with the United States. Tokyo is already hedging on that issue, seeking additional positive relationships and mutually supporting relationships with other Asian states.

Canada's navy is one such friendly force; Russia's is not; North Korea remains a hostile force. A particularly frustrating relationship with the ROK has been on display for several years, as Tokyo and Seoul have (so far unsuccessfully) sought to establish a military relationship in the face of domestic political opposition on both sides, opposition reinforced by the ROK president's August 2012 visit to Takeshima, the island disputed between Japan and South Korea. All of these nations' navies play roles in the North Asian maritime picture.

four

NORTH ASIA

INTRODUCTION

The United States, China, Japan, and India dominate maritime Asia, also known as the Indo-Pacific. The huge area is marked by distinct regions, each composed of significant nation-states that deploy considerable maritime forces—naval, coast guard, and commercial.

The subregion of North Asia stretches from the northwestern North American littoral across the Bering Sea and North Pacific to the Sea of Okhotsk. Its maritime picture includes Canada, Russia, and the two Koreas, as well as Japan, China, and the United States.

These latter three countries are subjects of separate chapters, as the major actors in the region's maritime, economic, and political life. Nonetheless, the other four countries of the region also play important naval, economic, and political roles; their interests and concerns will be addressed below. None of these is a world maritime power, although Russia's still-considerable arsenal of nuclear weapons earns it respect as "more equal" than the other nations of the region.

North Asia was described as "the cockpit of Asia" and a possible source of world war in 1931.[1] That observation acknowledged Japan's expansionist policies, the Soviet Union's revolutionary fervor, China's civil war, and Korea's suppressed nationalism. Those issues had already contributed to wars between Japan and China and between Japan and Russia, as well as to the Japanese colonization of Korea and Taiwan, and they would contribute significantly to the advent of World War II in Asia. Those conflicts were all characterized by major maritime conflict.

CANADA AND THE CANADIAN NAVY

Canada has the longest coastline in the world at 142,100 nm, large navigable waterways, and four coasts bordering the Atlantic, Pacific, and Arctic Oceans as well as four of the five Great Lakes. Canada published a long maritime policy in 1998 and a maritime strategy in 2002.[2] The 2002 strategy notes the increasing importance of the Arctic, in view of the shrinking ice cap, and the importance to Canada of maritime resources and commerce.

The navy's tasks include protecting the nation's sovereignty at sea and contributing to collective defense—particularly in conjunction with "traditional allies," especially the United States, and through international organizations, including the UN and NATO.

The Maritime Policy is a completely civilian document—that is, the navy and coast guard are not addressed directly as the enforcement arms of the nation's policies and priorities. The emphasis of this document is on integration, on maximizing the synergistic effects of Canada's maritime capabilities. This includes integrating naval and coast-guard efforts, as well as those of federal, provincial, and local governments. The Canadian policy emphasizes seeking nearly complete maritime domain awareness (MDA) as the basis of maritime watchfulness and control.[3]

It touts the United Nations Convention on the Law of the Sea as the leading document for the international management of the global maritime environment, and as supported by Canada in its "Oceans Strategy." Almost every federal department and agency in Canada addresses maritime issues; the Oceans Act provides the regulatory foundation for Canada's Oceans Strategy, providing the basis for oceanic governance by

- Defining maritime territory in accordance with the UNCLOS;
- Assigning a leadership role to the minister of fisheries and oceans; and
- Clarifying and consolidating federal oceans management and responsibilities.

One aspect of maritime management perhaps unique to Canada is the concern expressed and duties delineated for aboriginal treaty rights. The Ocean Strategy addresses fisheries, as it does maritime industries, including shipbuilding, oil and gas exploration and extraction, seabed mining, defense production, and port management. The strategy provides the basis for three policy objectives: understanding and protecting the maritime environment, supporting sustainable economic opportunities, and providing international leadership.

The Canadian navy is modern and capable but relatively small. Divided into Atlantic and Pacific Fleets, it deploys three destroyers, twelve frigates, twelve mine-warfare ships, and two oilers. A large fleet of thirteen icebreakers is operated by the Canadian Coast Guard. These last ships, of various displacement and capability, are key to Canadian concerns along its northern coast. This icebreaker fleet will be increasingly important as 2050 approaches, the year anticipated to see year-round navigation across the polar cap.

The navy has had remarkable difficulty in deploying submarines. Four *Victoria*-class boats were acquired from Great Britain in the late 1990s, but they have been, in the words of one Canadian observer, "glitch-prone," with accidents at sea and in port plaguing their operations. The navy hopes to acquire a new submarine flotilla, but budget and technical limitations make that problematical.[4]

The Canadian maritime forces are well trained for specific tasks, ranging from Arctic operations to fighting crime at sea. Canadian warships have regularly deployed to the Gulf of Aden to fight piracy and to the Mediterranean to combat terrorism.[5]

RUSSIA AND ITS MARITIME STRATEGY

An accurate, if perhaps harsh, characterization of Russia in the second decade of the twenty-first century is that it is no longer either an empire or a world power but a country caught between the United States and China, with gravitas due only to its remaining nuclear weapons stockpile and huge energy reserves. In 2012, however, Moscow assumed leadership of a major international organization, the Asia-Pacific Economic Cooperation

(APEC) group. Russia thus is trying to assume a more prominent role in economic Asia.[6]

Russia has a coastline of more than 15,500 miles, but its Asia-Pacific region accounts for only 1 percent of the nation's trade and contains less than 5 percent of the population.[7] Historically, only infrequently has either Russia or the Soviet Union deployed a modern, capable navy. That is not surprising, given the overwhelmingly continental nature of the national security threats faced by that nation over the millennia.

A notable attempt to become a world maritime power was launched in the 1960s, following Moscow's embarrassment in the 1962 Cuban missile crisis. Adm. Sergei Gorshkov, commander of the Soviet navy for almost thirty years, from 1956 to 1985, brilliantly led this effort.[8] Despite the impressive growth and increased capabilities acquired by the Soviet navy under Gorshkov, continued U.S. maritime dominance limited its primary strategic responsibility to protect its ballistic-missile submarines and defend "the USSR and its allies from strikes by enemy ballistic missile submarines and aircraft carriers." The overall Soviet naval strategy was defined in the West as one of 'sea denial,' specifically of adjacent seas and areas out to 2,000 km [1,080 nm] beyond Soviet territory."[9] (This characterization resembles current views of probable Chinese maritime strategic thought, focusing as it does on defense of the Yellow, East, and South China Seas— the three seas, or *san hai*—and perhaps the area out to the "second island chain," approximately 1,600 nm from China's coast.)

The emphasis on strategic deterrence and defense remained the Russian navy's focus at the end of the Cold War.[10] It remains a stated priority in 2012, although resources for accomplishing these missions are dramatically reduced. Current naval tasking addressed in the Russian Federation's 2010 Military Doctrine also includes combatting piracy and terrorism and "ensur[ing] the security of the economic activities of the Russian Federation on the high seas," but interestingly not operations in relief of humanitarian or environmental disasters.[11]

This document was preceded by the 2001 *Maritime Doctrine of the Russian Federation 2020,* updated in 2009. It describes Russia's maritime forces as comprising the navy, the Maritime Border Guard Federal Border Service, and the merchant fleet. Vital maritime interests include ensuring "the sovereign rights and jurisdiction of the Russian Federation, carried out in the exclusive economic zone and continental shelf . . . for the exploration, development, and conservation of natural resources, both living and non-living [and] freedom of the high seas, including freedom of navigation, operations, fisheries, research, freedom to lay submarine cables and pipelines; . . . [as well as] the control of the vital sea communications."[12] These missions, though without direct reference to the UNCLOS, are closer to those of the majority of that treaty's signatories than they are to those of China, India, Brazil, and a few other nations that have asserted excessive claims to rights in the EEZ and continental shelf.

The navy is tasked with maintaining the "necessary naval capabilities and [their] effective use" in support of the maritime doctrine. The navy is also directed to maintain "the Russian fleet in readiness to address challenges." Fleet modernization is emphasized, with particular reference to maintaining "world leadership in the construction and operation of nuclear icebreakers." Environmental protection is noted, in conjunction with preserving and maximizing fisheries production.

The navy is described as "the pillar and foundation of maritime capabilities [of] the Russian Federation," responsible for the "maintenance of military-political stability in the adjacent seas[,] . . . display[ing] the flag[,] . . . peacekeeping and humanitarian actions, [and] defending the interests of the Russian Federation." These maritime interests are described as reaching to the Atlantic, Arctic, Pacific, and Indian Oceans and to the Azov, Baltic, Black, Caspian, and Mediterranean Seas.

The phrase "Pacific Regional Direction" is given to refer to the "heavy economic and military development of neighboring countries in [the] Asia Pacific," notably the "long-term challenges" in adjacent seas. The Indian Ocean is addressed as an area of concern, because of Russian shipping and fishing, as well as the countering of piracy "together with other nations," research in the Antarctic, and a focus on ensuring Russia's periodic naval presence.

Russia's maritime strategy for its Pacific Fleet is unexceptional. In "peacetime" it is assigned the following goals:

- Creation of a maritime regime in littoral waters that is favorable for Russia and protection of the nation's Far Eastern maritime flank
- Maintaining a high degree of readiness for the fleet's ballistic-missile nuclear-powered submarines (SSBNs) for effective strategic deterrence

- Protecting merchant shipping and access to global maritime resources
- Protecting Russia's industrial maritime activity and its EEZ
- Supporting Russia's foreign policy in the region, to include "showing the flag"
- Participating in UN peacekeeping operations

In "wartime" the fleet's missions focus on strategic warfare and the "maritime defense of eastern Russia." These missions include

- Strategic-level tasks: area defense of SSBN operating areas;
- Operational/tactical-level tasks: operations against enemy battle groups and ASW operations against nuclear-powered attack submarines (SSNs) armed with cruise missiles; and
- Tactical-level tasks: ASW, anti-SLOC warfare, mine warfare, coastal defense, and limited amphibious operations.[13]

These missions and tasks attest to a Russian defensive focus, particularly in the seas of Okhotsk and Japan. This defense of littoral waters includes defending the fleet ballistic-missile (FBM) operating "bastions" in the Sea of Okhotsk. The defensive character of the Pacific Fleet's strategy reflects the lack of air support for maritime operations and concern about U.S. long-range cruise missiles. The Russian navy also apparently retains the concept of defensive maritime zones, evidenced by current Pacific Fleet focus on an area extending perhaps 2,500 nm from the Russian coast.

No specific naval strategy has been promulgated since 2001, but Moscow did issue a military doctrine in February 2010, one that emphasizes cooperation rather than confrontation.[14] The "main tasks for the military" include practicing multilateral cooperation, countering piracy, safeguarding Russia's economic activities, peacekeeping, and fighting international terrorism. Another significant document, the National Maritime Policy, issued in 2010, briefly addresses naval strategy, noting the importance of Russia's retaining "unfettered use of the world's oceans" to ensure freedom of shipping, fisheries, access to minerals and energy, and scientific activities.

The end of the Cold War saw a dramatic diminution of the former Soviet navy, especially its Pacific Fleet. Even this is an unjustifiably optimistic way of putting it—in fact, the strength of that fleet is likely represented in the seven warships it was able to deploy in support of an April 2012 exercise with China, its fourth since 2005.[15] Russia's Pacific Fleet numbers on paper four SSBNs, eleven SSNs, one cruiser, seven destroyers, ten frigates, fourteen corvettes, eight mine-warfare ships, four amphibious-warfare ships, and seven oilers. Of this inventory, none of the SSBNs, just three of the SSNs, and seven of the surface combatants of frigate size or larger were operable as of August 2012.[16]

A recent Moscow assessment states that by 2005 the Russian Pacific Fleet had been restored and that "naval activity has intensified; periodic deployments to forward areas have resumed; and the fleet has begun acquiring new platforms, weaponry and equipment."[17] As demonstrated by the actual state of the Pacific Fleet, however, this observation is aspiration, not reality, and periodic announced resurgences of that force have come to naught.[18] While limited budget allocations to the navy are the primary reason for these shortfalls, the shipbuilding industry itself continues to be inadequate. For instance, an announcement that "20 SSBNs" would be manufactured is followed by reports of "new subs made of old spare parts" and of "dozens of major flaws in newest submarine."[19]

Two priorities are apparent for the Pacific Fleet. The first is the Arctic, with concern for ensuring "complete control of the Northern Sea Route through an Arctic Ocean that has become ice-free for longer periods each successive year." Commercial and military use of the Arctic requires maintaining as a priority the world-leading superiority of Russia's nuclear-powered icebreakers.[20] Second is the Pacific, with attention to the safeguarding of trade, exploitation of seabed resources, and "development of coastal-port infrastructure in the Kuril Islands."

Both of these Pacific Fleet priorities are contentious. Moscow's Arctic sovereignty claims are in conflict with those of the UNCLOS, the other members of the Arctic Council (the United States, Finland, Sweden, Norway, Denmark, and Iceland), and probably China as well.

Developing the Kurile Islands will almost certainly be strongly opposed by Japan, which claims sovereignty of the southern Kurils (Habomei, Shikotan, Iturup, and Kunashir Islands).[21] Another noteworthy move by Moscow has been an announced allocation to the navy of 25 percent of the annual military budget—an allocation that has not occurred, leading to a series of contradictory statements about Russian naval modernization. Periodic announcements of renewed shipbuilding have not been borne out, although some submarine construction programs are making progress due to "resumption of regular funding of defense contracts and newly established industrial cooperation." New classes of frigates, some for export, also are under construction.

More worrisome is the lack of new major warships, despite periodic announcements of plans for new nuclear-powered aircraft carriers.[22] Much more likely as air-capable ships for the Pacific Fleet would be one or more of the four *Mistral*-class helicopter-capable amphibious ships Moscow is purchasing from France. These ships will provide the fleet with platforms ideally suited for both amphibious operations and humanitarian-assistance missions ashore.

Russian naval forces in Asia are currently weak, with future increases in capability focused on maintaining a seaborne nuclear deterrent, safeguarding the nation's Pacific littorals, and exploiting the Arctic. The Russian navy may regain a position of prominence in the nation's army-dominated military, but as of 2013 progress has been marked more by aspiration than by accomplishment. In the words of one analyst, Russia's "grand naval plans [are] not realistic."[23] Instead of a aiming at a globally capable navy, Moscow's maritime strategy will most likely follow its historical focus on strategic deterrence. The only probable Russian route to greater influence in East Asia will be via its vast energy supplies and its position on the Arctic Council.

THE DEMOCRATIC PEOPLE'S REPUBLIC OF KOREA

The navy of the Democratic People's Republic of Korea (DPRK, or North Korea) is dependent on twenty small submarines for most of its punch. It also deploys three small frigates and five corvettes. North Korea engaged in the landing of agents in Japan and kidnapping of Japanese citizens during the Cold War; today its mission is strictly anti–South Korean, with an emphasis on landing in, and extracting from, the South intelligence and special-operations personnel.

Pyongyang also has maritime boundary disputes with South Korea and fisheries disputes with both the South and China. A more serious maritime issue is Pyongyang's trafficking in WMD, using its merchant fleet as a conduit. That fleet consists of just over two hundred ships of all categories, but their material condition is uniformly poor and their accountability very weak.[24]

All this contributes to North Korea's role in East Asian, indeed world, politics as an economic basket case, a political provocateur, and a military aggressor.[25] The DPRK regime's focus on survival means that the navy is devoted directly to supporting it, sometimes through direct aggression against ROK forces or by transshipping WMD components or other illegal goods by sea.

North Korea's navy remains small in size and coastal in capability. Pyongyang may have constructed its southernmost hovercraft base, close to the disputed "Northern Limit Line," less than thirty nautical miles from the ROK's West Sea Islands.[26] The DPRK appears not to have a maritime strategy. Its merchant marine and navy episodically operate in support of the regime. These episodes are consistently disruptive to peace and good order on the seas.

REPUBLIC OF KOREA AND THE ROK NAVY

The Republic of Korea was shaken by unprovoked North Korean attacks in 2010 that sank an ROK Navy (ROKN) corvette and killed civilians on Yeongpyeong Island. Those incidents and the domestic political pressure on the government to react to such aggression contributed to defense reforms in South Korea. The Defense Reform Plan (DRP) 307 was promulgated in 2011.

The ROK had finalized a DRP 2020 in 2005, which envisioned a significant reduction of the size of the ROK armed forces in view of a perceived reduction of the North Korean military threat. This assumption became doubtful in 2009, and an expert panel was convened to review the DRP. After meeting for a year, it submitted in December 2010 its recommendations to the Ministry of Defense, which issued a revised DRP, known as DRP 307, which was approved in March 2011.

This plan reflects the concerns engendered by the sinking of the corvette *Cheonan* and the bombardment of Yeongpyeong. The sinking of the corvette particularly motivated the government and military to reorganize command and control and force structure and also to focus on doctrinal change to cope with the North Korean threat.

The new doctrine signaled a change from the previous policy of patience and "defense by denial" to one of "proactive deterrence." The new doctrine directs the armed forces to respond to North Korean provocation with "prompt, focused and proportional retaliation." ROK minister of national defense, Kim Kwan-Jin, stated that "if the enemy attacks our people and territory, I will use force to punish the enemy to make sure it doesn't even dare to think about it again. The enemy should be punished thoroughly until the source of hostility is eliminated. . . . Credible intimidation lies at the core of 'Proactive Deterrence.'"

Especially interesting is the DRP's apparent determination that the North Korean "autocratic system [and] totalitarian dictatorship" must be overthrown in favor of a "democratic state" before a unification process can succeed. This apparently was not a call for outright military action, but the plan does state that South Korea must "maintain military superiority to North Korea."

Key to reorganizing South Korea's military command-and-control structure is the planned 2015 turnover of wartime operational control from the U.S. Combined Forces Command (CFC) to the ROK military command. DRP 307 incorporates this shift and emphasizes the importance of ensuring true jointness among the army, air force, and navy.

The ROKN reportedly is not satisfied with all aspects of DRP 307, fearing that the document will limit its activities to deterrence and coastal defense, paying inadequate attention to safeguarding the SLOCs upon which the country is dependent for its economic well-being—almost totally so for energy supplies.[27] Another source of ROKN concern is China's increasing naval strength. This has been highlighted by incidents between Chinese fishermen and ROK coast-guard units, and more seriously over the disputed EEZ delimitation between the two countries.[28]

The ROKN also faces domestic difficulties in modernizing itself within a military dominated by the army. A particular issue is the navy's plan to build a new base on Jeju Island, in the Tsushima (Korea) Strait. This base, designed to berth more than twenty warships, would allow the navy easy access to the East China Sea and the Pacific beyond. Construction began in 2011 but faces legal and popular opposition from the island's inhabitants, in a scenario not dissimilar to that faced by the Japanese and U.S. governments over military installations on Okinawa.[29]

The ROKN's aspirations for increased open-ocean operational capabilities have been realized to an extent. Korean warships have participated in Gulf of Aden counterpiracy operations since April 2009. They have also participated in distant exercises with the navies of Japan, Singapore, India, Turkey, and several European nations. Additionally, the ROKN dispatched a large amphibious ship to participate in the humanitarian-assistance operations in Southeast Asia following the devastating tsunami that struck Indonesia in December 2004.[30]

The navy has been modernizing since the 1970s, albeit at a relatively moderate pace. But ROKN capabilities are already, with those of China and Japan, the most powerful in East Asia. The ROKN deploys twelve Aegis-equipped KDX-class destroyers, indigenously produced with U.S. assistance.

The ROKN also has acquired a modest force of modern submarines, with an indigenous capacity to build more. Nine Type 209 boats lead this force, with nine Type 214s, equipped with air-independent propulsion, in construction. Long-range plans call for up to twelve submarines built with vertical-launch systems (VLSs) for missiles.[31]

The ROKN is deploying a power-projection capability, with entry into service of the first of perhaps three landing helicopter docks (LHDs). The *Dokdo* class displaces 19,000 tons and will be accompanied by a new class of tank landing ships (LSTs). Three oilers and three or more mine-warfare ships are also in the fleet.

The name of the large new amphibious ship points to one of South Korea's most serious national security concerns—Japan, with which Seoul disputes the sovereignty of the small archipelago of Dokdo/Takeshima. Although barren and uninhabitable, these rocks constitute a serious point of contention, as neither country is flexible on the issue. This is due in Seoul more to historical Korean enmity toward Japan, especially as a result of Japan's harsh 1910–45 occupation of the peninsula, than it is to possible seabed resources in the waters around Dokdo.[32]

The ROKN continues to benefit from the modernization process within the South Korean military. Unmanned aerial vehicles (UAVs) are being acquired. Daewoo Marine & Shipbuilding has upgraded two Indonesian submarines, with follow-on contracts possible. South Korea ended 2011 with half of its major equipment renewal for its coast guard complete. This process focused on new patrol vessels, including a class of large (328-foot-long) ships.

CONCLUSION

Northeast Asia was described as the "cockpit" of Asia during the first part of the last century; it still presents international rivalries that could threaten peace and stability throughout North Asia. North Korea presents the most destabilizing factor in the region and beyond, at many levels.

Most dangerous is Pyongyang's determination to acquire nuclear weapons and the missiles with which to deliver them at least regionally, if not intercontinentally. Second is Pyongyang's engagement in the trafficking of illegal and counterfeit drugs and goods, a practice resulting from the regime's refusal to follow accepted rules of international behavior. This has resulted in incidents ranging from the bizarre kidnapping of Japanese citizens to terroristic acts against airliners and foreign officials to the sinking of a South Korean corvette.

Third is North Korea's treatment of its own citizens, with complete disregard for human rights as embodied in the UN Declaration of Human Rights.[33] This is more than a humanitarian issue, since large numbers of oppressed North Koreans fleeing across the Yalu River into China or across the demilitarized zone into South Korea could stimulate a breakdown in political control on the peninsula leading to outright conflict.

Apart from North Korean depredations and confrontation with South Korea, disputes among the region's nations are relatively minor, from an international perspective. Territorial disagreements over the southern Kuriles, over Dokdo/Takeshima, and over Socotra Rock (Ieodo to Seoul, Suyan Rock to Beijing) and fishing boundaries and catch limits are all the subjects of negotiation—no matter how prolonged—and not liable to lead to conflict.[34]

Canada's role in maritime North Asia rests largely on trade and diplomacy. Any naval involvement is likely to occur only as an adjunct of U.S. engagement.

Russia, however, has been striving since the middle of the nineteenth century to increase its role as a North Asian power. Tsarist Russia successfully expanded to the Pacific, to a significant degree at the expense of imperial China, but was then blocked at the Korean border by Japan in 1905. World War I, the Bolshevik revolution, and the invasion of Siberia by Western powers and Japan in 1918–20 constrained Soviet activities in the Russian Far East.

Moscow stationed large troop formations in eastern Siberia during the Cold War, especially following the 1960 split with Beijing and the brief period of combat with Chinese forces on the Amur River in 1969. These forces were greatly reduced in 1991 following a negotiated settlement with Beijing over the extensive Russo-Chinese boundary. A powerful fleet was also built up by Moscow during the Cold War, with headquarters at Vladivostok. This fleet was reduced and allowed to deteriorate in the 1990s and early 2000s; despite announcements of Russian naval rejuvenation, the Pacific Fleet remains weak and hard pressed to serve as more than a local force.

South Korea's immediate strategic concern is, of course, North Korea. Ameliorating that concern is the alliance with the United States and the continued UN commitment to the nation's independence. In the longer term, Seoul no doubt views Japan with concern. This strategic doubt arises from current issues—the status of Dokdo/Takeshima, for instance—and the enmity engendered by the memory of nearly half a century of extremely harsh Japanese occupation.

Indeed, Japan plays a role in North Asia defined by two very different phenomena. First is its heavy historical baggage, including Tokyo's assault on China from the 1890s to 1945, highlighted by the 1937 Rape of Nanking. Japan conducted, as noted, an equally notorious occupation of Korea from approximately 1895 to 1945; harsh Japanese occupation of Southeast Asia during World War II was underscored by the often horrific treatment of prisoners of war and civilian populations. All of this receives continued life in the Asian political environment; the victimized nations, especially China and the Koreas, seem unable to forget this tragic history. It is further kept alive by periodic Japanese waffling or outright denial regarding, for example, Nanking or the Korean "comfort women."

Countering this deplorable narrative is Japan's late twentieth- and early twenty-first-century role as economic banker and sometime benefactor to the developing nations of the region. Another ameliorating factor may be Japan's status as surrogate for the U.S. military presence in North

Asia and as a fellow treaty ally with South Korea. The U.S. presence serves as something of a bond between Tokyo and Seoul.

China, Japan, and the United States are preeminent in North Asia, but Canada, the Koreas, and Russia are nations around whom the former three define and pursue maritime policies. The region's waters are relatively constricted; the Okhotsk, Japan, Yellow, and East China Seas are bounded by Russia, Japan, and the Koreas; Canada and Russia share an Arctic border; while the Aleutian and Kurile Islands constitute a maritime pointer from North America into Asia.

The most powerful North Asian maritime powers, especially the United States and China, share similar concerns about sovereignty, energy, and SLOC security in Southeast Asian waters. Beijing is potentially a dominating maritime force in the region and the most important naval factor in the changing Indo-Pacific.

five

CHINA

INTRODUCTION

China has a long, if episodic, history as a naval power. Its best-known operations were the early fifteenth-century voyages of Zheng He, a Muslim eunuch who led fleets of large ships as far as Africa and the Persian Gulf. These were not primarily commercial voyages; Zheng He's fleets followed trading routes already frequently used. Rather, the renowned admiral conducted voyages that combined exploration with—despite the revisionist claims of current Chinese apologists—demonstration of Ming Dynasty China's military power. Hence, the well-armed expeditions included large contingents of soldiers who intervened in political contests in Southeast Asia.

Despite these and other notable periods of great maritime power, China historically has been a continental power, with land forces typically defending against threats from the northern and western reaches of Asia. Even today Beijing has promulgated no formal maritime strategy, a factor recently criticized by some Chinese analysts. Beijing has, however, published important documents addressing the maritime theater.[1] One is the 1998 *National Ocean Policy of China*.[2] Another is the series of biennial defense white papers first published in 1998, the most recent of which appeared in January 2011.

The 1998 ocean policy identified several maritime concerns that remain current. One is "safeguarding the new international marine order and [China's] marine rights and interests," outlined by the 1992 Law of the People's Republic of China on Its Territorial Seas and Adjacent Zones.[3] Another is the promise that "China will strengthen the comprehensive development and administration of its coastal zones . . . and protect the offshore areas," while participating in developing "international sea beds and oceans" in order to "form coastal economic belts and marine economic zones."

The Ocean Policy's second goal is simultaneously to plan and implement "the development of marine resources and the protection of the marine environment," while improving the "monitoring, surveillance, law enforcement, and management" of that environment. Third is "reinforcing oceanographic technology research and development," and fourth is "setting up a comprehensive marine management system." The final goal is to participate actively in "international cooperation in the field of marine development."[4]

One Chinese analyst has rephrased the Ocean Policy as "four coordinations."[5] The first is to "harmonize national and international maritime law." As will be discussed below, this is a crucial point of difference between China, which has passed as series of pieces of domestic legislation that diverges in some basic ways from the United Nations Convention on the Law of the Sea.

The second issue of coordination urges the integration of China's several agencies responsible for various aspects of maritime security. This is still very much a work in progress, and the "stove-piping" of the organizations dealing with security issues continues to cause confusion, both domestically and internationally.[6]

Third is coordinating traditional and nontraditional maritime security concerns. The former is obvious; the latter refers to operations other than war, such as reacting to economic and environmental problems, natural disasters, and incidents involving safety at sea.

The fourth coordination refers to traditional maritime issues, both national and international. Sovereignty disputes in the East and South China Seas on one hand and antipiracy deployments to the Gulf of Aden on the other mark the range of these issues.

Additionally, the Hainan, Guangdong, and Guangxi provincial governments have each directly addressed maritime economic objectives in formal documents. They have each listed "developing the ocean economy" as one of their key missions under the national development master plan, the twelfth five-year plan (2011–15) issued by the State Council.[7]

None of these provincial goals is explicitly naval, but all require deployment of a modern navy to support China's overall maritime development. A prime example is improving oceanography: a civilian-manned research ship conducting bottom surveys is producing data that may indicate the presence of seabed minerals but will also facilitate submarine operations.

Defense White Papers

In the absence of a "maritime white paper" or similar maritime strategic document, China's various defense white papers are important indicators of Beijing's strategic thought in the maritime arena. The 2010 version, published in January 2011, described the PLAN's role in a national defense focused on "safeguarding national sovereignty, security and interests of national development . . . tasked to guard against and resist aggression, defend the security of China's lands, inland waters, and territorial waters . . . [and] safeguard its maritime rights and interests." The PLAN is directed "to accelerate the modernization of its integrated combat forces, enhance its capabilities in strategic deterrence and counterattack, and develop its capabilities in conducting operations in distant waters and in countering non-traditional security threats." It is also to improve its "combat capabilities."

To ensure the success of combat and military operations other than war (MOOTW), the PLAN would continue developing and deploying "new types of submarines, frigates, aircraft and large support vessels." It would also try to "build a shore-based support system which matches the deployment of forces and the development of weaponry and equipment." Particularly important is "the Navy [accelerating] the building of surface logistical platforms [and] working to improve its surface support capabilities," to include "new methods of logistics support for sustaining long-time maritime missions."[8]

Assisting the PLAN in these responsibilities are "organs of maritime surveillance, fisheries administration, marine affairs, inspection and quarantine, and customs," as well as a recently "improved . . . border and coastal defense force system."

The growing out-of-area role for the PLAN in the Gulf of Aden is described as "in line with relevant UN resolutions," as "China takes a proactive and open attitude toward international escort cooperation . . . [joining] international regimes such as the UN liaison groups' meeting on Somali pirates, and the international conference on 'intelligence sharing and conflict prevention' escort cooperation."

Beijing also emphasizes the navy's increasing role in international efforts in general, striving "to maintain maritime security through multiple peaceful ways and means." It has highlighted PLAN ship visits to foreign ports, with "more than twenty naval ships" visiting "more than thirty countries." The PLAN first took prominent part in MOOTW in 2011, when the frigate *Xuzhou*, on antipiracy patrol in the Gulf of Aden, was dispatched into the Mediterranean to assist in evacuating Chinese citizens trapped by the civil war in Libya.[9] The fact that this Jiangkai II-class frigate did not actually evacuate any Chinese citizens is less significant that the fact that Beijing had sufficient confidence in its navy to dispatch a warship on such a mission and that the PLAN was able to execute it successfully.

The introduction to the 2010 white paper notes pressure for action "in preserving China's territorial integrity and maritime rights and interests," a complaint clearly aimed at the ongoing sovereignty disputes in the East and South China Seas. This theme—defending the security of inland and territorial waters—is repeated as integral to "National Defense Policy."

PLAN responsibilities were also included in President Hu Jintao's "Four Historic Missions" speech in 2004. The missions are as follows:

- Consolidate the ruling status of the Communist Party,
- Help ensure China's sovereignty, territorial integrity, and domestic security in order to continue national development,
- Safeguard China's expanding national interests and
- Help maintain world peace.[10]

The four historic missions include tasks for the PLAN, namely, maritime border issues, Taiwan's status, and "protection of China's expanding national interests," including missions other than war.[11] Hu followed this theme in a December 2006 speech to the party's Central Military Commission (CMC) in which he urged the People's Liberation Army

(PLA) "to develop capabilities to deal with many kinds of security threats and complete diversified military tasks."

The PLAN also is engaging regularly in one traditional naval mission not specifically addressed in these documents: presence, or naval support for diplomacy.[12] The 2010 defense white paper does address, however, the need for improved "maritime surveillance, fisheries administration, marine affairs, inspection and quarantine, and customs enforcement," as well as coastal defense.

On a cooperative tack, the PLAN's role in United Nations peacekeeping operations is touted, as are its exercises with foreign navies. These latter are described as occurring on a "regular basis." In fact they have numbered no more than a dozen over the past decade; the white paper takes a positive slant and is worded for the public. Nevertheless, it remains an important document, reflecting China's national security concerns.

Beijing's focus on maritime issues is understandable, given China's 10,250 nautical miles of coastline and more than 6,500 claimed islands. China also has eight of the world's ten largest harbors, while its shipping fleet is the world's fourth largest, and "ocean-related activities" constituted almost 10 percent of the nation's GDP in 2009.[13] Finally, Chinese government officials have listed as "core interests" only the sovereignty status of Taiwan, Tibet, and Xinjiang. Classifying the East and South China Sea disputes as "sovereignty issues," however, would suggest that under certain circumstances these also would be considered "core interests."[14] If so classified, these disputes would rise significantly in Beijing's security interest priorities and pose greater dangers of military escalation.

LIU HUAQING'S VISION

Liu Huaqing served as both an army general and a navy admiral in China's People's Liberation Army. As commander of the PLAN in the 1980s, he made his mark as the country's most influential modern flag officer, a standing similar to that of Admiral of the Fleet of the Soviet Union Sergei Georgiyevich Gorshkov, who revitalized that navy in the 1960s and 1970s. Liu continued his advocacy of Chinese naval power as vice chairman of the CMC into the mid-1990s, although he reverted to his army general's uniform for that tour.

Liu's plan for modernizing the navy was well thought out, recognized internal PLA budget priorities (his goal was to alter those so as to increase PLAN funding), and was essentially defensive. His strategy is conveniently described as a three-phrase process. First, by 2000 the PLAN would be capable of defending China's maritime security interests out to the "first island chain," a line drawn from the Kuril Islands through Japan and the Ryukyu Islands, then through the Philippines to the Indonesian archipelago. Second, by 2020 it would defend China's maritime security interests out to the "second island chain," a line drawn from the Kurils through Japan and the Bonin Islands, then through the Marianas Islands, Palau, and the Indonesian archipelago, with the implied inclusion of the island of Java, which would extend the navy's control through the Singapore and Malacca straits. Finally, by 2050 the PLAN would possess aircraft carriers and have the capacity to operate globally to support China's maritime interests.

Liu spent a significant portion of his long career as an army officer. It is not surprising that he would have thought in terms of "lines": armies operate in and across solid geography, cued to lines of defense, advance, and withdrawal, and logistics. However, Liu almost certainly was reacting to what he perceived as U.S.-imposed lines at sea; his "island chains" concept is a reactive strategic paradigm for the PLAN. It does not envision limiting naval operations to within the island chains until the dates specified; Liu viewed the chains as barriers to be overcome, not as limits on China's maritime objectives or as maritime defensive perimeters.[15]

Hence, in keeping with Maoist elements of his theory, the PLAN is free at any time to operate within or outside the island chains, as demanded by national security objectives and as enabled by its capabilities at sea.[16]

The immediate obstacle Liu faced in the 1980s was internal PLA budget politics: the Chinese military was (as it remains) dominated by the army in terms of leadership, numbers, and influence. This is due to both a traditionally continentalist view and the fact that the communist revolution's victory in 1949 was achieved almost solely by land forces. Liu had then to convince his civilian leaders that the navy needed to modernize if it was to fulfill new missions resulting from China's rise to regional and eventually global economic and political prominence. His first battle was an internal, bureaucratic struggle.

The First Chain

The initial goal of Liu's maritime power strategy, sea control out to the first island chain, was not realized by its target date of 2000—and indeed, one might argue, has not been realized yet. Liu did succeed, however, in the more important goal of gaining the commitment of China's civilian leadership to allocate to the navy the resources needed to develop into a twenty-first-century force that could deal with the country's maritime national security concerns.

Taiwan

The first measure of Liu's efforts was the 1995–96 situation vis-à-vis Taiwan. Two important events spurred a strong military reaction from Beijing on that occasion. First was Washington's granting of a visa to President Lee Tung-hui of Taiwan, who seemed to be favoring a pro-independence position, to visit the United States in 1995 Secretary of State Warren Christopher had assured his Chinese counterpart that Lee would not receive a visa, but because of domestic political pressure, President William J. Clinton directed that one be granted, which not surprisingly angered Beijing.

The second factor was Taiwan's holding of its first fully democratic—in a Western sense—legislative elections in December 1995 and presidential election in March 1996. Beijing conducted a series of air, ground, and maritime exercises near Taiwan in the late summer 1995 and in March 1996, in an attempt to influence Taiwan's voters not to reelect President Lee.

U.S. Intervention

Washington responded strongly to China's 1996 military demonstrations against Taiwan, deploying two aircraft-carrier battle groups to the region. Beijing was surprised by this very strong display of force.[17] The arrival of the carriers probably had little effect on the PLA's exercise—deteriorating weather was almost certainly more influential—but the crisis demonstrated that China still lacked the forces necessary to carry out Liu's plans

for maritime power. Beijing had initiated a process of military modernization following the PLA's troubled victory over Vietnamese forces during
China's invasion of that country in 1979. U.S. and Western success in the
Iraq War in 1990–91 demonstrated to the PLA how inadequate its capabilities remained. Those wars involved little naval involvement, however,
and it is likely that it was the 1995–96 Taiwan Strait crisis that spurred
naval modernization in China.[18]

Taiwan has remained the strategic focus of Chinese naval modernization since 1996. Chinese civilian and military analysts have repeatedly characterized Taiwan as vital to breaking through the self-imposed
"first island chain" and gaining free entry to the Pacific. Taiwan remains
Beijing's top maritime concern for the possible application of naval force.
It continues to survey the island's waters and to prepare for a conflict over
Taiwan's status.[19]

THE PEOPLE'S LIBERATION ARMY NAVY

The January 2012 assessment of "China's naval rivals" by a civilian analyst in Beijing focused on the U.S. Navy as "a strategic opponent of the
Chinese Navy" but boasted about the PLAN's progress, highlighting the
apparently successful sea trials of its first aircraft carrier, the ex-Russian
Varyag, renamed *Liaoning* (which joined the operational fleet in the fall
of 2012). Japan was then highlighted as the more immediate concern,
in light of "naval hatred stretching over 100 years, Diaoyu Islands sovereignty, maritime boundaries in the East China Sea, and the possibility
of Japanese military interference in the Taiwan issue and the South
China Sea."

Vietnam and the Philippines were listed as "local tactical opponents"
and India as a "potential blue water opponent." The analysis concluded
that the "Chinese Navy now faces a maritime competition structure that
involves a broad maritime region, great depth, and multiple opponents."[20]

To meet such opponents, Beijing is deploying today a large, modern navy capable of operating in the twenty-first-century maritime arena.
Three milestones mark the progress of this program. The first was Adm.
Liu Huaqing's plan to build a modern Chinese navy. The second was the
1995–96 diplomatic crisis just described, which brought home to Beijing

that U.S. acquiescence would be required if any application of naval or air power against Taiwan was to succeed.

The third, and most recent, has involved the successive deployments of Chinese naval task groups to the Gulf of Aden, deployments that began in December 2008 and continue today. The PLAN has been making out-of-area cruises since the mid-1970s, for political as well as operational reasons, but the counterpiracy deployments—the thirteenth task group departed China in December 2012—mark a new expanded scope for Chinese naval operations.[21] Although these events indicate that its navy has extended its reach, the question remains open as to whether China's maritime strategy of defending fixed and limited areas at sea will prove successful.

On 6 December 2011, President Hu Jintao met with deputies of the PLAN's Party Congress to discuss the navy's armament. Hu, who was chairman of the CMC, urged the deputies "to promote the fine traditions of the PLA, accelerate the transformation and modernization of the Navy in a sturdy way . . . in order to make greater contributions to safeguarding national security and world peace."[22]

Force Structure

China's naval modernization program began accelerating in the mid- to late 1980s and was further spurred by the 1996 Taiwan Strait crisis. PLAN platform acquisitions have continued at a steady but moderate rate, except for one type of warship, submarines, which have been more rapidly added to the fleet than any other ship type. The Houbei-class missile-armed fast-attack craft also has seen significant construction, with perhaps sixty to eighty now in commission, but these are designed for defensive missions in littoral waters. By 2013 the PLAN had a world lead in this category and was proceeding to build nuclear-powered boats as well, albeit slowly. The PLAN has acquired more than forty newly built submarines since 1995.

This construction program included China's second attempt to deploy a ballistic-missile submarine armed with intercontinental ballistic missiles (ICBMs). At least three Jin-class boats have joined the fleet, although the missile they are designed to carry remained in testing as of mid-2012. Their success will for the first time provide China with a sea-based nuclear deterrent force.[23]

New classes of frigates and destroyers have also been built, each class, though small, more technologically advanced and theoretically more operationally capable than its predecessor. These remain few in number, although not as few as the support ships necessary for the PLAN to execute long-range, long-term deployments on a regular basis. The ongoing operations to the Gulf of Aden, for instance, have been served by just two of the navy's five replenishment-at-sea ships supporting some of the navy's newest combatants.[24]

China's first aircraft carrier, *Liaoning,* completed sea trials in 2012 but has yet to receive a full air wing.[25] More important to Beijing's de facto maritime strategy than carriers, however, is shipbuilding for lesser naval missions. These feature construction of China's first dedicated hospital ship and a new class of landing platforms dock (LPDs). Both of these ship classes greatly enhance the PLAN's ability to conduct humanitarian relief operations ashore, as well as more traditional naval tasks. The hospital ship has completed significant missions to the Indian Ocean and the Caribbean Sea.[26]

China's naval building program supports the PLA's doctrine and remains focused on littoral missions. The PLAN is only gradually adapting to new missions in distant seas. Only the newer destroyers and frigates are being deployed on the Gulf of Aden mission, and according to the U.S. 2011 DOD report on the People's Republic of China (PRC), only 25 percent of China's surface forces are "modern," while approximately 56 percent of the submarine force is so categorized.[27]

There is little in China's decades-old program of naval modernization that would support an offensive maritime strategy. The numerical size of the force has not increased significantly, because as new ships are commissioned, older ones are being retired. Additionally, PLAN land-based anti-ship-cruise-missile (ASCM) coastal-defense units are being upgraded, and naval aviation's primary role remains air defense of the mainland, under PLA Air Force (PLAAF) control. Extensive operations in "blue water" or the "far seas" no doubt remain a PLAN ambition, but it is an ambition for the future.

Another significant addition to China's maritime capabilities is its ongoing effort to strengthen and regularize the many organizations performing coast guard–like functions. The China Maritime Surveillance force apparently will lead the way. The CMS plans to increase personnel from its present nine thousand to fifteen thousand by 2020. Its air arm will increase from nine to sixteen aircraft and its surface vessels from 260 to 520.[28] Beijing is making greater use of these forces, increasing their numbers and capabilities to carry out the nonmilitary missions that increasingly characterize China's maritime concerns. The PLAN may, however, be intent on at least influencing, if not controlling, these organizations' operations.[29]

Strategy and Policy

China's recent naval exercises demonstrate that the PLAN can deploy twenty-first-century ships to far seas. However, the current strategic theory espoused in public by Chinese analysts advocates a maritime paradigm based on island chains, a paradigm that does not fit with a navy capable of projecting global power.

More important than the number of advanced technology platforms joining the PLAN, however, is the strategic direction they indicate Beijing has adopted. The shorthand for this perceived goal has been labeled "anti-access and area denial" (A2/AD) by U.S. observers and "counterintervention," as a subset of "active defense," by official Chinese sources.

By whichever name, the concept is viewed as a Chinese operational plan to prevent other military forces from entering a given area that Beijing believes is vital to its national security. The "three seas" rubric—Yellow, East China, and South China—may describe this area, as may the waters within the first island chain. These definitions do not originate with American analysts but are taken from Chinese writings that have appeared in the open press. "Counterintervention" is not a strategy, however, but rather a defensive plan that reflects PLAN capabilities.[30]

The antiship ballistic missile (ASBM) is the new PLA weapon system for achieving A2/AD. The land-launched ASBM is seen as providing China with the means to attack moving, over-the-horizon targets, particularly U.S. aircraft carriers. China faces significant challenges in deploying and operating an ASBM system, apart from technical problems with the hardware itself. The broader problems include accurate targeting and, perhaps even more challenging, the joint issues attendant to the maritime employment of a system apparently assigned to and operated by the Second Artillery Force.[31]

From China's perspective, the U.S. military is responding with a new strategy designed specifically against China and its maritime interests, especially those vital to its national security.[32] The new U.S. development—known as Air-Sea Battle, part of the Joint Operational Access Concept—is viewed with particular suspicion. It remains much more of a concept than a reality, but Chinese analysts are treating ASB as a solid accomplishment.[33] They see it as a doctrinal descendent of the Air-Land Battle doctrine, which was designed to combat Soviet-bloc military superiority in Europe during the Cold War.

Furthermore, Chinese strategists and policy makers often accuse Washington of trying to contain China, to prevent it from achieving its rightful place in the world. It is not difficult to see how Beijing might draw such a conclusion, given the U.S. defense treaties and special arrangements with South Korea, Japan, Taiwan, the Philippines, Australia, Singapore, Malaysia, and Thailand. That conclusion may be buttressed by the improving U.S. relationships with Vietnam, Myanmar, and India, as well as by military facilities in various Central Asian nations.

There are "pragmatists and free marketers in China," however, who advocate a cooperative maritime strategy.[34] This school of thought might be described as fitting a more general Chinese concept of civil-military relations, one in which the PLA remains a party army and not a "national" army—devoted, that is, to ensuring that China's national security infrastructure remains firmly in the hands of the Communist Party leadership. This ties to the oft-repeated statements by Chinese leaders that their nation requires a peaceful world in which to continue growing its economy and overall development.

DEFENSE BUDGETS

China's defense budget first experienced a double-digit increase in 1989, but Beijing had realized in 1996 that not only had its modernization efforts failed to close the gap with the U.S. military but that in fact the gap had widened. U.S. forces continued to advance in terms of technology as well as in operational experience and expertise. Double-digit increases in defense spending have continued almost every year since the 1996 crisis, when, as noted, apparently the PLA learned a significant lesson.[35] The military at that time was unable even to detect the presence of the U.S. carriers on its own; by any measure, the PLAN remained a secondary force.

Ascertaining details of China's defense spending, including that for the navy, is difficult, for several reasons. First is the general lack of transparency to outside observers—and to Chinese analysts as well. Second is the diffuse nature of defense spending sources in China; for instance, local governments provide some of the funds required for mobilization preparations, conscription, and demobilization.[36]

Third, China's "defense spending" categories do not always match U.S. definitions. Research and development funding, for instance, draws on both the Ministry of Defense and the defense industrial sector. Foreign military sales and purchases too may not be included in Beijing's figures. Hence, accurate computation of the PLAN's submarine- and ship-acquisition programs founders on the question of how to account for the purchase of Kilo submarines and *Sovremenny*-class destroyers from Russia, a question further complicated by the unknown but surely significant costs of the training, supply, and maintenance that accompanied those purchases.

Most recently, Beijing announced a $106.4 billion defense budget for 2012, an 11.2 percent increase over that authorized for 2011.[37] This increase tracked with China's GDP increase for that year, evidence that the defense-budget increases, while certainly significant, are being tightly controlled by the CCP to ensure that the nation's economic development remains the number-one priority.

Beijing justified its 1994 defense-budget increase, estimated to have been as high as 29 percent, as required to counter inflation and to increase PLA salaries, especially for officers.[38] Similarly, recent defense spending increases have been explained as responses to higher equipment and consumables costs, personnel pay and benefit increases, improvements in personnel living conditions, and compensation for the requirement that the PLA rid itself of commercial business investments.[39] These explanations are probably accurate. In 1993, for instance, inflation was a problem; officer salaries were doubled for 1994. More recently, in 2011, noncommissioned officer salary and benefits were increased by as much as 40 percent.

Significant proportions, however, of these budget increases have been spent on new naval systems and platforms. Furthermore, during the past two decades the Chinese military has had much more money to spend on fewer troops than it did fifteen years ago.

The past two decades of frequent double-digit increases in the defense budget in fact appear to be coordinated with the growth of the Chinese economy, as past defense white papers have claimed. Defense spending is increasing, but not at a rate that would conflict with China's primary objective of economic development. If need be, if a vital national security interest appeared threatened, the government could increase spending even faster.

Most significantly, despite large annual defense-budget increases, China appears to be adhering to a goal of achieving by 2050 a completely modern military, one capable of defending the nation's maritime interests against even the United States. The PLAN probably sees itself at the halfway mark in its overall modernization program.[40]

China's most notable success in maritime modernization is that for the first time in modern history it has been conducting distant naval deployments to the Gulf of Aden in support of national security interests. What the impact of these deployments will be on future PLAN capability cannot be accurately evaluated, but it almost certainly will be significant. A "lessons learned" structure had been established by 2010, at the latest.[41]

Through these deployments, China has demonstrated, as we have seen, for the first time its capacity to operate twenty-first-century ships on distant deployment, giving their crews extended operational experience. But does this reflect Beijing's strategic priorities as laid out by Liu Huaqing in his quest for a global Chinese navy?

Defending China's Littoral

Of more relevance to the U.S. Navy is A2/AD, intended to prevent an opponent—the United States—from intervening in an armed Taiwan scenario or other military operations in East Asian waters.

Presumably China would rely primarily on submarines, cruise missiles, and ASBMs, likely between the coast and the second island chain. The effort would be an element of "active defense," a construct that a U.S. analyst might well consider "offensive."

The point here is that, as noted above, the PLAN will not be constrained by lines or Western defensive concepts in defending China's maritime interests.[42] Its doctrine has been described as a "strategically defensive and active self-defense counterattack," one that could be triggered "as soon as the enemy splits and invades China's territory, severely harming China's interests, . . . equivalent to firing the first shot at China at the strategic level." Furthermore, the PLA's mission is "to do all we can to dominate the enemy by striking first . . . as far away as possible."[43] None of this points to a linear Chinese maritime strategy. PLAN campaign planning appears instead to focus on the nonlinear character of naval warfare.

In its book *2006 Science of Campaigns,* the PLA describes its vision of maritime operations as marked by shifting battle lines and the maneuverability and offensive power of naval forces. Battles at sea are characterized as asymmetric operations occurring on, above, and beneath the sea. Naval campaigns are specifically discussed at length, taking note of the sea's openness and lack of defensive lines, a fact that requires taking the initiative with offensive operations to neutralize enemy forces. Flexibility and the clever employment of tactics and forces are emphasized. Even defensive naval operations should, in the PLAN's view, be imbued with an offensive spirit, that of always taking the initiative and attacking the opponent's weak points.[44]

These views reflect the PLAN's recognition of the inherent value of unconstrained, mobile naval power, limited as little as possible by geographic features or the capabilities of statically based weapons.

The island chains so often discussed may be a Western construct to which Chinese strategists are reacting. PLAN defensive plans acknowledge the limitations of platforms and systems, but at sea these are mobile—a primary attribute of naval forces. Hence, sensor and weapons ranges, capabilities, and vulnerabilities are not rigid factors in naval warfare. PLA planning is not based on drawing limiting lines at sea, as was Soviet naval thinking during the Cold War. Instead, the PLAN appears to recognize both its own and USN strengths and weaknesses.

PLAN strategists are focused on mobile, noncontiguous, nonlinear operations that can bypass the island chains to "reach out and touch" foreign forces in order to achieve specific objectives for specific periods of time. This concept is distinctly not that of Alfred Thayer Mahan; attempts to identify twenty-first-century Chinese naval thinking with that classic maritime strategist are not very useful.[45]

Strategic Intent

Despite the lack of a published maritime strategy, the PLAN almost certainly plans and operates along the lines of guidance from China's civilian and military leadership, the CCP's Politburo Standing Committee, guidance that equates to a strategy. Separate but under the same category is guidance provided to the ministries responsible for the fisheries and coast guard–like functions. The fact that at least five and possibly twenty-one separate government organizations are responsible for these economic and quasi-naval sectors complicates all their associated missions.

Representatives at the early spring 2012 meeting of the National People's Congress in Beijing vociferously criticized the lack of a maritime strategy, calling for the government to "formulate and promulgate a complete, comprehensive, and systematic maritime development strategy, with all the national political, economic, military factors being brought into consideration!"[46] This bureaucratic mess no doubt also hampers coordination with and by the PLAN.

A core principle in China's twenty-first-century maritime strategic thought is definition of the likely scope, or maritime arena, for which it must prepare. A PLAN focus on littoral and regional waters may be assumed, but Beijing's policy for the application of naval power in waters distant from China is unknown. The post–December 2008 antipiracy deployments to the Gulf of Aden are the only such long-range operational cruises to date.

In 2004 China's defense white paper stated that "the Navy has expanded the space and extended the depth for offshore defensive operations." This was augmented in the 2006 white paper with, "The Navy aims at gradual extension of the strategic depth for offshore defensive operations," replaced in the 2008 version with the statement that "since the 1980s the Navy has realized a strategic transformation to offshore defensive operations." Most recently, in the 2010 defense white paper the PLAN's strategic aim was described as "in line with the requirements of offshore defense strategy."[47]

The concept of offshore defense is reflected in Chinese writings about the first and second island chains. Further reading reveals three descriptions of maritime areas of primary concern: the exclusive economic zone, the "three seas" (*san hai*), and the "near seas" (*jin hai*). All indicate what the PLA considers a primary defensive zone, embracing the Yellow, East China, and South China Seas, but more practically based on distance from the homeland and by detection and weapon-system capabilities. Beijing may view this area as a maritime security zone in which it will attempt to prohibit foreign surveillance and reconnaissance activities or any other activities it finds objectionable.

If this concept is effective, it represents a formidable national-security-policy definitional process, one that focuses on maritime strategy while offering legal, national security, domestic political stability, and a fleet composition rationale. No matter which term is used, this thinking seems to have been a factor in Beijing's objections to the 2010 U.S. carrier deployments to the Yellow Sea following the North Korean sinking of the South Korean corvette *Cheonan*.

On 8 July 2010, a Chinese Foreign Ministry spokesperson stated, "We resolutely oppose foreign military ships and aircraft coming to the Yellow Sea and other Chinese adjacent waters and engaging in activities that influence China's security interests."[48] This view, combined with the aggressive actions against foreign fishing craft in the South China Sea during the past decade or more and with actions against U.S. surveillance aircraft and ships, all point toward a view of waters as "sovereign," or at least as of vital national security concern, far in excess of those delineated by the UNCLOS.[49]

United Nations Convention on the Law of the Sea

Beijing ratified the UNCLOS in May 1996. Many states included formal "declarations and statements" when ratifying. China listed four, with reasons including the view that international law historically had been used by Western nations for imperialistic purposes against developing countries and that the sea had often served as an avenue for the invasion and exploitation of China.

China's maritime claims are questioned by most UNCLOS signatories before they are even measured. That is, Beijing measures its zones from coastal baselines that are "straight" to a degree not permitted by the UNCLOS.[50] These UNCLOS-delineated zones are a nation's territorial sea, extending seaward twelve nautical miles from the nation's coastal baseline; its contiguous zone, extending seaward twenty-four nautical miles; its exclusive economic zone, which may be claimed as far out as two hundred nautical miles from a nation's baseline; and its continental shelf, which may be claimed to a maximum distance of 350 nm.

In its first qualifying statement when ratifying the UNCLOS, China claimed "sovereign rights and jurisdiction" over its two-hundred-nautical-mile EEZ and "the continental shelf." This claim appears to contravene both the UNCLOS limitation of sovereign rights over the EEZ and the UNCLOS definition of the continental shelf; Beijing is joined in its position by just fifteen of the 192 treaty signatories.[51] This statement is the basis of China's rationale for protesting—and on several occasions for employing military force against—U.S. surveillance aircraft and ships operating within the EEZ. Beijing maintains that foreign warships must obtain prior permission before entering China's claimed territorial waters, a requirement "inconsistent with the rules of innocent passage" delineated in the UNCLOS.[52]

China's second qualifying statement opposed the UNCLOS-suggested method of delineating contested EEZ and continental shelf claims by applying equidistance criteria, instead favoring bilateral negotiations by the parties concerned "on the basis of international law and in accordance with the equitable principle." Third, China reasserted "its sovereignty over all its archipelagoes and islands" listed in its 1992 Law on the Territorial Sea and Contiguous Zone.[53]

Fourth, China attempted to qualify the UNCLOS provision of innocent passage for foreign warships passing through territorial (i.e., sovereign) waters, stating that "foreign ships for military purposes shall be subject to approval by the Government of the PRC for entering the territorial sea" of the PRC.

The United States and the great majority of UNCLOS signatories object to China's claims that it has the right to control military vessels operating within its EEZ. Also disputed is Beijing's claim to sovereignty over all the islands it had named as sovereign territory in its 1992 Law on the Territorial Sea and Contiguous Zone. These include "Taiwan and all islands appertaining thereto," as well as the Penghus (Pescadores), Dongsha (Pratas), Diaoyu (Senkaku), Xisha (Paracel), and Nansha (Spratly) Islands, as well as other South China Sea land features. Beijing's position on this disputed land would remove from discussion exactly the sort of issues the UNCLOS was created to address.[54]

Beijing followed the 1992 law with a June 1998 law on the EEZ and the continental shelf. The Taiwan Legislative Yuan (LY) passed in January 1998 a similar law, laying out its maritime claims under the UNCLOS.

Two UNCLOS provisions are particularly important to China's maritime claims. First, the UNCLOS definition of an "island" as "a naturally formed area of land, surrounded by water, which is above water at high tide," affects Beijing's insular claims in the East and South China Seas. An island also must be "capable of sustaining human life," an admittedly ambiguous attribute. A land feature not thus qualifying as an island is entitled only to a territorial sea, not to the contiguous zone, EEZ, and continental shelf characteristics of a coastal state.[55]

Second is the UNCLOS provision for delimiting the EEZs between states less than four hundred nautical miles apart—and the CS between states less than seven hundred nautical miles apart. This clause particularly affects China's maritime territorial claims vis-à-vis North Korea, South Korea, Japan, and several Southeast Asian nations. These maritime disputes are but one facet of China's relations with the Southeast Asian nations. Such differing interpretations by China and other UNCLOS signatories represent potential maritime conflict scenarios.

CHINA AND MULTILATERALISM

Beijing historically has been reluctant to engage in multilateral approaches to resolving contentious issues, including those in the maritime realm. This has been most graphically demonstrated in the South China Sea, where, despite agreeing to the 2002 Code of Conduct, on peaceful resolution of the conflicting sovereignty claims in the South China Sea, Beijing has simply carried on fortifying claimed land features and refusing to negotiate. Beijing continues to express cooperative intent about disputed South

China Sea land features but then fails to acknowledge questions of sovereignty. China's efforts to resolve this dispute, embodied in the 2002 agreement, have accomplished little except to provide a platform for Beijing's continued refusal to engage in multilateral negotiations over those claims.

Nonetheless, China seems to have decided to join as many multilateral organizations as possible.[56] These have included formal and informal organizations addressing issues ranging from environmental pollution to maritime security. Chief among regional organizations is Beijing's participation in various forums of the Association of Southeast Asian Nations. Also notable is China's participation in the Container Security Initiative (CSI), an effort begun by Washington and the Northwest Pacific Coast Guard Forum, also initiated by the United States.[57] China participates in the Partnership in Environmental Management for the Seas of East Asia (PEMSEA), the Northwest Pacific Action Plan (NPAP), and of course in the South China Sea Code of Conduct.

Beijing has been selective in this, however, refusing for instance to participate in the Proliferation Security Initiative (PSI) organized by the United States.[58] Still, China has made great strides increasing its political and economic relations with the member states of the ASEAN, which includes all ten of the region's major states: Brunei, Cambodia, Indonesia, Laos, Malaysia, Myanmar, the Philippines, Singapore, Thailand, and Vietnam. The PLAN has played a positive role enhancing this relationship, conducting port calls in the region and limited naval exercises with several regional navies, although these all have been very rudimentary.

China's sensitivity to sovereignty issues is a typically nationalistic trait, in its case probably heightened by the "hundred years of humiliation," the period from approximately 1840 to 1949, during which the country was at the mercy of foreign intruders. Also, as long as Taiwan refuses to accede to Beijing's control, the Chinese consider their 1949 revolution incomplete and the homeland still not unified. Further, problems of "national territorial sovereignty" remain in the East and South China Seas; hence, the "core interest" of sovereignty remains in doubt. This latter point refers not just to islands and other land features but also to "territorial waters," including "relevant continental shelf waters" and exclusive economic zones contested by eight other nations and covering an area of up to 1.5 million kilometers, "accounting for about half of China's maritime jurisdiction."[59]

CONCLUSION

In a long 2010 article, Vice Minister of Foreign Affairs Dai Bingguo argued that China had been and would continue following a national policy of "peaceful development," rather than "the western powers' practice of invasion, plunder, war and expansion." That is, to say the least, a very selective view of China's history, from the Qin Dynasty's use of military force to the PRC's invasion of Vietnam in 1979 and even more recent uses of maritime force in the East and South China Seas. Furthermore, as noted by a professor at China's National Defense University, "peaceful development . . . does not mean that military means are not employed."[60]

Will Dai's discourse affect the future composition, capability, and employment of the PLAN? Beijing's mantra about future military growth, with a specific focus on its naval modernization, is that China has never been expansive or aggressive or stationed military forces overseas. All of these claims are either demonstrably false or at least extremely debatable, given China's dynastic history of expansion and foreign expeditions, but it is too soon to know to what extent current PLAN modernization will take Chinese forces overseas.

Future out-of-area PLAN operations are certain and will likely expand, particularly after the Taiwan issue is resolved. Such operations will likely to be aimed nominally at securing the SLOCs but more practically will reflect the historically typical moves by a nation gaining global economic status, one of which is to deploy a global navy. Two issues of particular concern to the PLAN are, first, India's apparent maritime strategy of effectively controlling the Indian Ocean. Second is the potential for the United States to control navigational choke points crucial to China's trade and hence to its economy.

Both concerns may be exaggerated by Beijing, but that does not reduce their influence in the development of China's maritime strategic thought, which seems to assume that the United States is determined to contain and encircle China.[61] One analyst at the influential PLA Academy of Military Science (AMS) recently described the PLAN as "relatively weak," with "China's maritime security at the mercy of . . . the United States Navy."[62]

China may be engaging in the difficult transition from continental to concurrent maritime power, attempting to gain the latter without losing the former.[63] A former U.S. commander of Pacific forces, Adm. Robert

Willard, has opined that China "aspires to become a 'global military [power]' by extending its influence beyond its regional waters."[64] One analytical view holds that a Chinese drive to global power will lead to conflict with the United States.[65] That is far from certain, however; the phrase *san hai* better explains Beijing's current maritime ambitions.

Future maritime expansion will in large part depend on continuing Chinese GDP growth and a continued absence of threats to the nation's very long land borders. In fact, China is already a global maritime power, if one considers the nation's existing navy, globally ranked merchant fleet, shipbuilding industry, and cargo-handling seaports.

Beijing without doubt is reassessing how much to invest in and how to employ its modernizing PLAN. Previous examples of developing nations emerging as global powers indicate that if China's global economic impact continues to grow, its navy will also grow.

China's current national security concerns are traditional and include defense of the homeland and repulse of potential threats in the near sea, as well as, especially, Taiwan's status. At present, a PLAN built for missions beyond the *san hai* would be a "prestige fleet" similar to that built by France in the late nineteenth century or Germany in the early twentieth.[66] That said, the PLAN is already active in noncombat naval missions, including counterpiracy operations, evacuation of Chinese citizens in danger zones, disaster relief, and UNPKOs.[67]

The argument against global naval ambitions poses a serious domestic issue for China's government. Naval ambitions involve long-term, basic issues of food and water, energy, and environmental threats, all of which must be dealt with if the CCP is to remain in power. Regardless of the scope of GDP growth, as long as no perceived vital national security interest is threatened, Beijing's focus will remain on the domestic scene.

A significant question, the answer to which remains uncertain, is to what degree the PLAN itself influences the setting of national security policy in Beijing. The navy commander, Adm. Wu Shengli, first became a member of the CMC in 2007, but not since Adm. Liu Huaqing retired in 1997 has any PLA officer served on the important Politburo Standing Committee (PBSC). The PLAN has almost certainly gained influence within the PLA during the past two decades, and the PLA in general seems to have become a more professional force. But its increased professionalism does not necessarily mean a less ideological orientation; loyalty to the CCP is uppermost.[68]

Beijing views the United States as the primary threat to its national security interests, especially in view of the 1979 Taiwan Relations Act and the 1996 Taiwan Strait crisis, as well as the updating of American defense treaties with Japan, South Korea, the Philippines, and Australia and a policy of strengthening relations with Vietnam, Singapore, and India.

A 2007 report estimated that Chinese energy companies had $27.178 billion invested in 120 international projects, including $13.379 billion in Russia and Central Asia, $7.98 billion in Africa, $2.749 in North and South America, $1.083 billion in East Asia, and $1.259 billion in the Middle East and North Africa.[69] These data would seem to support another concern often voiced by Chinese analysts—that the United States might intervene in navigational choke points to intercept seaborne energy supplies destined for Chinese ports. This "Malacca Dilemma" is baseless from a naval operational perspective, but it is apparently real at least to some in Beijing.

In other words, to a Chinese maritime strategist in 2012 the region is not without risks, and most of those are attributable to U.S. containment. This accusation is verbalized in terms of arms sales to Taiwan, surveillance flights and ship operations in China's EEZ, congressional restrictions on Sino-American military relations, and maintenance of U.S. defense treaties and agreements with China's neighbors.[70]

History does not offer ready examples of land powers also becoming sea powers. France, Germany, and Russia all failed to do so. If China succeeds in building and deploying an effective, global navy, it will have beaten the historical odds. That ambition is far from established in Beijing, however, which seems more likely to build and maintain only a navy able to defend its national security interests within the three seas.[71]

Beijing's primary national security concerns are in the domestic arena, one in which the nation's new and growing navy plays only a very marginal role. Historically, global ambitions demand a leadership eye on the international arena, and in Asia that means maritime. Hence, China continues to modernize and expand its navy as its economic and political maritime interests increase.

Threats to those interests are mostly nontraditional, but PLAN planners, like planners of all navies, look at the most likely opponents at sea.

That selection is easy for Beijing—the United States is arguably the only maritime power capable of frustrating China's national security interests. Japan, however, is the historical enemy, very much a maritime nation, and hence a primary concern to PLAN planners and strategists.

Incidents at sea confronting China's navy and coast guard have occurred in the East China Sea and, particularly, the South China Sea. Beijing's maritime interests in the latter are contested by several Southeast Asian nations, most of whom are pursuing their own naval modernization programs.

SOUTHEAST ASIA

INTRODUCTION

Southeast Asia, except for Australia and New Zealand, is centered on the South China Sea. Perhaps no body of water in the world is either more important to its surrounding region or the global maritime commons or more contested. The South China Sea contains valuable fisheries, producing energy resources in its peripheral waters and potential energy reserves in the areas around the Spratly Islands, located roughly in its center. These reserves, if they exist, would be deep within the seabed and expensive to extract with today's technologies.

The energy reserves in the central South China Sea are almost certainly greatly exaggerated by Chinese analysts. The true energy and economic value of the South China Sea lies in its vital sea-lanes between the energy-rich Middle East and energy-starved Northeast Asia.[1]

Conflicting national claims in the region focus on the islands and land features that dot the South China Sea. Almost none of these bits of land have any intrinsic value, but they do serve as markers for the nations claiming some or all of them, chiefly because of the maritime areas they may include under the UNCLOS.

The ten Southeast Asian nations are members of the Association of Southeast Asian Nations, formed in 1974 initially for the purposes of coordinating economic interests; it has since added wider international concerns to its portfolio and has grown to include extraregional nations, albeit under the "ASEAN+3 formula." This has added China, Japan, and South Korea to semiofficial membership in the organization, and the United States and other countries send observers to some of ASEAN+3's meetings.

Although often seen as little more than a venue for discussion, the ASEAN has spawned other Southeast Asia–centered organizations, including the ASEAN Regional Forum, the ASEAN Defense Ministers Meeting Plus (ADMM+), and the ASEAN Maritime Forum (AMF).[2] The latter met for the second time in August 2011, when its chief accomplishment appears to have been an agreement to work together to address transnational issues and environmental disasters. The most recent ADMM+ meeting, in May 2012, produced a similar goodwill message. These organizations' real accomplishments are simply the furtherance of a regional approach to maritime problems.[3]

Australia and New Zealand may usefully be classified as Southeast Asian nations. Their economies are inextricably linked to those of Asian countries, especially China's. Australia's strategic position is in one way similar to Japan's—extensive economic interdependence with China but greater interdependence with the United States for defense and security issues. This strategic situation exists for most Southeast Asian nations.

REGIONAL NAVIES

Most of the region's nations are embarked in a naval modernization effort, although none of them realistically aspires to more than an increase in defensive capability. One common factor is a desire to acquire submarines, perhaps with the view that this weapons platform offers the most "bang for the buck" for a small navy possibly confronting a much larger, modern naval force.[4]

The first priority of all of them is defense of national security interests. For the ASEAN nations, save Laos, this includes maritime concerns ranging from cross-border terrorism to striving for a fair share of biological and mineral resources from the sea. Second is an emphasis on deploying forces capable of executing a multifaceted maritime strategy focusing both on traditional national security threats and on maritime support for humanitarian and other nontraditional problems ashore.

Australia

Canberra issued a new defense white paper in 2009, calling for the most significant increase in its military capability since World War II, and assigning to the Royal Australian Navy (RAN) the main task of deterring or defeating an enemy: "Australia might need to be prepared to engage in conventional combat in the region . . . in order to counter coercion or aggression against our allies and partners and armed attack on Australia."[5]

The white paper emphasizes the need for "control of the air and sea approaches to Australia." It specifically addresses the need for destroyers, frigates, and submarines "to establish sea control, and to project force in our maritime environment (including . . . maintaining freedom of navigation, protecting our shipping, and lifting and supporting land forces)." Future naval growth by 2030 is described as doubling the size of the submarine force from six to twelve boats, replacing the current Australia–New Zealand (ANZAC) frigates with a new design, and enhancing "our capability for offshore maritime warfare, border protection, and mine countermeasures."[6]

The future maritime force will focus on Australian industry involvement, although engaging with "a number of overseas partners during the design and development phase." The new surface combatants are referred to as "Air Warfare Destroyers," implying that the ships will possess the Aegis air-defense system. Eight new "Future Frigates," with a primary antisubmarine warfare mission, will join them.

The 2030 force plan also includes "at least 24 new naval combat helicopters [and] 46 MRH-90 helicopters," the latter shared with the army. Eight new aircraft of an as-yet unspecified model and "seven large high-altitude, long-endurance UAVs" will replace the current P-3C patrol plane force.

Twenty new offshore patrol vessels (OPVs) will be tasked with mine warfare, hydrographic tasks, and transnational problems. Two new, large amphibious ships capable of operating helicopters are on schedule to join the fleet during the next decade, as are two new replenishment-at-sea supply vessels.

The white paper emphasizes that Australia's most important defense relationship is with the United States.

Canberra signed and ratified the UNCLOS in 2002. Its maritime claims in the UNCLOS-delineated zones cover an area greater than the continent itself and are the largest in the world. Australia has sovereignty disputes with Timor-Leste; the two nations' EEZ claims conflict. Australia also does not agree with the views of China and a few other nations regarding naval ship and aircraft operational limits within a country's EEZ.

Australia's already impressive defense capacity will be significantly enhanced by its new destroyers' ability to engage in a networking paradigm, the "cooperative engagement capability" (CEC). Three Aegis-equipped ships will also provide a ballistic-missile-defense capability. The RAN's two large landing helicopter dock ships under construction will join its fleet of nine amphibious-warfare vessels, six submarines, three destroyers, twelve frigates, eight mine-warfare ships, and two oilers.[7]

The RAN has experienced difficulties with several important platform and system acquisition programs. The Department of Defense published a list of "Projects of Concern" in 2011, which addressed late and canceled defense systems. The list was headed by the canceled LCM 2000 Watercraft and included the *Collins*-class submarine, as well as several other navy systems.[8] In at least one case, material shortfalls caused the navy to miss a commitment, an occasion when its amphibious capability was reported as "at a crisis point."[9]

The Australian air force is also seeking a replacement maritime strike aircraft for its very old F-111s. The F-35 has been selected; indeed, it is the only Western-built, fifth-generation strike/fighter option, but it is criticized as not capable of matching either Russia's T-50 PAK-FA or China's Chengdu J-20 series fighters. The F-35 also offers a problematic ordnance-load/strike-range capability, as well as suffering from production delays and increased costs.[10]

Finally, the fleet's submarine force of *Collins*-class boats has experienced a series of difficulties throughout its life, and Australia is seeking a long-term replacement. The *Collins* class's expected retirement date is not until 2025, but a replacement decision is required by 2014 to allow for an orderly replacement process. A Japanese-built submarine is a serious candidate for Australia's new undersea fleet.[11]

Australia's navy should not be judged as an independent force, however; significant synergistic effects result from its close relationship with, and ability to operate in an integrated fashion with, the U.S. and New Zealand navies. The RAN's demonstrated professionalism and competence in combat will also be a factor in any mission it undertakes.

The navy apparently has shifted from its historical focus to the north and east, toward Indonesia, to a western orientation, recognizing the increasing importance of the Indian Ocean SLOCs and the potential role of the Indian navy in balancing China's modernizing navy.[12] This concern was indirectly addressed in the September 2011 joint communiqué that followed Australian-U.S. ministerial consultations. The communiqué reaffirmed the Australia–New Zealand–United States pact, emphasized "trilateral policy coordination" with Japan, and "welcomed India's engagement in East Asia," while "constructively managing differences with China."

The two nations also discussed increasing U.S. access to Australian facilities, which has led to establishing a training facility for U.S. Marines in northern Australia. The final note in the communiqué addressed Australia's continued participation in U.S. ballistic-missile-defense efforts, reflecting concern about China's reputed ASBM program.[13]

Prime Minister Julia Gillard nicely summed up the Australian national security situation in September 2011. In codifying her nation's national interests in Asia, the prime minister listed both "space for a rising China" and "a robust alliance between Australia and the United States."[14] Australia's navy outlook is distinctly international, however; the chief of the navy, Vice Adm. Ray Griggs, spoke to that view in August 2012. Griggs described "a key issue" for the navy as "how we can contribute to ensuring that the use of sea, for a multitude of activities, remains free and interrupted." Furthermore, he stated, "like most things at sea, security on this scale must be a cooperative and collaborative venture."[15]

Brunei

This oil-rich sheikhdom on the north Borneo coast has extensive interests in the energy resources in the South China Sea. It signed and ratified the UNCLOS in 1996 and claims a two-hundred-nautical-mile EEZ. This includes one land feature that emerges only at low tide, Louisa Reef, also claimed by China and Malaysia.

Four missile-armed corvettes lead Brunei's navy, with three OPVs in the offing. The navy is tasked with securing the kingdom's maritime claims, including its EEZ and 350 nm continental shelf, a mission it is incapable of executing.

Cambodia

Cambodia's qualification when it signed the UNCLOS was to claim "control of all foreign activities on [its] continental shelf," to include the passage of military vessels. This clearly is not in accordance with the UNCLOS, which awaits final Cambodian ratification. The country has no navy, only small craft to attempt to enforce its claims over its twelve-nautical-mile territorial sea, twenty-four-nautical-mile contiguous zone, and two-hundred-nautical-mile EEZ and "fishing zone." Cambodia has one maritime sovereignty dispute of note, with Thailand over conflicting continental shelf claims; the two nations signed a Memorandum of Understanding for Joint Development in 2001.[16]

Indonesia

Indonesia's military was established with an officer corps whose members could serve in civilian government positions while on active duty. This political role has ended for military officers, but the process of reform continues, affecting the navy, as well as the other armed forces. The Indonesian navy has other historical baggage as well, including the abortive modernization campaigns that have occurred periodically since independence.

Indonesia's geography—the nation borders the Malacca Strait and contains the Sunda and Lombok Straits, as well as other important straits—makes an effective navy vital to national defense. Maritime strategy since independence was gained in 1947 has been two-sided. First priority is assigned to maintaining peace and stability in an archipelagic nation of several thousand islands. Second have been the traditional maritime concerns of so intensely maritime a nation. These include a concern in the sovereignty disputes that plague the South China Sea.

As the twenty-first century moves into its second decade, the Indonesian navy appears to have hit upon a viable manner in which to serve both domestic and regional concerns. In 2005 the navy announced its goal of deploying a "green-water navy" by 2024. This concept conveys a maritime strategy that will allow defense of both domestic and international interests.[17] It has been followed by calls for a "navy second to none in Southeast Asia"—a very achievable goal, given Indonesia's economic potential and the interest shown by its civilian leadership.

Indonesia's defense budget increased by 28 percent in 2010, with the navy's share sized by a target of acquiring a 274-ship fleet, divided into Striking, Patrolling, and Supporting Forces.[18] This goal attests to the existence of a considered, although unwritten, maritime strategy relying on seagoing surface combatants and submarines for green-water defense. It will also employ vessels well suited for the nontraditional naval missions so crucial to Indonesia, given its location at the hinge of East and South Asia. The 2004–5 multiple disaster resulting from earthquake, tsunami, flooding, and volcanic eruption underscored the criticality for the Indonesian navy of the mission of humanitarian relief of disasters ashore.

The navy historically has struggled to acquire and effectively operate forces capable of patrolling its extensive national waters, which include more than 14,000 islands, and maritime boundaries with no fewer than ten nations: Australia, India, Malaysia, Palau, Papua New Guinea, the Philippines, Singapore, Thailand, Timor Leste, and Vietnam. Recent steps include acquisition of four *Sigma*-class corvettes of stealthy design. They join a fleet of two submarines, twenty-four other frigates, twenty-three corvettes, and two oilers.

The Indonesian navy also plans to acquire two LPDs, in addition to the three Korean-built LPDs it already operates. These new *Makassar*-class ships displace 8,400 tons and will serve admirably both for combat and humanitarian missions.

Jakarta's ratification of the UNCLOS in 1986 included a stipulation that "warships and all vessels other than merchant ships must announce their passage in advance," which reflects concern about the country's particular maritime defense issue—its very complex archipelagic character.[19]

Indonesia faces a strategic situation similar to Australia's. It has increasingly close economic ties with China but wants to continue developing a positive security relationship with the United States. Jakarta has been successfully pursuing this dual strategy, but problems loom in the future, particularly with respect to China's apparent claims on waters well within Indonesia's EEZ. So far, Chinese activities in the area of the Natuna natural-gas fields have been limited to fishing craft, but Indonesia's concerns over Chinese incursions into its EEZ are real, if seldom expressed.[20]

Indonesia has long been one of Southeast Asia's strongest supporters of multilateral, regional efforts to enhance economic, political, and maritime security. In recent years this has expanded to include encouraging greater U.S. involvement in the region and a reaching-out to India, a policy that ties in with New Delhi's "Look East" program.[21]

Malaysia

When Kuala Lumpur signed the UNCLOS in 1996, it stipulated that "prior consent" had to be acquired by foreign ships engaging in military exercises and maneuvers in its claimed EEZ and continental shelf areas. In doing so, it joined several other coastal states in this partial agreement with China's excessive claims. Malaysia's navy faces a geographic challenge almost as complex as Indonesia's; Kuala Lumpur's territory is both peninsular and insular, spread over great distances across twenty degrees of longitude.

Hence, the Malaysian navy's missions include a full range of defense-of-the-homeland challenges. To meet one facet of this problem, Kuala Lumpur has acquired a force of two conventionally powered submarines and two oceangoing frigates. It also deploys twelve corvettes, four mine-warfare ships, and two oilers. The insular challenge confronts a Malaysian patrol force that is moving to increase its capacity in patrol, surveillance, port and littoral waters security, and maritime domain awareness.

Kuala Lumpur emphasizes the importance of the ASEAN as a security forum but maintains consistent, low-key relations with the U.S. Navy. Port calls, exercises, and training initiatives have increased in recent years, a trend expected to continue.[22] The Malaysian navy is moving to acquire more submarines, although it apparently lacks a comprehensive strategy for employing an expanded submarine fleet.[23]

Myanmar

Myanmar too signed the UNCLOS in 1996, at which time it stated a requirement that warships obtain prior authorization to enter its EEZ. It also "claims the right to restrict the freedom of navigation and over flight in its exclusive EEZ."[24] Myanmar's navy is ill equipped to enforce these provisions, being focused on riverine operations. It includes one frigate and three corvettes of dubious reliability, all acquired from China, with additional frigates in the offing.[25]

New Zealand

New Zealand is an outlier to the Southeast Asian political environment, having close defense ties to Australia and significant economic ties with China. New Zealand also is an enthusiastic supporter of Washington's Trans-Pacific Partnership (TPP) and has signed a free-trade agreement with China.[26]

New Zealand was suspended from the 1954 ANZUS Pact in 1986, when it refused to allow vessels or aircraft to enter its territory before first declaring whether or not they were carrying nuclear weapons. The U.S. Pacific commander at the time, Adm. William Crowe, forced the suspension.[27] Wellington thereafter codified this restriction into a law that remains in effect. Since that time New Zealand has relied on Australia for defense support, although some informal relations have been maintained between New Zealand military personnel and their U.S. counterparts. New Zealand, however, has been a firm supporter of U.S. military efforts in Iraq and Afghanistan since 2001.

In 2010 Wellington issued its first defense white paper since 1998. The white paper directly addresses present and planned maritime forces, focusing on the plan for replacement of its two destroyer-sized combatants, its single replenishment-at-sea and amphibious vessels, and limited mine-warfare and offshore patrol forces.[28]

The white paper was followed late in 2010 by the Wellington Declaration, which "provides for a new strategic partnership between New Zealand and the United States." These two documents appear to herald a revised security position for New Zealand. The white paper identifies the Five-Power Defense Arrangement as the nation's number-one security relationship and a "valuable anchor" for its relations in Southeast Asia. It focuses on dealing with security challenges in the country's maritime zones and in the South Pacific, where it has special relationships with some of the island nations.[29]

The Royal New Zealand Navy (RNZN) continues to shrink; as of 2013 it numbered just two frigates, one oiler, and a number of OPVs. The navy's missions are to ensure the nation's sovereignty over its EEZs, serve its interests in the "Southern Ocean and Ross Dependency," counter threats of terrorism or sabotage, support "civil defense and other emergencies," and "contribute to the Government's social and economic priorities."[30]

Philippines

The foundation of Philippine international defense has been the 1951 mutual defense treaty with the United States, although even at the height of the Cold War there were no existential foreign threats to the Philippine democracy.

The Republic of the Philippines' primary national security threat since it achieved independence in 1946 has been domestic. The Hukbalahaps (the Huks), the New People's Army (NPA), various Islamic groups, and Philippine army officer cliques have all posed threats to the government.[31] As one Philippine senior military officer put it, "we always have insurgencies in the Philippines."[32]

Currently, the United States is assisting the Philippines in suppressing insurgencies by the NPA and various Islamic and terrorist groups, but it has not committed to defense of the few Spratly Islands claimed by the Philippines. These land features, called the Kalayaan Islands by Manila, were first claimed in 1956, five years after the signing of the mutual defense treaty with the United States.[33]

In addition to an active advisory role and mutual training events, U.S. Navy vessels made more than a hundred port calls in the Philippines in 2011, and U.S. forces continue to participate in exercises with Philippine forces, including an annual, significant exercise named Balikatan. The most recent iteration of this exercise took place in March 2012. The field phase occurred on the island of Palawan, close to the disputed Spratly Islands.[34] The Ministry of Defense in Manila even announced that U.S forces could use their former bases in the Philippines, "provided they have prior coordination from the government."[35]

The Philippines signed the UNCLOS in 1982 and ratified it in 1984. In doing so, Manila issued eight "understandings." These include the statement that "signing shall not in any manner impair or prejudice the sovereignty of the Republic of the Philippines over any territory over which it exercises sovereign authority, such as the Kalayaan [that is, the Spratly] Islands, and the waters appurtenant thereto."

The Philippine navy remains more a vision than a fleet in being. It nominally deploys two frigates, eleven corvettes, and fifty-eight patrol craft. The average age of the corvettes is fifty-seven, however, and the newly acquired ex–U.S. Coast Guard cutters are more than forty years old. Even these old ships, however, represent a significant increase in force to that navy.[36] The Philippine Coast Guard, reorganized in 2003, is the nation's most capable maritime force. It operates vessels acquired from Japan and Australia and has received training support from the former.[37]

In 2001 the Philippine president warned China of "an arms race" in the South China Sea and authorized a significant increase in the navy's budget.[38] Despite this initiative, however, Philippine defense spending declined in 2009 to 0.8 percent of GDP, less than half the average spent by all Southeast Asian nations.[39] Furthermore, the Philippine defense secretary recently complained that "until such time that we can upgrade our [military], we can't do anything but protest and protest." He described the condition of the navy as "deplorable but plain reality."[40]

The inadequacy of naval capability significantly affects Philippine foreign relations, particularly maritime sovereignty claims in the South China Sea and the security of even the nation's own archipelagic SLOCs, let alone the maritime transportation sector on which so many of its citizens depend for their livelihoods. Hence, Manila's inherently contradictory policies of neither ceding its sovereignty claims in the "West Philippine Sea," as it has recently been calling the South China Sea, nor antagonizing Beijing rests in the final analysis on support from Washington.

Without this problematic U.S. support, Manila has little hope of prevailing against Chinese, Malaysian, or Vietnamese sovereignty claims in the South China Sea. Instead, it likely will use its 2002 agreement with Beijing as a first step in accommodating Chinese demands, as the Philippine oligarchy throughout history has accommodated itself to the Spanish, the Americans, the Japanese, and again the Americans.[41]

Singapore

Singapore is perhaps the most strategically aware and stable state in East Asia, pursuing a defensive strategy of rare coherence. The city-state is self-dependent to the extent possible, but it also pursues a balanced policy between China and the United States, currently with a strong "lean" toward the latter.[42] The navy particularly focuses on multilateral cooperation in training and dialogue in areas including maritime security, disaster relief and humanitarian assistance, counterterrorism and protection against other maritime crime, and defense of the homeland.[43]

These have been described as elements in Singapore's "Total Defense." This in turn is set within a framework of five pillars: military, civil, economic, social, and psychological defense.[44] Singapore also draws on required national service, which makes the maximum number of young citizens stakeholders in the state's defense.

Singapore lies at the heart of the world's busiest SLOCs, from the Indian to the Pacific Oceans via the South China Sea. The city-state ratified the UNCLOS in 1994.

Singapore has a well-deserved reputation for seeking state-of-the-art naval technology; its six new *Formidable*-class frigates embody this trend. These 3,200-ton-displacement ships are full participants in Singapore's integrated command-and-control system, which in turn plays a key role in the city-state's admirably coherent defense posture. These are stealthy ships, equipped with phased-array multifunction radars and vertical-launch missile systems. Six corvettes and one oiler are also in the fleet.

The Singapore navy includes four *Endurance*-class LPDs, each displacing 8,500 tons and capable of operating two helicopters. These are ideally suited for the maritime support of operations ashore, both humanitarian and combat. Four submarines and four mine-warfare ships are also in service. The most recent two submarines, of the *Archer* class, were acquired from Sweden and are equipped with air-independent propulsion systems.[45]

The navy pursues an active program of domestic and international exercises, including participation in the U.S. Cooperation Afloat Readiness and Training (CARAT) exercise series, India's multilateral exercises, and bilateral training with other Southeast Asian nations.[46]

The government consistently strives for a multilateral approach to bolster the nation's security. The navy has participated in Gulf of Aden antipiracy patrols as a member of multinational task groups, while the government has served as a leader in forming ASEAN, the ARF, the Asia-Europe Meeting (ASEM), and the East Asia–Latin America Forum (EALAF).

Taiwan

Taiwan maintains a small navy that is only marginally capable of a meaningful contribution to the island's defense. Four large *Kidd*-class guided-missile destroyers, twenty-two frigates, and two large amphibious warfare ships are the mainstays of the Taiwan navy (TN). The navy also includes twelve mine-warfare ships and one oiler. It deploys four submarines, the newer pair of which are more than twenty years old.

The TN is unable to oppose the Chinese navy effectively, not least because its major naval base at Tsoying is small, shallow, and directly opposite the mainland, less than a hundred nautical miles distant. The navy's main strength is its personnel, who are dedicated, well-trained men and women. Taipei is working to improve its C4ISR (command, control, communications, computers, intelligence, surveillance, and reconnaissance) capability, expand its cruise-missile inventory, and acquire new submarines, although success in this latter step is very doubtful.

These ambitions remain frustrated by a government in Taipei that apparently does not take seriously a Chinese military threat, notwithstanding the president's statement that "we must maintain a viable level of military power to deter aggression [by China]." Clear evidence of this is the administration's determination to end compulsory military service.[47] It has not been able to provide the leadership necessary to convince the legislature to provide the budgetary resources required by the navy to develop a more creditable defensive capability.

Taipei makes the same sovereignty claims in the East and South China Seas as does Beijing. Taiwan occupies and has fortified just one of the Spratlys—Itu Aba, called Taiping by Taipei—as well as the Pratas Islands, a very small atoll at the northern end of the South China Sea.[48]

Thailand

Thailand has at least temporarily resolved its sovereignty claims in the Gulf of Thailand that conflict with those of Malaysia, Myanmar, and Vietnam.[49] Its navy is led by a small aircraft carrier, the *Chakri Narubet*, but this ship rarely goes to sea, and Thailand no longer possesses fixed-wing carrier-capable aircraft. The Thai navy also numbers eleven frigates, nine corvettes, seven mine-warfare vessels, seven amphibious-warfare ships, and one oiler. A new, small LPD recently joined the fleet but was described as a support vessel for the relatively inactive *Chakri Narubet*. The navy has successfully conducted antipiracy patrols in the Gulf of Thailand, while Thai aircraft have taken part in antipiracy patrol exercises in the Straits of Singapore and Malacca.[50]

Thailand has not formulated a maritime strategy but has drafted a *National Coastal and Marine Policy*. While not formally approved, this body of laws and policies effectively addresses managing and conserving the nation's maritime economic sector. It does not amount to a military doctrine, with the navy mentioned only in connection with support of law enforcement.[51]

Vietnam

Vietnam has not issued a maritime strategy, but it is extremely conscious of its reliance on the seas for food, energy, transportation, and trade. Hanoi also has maritime disputes with several neighboring countries: Cambodia, Indonesia, China, Taiwan, Thailand, Malaysia, and the Philippines, the latter five over the sovereignty of the South China Sea islands.

Hanoi is attempting to defend its maritime interests, particularly those contested by China, while also reducing the chances of conflict. It has been only partially successful, since Beijing has maintained a rigid policy with respect to fishing-boat incursions and energy drilling sites in contested waters.[52] Vietnam asserts "undisputed sovereignty over [Paracel and Spratly] archipelagos" but engages diplomatically with China to resolve these disputed islands. Furthermore, the two nations have since 2005 conducted a series of joint patrols, and they repeatedly hold discussions, which consistently end with statements of peaceful resolution, however little was accomplished at sea.[53]

When Vietnam signed the UNCLOS in 1994, it claimed straight baselines in excess of common practice; it also stipulated that warships must obtain authorization "at least 30 days prior to passage" through its twenty-four-nautical-mile contiguous zone. Hanoi further claims extension of the UNCLOS restriction on warship operations for the twelve-nautical-mile territorial waters throughout the contiguous zone. More seriously, Vietnam places restrictions that are unlawful, even in its territorial sea, on the numbers and activities of visiting military vessels.[54]

The nation has passed a body of domestic legislation to support its UNCLOS claims. These have included the 1989 Ordinance on Protection and Development of Aquatic Resources, the 1990 Maritime Code, and the 1993 Petroleum Law. The UNCLOS was ratified in 1994 with a note about Vietnamese sovereignty over the Paracel and Spratly Islands.[55]

Vietnam feels pronounced historical enmity toward China, despite that country's assistance during wars against France and the United States. China is accused of threatening behavior, "bullying," and unjustifiably "showing groundless demands against international law."[56] Hanoi in the past decade has moved to establish closer relationships with nonregional powers, particularly the United States and India. It has also joined South Korea in an "overall joint proposed plan."[57]

Vietnam deploys a significant, modernizing navy. It warships include six Kilo-class submarines on order from Russia; seven frigates, with two more under construction; nine corvettes, with as many as nine more planned; three amphibious-warfare ships; and four mine-warfare vessels. Responsibility for Vietnam's maritime security is shared by the maritime element of its Border Guard, organized in 1997, and its coast guard (Marine Police), organized in 1998. The 1996 Committee for Search and Rescue was established in 1996 and has supported increased cooperation with Thailand, Cambodia, and China to address search-and-rescue (SAR) and fisheries issues.

These incremental steps have led to a call for a national maritime strategy. Senior government officials met in 2011 to discuss a maritime strategy for 2020, but that continues to be a work in progress.[58] The nation did issue a third defense white paper in 2009, which, while emphasizing "a defense policy of peace and self-defense," noted the importance of defending sovereignty claims in the "East Sea," as Hanoi calls the South China Sea, and the "tensions over Mekong water resources."[59]

CONCLUSION

Southeast Asia is caught inextricably in the rivalries of the greater Asia region, from the North Pacific to the western Indian Oceans. Competition between China and the United States imposes a political, economic, and military environment that envelops and sometimes drives events in the region. India's Look East policy interposes a third maritime power's interests into Southeast Asia, while Japan may be on the verge of increasing its presence in the region's waters.[60]

Regional efforts to resist the pressures from outside powers have tended toward multilateral organizations, such as the ASEAN, but these have been of dubious effectiveness. In 1996 ASEAN ministers agreed to formulate a regional code of conduct that would permit such activities as conducting scientific research, combating piracy, and thwarting drug trafficking without invoking the issue of sovereignty. China and the ASEAN member states signed in November 2002 a Joint Declaration on the Conduct of Parties. They agreed to "undertake to resolve their territorial and jurisdictional disputes by peaceful means" without "resorting to the threat or the use of force." This was a positive step but crucially did not contain an agreement not to further fortify any of the disputed land features.

Associated with the ASEAN is the ARF, which focuses on security issues. The twenty-two-nation ARF includes non-ASEAN members, however, including the United States. Meetings between Vietnam and China in December 2000 resolved the two nations' boundary dispute in the Gulf of Tonkin (Beibu Wan in Chinese, Vinh Bac Bo in Vietnamese). The disputed Paracel Islands were not addressed by the 2002 agreement, in part because they are disputed only between Vietnam and China. In 2007 the two nations conducted at least five joint patrols of the Gulf of Tonkin.

Malaysia and Brunei held talks in 2003 regarding their conflicting EEZ claims but have yet to reach an agreement. In 2003 naval vessels from Malaysia and Brunei prevented (without the actual use of force) exploration vessels from working in the disputed area. In 2004 China and the Philippines agreed to exchange seismic data resulting from their individual seabed explorations. Vietnam joined this agreement in 2005. Apparently no data was exchanged before this agreement ended, without renewal, in 2008.

Apart from the Taiwan situation, the South China Sea disputes present the most dangerous potential for conflict in maritime Asia. The primary obstacles to settlement are the claimants' rigidity on their own claims and China's unwillingness to negotiate on anything more than a time-delay basis. Time is in Beijing's favor, given China's steadily increasing economic and naval strength.

The other claimants welcome increased U.S. and Indian involvement in Southeast Asia, as possible counterweights to China.[61] In particular, the maritime Southeast Asian nations are watching with concern the growth and changing policies of China and the United States. These are the two elephants of the region; the lesser states want to balance both and offend neither.

Australia is a firm U.S. ally, of course, and its modernizing navy should be counted among U.S. maritime assets. New Zealand is more independent but supports U.S. maritime efforts across the Indo-Asian maritime arena.

Particularly important is the South China Sea's bridging position between East and South Asia. It serves as a natural region of interest to New Delhi and to the maritime nations of the Indian Ocean region. The Indian navy's Look East policy acknowledges Southeast Asia's importance.

seven

INDIA

INTRODUCTION

The Indian Ocean covers 20 percent of the earth's water expanse, while its littoral states contain more than one-third of the earth's population. It is dominated by India, which has been a maritime nation for millennia, periodically commanding the vital sea lines of communication between the Middle East and Asia. The subcontinent has a coastline of more than 3,396 nm, with an additional 765 nm of island coastline. These island groups include the Lakshadweep to the west of the great Indian peninsula and the Andamans and Nicobars to the east. They define the most heavily traveled Indian Ocean SLOCs, through the Nine Degree and Eight Degree Channels in the west and the Malacca Strait in the east.

India depends on the sea for a stunning 97 percent of its international trade, which accounts for 10 percent of its GDP.[1] Major maritime economic interests also include fisheries, a large and growing port infrastructure, and seabed minerals, especially oil and natural gas. China is already seeking these seabed resources; the International Seabed Authority has allotted a 3,900-square-mile exploration area on the Indian Ocean's Southwest Ridge to Beijing, to search for polymetallic sulphides.[2] India's protective attitude toward the Indian Ocean—and its extensive hydrographic explorations throughout the ocean—will contribute an additional element of competition, if not hostility, between the two countries.[3]

It is no exaggeration to say that Indian maritime strategists take the name "Indian Ocean" literally. An Indian naval strategist has categorized India's security concerns as "global, regional, and local," focusing on secure sea lines of communication, especially with respect to energy security.[4]

India has expressed sovereignty claims similar to China's, in excess of the most widely held interpretation of the UNCLOS, which it signed and ratified in 1995. For instance, New Delhi requires that foreign warships provide notice before entering the Indian territorial sea, asserts security jurisdiction over the contiguous zone, and restricts military activities in its exclusive economic zone along the lines advocated by China.[5]

New Delhi's concern with the maritime zones delineated in the UNCLOS is expressed in its assignment of missions to the Indian navy— and in the limitations on that force's ability to execute its missions within the UNCLOS zones. The key to successful mission accomplishment is correctly identified by the Indian navy as maritime domain awareness.

THE EVOLUTION OF INDIA'S MARITIME STRATEGY

Modern India expressed a maritime vision soon after independence, in its 1948 Naval Plans Paper.[6] The "first" Indian navy (IN) featured cruisers, destroyers, and small aircraft carriers; its primary mission was protecting India's SLOCs. Maritime threats were envisaged to come from aircraft and submarines trying to interrupt the SLOCs.

Pakistan has dominated New Delhi's security concerns since that time; as a result, the army and air force understandably take the lead in India's defense establishment. This characterized India's early military development and dominated the remainder of the twentieth century, "with maritime affairs being perceived merely as an extension of" land warfare.[7] The IN early addressed the nation's maritime interests, of course, and has maintained its focus on developing a force capable of defending the nation's maritime interests. This involved a fleet centered on aircraft carrier battle groups, with the 1961 acquisition of India's first aircraft carrier, INS *Vikrant*.

Carriers remain the centerpiece of the navy's organization. While the IN did not play a significant role in the 1965 war with Pakistan, the 1971 conflict featured a *Vikrant* task group blockading the Pakistani coast, while combatants launched cruise-missile attacks. Lessons learned from these wars included the need to acquire additional submarines and aircraft, combatants capable of spending extended time at sea, and the logistics ships and infrastructure necessary to support those extended operations. The navy in the 1970s identified its goals as defending against surprise attack on "maritime interests," deterring Pakistan from further military conflict, and winning a war at sea.

IN operations since the conflicts with Pakistan have run the gamut of naval missions. The navy's role in the long Sri Lankan civil war was largely to support Indian army efforts on that island between 1987 and 1990. New Delhi's efforts to resolve this long-standing conflict were unable to bridge the extreme hostility between the ruling Sinhalese majority on the island and the rebelling Tamils, who sought independence, possibly supported by India's own Tamils. Indirectly associated with the Sri Lankan civil war was the 1988 attempted coup d'état in the Maldives—a coup suppressed with the effective assistance of the IN.

Lessons learned from efforts during the Sri Lankan conflict included the need for more effective capability to transport troops for amphibious operations and for an increased ability to provide fire support to troops ashore. The Indian 2007 maritime strategy also noted the difficulty—perhaps the impossibility—of effectively isolating the Sri Lankan rebels from the sea with a blockade, despite the conflict's insular nature.

The navy even drew lessons from Operations Vijay in 1999 and Parakaram in 2001–2, although both actions centered on the dispute with Pakistan over Jammu and Kashmir. These were two episodes in the Indian and Pakistani conflict over these areas dating to 1947. One lesson learned was that conventional maritime operations were possible even in the shadow of a nuclear threat; another was that maritime forces could affect combat ashore. These should more properly be described as lessons relearned, but nonetheless they apparently have impacted the continuing development of maritime strategy in New Delhi.

The past two decades have underscored for many Indian strategists the importance of maritime security. Freedom to use the seas is the core of India's maritime strategy. This developing realization has been punctuated by several significant events and trends. First is the globalization phenomenon, including the importance to India's economy of overseas trade and its increasing need for imported energy. Second is the increased danger of international terrorism, epitomized in the maritime infiltration of India by the terrorists who attacked Mumbai so devastatingly in November 2008.

Third is China's economic and military rise, including its navy's modernization and expansion. Many Indian analysts believe the Chinese navy has a goal of dominating the Indian Ocean. Fourth and perhaps most crucial is the IN's need for significantly increased financial resources if it is to achieve the operational effectiveness necessary to carry out its national security missions.[8] These conditions are often couched in terms of the increasingly capable Chinese navy and a U.S. Navy that is some-times viewed as growing weaker in numbers and capability, and of the way in which both developments cast an ever heavier responsibility on India's navy.

India's strategy arises from classic maritime strategy, particularly as discussed by Julian Corbett. The IN also uses, interestingly, the concept of "people's power" to delineate the interests of the Indian state to be defended by the navy in time of war. This in turn leads to a discussion of geographic areas of responsibility.

2009 MARITIME STRATEGY

The 2009 maritime strategy lists maritime geographic areas of interest; "primary areas" include the Arabian Sea and the Bay of Bengal, which largely encompass India's claimed continental and island territory EEZs, and IOR choke points. To secure these waters, New Delhi has reached agreement on continental shelf limits and other maritime boundaries with Indonesia, Thailand, Bangladesh, Myanmar, Sri Lanka, and the Maldives.

The maritime strategy states up front that India is historically a con-tinental nation in terms of national security threats—a situation unlikely to change in the future. Hence, it declares, the IN should focus its war-time efforts at affecting an opponent's national interests ashore, as well as denying it use of the sea. The most direct way to do this, the strat-egy notes, is also the simplest—"target the adversary's territory from the sea by the delivery of ordnance."[9] Both enemy combatants and material assets are listed as legitimate targets, while expeditionary operations are given, in addition to ordnance fired from sea-based platforms, as means of projecting naval power ashore.[10]

Defense of the homeland also occupies pride of place in the new Indian naval strategy, to include defending coastal and offshore installations, as well as coastal merchant-ship traffic. These tasks, especially the latter, may require projecting defensive naval power far out to sea, a similarity between the maritime strategies of India and China, that latter of which promulgates the strategic element of "active defense."

The 2007 maritime strategy subsumed the nation's maritime doctrine, which addresses the IN's missions. These are unexceptional but seem to have been based on achieving improved maritime domain awareness, described as key to maintaining national security.

The navy today describes its strategic goal as simply "to promote a secure and stable environment in the IOR."[11] This may be rephrased as ensuring that India can use the sea for its own purposes while preventing similar use to hostile states. This subsumes the navy's role in serving as a "catalyst for peace, tranquility and stability" in the IOR, as well as a deterrent to conventional or strategic conflict.

Specific missions include a constabulary role with the Indian Coast Guard (ICG), combating piracy and terrorism at sea, performing hydrographic surveys, carrying out search and rescue operations, coordinating navigational warnings, evacuating Indian citizens from zones of danger, and conducting humanitarian relief operations. Finally, India's maritime strategy has three major facets: peacetime missions, conflict operations, and force buildup.

THE INDIAN NAVY

India's navy numbers no more than 55,000 personnel. These man an impressive fleet, including two aircraft carriers, with a third under construction. Its submarine fleet in 2013 included one nuclear-powered submarine, with another under construction. Five SSNs are planned for the fleet in 2020, joining at least fifteen conventionally powered attack submarines, although delivery of the most recent acquisitions have been delayed until at least 2013. The surface force includes eleven destroyers; twelve frigates, with eighteen under construction or in planning; twelve corvettes under construction or planned; one large and eight small amphibious-warfare vessels; and two underway replenishment ships.[12]

Capability Prioritization

India's maritime strategy includes concern about future fleet composition, noting "that at the current rate of growth of our economy, allocations of funds for naval budgets will be just sufficient for induction of destroyers, submarines, aircraft and space-based assets." This implies obvious budgetary concerns, but the navy is planning nevertheless to acquire hoped-for state-of-the-art equipment.[13]

The first operational SSN is finally at sea, an Akula II–class boat acquired from Russia on a ten-year lease. The first indigenously constructed SSBN will join the navy in 2015: INS *Arihant* will be armed with twelve short-range Shaurya ballistic missiles capable of carrying a nuclear warhead to a range of 435 miles, which would reach far into China.[14]

Building on a reported 17 percent increase in defense spending for 2012, the navy is planning—almost certainly unrealistically—on a huge, 74 percent budget increase in 2013. This increase, however, would not be enough to complete acquisition of the ex-Soviet aircraft carrier *Admiral Gorshkov,* renamed *Vikramaditya*; to accomplish its program for acquiring French-built *Scorpène*-class submarines; and most important, to continue indigenous construction of destroyers, frigates, and nuclear-powered submarines.[15]

A significant factor in the navy's ability to expand and maintain readiness is its shipyard capacity, which is an issue of concern to its leadership. The IN makes extensive use of four major shipyards, at Visakhapatnam and Kolkata on the east coast and at Goa and Mumbai on the west coast. A fifth yard, Hindustan Shipbuilding, also located at Visakhapatnam, was transferred from the Ministry of Shipping to the Ministry of Defense in 2009. In fact, this yard is constructing the first of the three planned *Arihant*-class submarines.[16]

A former navy chief of staff, Adm. Arun Prakash, discussed his concern in a 2006 article, in which he wrote that of "all the Indian flagged vessels, only about 10 percent have been built in Indian shipyards because of higher costs, lengthy delivery times and indifferent quality." He also expressed frustration that shipbuilding did not share in India's "cutting edge" capabilities in information technology (IT) and other industrial sectors.[17]

If the desired budgetary resources are allocated, the navy's plan would mean acquisition of approximately forty ships by 2020, including two aircraft carriers and at least six submarines, in addition to other combatant and support vessels.[18] This budget increase, however unlikely, is required to improve notable weaknesses in the navy's antisubmarine warfare and antiair warfare (AAW) capabilities, as well as in C4ISR.[19]

Present Concerns

The maritime geography within which the IN operates dictates its traditional mission: defense of the homeland. India has more maritime than continental borders with other countries. The maritime boundaries with five countries—the Maldives, Sri Lanka, Myanmar, Indonesia, and Thailand—have been established, but differences remain with Pakistan and Bangladesh.

No nation concerns Indian naval strategists more than China. In the words of one analyst, "China aspires to grow into a dominant player in the maritime domain in furtherance of its aim to become a global superpower [and] seeks to vehemently extend its maritime control domain as far away from its shores as possible."[20]

While Pakistan is still seen as the primary threat to Indian security in general, China is widely viewed as an economic and political competitor and its modernizing navy as a force with which India will potentially have to deal. Indeed, New Delhi is making moves that indicate rebalancing from Pakistan to China as the threat of consequence, at least for the navy. Nowhere does the "string of pearls" phenomenon have more credibility than in India.

This catchy name reportedly originated not in a maritime study conducted by an American contractor but as an epithet by an unknown individual in the Office of the U.S. Secretary of Defense accusing Beijing of building a series—a "string"—of naval bases across the Indian Ocean. These are often named as Hainggyi, Bassein, Kyaukpyu, or Mergui, in Myanmar; Hambantota, Sri Lanka; Chittagong, Bangladesh; and Gwadar, Pakistan.[21]

New Delhi's approach to national security measures during the past twenty years has included a Look East policy. India's Eastern Naval Command has been allocated additional resources to assist in "the competition for strategic space in the Indian Ocean region." This has already included adding twenty "major warships" since 2005, nearly doubling the total assigned to that fleet, whose commander has been raised from rear admiral to vice admiral.[22] Furthermore, the navy reportedly wants to build additional naval bases on India's east coast.

Another move to the east is a buildup of naval facilities in the Andaman and Nicobar Islands, at the western entrance to the Malacca and Singapore Straits. The new command there has been assigned six primary duties:

- Defending the territorial integrity, waters, and airspace of the islands
- Ensuring that eastern approaches to the Indian Ocean remain free from threats to the unhindered passage of shipping
- Monitoring SLOCs in designated areas of responsibility (AORs)
- Exercising surveillance over the EEZ
- Establishing an air defense identification zone (ADIZ) for air defense and airspace control
- Undertaking joint planning for contingencies and infrastructure planning[23]

The Look East policy is described in the maritime strategy as "an essential element of India's foreign policy." India's partnership with the ASEAN and its active engagement with the Bay of Bengal Initiative for Multisectoral Technical and Economic Cooperation are part of an irreversible process of integration of India's economy with that of Southeast Asia. A highlight of this interest was New Delhi's signing of the 2009 free-trade agreement with ASEAN.

Thailand especially has been a partner in this process, potentially serving New Delhi as a point of entry and egress to and from the South China Sea. The two navies have conducted joint maritime patrol exercises, disaster management drills, and officer exchanges.

India and Thailand are both members of the BIMSTEC and the Mekong Ganges Project (MGP). Additionally, India attends the ASEAN Defense Ministers Meeting Plus, of which Thailand is a full member, as it is of the ASEAN Regional Forum, the meetings of which India attends. New Delhi and Bangkok are also integral members of the East Asia Summit (EAS) and the Asia Cooperation Dialogue (ACD).

A recent visit to New Delhi by the Thai prime minister resulted in a joint statement that signaled "India's growing geopolitical interest" in Southeast Asia. "Both sides expressed the desire to work together," the statement noted, to combat "maritime and terrorism threats," as well as to cooperate in "defense, science, and technology."[24] An important element in the Look East policy is an increased attempt to construct a closer relationship with Myanmar, an option made more attractive by the loosening of reins by the military junta that has ruled that unfortunate nation for half a century. This apparent change should reduce China's extensive influence in the country, to the benefit of India.[25]

The Look East policy has included Indian navy deployments to Northeast Asia, with port calls in and exercises with the navies of Vietnam, South Korea, and China. Closer to home, the navy has exercised with and conducted port calls in Vietnam and Indonesia.

The most recent naval "long-range overseas deployment" (LROD) began in May 2012, as a four-ship task group departed India for Japan, with port calls en route in Malaysia, Philippines, Singapore, and Shanghai.[26] New Delhi has also signed an energy agreement with Hanoi and agreed to a "strategic partnership" with Tokyo.[27]

Maritime Domain Awareness

MDA is a particular concern for the IN because the Indian Ocean contains some of the world's busiest sea-lanes. The presence of neutral warships and mercantile traffic obscures the clarity of the maritime situation with which the navy must be concerned. The Indian Ocean contains the busiest SLOCs in the world, including passage of two-thirds of the world's oil shipments, one-third of bulk cargo traffic, and half the world's container shipments.

Maximizing MDA demands effective utilization of maritime airpower, as well as establishment of a coastal radar network on the Indian Ocean littoral and of space-based assets.[28] Maritime power in space and in the air are viewed as enabling synergistic effects for enhanced surveillance, net-centric effects, and maritime strike.

MDA is a universal requirement for conducting maritime operations across the spectrum of naval operations. These include conventional conflict with another state, with Pakistan and China most often on the mind of Indian naval analysts; support of a neighboring country, such as Sri Lanka or the Maldives; counterpiracy and counterterrorism; assistance to Indian citizens and interests abroad; United Nation peacekeeping;

humanitarian assistance and disaster relief; and deterrence, both conventional and nuclear.

MDA is crucial for the execution of the navy's traditional wartime role as well as its diplomatic and peacetime constabulary roles. All the navy's roles are in support of the nation's political objectives and foreign policies.

NATIONAL MARITIME ISSUES

India's maritime strategy recognizes the merchant marine's contribution to India's strength as a maritime nation. Similarly, the shore-based maritime infrastructure—shipyards, port facilities, personnel training systems—is also recognized as an important supporting leg of the nation's maritime strength.

Indian Ocean Choke Points

The focus of the navy's concern is the vital navigational choke points through which passes most of the Indian Ocean's ship traffic. These are the Strait of Hormuz, connecting to the Persian Gulf; the Bab el-Mandeb, which leads to and from the Red Sea; the Nine Degree Channel, through the Lakshadweep Islands southwest of India; the Six Degree Channel, the primary passage through the Andaman and Nicobar Islands, just west of the Malacca and Singapore Straits; and the Malacca and Singapore Straits themselves, which connect the Indian Ocean to the South China Sea.

The Persian Gulf and West Asia

India also has a "Look West" policy, although it has not received as much attention as the Look East program. The former is focused on the Persian Gulf region, host to more than 4 million Indian expatriates and the most important source of India's imported petroleum. The IN has built a large new base at Karwar on its west coast, closer to the navy's concerns in the waters to the west and enhancing its ability to confront Pakistan.

The Look West policy includes IN efforts to counter both piracy and terrorism in the western Indian Ocean and Arabian Sea, as well as arms, drugs, and human trafficking. To this end, the navy is supporting New Delhi's extensive diplomatic efforts with the nations of the Persian Gulf and eastern Africa. There is no doubt that the navy will continue to face challenges in carrying out these missions in addition to maintaining a force ready to defend the country against the more traditional maritime threat potentially posed by Pakistan.[29]

India is acutely aware of extraregional navies operating in the IOR. These forces are for the most part operating against piracy in the Arabian Sea, especially in the Gulf of Aden. The counterpiracy campaign in the GOA means that India's maritime picture includes efforts by at least a dozen major navies, including those of Australia, China, Japan, Pakistan, South Korea, the United States, and members of the European Union. Especially notable, of course, is the continuous presence of at least one and usually two U.S. aircraft carrier strike groups.

India has proposed a standard operating procedure for the naval forces conducting antipiracy operations in the Indian Ocean and attendant bodies of water. This proposal was offered at the 2012 meeting of the Indian Ocean Naval Symposium (IONS) in South Africa. The proposal was "well received" but had not been acted upon when the meeting closed.[30]

These foreign naval units have the same broad operational objectives as those of the Indian navy in the Gulf of Aden but nonetheless have altered the basic IOR strategic picture. Central to these objectives from India's perspective is the security of the SLOCs and the concomitant security of India's maritime trade.

India's navy is not large enough to secure these SLOCs by itself—hence the plans for future growth that will require such increased budgetary allocations as discussed. SLOC security became significantly more worrisome following the 9/11 terrorist attacks, which heralded a new, global era of terrorism. New Delhi has been fully supportive of International Maritime Organization efforts to improve maritime security, including implementation of the International Ship and Port Security Code and the Port State Control.

Within the general dependence on the sea for its trade, India is dependent on the SLOCs particularly for the energy supplies that are crucial to its economic health. India is the sixth-highest energy consumer in the world, with 90 percent of its oil coming either from offshore fields or foreign sources, overwhelmingly the Persian Gulf. As a subset of SLOC security, the Indian maritime force, particularly the coast guard, has responsibility for ensuring the security of the very considerable offshore oil production so important to the country.

Nuclear Deterrence

Conventional deterrence is a primary mission for the Indian navy; nuclear deterrence remains in the future, pending deployment of the new *Arihant*-class nuclear-powered ballistic-missile submarines carrying a nuclear warhead. India follows a no-first-use (NFU) policy with respect to the employment of nuclear weapons; the sea-based deterrent is intended to guarantee survival of a retaliatory capability in the event of attack by another country—again, usually envisioned as either Pakistan or China.[31]

Maintenance of a seaborne nuclear deterrence requires robust command-and-control systems, effective surveillance, good intelligence, sound planning, and proper training. The NFU doctrine also requires conventional forces capable of ensuring that the nuclear threshold remains high. India recognizes these requirements, but how effectively it currently fulfills them is not clearly known to outside observers.

Conventional Deterrence

Conventional deterrence is a routine, almost unspoken mission for any navy that, being as large and capable as India's, serves as a primary instrument of statecraft. The task requires maritime forces with sufficient capability in all naval warfare domains to impress potential adversaries. This in turn requires material capability, as well as personnel readiness demonstrated in peacetime exercises and operations.

Acceptable levels of readiness result from a cumulative process involving essentially all naval activity conducted during peacetime. The IN believes that by definition all peacetime activity contributes to readiness for wartime operations at sea. Therefore, exercises and operations aim to simulate wartime conditions, to include elements of uncertainty, stress, and disorder. Also required is the less intense but historically important mission of "presence," conducting port visits and ship deployments in support of New Delhi's diplomatic policies and priorities.

India's maritime doctrine emphasizes the importance of information operations (IO), the ability to effectively gather, analyze, and implement intelligence, including that gained by surveillance operations and implemented through networking. IO serves as a measure of a navy's technical and organizational capabilities, as India's naval leadership clearly recognizes.[32]

Building Partnerships

India has long and successfully sought to build partnerships among other IOR nations. More recently, though dating back at least to 2001, New Delhi has increased this effort, with the notable addition of the United States, which has been seeking a closer maritime relationship with India since the mid-1980s. As of 2013, the Indian and U.S. navies have conducted a series of major complex exercises as one facet of a closer operational and strategic relationship.

New Delhi does not seek alliances, particularly not with the United States, but it does see common strategic interests with certain foreign nations—including the United States. These interests are related, first and foremost, to concern about China's naval modernization; the belief is common among senior Indian naval officers that Beijing is building a global navy with which it intends to challenge for control of the Indian Ocean.[33] Second, they are related to constabulary missions in which both navies are engaged. These include operations to counter piracy, terrorism, and illegal trafficking of persons and materials, and to maintain the comprehensive security of the SLOCs into and through the Indian Ocean and adjacent seas.

Coast Guard

The constabulary mission is a major element of twenty-first-century maritime strategy. This less-than-full-combat role includes several tasks, from containing pollution to chasing down fishing boats illegally intruding into Indian waters. It includes law enforcement in the nation's UNCLOS-defined sovereign waters, out to a distance of a maximum 350 nm from India's coastal baseline.

Another characteristic of the constabulary mission is that it almost always involves nonstate actors, ranging from individual polluters to well-organized terrorist groups. The IN must be prepared to participate with the ICG in constabulary operations, particularly antismuggling, antipiracy, and coastal security missions.

The navy further describes its "benign tasks"—humanitarian assistance, disaster relief, hydrography and navigation, search and rescue, pollution control—as primarily assigned to the coast guard but as functions in which the navy must be prepared to assist. Noncombatant evacuation operation is ideally a benign mission that almost always requires naval forces for effective execution. For example, in 2006 the IN participated in rescuing foreign citizens from Lebanon.[34]

Maritime Cooperation

India pursues maritime cooperation with other nations, to include establishing maritime partnerships. This policy is subcategorized into strategic defense-security cooperation, defense industry and technology cooperation, and navy-to-navy cooperation. The navy envisions maritime cooperation to include surveillance of areas of interest, utilizing ships, aircraft, unmanned aerial vehicles, and space-based assets. Thus, active engagement with the countries on the IOR littoral is an element in the mission of safeguarding India's national interests at sea. This cooperation with IOR countries is joined with engagement of nonregional powers whose navies operate in the IOR or other maritime areas of interest to New Delhi.

A particular feature of readiness to execute constabulary operations is the synergy gained from operating with foreign—both regional and extra-regional—maritime forces concurrently engaged. This requires detailed attention to the standardizing of operational methodology, ranging from simple bridge-to-bridge communications to the coordination of complex search-and-rescue operations involving surface ship, aviation, and special forces units.

The IN categorizes its constabulary role into "low-intensity maritime operations" (LIMO) and "maintaining good order at sea" (MGOS). These seem indistinct in both objective and methodology, of necessity addressing such standard high-seas issues as piracy, terrorism, and trafficking in persons and illegal goods. MGOS also implies that India has taken on itself the role of IOR police, assisting or perhaps even superseding other states, as indicated in the statement that "as a major maritime power, the Indian navy is duty-bound to work towards improving the maritime security environment in the region."[35]

Strategic communications is considered an important element in all IN missions. The maritime strategy unabashedly states that "the ultimate aim of strategic communications [is to] influence the perception of our target audience," to include "retaining the support of the home population [and] turn[ing] hostile or neutral public opinion."[36]

The navy's Hydrographic Department is a very active arm, conducting hydrographic surveys, printing charts, and coordinating maritime warnings. Recent surveys have extended beyond Indian waters to the support of surveys by Indonesia, Oman, Mauritius, the Maldives, and Seychelles.

Wartime Employment

The 2007 strategy directly addresses classic wartime employment, which remains the primary mission for an IN confronting a hostile Pakistan. By 2012, however, Indian naval officers and analysts had become deeply concerned about the improving Chinese navy. They cited the PLAN's acquisition of aircraft carriers and nuclear-powered submarines as evidence that Beijing is intent on establishing a (perhaps dominant) maritime presence in the IOR.[37]

Joint Operations

Senior Indian naval officers seem well aware of the position their service holds in India's army-dominated military. They also recognize the virtues of joint warfare. The Integrated Defense Staff was established in 2001, and *Joint Doctrine—Indian Armed Forces* was published in 2006.[38]

While jointness remains much more a goal than a reality, the navy is preparing to operate in support of Indian troops ashore by striving for readiness to operate in littoral waters.[39] Furthermore, the relatively new Andaman and Nicobar command is joint, involving army, air force, and navy forces.

IN doctrine recognizes the need to gain and maintain information dominance; to exercise sea control, possibly including sea denial; and to render effective support of operations ashore. Indian experiences during the long civil war in Sri Lanka brought home the difficult realities of operating in such waters, as well as the exigencies of supporting troops actively engaged ashore.

Force Buildup

India's navy is the most powerful in South and Southeast Asia, but long-term force-building plans exist, based on the navy's perceived inadequacies to carry out all missions successfully in the mid-twenty-first century. Reaching the necessary force size, of course, will depend on resources allocated by the national command authority, but it is recognized that the attempt will require taking maximum advantage of the revolution in military affairs. Technological advances must be combined, according to the strategy, with maximizing the navy's infrastructure, maintenance, logistics, and continual improvement of personnel. Self-reliance and indigenous capabilities are highlighted as service goals.

The future force must not only possess the capabilities to carry out all assigned missions, the Indian navy believes, but also demonstrate those capabilities to the military and civilian leadership. That is, the service is required not only to reach and maintain the desired state of readiness but also to demonstrate its worth to those allocating the resources and its ability to carry out national security missions of the first priority.

A particularly analytical section of the maritime strategy notes the requirements for technological advances that exceed indigenous resources allocated to the navy. This, it notes, will require not just the synergistic employment of available technological and other resources but also seeking "leapfrogging" technologies to save both time and money. Second, commercial off-the-shelf (COTS) technologies may offer time- and resource-saving paths to the technological enhancement of operational capabilities.

Strategy Plus

The 2007 document goes beyond maritime strategy, often discussing operational art and even tactical issues. Hence, enhanced operational capabilities are emphasized for intelligence gathering, antiair and antisubmarine warfare, and the employment of carrier-based aircraft. In support of these and other basic naval warfare areas, programs are advocated to improve mine warfare, strategic sealift, and heavy lift by helicopters and air-cushion vehicles, the latter in support of the "close integration of amphibious, Marine, and Special Forces" employed jointly.[40]

The navy recognizes both the need for geographically extended operations and its current budgetary shortfalls. This awareness is evident in the call for support facilities in "the farthest littoral reaches of the IOR" and a statement of the need for ships, submarines, and aircraft able to operate with reduced maintenance.[41]

This ambitious long-term policy has obvious implications; it provides a rationale for gaining the support of not only the government but also the public that elects the government. This latter point is described as "bringing home a maritime consciousness to the intelligentsia as well as to the people as large" and ties directly to the previously discussed concept of strategic communications. The IN, the strategy's authors state, "needs to be viewed in the correct perspective."[42]

CONCLUSION

New Delhi's concern with Southeast Asia and the Pacific as strategic extensions is evidenced in recent naval deployments and exercises. The annual Malabar and biennial Milan exercise series have developed into major multilateral events. They each have involved participation by more than a dozen foreign navies.

The April 2012 Malabar exercise included participation by fourteen maritime forces—from Australia, Bangladesh, Brunei, Indonesia, Malaysia, the Maldives, Mauritius, Myanmar, the Philippines, Seychelles, Sri Lanka, Singapore, Thailand, and Vietnam. It was conducted in the eastern Indian Ocean and was focused on defense of eastern Indian Ocean SLOCs.[43]

Another Indian multilateral initiative of note is the IONS defense forum, which meets biannually. Twenty-six navies were represented at the first IONS session, in 2008 in New Delhi; thirty-two attended the second, in 2010 in Dubai. The third meeting was hosted by South Africa in April 2012. In words strikingly similar to the justification that Adm. Michael Mullen of the U.S. Navy offered for his "thousand-ship navy" initiative in 2005, the IONS describes its purpose as promoting the "cooperation of the willing" to establish "a variety of transnational, maritime, cooperative mechanisms to mitigate maritime security concerns."[44]

New Delhi maintains a maritime focus on the Indian Ocean writ large. From Malacca to the Bab el-Mandeb, the IN is concerned with homeland security, with a particular eye on Pakistani threats; on counterterrorism, counterpiracy, and humanitarian assistance; and on cooperative efforts with other regional nations. In addition to expanding naval relations east of Malacca, India is moving to increase cooperation and shared responsibility for maritime security with Middle Eastern and African countries. For example, India and Saudi Arabia have discussed establishing a Joint Defense Committee, with a focus on increasing cooperation in the counterpiracy mission in the western Indian Ocean. New Delhi is also maintaining a keen interest in the Antarctic, clearly viewing its security concerns as extending to the very limits of the Indian Ocean and adjacent seas.

India's economic growth has been spurred its trade with Africa and by Chinese competition in that continent. Trade with Africa grew dramatically from $3.39 billion in 2000 to more than $30 billion in 2007, a trend that continues.[45] India deploys the world's fifteenth-largest merchant shipping fleet, but it is an aging fleet, already inadequate for India's needs.

Interest in China's naval modernization and assumed incursions into the Indian Ocean dominate the navy's strategic thinking. India views "its" ocean as vital to its national security, while China is viewed as the most serious threat to its maritime interests.

Clearly, the IN has garnered the support of its nation's civilian leaders for its intention to continue deploying a navy with aircraft carriers as the capital ship.[46] Navy leaders appear to realize that resource limitation will not in the foreseeable future allow their force to "go one-on-one" against the Chinese navy, either in terms of numbers or strategic assets—hence the ongoing policy of forging strong relations with other navies, particularly those of the United States, Japan, Singapore, and Vietnam.[47]

New Delhi's strategic focus in 2012 is on the IOR. Future naval expansion depends in significant measure on whether the Look East policy becomes firmly emplaced—that is, on whether New Delhi decides to become an Indo-Pacific power. If made, this political decision will boost the IN's ambitious building plans for a navy capable of operating routinely in the ocean areas east of Malacca.

Within the Indian Ocean, the IN faces only one significant opponent, the Pakistani navy. It is actively pursuing a policy of alliance and cooperation with other South Asian navies to solidify its commanding position in South Asia.[48]

eight

SOUTH ASIA

INTRODUCTION

T
he Indian Ocean is dominated by India, as discussed in the previous chapter. This chapter will address other Indian Ocean nations, as well as the naval situation in and attendant to the Persian Gulf. Iranian maritime forces, both naval and Republican Guard, potentially dominate that vital body of water.

The Indian Ocean is characterized by several factors. Most important is its domination by a regular, dramatic weather pattern: the monsoons, which both support and endanger human existence at sea and ashore. Another is the importance of the sea lines of communication that cross the ocean. These historically important SLOCs are perhaps more important today than ever before, given their crucial role in the security and availability of energy resources globally.

An equally long-standing factor has been piracy as a threat to these SLOCs. In the words of the novelist Patrick O'Brian, "Every second vessel is a pirate in those seas, or will be if occasion offers, right round from the Persian Gulf to Borneo."[1] Piracy remains a problem in the current century, when the uneven economic situation in much of the Indian Ocean region littoral, marked on the Horn of Africa by extreme poverty and lack of governance, has made piracy almost an organized industry, particularly in the waters of the Gulf of Aden and the northern Arabian Sea.

IRAN

Iran has both the region's most powerful navy and the most menacing security posture; it has even threatened to close the Strait of Hormuz. A major reorganization of Iran's maritime forces occurred in 2007. The nation's two navies—the Islamic Republic of Iran Navy (IRIN) and the Iranian Revolutionary Guard Corps Navy (IRGCN)—adopted in that year a modernization program that included updating the country's military industrial infrastructure. The reorganization also redefined each naval force's missions, to eliminate duplication and increase mission effectiveness.[2]

The international community, led by the United States, continues to target Iran with economic sanctions to convince Tehran to end its nuclear-weapons development program. Tehran has been defiant in response. Exercises have been conducted in the area of the strait, clearly intended to send threatening messages. "Iran," claims the naval commander of the Revolutionary Guard, Maj. Gen. Mohammed Ali Jafari, "has full domination over the region and controls all movements within it."[3]

The IRGCN is now assigned responsibility for defending Iranian interests in the Persian Gulf; the IRIN has responsibility outside the Strait of Hormuz, extending as far out into the Indian Ocean as Tehran might think necessary to safeguard Iranian interests. The IRIN commander, Adm. Habibollah Sayyari, declared in 2008 that Tehran aims "to influence the strategic maritime triangle that extends from the Bab el-Mandeb to the Strait of Hormuz," following this ambitious goal with the stunning phrase, "and even across the Indian Ocean to the Malacca Strait."[4] The more practical mission of Iranian maritime forces is to, "if necessary[,] . . . prevent any enemy ship from entering the Persian Gulf."

This mission is subsumed within Iran's historical maritime strategy, dating back to the shah of Iran's arms-spending spree in the 1960s and 1970s; that strategy aimed for Iranian domination of the region, both within and outside the Strait of Hormuz. Ironically, the shah was encouraged and armed by the United States, which now faces the heritage of its policy from the other side of Tehran's maritime power.

The IRIN has, however, been participating in antipiracy operations in the Gulf of Aden and is conducting the navy's diplomatic mission.[5] Two Iranian ships passed through the Suez Canal in February 2011 en route to a port visit to Latakia, Syria. Given the domestic political unrest in Syria and the attendant international isolation of President Bashar al-Assad's regime, this deployment was a strong signal of support.

Both maritime forces continue to grow; the IRGCN numbers more than twenty thousand personnel, including a five-thousand-man marine corps and a coastal-defense brigade manning antiship missile batteries. In terms of platforms, Tehran is seeking to build a local defensive force based on relatively small craft and submarines.

The IRIN's three Kilo-class submarines, acquired from Russia, are joined by nearly twenty miniboats. Iran is also reportedly building a class of slightly larger submarines that will bridge the gap between the Kilo and minisub classes.[6]

In its surface fleet, the Iranian navy deploys three British-built *Alvand*-class light frigates that were acquired in the 1970s. It is building a class of *Mowj*-class light frigates, with two in inventory at the end of 2012. Both classes are capable of operating small helicopters and are armed with ASW torpedoes, 76 mm guns, and antiship cruise missiles acquired from China. The *Alvand* class reportedly carries the C-802, while the *Mowj*s are armed with the indigenously produced Noor ASCM and the U.S.-designed SM-1 antiaircraft missile.

The IRGCN does not aspire to add large combatants to its fleet because its mission lies in the internal waters of the Persian Gulf. It is instead enhancing its missile and sensor capabilities, exploiting its local geographic advantages by joining shore-based and sea-based assets into an effective sea-control force.

PAKISTAN

Islamabad's most important national security concern should be Pakistan's coherence as a nation-state. On the military front, the dispute over Kashmir headlines the country's confrontation with India. The two states' mutual history since separation in 1947 has been marked by major wars—in 1947–48, 1965, 1971, and 1999—as well as by nearly continuous low-level combat in Kashmir, including an armed conflict commonly known as the Kargil War in May–July 1999. Attacks on India by terrorist groups apparently sponsored by Pakistan continue to make the confrontation between two nuclear-armed states extremely dangerous, both to themselves and to the region generally.

UNCLOS

When Islamabad signed and ratified the UNCLOS in 1997, it issued three declarations. It agreed in general with the excess sovereignty claims expressed by China for the EEZ and continental shelf, stating that "military exercises or maneuvers by other states, in particular where the use of weapons or explosives is involved" require Pakistan's prior consent. Islamabad also stated that warships had to obtain authorization before passing through its claimed EEZ, inferring an extension in that zone of the rights stipulated by the UNCLOS for territorial waters.[7]

Pakistani Navy

Pakistan deploys the second-strongest navy in South Asia, following only India. It includes five conventionally powered submarines, eleven destroyers and frigates, three mine-warfare ships, and two oilers. Islamabad continues to rely on France for submarines and on China for surface combatants.

Beijing remains Islamabad's primary source of arms and its major political ally. China has provided everything from personal weapons to near-state-of-the-art tactical aircraft and surface combatants. In a typical transaction, Beijing provided a modified Jiangwei-class frigate, several of which now are being constructed in Pakistan.[8]

China also played a major role in constructing the port of Gwadar, which lies on the Indian Ocean coast east of Karachi. Gwadar is potentially a naval base but is intended primarily as a port for containerships, with its four thousand-foot-long berths. Its relative isolation in disturbed Baluchistan Province, however, limits its usefulness. A further concern is the terrorist activity that has already directly affected Chinese citizens working in Pakistan.[9]

The Gwadar project has not yet worked to Pakistan's advantage, apart from its lack of economic viability in 2012. First, Beijing rebuffed the Pakistani prime minister's attempt to have a Chinese company assume its management from the Singapore Port Authority. Then a Chinese company did take on the port-management task in February 2013.[10] Second, at least partially in response to the new port facility, India expanded and constructed a new naval base at Karwar, located on India's west coast, facing Pakistan; it then assisted Iran in developing the port of Chabahar as an economic competitor, just forty-five miles west of Gwadar.[11] The question of whether Gwadar serves as one of a supposed "string of pearls" to support Chinese naval encroachment throughout the Indian Ocean must be answered in the negative, for several reasons. First is the lack of a local transportation infrastructure and the port's isolation from the interior of Asia; second is the location of India, in a position to effectively blockade and if necessary attack the port; third is Islamabad's apparent lack of interest in homeporting naval vessels at Gwadar; finally, no PLAN ships have called at the port.

Pakistan's navy numbers approximately 22,000 active-duty personnel, including approximately two thousand marines.[12] There are also five thousand navy reserves, approximately two thousand personnel in the Maritime Security Agency, and 2,500 in the coast guard. These last two organizations support navy operations. Naval aviation operates three Westland Lynx, six Westland Sea King Mark 45, and eight Aerospatiale SA-319B Alouette III helicopters, and eight Fokker F27–200 and two or three Breguet Atlantique I patrol and antisubmarine warfare aircraft. The Pakistan air force operates a wing of Mirage-V antiship fighter aircraft in support of navy operations.

Islamabad has purchased eight P-3C long-range patrol and ASW aircraft from the United States. The first two, received in 2010, were destroyed in an embarrassing terrorist attack in 2011; two more arrived in February 2012.[13]

Pakistan's future navy acquisitions are focused on increasing its fleet of French-built submarines or possibly opting for German-designed Type 214 boats. It is acquiring four Jiangwei II–class frigates from China, with four more to be built in Pakistan, and has requested the sale of six *Oliver Hazard Perry*–class frigates from the United States. New corvettes are being planned, as are a number of small craft. The navy also is acquiring F-22P frigates with six Z-9C antiship/antisubmarine helicopters. Finally, some of the JF-17 fighter aircraft acquired from China may be assigned naval missions.

In strategic terms Pakistan is not a maritime power, although its navy has participated in the CTF-150 and CTF-151 antipiracy task forces in the Gulf of Aden. The navy's submarines would cause some discomfort to its likely opponent, India. Pakistan's military remains dominated by its army—understandably, given the continental nature of the threats to its national security. Hence, the army has enjoyed dominant political and economic power during the nation's history.

A major limitation on Pakistan's maritime power is its short coastline, just 650 nautical miles on the Indian Ocean. This in turn limits the creation of large ports, for both naval forces and merchant shipping. Karachi is the nation's only major seaport; Gwadar remains underutilized.

BANGLADESH

The Bangladesh navy (BN) is small and modestly outfitted but manned by well-trained professionals. It is centered around five frigates and includes five mine-warfare ships, forty-three patrol craft, eleven amphibious vessels, and two helicopters. The navy numbers 19,000 personnel, including four thousand civilian employees. Its operations are focused on littoral operations.

Parliament approved a ten-year naval modernization plan in 2009, but financial constraints have halted the program. Some steps, however, are in progress, such as replacing old frigates acquired from Great Britain with more capable craft armed with state-of-the-art missiles. The plan is designed to modernize the navy's ships and aircraft, rather than significantly to expand their numbers.

China is Bangladesh's largest arms supplier and has called for closer navy-to-navy relations.[14] This results from a general Chinese desire to gain better commercial access to IOR countries and their ports. Hence, the possibility exists of Beijing assisting Dhaka in modernizing Chittagong, which, although shallow and relatively restricted, is the country's only major port. Mongla is a smaller but significant port.

Bangladesh is a signatory of the UNCLOS and issued no fewer than twelve declarations qualifying its ratification in 2001. Most significant of these is the unusual claim requiring warships to request permission to enter an eighteen-nautical-mile contiguous zone. This is not in accord with either the UNCLOS principle of innocent passage or the treaty's definition of the contiguous zone, which extends twenty-four nautical miles from a nation's coastal baseline.[15]

Bangladesh's small navy has an inadequate number of ships to patrol even its EEZ, extending from its relatively limited coastline of 378 nm on the Bay of Bengal. Dhaka has not published a maritime strategy, but one analyst has described a "perceived maritime strategy," one that aims "to safeguard the [nation's] maritime sovereignty and maintain peace and stability in the region."[16]

Dhaka has published a list of missions for its navy. This "Role of the Bangladesh Navy" is a model of naval missions, lacking only the nuclear-deterrent role of the Indo-Pacific's largest naval powers. The BN is tasked with the following:

- Safeguarding the nation's territorial seas
- Keeping the SLOCs open during peace and war
- Keeping the sea ports open during wartime
- Protecting the fishing fleet
- Patrolling riverine water
- Search and rescue at sea
- Cyclone warning
- Protecting Bangladesh merchant ships on the high seas
- Assisting the civil administration in maintaining internal security and peace
- Assisting the civil administration in the event of natural calamities
- Naval control of shipping (internal and external, inland or foreign)
- Oceanographic survey
- Any other task that the government may deem necessary.[17]

The navy's overall mission is to "safeguard the sovereignty over the internal waters and territorial sea, and sovereign rights over the Contiguous Zone, EEZ and Continental Shelf of Bangladesh while supporting riverine and maritime economic activities including free flow of riverine and sea borne trade."

The Bangladesh coast guard began operating in 1995. Its missions include many of the navy's tasks but focus on maintaining coastal security and safety at sea.[18]

MYANMAR

Although a member of the Association of Southeast Asian Nations, Myanmar also has deep roots in South Asia. Geographically, it lies west of the Malacca and Singapore Straits, which may be viewed as dividing Southeast and South Asia.

Much has been written about China's political, economic, and military encroachments into Myanmar. The first two categories of the relationship are accurate; in fact, Beijing's economic policies have engendered a quasi-colonial relationship with its southern neighbor. Myanmar's military relationship, however, is more complex. China has for decades served as the source of the majority of the country's armaments, from missile-armed frigates to sidearms. There has also been much written about Chinese military facilities in Myanmar, although these suppositions are for the most part without substance, as will be discussed later in this chapter.[19]

Myanmar faces a seminal moment in its internal political and social development and appears to have taken a path of major change in its international relations. This is occurring, first, because of the release from imprisonment of the activist Aung San Suu Kyi and the holding of democratic elections, constituting between them a moment that may turn out to be as significant as was the release from prison of Nelson Mandela for the ensuing political developments in South Africa.

Second, spurred by these domestic developments, the United States decided to end or at least greatly reduce the sanctions against and attempted isolation of Myanmar, previously ruled since 1962 by military dictatorship. This was signaled by Secretary of State Hillary Clinton's visit to Naypyidaw, the country's new capital, in November 2011 and the appointment in April of Derek Mitchell as the first U.S. ambassador to Myanmar since 1990. The new U.S. policy was capped by the November visit to Myanmar by President Barack Obama.

Third has been India's renewed interest in extending its economic and political relations with Myanmar. New Delhi is motivated by several factors, not the least of which is concern at China's incursions into that country and its projected economic, political, and possibly military presence on the Indian Ocean littoral. India is also attempting to garner economic benefits from a Myanmar now reaching out to become an active member of the globalizing economy, and also from entrée into that nation's very considerable offshore energy resources. Finally, there reportedly exists long-standing popular Burmese resentment of the Chinese presence.

These developments should allow Myanmar to loosen its ties with China. For one thing, Beijing will find it more difficult to deal with a liberalizing polity than with military strongmen. For another, Myanmar's willingness to engage more robustly with the United States and with India places China in a triangular, if not outright subsidiary, position as Myanmar becomes a much more active participant in the regional and world community and improves its trade and geopolitical options.

This does not negate the prospect of a Myanmar future of continued, serious challenges, both domestically and internationally. Ethnic discord, an underdeveloped economy with an artificially suppressed agricultural sector, the absence of rule of law, transition from autocracy to democracy, and an inwardly focused military are all difficult problems confronting Myanmar's leaders. Internationally, they face a historic balancing act between their two neighboring giants, China and India, a process that will include seeking support for the continued modernization of maritime forces needed to ensure the security of offshore resources and littoral trade routes.

Additional national security concerns confront Myanmar. These included, until nominally resolved in 2012, maritime boundary disputes with Bangladesh and Thailand. Fisheries issues and criminal activity in the Bay of Bengal and Andaman Sea, however, continue to be troublesome.[20]

SOUTH AFRICA

South Africa occupies the IOR's southwest corner, a position from which it can monitor all ship traffic transiting between the Indian Ocean from the South Atlantic. It ratified the UNCLOS in 1997 without significant reservations.

The South African navy is small but modern. It deploys three Type 209/1400 submarines, two *Valour*-class frigates, and one replenishment-at-sea ship. Johannesburg has joined with New Delhi in multilateral efforts to secure Indian Ocean SLOCs. South Africa's navy commander addressed the country's Strategy for Maritime Security in March 2012. It emphasizes "global governance of the sea." Piracy, terrorism, and environmental degradation are listed as primary threats, which must be combatted through increased maritime domain awareness and international cooperation.[21]

ISLAND STATES: SRI LANKA, MALDIVES, SEYCHELLES

None of these nations possess oceangoing navies, but all deploy coast-guard forces to enforce their claims under the UNCLOS. Sri Lanka and Maldives require that warships obtain prior authorization before entering their contiguous zones, while Seychelles requires notification in advance of transit.[22]

Seychelles, located northeast of Madagascar, is composed of more than a hundred land features, but approximately 90 percent of the nation's population of 90,000 lives on the main island of Mahe. This island has a central range of hills reaching to an elevation of three thousand feet, but the island state's most pressing problem is the sea rise caused by global warming.

Seychelles, having no navy, has not published a maritime strategy but has issued a "Strategy 2017," which emphasizes the importance of fisheries and tourism, both of which require control of its maritime zones, claimed under the UNCLOS.[23]

The nation does deploy the Seychelles Coast Guard (SCG), organized in 1992 and operating four primary vessels, obtained from Italy, India, and Spain. Its missions are typical of coast guards, including search and rescue, environmental protection, and counterpiracy in the nation's EEZ. The SCG has been particularly engaged in counterpiracy operations. The island nation has also been reported as the possible location of a support facility for the Chinese navy ships engaged in antipiracy patrols.[24]

Maldives has a coast guard but not a navy. Known as the Maldives National Defense Force (MNDF), it operates about a dozen patrol craft and is assigned typical coast-guard missions, specifically to

- Defend the nation and its territorial integrity,
- Protect its territorial waters and EEZ,
- Safeguard the marine environment,
- Enforce maritime law,

- Assist the people and conduct search-and-rescue missions,
- Respond to national emergencies and crises, and
- Support the national defense force.[25]

Sri Lanka has perhaps the most combat-experienced littoral navy in the world, having been fighting insurgents armed with the world's only substate naval forces almost continually between 1971 and 2009.[26] The navy deploys more than two dozen patrol vessels ranging from OPVs of nearly two thousand tons' displacement to eight-hundred-ton missile boats to rigid-hull inflatable boats (RHIBs) and various landing craft. Three helicopters constitute the navy's air arm.

With the end of the drive by the Liberation Tigers of Tamil Eelam (LTTE) to establish a separate Tamil state, the navy is concerned primarily with typical coast-guard missions in Sri Lanka's littoral waters. These include safeguarding offshore resources, both biological and mineral; enforcing environmental laws; ensuring safety at sea, including navigational safety and hydrography; and enforcing the maritime rule of law, to include customs enforcement, countering acts of piracy and terrorism, and combating the illegal trafficking of people and drugs.[27]

Sri Lanka recently has been in the maritime news as a result of the modernization of its main port, Colombo, and the construction of a large new port at Hambantota, on the island nation's southwest coast. The first phase of the Colombo project began in 2008 and has been financed by South Korea and China, as well as by indigenous concerns. The first phase was scheduled for completion in April 2012 but is now scheduled to begin operations in 2013.[28]

The second major port development project, at Hambantota, has been especially newsworthy as one of the Chinese "string of pearls," a series of potential naval bases some observers credit Beijing with building across the Indian Ocean. While 85 percent of the cost is being financed by China, the location was chosen in part because Hambantota is in the home district of Sri Lanka's president and in a relatively unpopulated area of the island. The first of the project's three phases was completed in November 2011 and provided berths for three ships. The entire project is scheduled for completion in 2018.[29]

The harbor facilities there are being built with considerable Chinese investment—obtained by the Sri Lankan government only after both India and the United States declined to take on the project. A Chinese company also is building a new airport fifteen miles from the port; that project is also scheduled for a 2018 completion. An adjacent international convention center, due for 2013 completion, is being built by a South Korean company.

The primary vehicle through which Beijing gained influence in Colombo was the provision of arms during the government's fight with Tamil insurgents, when the great majority of other nations refused, largely because of Sri Lanka's disreputable human-rights policies. By the end of 2011 China trailed only India as Sri Lanka's largest trading partner. Colombo, however, is trying to diversify its international economic stakes, inviting companies in Australia, India, Russia, and Dubai to invest in shipbuilding, repair, and warehouse facilities in Hambantota.[30]

The island nation's ties with Beijing have deepened in economic terms, but the government is concerned about overreliance on China. Colombo seems reluctant to establish a close strategic relationship with Beijing. India is very close; China is far away.

MULTILATERAL ORGANIZATIONS

Due in part to the dearth of capable navies in South Asia to secure the sea-lanes, that region's nations are employing multilateral organizations in their security interests. These include the Indian Ocean Rim Association for Regional Cooperation, the Bay of Bengal Initiative for Multisectoral Technical and Economic Cooperation, the South Asian Association for Regional Cooperation, and the Indian Ocean Zone of Peace Declaration (IOZP).

These organizations have accomplished little more than establishing themselves as discussion venues, but that in itself is a commendable achievement. The IOR-ARC was founded to increase economic intercourse among nations bordering on the Indian Ocean but has granted "dialogue partner" status to China and to the United States. The BIMSTEC has the same, although a geographically more limited, mission. Its members are Bangladesh, India, Maldives, Myanmar, Nepal, Sri Lanka, and Thailand. Interestingly, Pakistan has joined neither group, perhaps because of New Delhi's leading role in both.

The SAARC focuses on maritime issues. China, the European Union, Japan, Iran, Mauritius, the Republic of Korea, and the United States attend SAARC meetings as "observers." The IOZP recommends that Indian Ocean states, UN Security Council permanent members, and "other major maritime users" work to establish "a system of universal security without military alliances." Rather, it argues, international security should be enhanced through "regional and other cooperation; guarantee[d] free and unimpeded use of the India Ocean zone by vessels of all nations, and establishing the Indian Ocean as a zone of peace."[31]

PERSIAN GULF AND THE PERSIAN GULF STATES

The Persian (or Arabian) Gulf region is the world's most valuable source of petroleum. It is also an extremely complex maritime environment in a UNCLOS context. The narrow waters of the Gulf yield a spiderweb of national maritime claims. These are trumped by the single, narrow exit to the high seas: the Strait of Hormuz, connecting to the northern Arabian Sea and the Indian Ocean. The Gulf States include large geographic powers, such as Iran, Iraq, and Saudi Arabia, with formidable navies, and several very much smaller nations, including Bahrain, Kuwait, Oman, Qatar, and the United Arab Emirates. These smaller states are members of the Cooperation Council for the Arab States of the Gulf (also known as the Gulf Cooperation Council, or GCC) as are Iraq and Saudi Arabia. This regional group announced in March 2012 that it would be moving toward becoming a confederation.

The GCC was established in 1981 and is headquartered in Riyadh, Saudi Arabia. It was formed for two reasons: internal security and fear of the spread of the Iranian revolution. The GCC has made minor strides in establishing joint military organizations, and its continued existence relies primarily on Saudi Arabia for financial support and, arguably, on the United States for military and political support.

Iran poses the greatest political and maritime threat in the Persian Gulf and northern Arabian Sea. Tehran's public face all too often is one of aggressive, radical Islam; its maritime forces are dominated by the IRGCN, which operates at the behest of Iranian religious authorities and hence is an anomaly in the normal structure of civil-military relations.

This factor significantly complicates understanding and predicting the Iranian political and military decision-making processes.

Except arguably for Saudi Arabia, none of these nations deploy significant navies, despite their dependence on the sea-lanes through the Strait of Hormuz for their exported oil and hence for their economic well-being. All of them do possess smaller combatants.

Saudi Arabia leads the way, with seven frigates, four corvettes, three mine-warfare ships, and two oilers. The United Arab Emirates is building six corvettes and has two mine-warfare ships; Bahrain has one frigate and two corvettes; Oman deploys one corvette; and Iraq is trying to rebuild a navy capable of protecting its ports at the head of the Gulf.

CONCLUSION

South Asia as a strategic region remains a concept in development. The IOR, the term favored by Indian naval analysts, bridges Europe and Asia and is dominated by three geographic centers.

First, at the IOR's eastern terminus, are the Malacca and Singapore Straits, leading from the Pacific into the Indian Ocean, a huge body of water stretching from Australia to Egypt and from India to Antarctica. Second, in the center of and dominating this oceanic expanse lies India itself, the region's largest country, possessing its most powerful navy, largest population, and most dynamic economy. Third, at the western terminus of the IOR lies the world's largest source of energy, the area surrounding the Persian Gulf and Red Sea.

The IOR contains two acknowledged nuclear-weapons states, India and Pakistan, with Iran striving to achieve that capability. That country is currently the center of an international maelstrom of concern over its nuclear aspirations; its determination to develop the maritime power to dominate Southwest Asia, especially the Persian Gulf; and its status as a center for spreading religion-based terrorism.

The region contains the world's most important SLOCs, particularly for the transportation of energy; those SLOCs are threatened by piracy and terrorism. The Persian Gulf and Red Sea energy-producing states are not capable of defending their maritime interests against either Iranian ambition or transnational threats. Instead, they rely on their customer nations to guarantee their security, which explains in large part the extensive foreign naval presence in the region.

Current international efforts to combat piracy and terrorism, and to provide a counterbalance to Iranian attempts at domination, have been effective in the sense of fending off any critical damage to international commercial reliance on IOR sea-lanes. This has engendered increased naval entry into the region by U.S., Chinese, and other navies, a development that concerns Indian and Iranian strategists.

India appears to be accommodating itself to a changed strategic balance in the IOR, although with much unease. Iran, however, apparently views increased foreign naval forces in its area as a direct threat to its international policies—policies ameliorated in the eyes of China and other energy-hungry states only by Tehran's ability to provide those resources in the face of international sanctions.

The renowned American maritime strategist Alfred Thayer Mahan discussed the importance of the Indian Ocean in his 1906 work *The Problem of Asia*. He did so, however, not in terms of the importance of the ocean itself but of the then-prominent "Great Game," the Russo-British contest for control of Central Asia and, by extension, India. More recently, as Henry Kissinger argued in 2008, "the center of gravity of world affairs has left the Atlantic and moved to the Pacific and Indian Oceans."[32]

That emphasis on the Indian Ocean's importance is exaggerated at present, but there is no doubting its importance, both as maritime highway and as a potential future scene of armed conflict, possibly involving Iran, India, Pakistan, or China. Any such conflict would almost certainly involve the United States, because of its own security interests and status as the world's most powerful maritime nation.

The IOR is just one of several areas containing potential missions for Asian navies. Conventional scenarios remain, but in the twenty-first century nontraditional missions are likely to predominate. These include the full range of transnational issues, from countering piracy to reacting to environmental disasters. These transnational issues contribute to many instances of possible conflict and cooperation in Asian waters, instances that we will discuss in the following chapter.

nine

CONFLICT AND COOPERATION

INTRODUCTION

There are few major maritime issues in Asia that do not offer possible venues for both cooperation and conflict. The world's sealanes carry more than 80 percent of international commerce. They also, unfortunately, account for the primary flow of illegal activities, including terrorist activities, narcotics trafficking, and illicit immigration. Containerization has revolutionized both legal and illegal international commerce, making even nonmaritime nations and nonstate organizations able to take advantage of globalized commerce.[1]

Maritime disputes are present on all the Asian seas. Many of the issues are minor, but all are subject to misunderstandings and possible unintentional or unpredictable political and military escalation. The strategic environment at sea and ashore in Asia is problematic, despite continued U.S. naval domination throughout much of the Pacific and Indian Oceans in 2012. North Asia is marked by at least six strategic maritime factors:

- China's dramatic economic and political influence
- Japan's reduced and further diminishing economic clout
- Fiscal crises in Japan and the United States
- Increase in South Korean economic and naval strength
- Growth in Chinese defense budgets and naval strength
- A rebalancing of U.S. diplomatic and naval focus to Asia

POINTS OF CONTENTION

The following discussion addresses only maritime disputes of significance to nations in addition to the direct disputants. Many minor disagreements over fisheries, for instance, are not included. Relations between South and North Korea are also omitted, due to the primarily continental character of that unhappy situation.

Kuril Islands

In the boundary waters between the Sea of Okhotsk and the North Pacific, Russia and Japan continue their dispute over the sovereignty of the southern Kuril Islands, a dispute dating to before the 1905 Russo-Japanese War. As discussed briefly in chapter 4, Russia occupied the four southern Kuril Islands at the end of World War II.

Although these islands had not been occupied by Japan on a full-time basis, they had historically been considered part of that nation. After many decades of episodic negotiations between Moscow and Tokyo, the islands remain firmly in Russia's grasp, with no indication that their status will change. The fact that their relative geographic and economic importance is minor is outweighed by Russian rigidity and Japanese nationalism, which raise the islands' potential as a casus belli.

East China Sea

International disputes in this vital maritime area, bordered by Japan, the Koreas, China, and Taiwan, are important to the disputants for economic, military, and political reasons. Their resolution has been especially difficult because of the nationalist pride and historical enmity with which they are deeply infused. Resolution also is complicated by the lack of any Northeast Asian regional organization to serve as a resource for discussion, let alone settlement.

Korea-Japan: Sovereignty over Dokdo/Takeshima

Sovereignty of the small islets called Dokdo by South Korea and Takeshima in Japan has become a constant irritant in the relations between these two allies of the United States.[2] South Korea currently occupies and administers them in what Japan calls the Sea of Japan and Korea the East Sea.

The seriousness of this dispute is indicated by both countries' intransigence. Seoul has been the more active about its claim to Dokdo/Takeshima, naming its navy's first large amphibious warship *Dokdo* and building "research facilities" on the disputed land features. In Japan, meanwhile, rallies are held to support Tokyo's claims to Dokdo/Takeshima, which, as Foreign Minister Koichiro Gemba stated, Tokyo will "never abandon." In that, he was supported by Prime Minister Yoshihiko Noda's statement that "we cannot accept [Seoul's] demand for withdrawal" from the disputed territory.[3]

These barren islets have little economic or military value but have become nationalist symbols for both Korea and Japan. Additionally, the Dokdo/Takeshima Islands have become inextricably part of Korea's resentment and enmity resulting from Japan's harsh occupation of Korea and its treatment of Korean "comfort women" during World War II.

The Japanese ambassador to the ROK claimed in 2005 that "the Takeshima Islands are Japanese territory historically and in terms of international law." Japanese newspapermen then hired a private plane to overfly the islands, but they were intercepted by four ROK air force fighters. The ROK foreign minister, Kim Sung-Hwan, canceled a scheduled visit to Japan as a result, making the stunning statement that the issue of sovereignty over the islands was more important than ROK-Japan relations. Foreign Minister Kim announced that Seoul would take military action in response to any provocation from Japan. As with other regional territorial disputes, the United States has taken no position on sovereignty of Dokdo/Takeshima and thus urges a calm approach and peaceful settlement of the dispute.

China–South Korea

Beijing and Seoul have not agreed on how to delimit their claimed exclusive economic zones, which overlap. One point of contention is whether a submerged rock called Ieodo in Korean and Suyuan in Chinese is located in South Korea's or China's EEZ. The UNCLOS does not grant EEZs to underwater formations, so South Korea built a "maritime research station," including a small helicopter landing platform, on the rock. China protested and then threatened to send ships to patrol the surrounding waters.[4]

China-Japan: Oil, Fish, and Sovereignty

The East China Sea is the site of two equally complex and marginally related disputes between China and Japan. First is the dispute about the sovereignty of the Diaoyu, or Senkaku, Islands, as called by the two nations, respectively. This group of eight rocks—five of which may generously be termed "islets"—are no more inhabitable than is Dokdo/Takeshima.

Despite their problematic economic and military value, these land features remain very much in dispute, for at least three reasons. First and most important is national pride. Second is the possibility of large energy reserves in the seabed within the islands' EEZs (assuming they are entitled to EEZs under the UNCLOS).[5] Third, and important to Chinese strategists, is their location in the "first island chain" (discussed in chapter 5). These islands, running from Japan through the Ryukyus, Taiwan, and the Philippines, are regarded by some strategists as forming a barrier to the ability of China's PLAN to sortie its ships from the East China Sea into the Pacific Ocean. These observers believe that Chinese possession of the Diaoyu/Senkaku Islands is vital to China's naval freedom of action.[6]

When Tokyo announced in January 2012 its intention to assign formal names to the individual Senkakus, Beijing immediately protested this as an illegal act, averring that these features had "always been part of Chinese territory" and announcing its own names. At the same time, Tokyo rejected a South Korean protest over the Japanese prime minister's reiteration of its claim to Dokdo/Takeshima.[7] Both Beijing and Tokyo have announced increased maritime presence in the waters around the disputed land features. This will apparently take the form of coast-guard assets rather than naval vessels.[8]

Proven seabed energy fields in areas claimed by both Tokyo and Beijing are the center of the second significant East China Sea sovereignty dispute. Resolution of this sovereignty issue rests on delineation of the continental shelf of each claimant. Both Japan and China have appealed to the UN Commission on the Limits of the Continental Shelf, which is currently meeting to provide advice on conflicting claims, worldwide, on delimiting continental shelves.[9]

The UNCLOS describes the continental shelf as determined by sea-bottom topography, to a maximum of 350 nautical miles from the claiming nation's coastal baseline. This definition is inadequate, however, when less than seven hundred nautical miles lie between two nations, as is often the case. Hence, a new CLCS for resolving conflicting continental shelf claims was convened by the United Nations in 2010.

Japan presented a submission to the CLCS in 2008 claiming a continental shelf in excess of two hundred nautical miles from its coastal baseline for seven regions to the south and southeast of its home islands. While some of these lie in areas subject also to claims by the United States or the Republic of Palau, China is the main disputant to Japan's claims.[10]

China had submitted its survey to the CLCS on 11 May 2009, claiming a continental shelf beyond two hundred nautical miles in the East China Sea—in fact, all the way to the western slope of the Okinawa Trough. China based this claim on data collected over ten years of marine scientific research undertaken by China's Academy of Sciences, the State Oceanic Administration (SOA), and the PLAN.

The Japanese and Chinese claims will further exacerbate the dispute between Tokyo and Beijing over these waters. The CLCS is not authorized to decide the issue; it can only evaluate the scientific merits of a state's claim to a continental shelf beyond two hundred nautical miles, as permitted under article 76 of the UNCLOS. Even if the commission were to rule that Beijing had demonstrated the scientific basis for a continental shelf claim beyond two hundred nautical miles, it would not be the same as granting China exclusive jurisdiction over the area. Japan is still entitled to claim an EEZ as far as two hundred nautical miles as well, although to date it has only claimed one as far the median line between the waters it claims and those claimed by China.

Only the two parties, therefore, can resolve the dispute. Furthermore, a CLCS ruling would not resolve the Sino-Japanese dispute over the Diaoyu/Senkaku Islands because that issue lies outside the commission's authority. Additionally, China's claim to the CLCS may overlap with the extended continental shelf claimed by South Korea.

Nonetheless, in June 2012 Beijing and Seoul prepared a joint submission to the CLCS, jointly opposing Tokyo's claim.[11] It is somewhat encouraging to see these capitals employing, even if imperfectly, the available UN instruments to aid in dispute resolution rather than making further resort to gunboat diplomacy.

South Pacific

Australia submitted a claim to the CLCS in 1994. Sydney's claim focused on nine areas, the most contentious of which concerns the Timor Sea and is disputed by Timor-Leste.[12] New Zealand also submitted a claim, in 1996, involving negotiations with Fiji and Tonga over continental shelf delimitations.

These disputes illustrate the complexity of continental shelf claims, which typically are geographically erratic because of irregular sea-bottom topography. Other Asian nations that have made submissions to the CLCS are Vietnam, the Philippines, Indonesia, Malaysia and Vietnam in a joint claim, Myanmar, Bangladesh, Sri Lanka, India, and Pakistan.

Indian Ocean

In the Indian Ocean, maritime disputes include both seabed resource disagreements, such as that between Bangladesh and Burma, and competing territorial sovereignty claims, such as that over the Chagos Archipelago. More threatening than either to the safe conduct of maritime operations in the Indian Ocean are the nascent national conflicts lurking just over the horizon. These include long-standing Indo-Pakistani hostility, Iranian policies, and failing or near-failing states.

Resolution is yet to be achieved for any of the submissions to the CLCS. Meanwhile, China and Japan have come to an understanding of sorts, at least as to the most prominent issue currently in dispute, recovering energy reserves from the natural-gas field called Chunxiao by Beijing and Shirikaba by Tokyo.

The two nations agreed in 2008 to a "China-Japan Principled Consensus on the East China Sea" and continue to engage in diplomatic discussion of their differences. Meanwhile, however, both nations continue drilling for energy resources in the disputed areas of the East China Sea, and neither is flexible about its respective claims under the UNCLOS. Talks between Tokyo and Beijing continue, then, but resolution is not in sight.[13]

The most notable maritime concern relating to these two disputes is the surveying and operational transits of Chinese warships and surveillance vessels through the various straits that penetrate the Ryukyus and other islands separating the East China Sea from the Pacific Ocean. Tokyo often complains about PLAN ships operating in its claimed EEZ; Beijing insists it is exercising freedom of navigation—a rather ironic argument, given its opposite position on U.S. naval vessels conducting surveys in its own EEZ in the East and South China Seas.[14]

Serving as a land link between the East and South China Seas, Taiwan poses the most contentious and potentially dangerous sovereignty dispute for Beijing. Only twenty-three nations recognize the Republic of China government in Taipei, but the American commitment to ensure a peaceful future for Taiwan makes the island the most important "sovereignty" issue in Asia.

Although tensions have eased in recent years, the island's status is the only issue with serious potential to draw China and the United States into armed conflict. Beijing insists that the island is part of China and that its de facto independence is solely a consequence of interference by Washington in internal Chinese matters. The Taiwan Relations Act, passed by Congress in 1979, remains a significant domestic political force in the United States, strongly implying U.S. support for Taiwan's de facto independence and enjoining the American president to ensure that the island is capable of defending itself.

Despite that imbroglio, however, recent events between Taiwan and the mainland, especially the economic relationship that has grown since the end of the independence-leaning administration of Chen Shui-bian's Democratic Progressive Party (DPP) in 2008, indicate that a peaceful resolution of the island's status will occur. Nonetheless, Taiwan remains a significant issue in the bilateral relations and domestic politics of China and the United States, both of which confronted contentious leadership changes in 2012.

The economic, political, and security importance of the U.S. relationship with China would seem, rationally, to dwarf that of the American position with Taiwan. There are three important counterbalancing factors, however. The first is Taiwan's status as a Western-style democracy. Second is that U.S. failure to live up to the commitments of the TRA, perceived or actual, would shake the confidence of friends and allies of the United States throughout Asia in the validity of Washington's commitments. Finally, U.S. support for Taiwan may constitute a useful element in the conduct of relations with China and with the overall American position in Asia.[15]

The 2012 elections in Taiwan were encouraging to Beijing, as the Kuomintang (KMT) kept its hold on the presidency and the legislature. The future of Taiwan is very high on the list of Beijing's vital national security concerns—or "core national interests," as they have been termed. The latter insists on Taiwan's eventual reunification with the mainland, refusing in the meantime to forsake the employment of military force to achieve that aim.

Although, as noted, such use of force does not currently appear likely, as economic and social integration continue to grow, PLAN modernization, centered on a modernizing submarine force, remains focused on this mission, as against both the Taiwan military and the U.S. military intervention that the PLA is confidant would occur. Far less attention is given nowadays to the threat of an amphibious assault on Taiwan, apparently because of the vulnerability of such a force in today's C4ISR environment, where neither strategic nor tactical surprise could be achieved, thus affording the United States and Taiwan forces ample opportunity to disrupt and destroy an assembling or sortieing amphibious force.

The PLA's enormous advantage in ballistic and land-attack cruise missiles and the supposed resultant capability to follow up with massive and largely unopposed air strikes may be seen as an adequate alternative to an initial amphibious assault. Demoralizing Taiwan and severely degrading its defenses and command and control seem to be part of Beijing's thinking; smaller amphibious and airborne forces, of the size China possesses, might then secure lodgments (ports and airfields) for the "administrative" landing of an occupying force.

South China Sea

There are seven claimants to South China Sea land features and three facets to their disagreements. These are disputes over the territorial sovereignty of land features, disputes over jurisdiction of waters and seabed, and disputes over coastal-state and international rights to use the seas.

The first of these three receives the most public attention, because South China Sea sovereignty disputes are both the best known and most complex and troublesome issues in maritime Asia. They center on the hundreds of land features—some of them submerged at high tide—that dot the sea. These islands, islets, reefs, sandbars, and rocks are grouped into three primary archipelagos, the English names for which are the Paracel Islands (in the northern South China Sea), the Spratly Islands (in the central part of that sea), and the Macclesfield Bank (in the eastern part). These groups, as well as the individual land features, are called by different names by the different claimants—as many as five, in some cases.

The sovereignty disputes in the South China Sea are based on several factors. Least quantifiable but perhaps most important is national pride. Second are the biological resources of the sea; third are the vital SLOCs that pass through those waters. Potentially most valuable in economic terms are the possible, but unproven, energy resources in the seabed.

Estimates of these reserves vary widely: the U.S. estimate is no more than 28 billion barrels of oil in the sea, while some Chinese estimates reach 105 billion barrels, even describing it as a second Persian Gulf.[16] The latter estimate is not likely, because oil exploration in the South China Sea has been undertaken since at least the mid-1930s, but the mere idea of vast reserves is enough to heighten national interest in sovereignty claims.

China and Vietnam claim sovereignty of essentially all the land features in the South China Sea. The Philippines, Brunei, and Malaysia claim individual features. Indonesia has sovereignty, which is not contested, over the Natuna Islands, in the far southwest of the sea. However, the often published "nine-dash line" used by China to denote its claims does intrude upon Indonesia's Natuna gas fields. Taiwan, as mentioned above, agrees with Beijing's claims. Fishing rights are also often disputed, sometimes to the point of gunfire, among the nations bordering the South China Sea.

China and Vietnam are the most contentious claimants to disputed South China Sea land features, not least because they are the only two countries claiming virtually all those bits of land, but also because of Vietnam's age-old animosity toward China. Efforts between Beijing and Hanoi to resolve their differences peacefully date back at least to 1955 but have yet to bring final closure. A recent visit to Hanoi by Xi Jinping, the Chinese vice president and putative future president and Chinese Communist Party secretary, produced no significant agreement, only a renewed statement on "maintaining regional peace and stability in the South China Sea."

Even more telling is the failure of national representatives at the July 2012 ASEAN meeting to issue a closing communiqué, an unprecedented event. Cambodia chaired this meeting and reportedly yielded to Chinese requests to quench the communiqué because of Beijing's insistence that it contain no mention of the South China Sea disputes.[17]

China casts a pall over the South China Sea, backing its claims to all of the land features in a wide swath of the sea with powerful economic and diplomatic policies—and with the region's most powerful navy just over the horizon, often much closer. Beijing has increased its maritime engagement by various coast-guard agency vessels in the South China Sea significantly since 2000. This reflects China's increased concern for its sovereignty claims and inevitably has led to an increased number of clashes with other claimants, particularly Vietnam and the Philippines.

As China has eased off from its assertive 2009–10 actions in the South China Sea, the Philippines has adopted a more insistent position about its claims. This challenge to Beijing's rigid position on sovereignty has focused on Scarborough Shoal, called Bajo de Masinloc by the Philippines and Huangyan Island by China.[18]

A series of incidents involving Philippine research and fishing vessels, on one hand, and Chinese patrol craft and fishing boats, on the other, occurred regularly in 2011 and 2012. These culminated in a standoff between a Philippine naval vessel and Chinese Marine Surveillance patrol craft in 2012 but were resolved peacefully when the Philippines withdrew in June. The Chinese remained in the vicinity until September, however, roping off the entrance to the lagoon.[19]

In fact, the warship *Manila*, dispatched to the scene of this confrontation, was the only operationally significant warship in the Philippine navy. This sad state of affairs has contributed to the Philippines' appealing to the UN, to the ASEAN, and especially to the United States for assistance in its territorial claims in the South China Sea. Little substantive help has been forthcoming.

The sharpest differences and the most frequent and deadly clashes over fishing rights and sovereignty issues have occurred between China and Vietnam. The relationship of these two nations is marked by a curious mix of assertiveness and compromise, perhaps colored by historical Chinese aggression against Vietnam, but also by Bejing's considerable assistance to Hanoi during the latter's fight against the French for independence and against the United States for unification.

A hedging aspect of Vietnam's attitude is reflected in China's willingness to discuss means for working around conflicting sovereignty claims but not the claims themselves. Beijing and Hanoi seem intent on not yielding on questions of sovereignty but equally intent on containing clashes at sea. This was evidenced in October 2011, when the two nations signed an "agreement in guiding principles for resolving maritime disputes."[20]

Hanoi clearly is trying to use Washington to counterbalance China's military might while hedging against an uncertain future. Washington's announced rebalancing toward Asia seems welcome by Hanoi. The American secretary of defense characterized this rebalancing, originally called a "pivot" toward Asia, as partnership and training, but it is being backed by definite military moves.[21] These include increased U.S. Navy ship visits to Manila; establishment of a U.S. Marine Corps training facility near Darwin, in northern Australia; and the stationing of warships in Singapore on a long-term basis.[22] A capstone of sorts to these moves was Secretary of Defense Leon Panetta's visit in June 2012 to Cam Ranh Bay, site of a massive U.S. military base during its war in Vietnam.

Beijing in 2013 has chosen a relatively nonaggressive path toward its South China Sea claims but does not hesitate to apply pressure to influence other claimants to South China Sea land features when it deems necessary. That pressure has been sometimes diplomatic, sometimes heavy-handed, in the form of civil maritime law-enforcement units (to contest foreign fishers in international waters) or demonstrations by the modernizing PLAN and coast-guard organizations.

The ASEAN nations have for the most part trod softly in the face of continued Chinese opposition to a multilateral approach to sovereignty disputes. The ASEAN member states are not unified but have resisted Beijing's pressure individually, especially when U.S. support is apparent.[23]

Vietnam and the Philippines have been the most active in contesting China's position. Hanoi draws on its own historical evidence and occasionally on armed force. The Philippines' claims to some of the land features in the Spratly Islands group are weak and its navy and air force even weaker, but Manila is attempting to draw on its defense treaty with the United States to support its claims and prospectively in the event of a clash with China. Washington, however, refuses to commit to such support. In fact, the defense treaty was signed in 1951, but the Philippine claim to some of the Spratly (called Kalayaan by Manila) Islands was not made until 1956. The Philippine attitude certainly has irritated Beijing, however, which apparently believes Manila is acting as a surrogate for Washington in containing China unjustly.[24]

China's irritation increased when Secretary of State Hillary Clinton referred to the South China Sea by the Philippine name of "West Philippine Sea."[25] The United States even more recently expressly stated its interest in the South China Sea disputes and their peaceful resolution. In an August 2012 statement, the Department of State (DOS) declared that the United States "has a national interest in the maintenance of peace and stability, respect for international law, freedom of navigation, and unimpeded lawful commerce in the South China Sea. . . . [W]e believe the nations of the region should work collaboratively and diplomatically to resolve disputes without coercion, without intimidation, without threats, and without the use of force." This is a long-standing U.S. position, but the DOS spokesman then criticized China, noting that the United States is

> concerned by the increase in tensions in the South China Sea and are monitoring the situation closely. Recent developments include an uptick in confrontational rhetoric, disagreements over resource exploitation, coercive economic actions, and the incidents around the Scarborough Reef, including the use of barriers to deny access. In particular, China's upgrading of the administrative level of Sansha City and establishment of a new military garrison there covering disputed areas of the South China Sea run counter to collaborative diplomatic efforts to resolve differences and risk further escalating tensions in the region.

Beijing's reaction was rapid and harsh. The American chargé d'affaires in Beijing was called in on a Saturday night by the vice foreign minister and berated. The Ministry of Foreign Affairs publicly derided Washington's "so-called statement" as showing a "total disregard of facts, confounding right and wrong, and sending a seriously wrong message."[26]

This exchange illustrates a serious lack of empathy in Beijing and Washington for each other's position throughout Asian waters. The former is seriously concerned about U.S. support for Tokyo's view of China as an increasing threat. With respect to the South China Sea, Beijing views the American position as part of an overall containment strategy directed against China. The latter keeps protesting that conclusion, but recent U.S. actions and statements in apparent support of Philippine and Vietnamese positions in the South China Sea do make it look like the United States has taken sides against China.[27]

Manila's claim to U.S. support under the Philippine-U.S. Mutual Defense Treaty is moot; the treaty was signed in 1951, and Manila did not make its first claim over sovereignty of the South China Sea Islands until 1956. Washington has not agreed that the treaty covers these islands.

Taiwan agrees with Beijing's sovereignty claims in the South China Sea; Republic of China analysts originally drew the well-known nine-dash line in the early 1930s. The area enclosed by this line includes most of the South China Sea, but its enclosed territory is exceeded by a claim in a May 2009 letter from the Chinese foreign minister and an April 2011 memorandum to the UN secretary-general to sovereignty over not just "the islands in the South China Sea" but also in "adjacent waters"; China also claimed "sovereign right and jurisdiction over the relevant waters as well as the seabed and subsoil thereof." That is, China appears to be claiming all the sovereign zones delineated in the UNCLOS for islands, not just the uninhabitable rocks and shoals in the South China Sea.[28]

The United States has long maintained a position of neutrality with respect to sovereignty of these various islands and land features, but its recent heightened interest in the South China Sea disputes has resulted from Beijing's demonstrated determination to change "the norms that govern military activities at sea."[29]

Secretary of State Clinton's statement at the July 2010 Hanoi meeting of the ASEAN Regional Forum did not state a new U.S. position but reiterated American insistence on freedom of navigation through the South China Sea, with sovereignty rights decided in accordance with the UNCLOS. Clinton also offered U.S. willingness to help negotiation of a "binding code of conduct" for the area rather than the 2002 agreement, which lacks substance. The United States had previously stated its interest in maintaining pace and stability in the South China Sea, in May 1995, following the February Chinese fortification of Mischief Reef, which is claimed by the Philippines.[30]

China's senior representative at this meeting, Foreign Minister Yang Jiechi, seemed surprised by this statement and reacted angrily, accusing the United States of interfering in matters that were not its concern. Ominously, he then warned the ASEAN member states "not to become involved in a cabal organized by an outside power," adding in an intimidating tone that

"China is a big country, bigger than any other countries here."[31] This performance marked the height of China's assertiveness regarding the South China Sea—at least to date—and ironically, no doubt had a result opposite to Yang's intent. His threats have prompted greater efforts by the other South China Sea claimants, particularly Vietnam and the Philippines, to draw closer to the United States as a counterweight to China.

Beijing seems to have realized the negative effects of its heavy-handedness and in 2011 adopted a lower-key, more cooperative attitude toward these issues. In 2012, however, Beijing reverted to a more assertive policy, using force to take possession of Scarborough Shoal, which is also claimed by Manila as sovereign territory.

The ARF member states did not heed this threat but are well aware of the new naval weight China is capable of throwing around. The ASEAN defense ministers in 2010 formed a new organization, the ASEAN Defense Ministers Meeting Plus. The intent is to increase defense coordination among member states and to try to develop a coherent approach to South China Sea issues.[32] Efforts continue to complete a code of conduct to manage disputes.[33]

Several lesser maritime disputes also exist in Southeast Asian waters, but the only significant contretemps involves the Gulf of Thailand. Thailand and Cambodia are the primary opposing claimants in his complex situation, but Malaysia and Vietnam are also involved. All of the contending parties have joined to some extent in resolution of their disputes.

Although extending far beyond the maritime arena, the India-Pakistan conflict affects the vital northern Arabian Sea, the entry and departure area for the energy supplies utilizing the Straits of Hormuz and Bab el-Mandeb. Finally, Iran's threatened stranglehold on the Strait of Hormuz has the potential to blockade the nations of the Persian Gulf, thus seriously affecting the energy-importing nations of East Asia.

Fisheries

The following headlines appeared in Asian newspapers during just one recent month: "Foreign Fish Poachers Detained in Sumatra," "Chinese Fisherman Killed in Palau Shooting," "Palau Urged to Address Chinese Fisherman Death," "Standoff Near Philippines Over; Chinese Boats Keep Catch," "China Releases Vietnamese after Maritime Row," "Fishermen

Detained for 'Pair Trawling,'" "Nations Agree on Tackling Illegal Fishing," "Embassy Takes Custody of Chinese Fishing Crew," and "Russian Coast Guard Fires on Chinese Boats in Sea of Japan."[34] A senior U.S. government official aptly described the general fisheries issue as "too many boats chasing too few fish," further identifying overfishing, marine pollution, and environmental destruction as significant problems.[35]

On 13 April 2011 the United Nations Office on Drugs and Crime (UNODC) launched a report on transnational organized crime in the fishing industry. It focused on trafficking in workers in the fishing industry, people smuggling, and drug trafficking, although also noting linkages to environmental crime, corruption, and piracy. The findings have particular relevance for Asia, which accounts for 85 percent of the world's fishers and 75 percent of motorized fishing vessels.

The UNODC has highlighted a general lack of governance and rule of law in the fishing industry, creating a climate in which transnational organized crime can infiltrate. Fishing boats and their crews are far less regulated than the merchant marine. For instance, fishing vessels are not included in the International Maritime Organization identification-numbering system, making them that much more attractive as vehicles for drug and illegal-migrant smuggling.

Fisheries disputes are ubiquitous throughout Asia, as indeed they are globally. Fishers appear to be the most independent of entrepreneurs, willing to break any rules and take any steps necessary to maximize their catch. Conflicts exist among all of the nations of Asia, from Russia around to Iran, but are most dangerous in terms of arms clashes between Japan and China, between South Korea and China, among China and the ASEAN nations, and among the ASEAN nations themselves.[36]

They are an especially important issue in Southeast Asia, the principal location for the illegal trafficking of individuals for forced labor in the fishing industry. Thailand is the main destination country, and many of those trafficked are from Myanmar, Cambodia, or Laos. Thailand and the Philippines also provide illegal workers to the Malaysian and Indonesian fishing industries. Fishing vessels are a favored means of smuggling illegal migrants from the Middle East and South Asia through Southeast Asian waters to other destinations.

Fisheries crimes directly impact food security, especially pressuring Southeast Asia's strained fisheries. There also are broader security implications. The potential for armed confrontations grows as fishing fleets increase their competition for dwindling fish stocks. The disputed sovereignty claims in the South China Sea are recurrent triggers for clashes among the many littoral states, most of the clashes involving China.

China has led the world in fisheries production since 2004, and Beijing has taken the lead in attempting to conserve South China Sea fisheries stocks. It worked actively with the UN in 1995 to develop its Fish Stocks Agreement and has struggled to impose order on the South China Sea fisheries industry, but with little success, even among its own fishers.[37]

These problems cannot be solved without the participation of the competing states, at the national and regional levels. The ASEAN could be a useful vehicle for targeting illegal trafficking networks.[38]

POINTS OF COOPERATION

All maritime nations support general humanitarian rules at sea, chief among which is saving the lives of mariners at risk. Another is rendering assistance ashore in time of natural disaster. A third is fighting piracy and other illegal acts at sea. Open conflict too often changes adherence to these rules, but they always remain part of the maritime environment.[39]

Sea Lines of Communication

Few maritime concerns are mentioned more often than sea lines of communication. These gained immense attention in the writings of the late nineteenth- and early twentieth-century maritime strategists—Alfred Thayer Mahan, Julian Corbett, and advocates of *guerre de course,* such as Theophile Aube—although not all agreed on the priority of the SLOCs in the pantheon of maritime strategy.

The SLOCs are increasingly vital to all the Asian nations, especially China, Taiwan, Japan, and the Koreas, because they are the primary highways of commerce, both inter- and intra-regionally. Discussion of dangers to SLOC security tend to focus on military threats, but more germane on a daily basis are nonmilitary threats from crime at sea, often categorized as piracy, accidents, and competing sovereignty claims.

Antipiracy, Disaster Response, and Antiterrorism

Incidents of piracy seldom seriously threaten the flow of merchant ships over the SLOCs, but they can pose significant challenges to maritime forces. Natural forces too may threaten SLOC security; the disastrous earthquake and tsunami of 2004 was one such instance. This danger is ongoing; in Southeast Asia, for example, an average of nine typhoons occur annually.

Incidents of terrorism at sea have been few, but its threat to SLOC security can easily overlap with other threats, such as piracy. Not only may criminal activity and terrorism form a continuum of threat, but the spread of technology (witness drug-cartel use of relatively advanced submersible craft to transport drugs) and failing states (the Horn of Africa's descent into piracy havens for instance) add up to a disturbing twenty-first-century picture of a merging of traditional missions for national maritime forces with those traditionally assigned to domestic police forces.[40]

Many incidents described as "piracy" do not occur in international waters and hence actually represent other forms of criminal activity, such as robbery and kidnapping. That said, in the words of Adm. Michael Mullen, former chairman of the U.S. Joint Chiefs of Staff, piracy "can no longer be viewed as someone else's problem. It is a global threat to security because of its deepening ties to international criminal networks, smuggling of hazardous cargoes, and disruption of vital commerce."[41]

The sensitivity of SLOC security is heightened in Asia by the presence of the world's most heavily traveled navigational straits for the transport of oil and gas. These are the Straits of Hormuz, Malacca, and Singapore, and the Bab el-Mandeb.[42] These and the numerous other Asian navigational choke points discussed in the introduction of this book are by definition the most susceptible points on the primary Asian SLOCs.

Maintaining SLOC security is in the economic and national security interests of all the Asian states, but this fact may not, in time of crisis, prevent sea-lane security from being threatened. Hence, all the naval powers in the region must assign their forces as a primary duty to securing their sea lines. For smaller powers, this may require just riverine and coastal navies, but for global powers, such as Japan and China, more capable and farther-ranging naval forces are needed.

Responses to transnational threats include the antipiracy efforts under way in the theater, especially in Southeast Asian waters and the

Gulf of Aden. Piracy in the South China Sea has a very long history but has in recent years faded from public attention, given the media focus on the Gulf of Aden. A dramatic decrease in criminal incidents at sea occurred following the 2004 earthquake and tsunami, but such activity has resurged.

The seventeen incidents that occurred in 2010 represented a 55 percent increase over 2009.[43] Despite this increasing trend, Malaysia and Indonesia remain resistant to outside assistance to its ongoing efforts in conjunction with Singapore and Indonesia to fight piracy under the 2004 Malaysia-Singapore-Indonesia (MALSINDO) agreement. Their effort has, however, received financial and operational support from Australia and Japan.

The three local nations support the Regional Cooperation Agreement on Combating Piracy and Armed Robbery against Ships (ReCAAP), formed in 2006 and signed by fourteen nations. ReCAAP established the Information Sharing Center (ISC) in Singapore and has significantly enhanced information sharing among the maritime nations using the Singapore and Malacca Straits and surrounding waters. A new cooperative arrangement was announced in June 2012 designed to improve maritime safety and protect the environment.[44]

The counterpiracy campaign in the Gulf of Aden and associated waters offers a picture of multilateral naval cooperation rarely seen. While not all countries with forces in the area participate in organized task forces, all participate to a degree in information exchanges and, when circumstances dictate, in cooperative rescue activities. Five task forces were active in the fight against piracy by 2012.

Combined Task Forces (CTFs) 150, 151, and 152 are multinational organizations that operate in designated geographic areas of the northwestern Indian Ocean and the Persian Gulf. CTF 150 is headquartered in Bahrain; CTF 151 was organized in 2009 and operates in the Gulf of Aden and off the Somalia coast; CTF 152 was organized in 2004 and operates in the Arabian Gulf. Ships from the navies of European Union and NATO member countries comprise Combined Task Forces 465 (Atalanta), formed in 2008, and 508, formed in 2009.[45]

This rather complex presence of foreign navies has had some success but is far from solving the piracy problem. Despite all these efforts, piracy in the western Indian Ocean (or, WIO, a region that includes the Gulf of

Aden) remains a significant, if annoying rather than disabling, threat to seaborne traffic. The International Maritime Bureau (IMB) received in 2009 reports of 406 piracy attacks, 217 of those occurring in the WIO. These attacks grossed the pirates $60 million in ransom—an increase over $55 million reported for 2008.[46] Such figures are inaccurate, however, given the propensity of shipowners not to report such payments.

The commander of India's navy recently proposed a standard operating procedure (SOP) for these navies, but such an SOP remains a work in progress. A similar call for strengthening "international naval cooperation" was made recently by the PLAN deputy commander.[47]

The IMB reported a decrease in global pirate attacks for the first six months of 2011 from 196 during the same period of 2010 to 166; 60 percent of the 2011 attacks occurred in the WIO. Sixty-one incidents were reported for the WIO for the first six months of 2012, of 157 globally. This indicates a decreasing trend, perhaps explained less by counterpiracy forces than by an increase to eighteen knots of the speed of ships transiting dangerous waters and to increased employment of armed guards.[48]

International efforts to suppress piracy suffer from nations' reluctance to attack pirate havens ashore, although the relevant UN resolution authorizes such attacks. The chaotic conditions on the Horn of Africa, graphically demonstrated by unsuccessful American and United Nations efforts in the early 1990s, no doubt discourage such operations, despite acknowledgement of their necessity and successful small-scale forays ashore.[49]

Natural disasters and accidents at sea routinely evoke multinational relief efforts, while increasing international cooperation against the possibility of maritime terrorism is manifest in the Proliferation Security Initiative and the Container Security Initiative. Other multilateral efforts to enhance maritime security include the International Ship and Port Security Code, installation of automatic identification systems on ships displacing more than five hundred tons, the Convention for the Suppression of Unlawful Acts against the Safety of Maritime Navigation (SUA), the Customs-Trade Partnership against Terrorism (C-TPAT), and enhanced information management.[50]

The employment of a nation's navy to disrupt an SLOC is not likely in the near to middle term. Many, perhaps most, merchant ships fly flags of convenience, their masters are from nations other than the flags', their crews are almost certain to be of mixed nationality, and ship ownerships are so convoluted as to defy description by nation. Cargo ownership also is likely to be difficult to determine during an interception on the high seas, especially for petroleum carriers, whose cargoes may be sold on the international "spot market" two or more times during their transits from loading to delivery ports.

Other common threats are combated through joint antipollution efforts, fisheries conservation programs and patrols in the North Pacific, cooperative efforts for navigational safety and salvage, and support for enhanced safety measures authored by the International Shipping Organization (ISO) and national coast guards. Agreements for maritime search and rescue and for maritime immigration law enforcement are not uncommon. Additional instances of bilateral cooperation include an emerging Philippine-Australian military training agreement, a similar agreement between Singapore and India, a long-standing pact between Singapore and the Philippines, and an Indonesia-Singapore submarine rescue pact.[51]

Arctic

The Arctic Ocean is the area of the most recent maritime sovereignty concern and potential conflict. Most directly concerned are the members of the Arctic Council: Iceland, Denmark, Norway, Sweden, Finland, Russia, Canada, and the United States. China, Japan, and South Korea are "ad hoc member states."[52] Russia and Canada have taken the most aggressive positions regarding sea-bottom mineral rights in the Arctic, but any solution to the conflicting claims will almost certainly have to be unanimous among the council members, with the ad hoc member strongly interested as well.

Although somewhat tangential to the Indo-Pacific region, the Arctic is viewed with concern by Russia, Canada, and the United States, all members of the Arctic Council with stakes in the Indo-Pacific. Japan, China, and India are also intensely interested in placing themselves in positions to exploit the year-round navigation of the Arctic Sea forecast to become a reality by 2050.

Russia has taken a leading position in this cooperation/conflict test. Moscow has announced formation of a military force to guard its Arctic interests, to include operation of its new class of ballistic-missile submarines, the *Borei*s, in Arctic waters.[53] Chinese premier Wen Jiabao signified Beijing's interest when he signed an agreement with Iceland for access to Arctic minerals. China has also begun calling the Arctic "international territory," while participating in a series of conferences addressing future Arctic sea routes, and it has built a formidable fleet of icebreakers.[54]

Cooperation in exploiting newly accessible Arctic resources is addressed by all members of the Arctic Council. Talk of the Arctic as a "global common" is not unusual, but it comes mostly from non–council members.[55]

Military conflict is not likely, but naval operations have been conducted in Arctic waters by Russia, Canada, and the United States for many years. Moscow, possibly because of its serious domestic problems, seems determined to maintain an assertive, even hostile, attitude toward the expanding maritime developments in the Arctic. Cooperative steps include regular council meetings and a May 2011 legally binding treaty "to divide responsibilities for search-and-rescue activities in the Arctic."[56]

Indian Ocean

This centrally located ocean is the scene of both cooperation and competition. The national contests, led by that between India and Pakistan, are long-standing and not susceptible to early resolution. Also significant, if less certain, is the prospect of a contest between India and China. Many Indian analysts think that a PLAN push into the Indian Ocean is inevitable; Chinese analysts deny this. They acknowledge the obstacles of the Indian navy and of the geography involved. Beijing almost certainly is not intending significant naval penetration of the Indian Ocean but seeks to ensure commercial access and preserve its ability to participate in transnational campaigns, such as the current antipiracy efforts in the Gulf of Aden.[57]

United Nations Convention on the Law of the Sea

The beginning of the twenty-first century has seen Asian nations adopt an increasingly rigid, sometimes bellicose attitude toward maritime sovereignty claims. The UNCLOS was completed in 1982 and ratified by all of the contending Asian nations. The United States did not ratify;

Washington, however, has repeatedly stated that it will abide by the treaty, pending eventual Senate ratification.

Whether or not the Senate ratifies the UNCLOS, the United States has established its navy as the final arbiter of disagreements in the South China Sea. Its 2007 Maritime Strategy states unequivocally that it "will not permit conditions under which our maritime forces will be impeded from freedom of maneuver and freedom of access . . . nor permit an adversary to disrupt the global supply chain by attempting to block vital sea-lines of communication and commerce." This statement also drives U.S. maritime strategy with respect to Iran and its threats to close the Strait of Hormuz.

The UNCLOS certainly is a commendable multilateral effort, but in one sense it has been disruptive of the previously existing maritime legal paradigm, because it completely redefined maritime zones and degrees of sovereignty. Furthermore, it lacks strong mechanisms for either enforcement or conflict resolution. China's attitude toward sovereignty claims in dispute is hardly unique, but it discloses a sensitivity to domestic political concerns and apparent refusal to negotiate that does not bode well for near-term resolution of the most troublesome maritime disputes, those in the East and South China Seas.

Perhaps key to the long-term viability of the UNCLOS and to Sino-American maritime cooperation instead of conflict is resolution of differing views of the EEZ. The United States, along with approximately 133 of the 157 UNCLOS signatories, believes that "it is essential for security at sea . . . that in a globalized era all states remain possessed of the navigational rights and freedoms to undertake military activities in foreign" EEZs.[58] China disagrees, however, as does India. This is a very serious issue, because almost 38 percent of the global seas are covered by coastal-state jurisdiction.

CONCLUSION

The maritime sovereignty disputes in Asia are defined by geography, in what Mackinder called the "geographical pivot of history."[59] Since geography rarely changes, contesting nations must find ways to adjust maritime claims to satisfy both their own national security, economic, and political concerns and those of their disputants.

While China usually is cast as the villain in the South China Sea sovereignty disputes, all the claimants, particularly Vietnam and the Philippines, press their positions uncompromisingly. Furthermore, none of the claimants has demonstrated a convincing case; indeed, to a layman who has studied the various claims, China's arguments outweigh those of at least the Philippines and Vietnam.[60]

Manila's claim is relatively recent and appears to lack significant historical justification. Hanoi cites fifteenth-century historical evidence in support of its position but relies on a more modern series of nineteenth- and twentieth-century factors, particularly a 1933 claim by France, whose colonial regime in Vietnam established administrative control over the South China Sea islands. This assertion is undercut, however, by China's 1887 treaty with France, an instrument that included a map showing the Spratly Islands as within Beijing's jurisdiction. Furthermore, Hanoi twice in the 1950s acknowledged China's sovereignty over these islands.[61]

Beijing hurts its own case, however, by a lack of coordination among the eleven or more government agencies that have an interest—and apparently authority over—South China Sea issues. No effective coordinating body among the various ministerial offices and law-enforcement agencies exists. Several attempts to correct this dysfunctional situation have been made in Beijing, even by President Hu Jintao himself in 2005, but with marginal success.[62]

Another cause of the contentious situation in the South China Sea is Beijing's unwillingness or perhaps inability to clarify the meaning of the nine-dash line. This line appears to represent a Chinese claim of sovereignty over nearly all of the water areas, as well as the land features in the sea. The clearest statement is that of a Foreign Ministry spokesperson in February 2012 that "no country including China has claimed sovereignty over the whole South China Sea."[63]

Opportunities for maritime cooperation are apparent, as noted above, but many depend on common interpretations of policies that are politically and economically beneficial to participating maritime states. Unfortunately, this commonality is not always present. For instance, Beijing, despite China's rapidly growing economy and emergence as a world power, remains distrustful of market mechanisms, seeking to maintain central-government dominance. Whether this can be a successful policy structure is problematical, but it means that it cannot be assumed that China will adopt or agree to policies that other Asian nations deem "logical" to maintain maritime security and economic well-being.

Beijing's actions generally exemplify the calculus inherent in this chapter's title of "conflict and cooperation." In the East and South China Seas, as well as in the Indian Ocean, Beijing opposes and cooperates, as its national security views dictate.[64] The same can be said for all Asian powers, including the United States.

CONCLUSION

INTRODUCTION

Asia's maritime geography includes long coastlines and extensive insular topography. It features many vital straits and navigational choke points, delineating the great maritime sweep from the Sea of Okhotsk to the Persian Gulf and the Red Sea. Few Asian nations have coherent maritime strategies or ocean policies that reflect both truly vital national interests and defense-budget realities. Published versions appear to be intended not so much to provide strategic direction as to garner public-sector and governmental support. This is particularly true of the Australian, New Zealand, and Indian published strategies. The Japanese and U.S. strategies are more directive, but they too are clearly aimed at garnering domestic support. The Canadian maritime strategy appears to be the most coherent and inclusive of the maritime strategies published by Pacific nations, virtues enhanced by its brevity.

None of the published maritime strategies, or white papers, reflect what one American strategist has called the "tactical transformation from the carrier era to the missile era of warfare, along with two additional complications: the impending influence of robotic systems and of cyber operations."[1] All continue to rely primarily on manned warfare systems.

Additionally, Asia may be facing a true strategic "sea change" in its power balance. The United States remains the region's dominant maritime power, in terms of both naval and economic strength, but it confronts very serious economic challenges that are directly affecting the nation's maritime strength and ability to modernize its globally preeminent navy.

China is the possible U.S. successor. If Beijing is not satisfied with the current international order in Asia, it will continue seeking regional preeminence. China's sheer size, human and material resources, growing economic power, and modernizing military, as well as the history of modernizing superpowers and a Chinese worldview that is at least as egocentric as that of the United States are all factors in the changing Asian strategic venue.

A hostile China-U.S. maritime relationship is not foreordained. Domestic political concerns dominate in both nations; neither currently perceives benefits in employing its military against the other or against the other's interests. There are points of potential conflict, however, as well as of possible cooperation.

The larger question may be phrased as, "Is China determined to replace the United States as the dominant military power in Asia?" Several quotes are available from Chinese maritime strategists to the effect that "China 'never intends to challenge the U.S.' and welcomes its role maintaining peace in the Asia-Pacific region." The United States, in the words of President Obama, has a military strategy that "seeks a positive, cooperative, and comprehensive relationship with China."[2]

While the United States and China are Asia's major naval powers, Japan, South Korea, and India deploy capable, twenty-first-century navies. Their cooperation on transnational issues and negotiations on contentious issues will go far toward ensuring continued peace and stability on the vast Asian seas.

This book has examined both the maritime national-defense interests of Asian nations and the security of the maritime commons, including the sea lines of communication. All maritime Asian states—a list that omits only Mongolia and Laos—are concerned about protecting their maritime interests, ranging from littoral law enforcement to countering piracy thousands of miles from home ports.

Underlying Factors

The maritime Asian nations are all parties to many opportunities for both conflict and cooperation scenarios.

History

The concept of the global maritime commons is the background for any maritime nation's security concerns. In Asia, that commons has been marked by many significant historical events that affect current perceptions of economic and security issues. These include the massive Mongol attempt to invade Japan in the thirteenth century; the fact that its failure was due primarily to environmental disruption attests to the power of nature in the maritime arena.[3]

The second is the series of fifteenth-century voyages of Zheng He, the great Chinese explorer. Third is the Western subjugation of most of maritime Asia by virtue of European maritime power. Fourth is World War II, the world's greatest war, which for eastern Asia lasted fifteen years, from 1931 to 1945. Fifth, and most enduring, is the ocean's foundational role in sustaining the commercial and economic life of the Asian nations.

Theory

The region's great maritime and economic powers can all be viewed through the lens of classic maritime strategic theories, particularly those advanced by Adm. Alfred Thayer Mahan and Sir Julian S. Corbett. The latter is especially applicable to Asia in the twenty-first century, because of his emphasis on the limited use of naval power, akin to the great German strategist Karl von Clausewitz's argument that limited objectives may be achieved with limited military force.

Corbett's emphasis on safeguarding one's SLOCs to cement the vital linkage between secure maritime communications and economic well-being is as applicable in peacetime as it is in wartime. SLOC security is especially vital in Asian waters in the twenty-first century, given the maritime dependence of nearly all the region's nations. This is demonstrated throughout the Asian trading arena; the region contains the world's three largest shipbuilders, eight of the world's ten largest containerports, and the center of global energy production and shipping.

Accompanying this huge civilian maritime infrastructure is the process of near-ubiquitous naval modernization across Asia, as the region becomes the world's most important commercial center. Australia, Iran, Japan, Pakistan, and South Korea are renewing and strengthening their already-capable navies, while smaller nations are acquiring twenty-first-century systems, especially submarines. China continues modernizing what promises to become, perhaps by midcentury, Asia's most capable maritime military force, while India's navy struggles against bureaucratic inertia and budgetary constraints to deploy a force that, centered on three aircraft carrier battle groups, would be dominant in the Indian Ocean. The U.S. Navy meanwhile remains the region's strongest maritime force, although Southwest Asian commitments and budget uncertainties at home are casting a shadow on its future presence and influence.

The importance of Asia's maritime character is underlined by Japan's naval wars with China and Russia, in 1895 and 1905, respectively. Even more significant as an example of maritime strategic development was the U.S. World War II strategy against Japan, which culminated in the latter's 1945 surrender aboard a U.S. battleship.

The last case remains a prime example of the long-term development of a maritime strategy followed by its actual application to a long, intensely maritime conflict. The application of strategy in Asia in World War II was molded maritime geopolitics. It was primarily an American construct, but its execution was aided by alliance relationships.

Treaties and Alliances

Indeed, the Cold War, which soon followed victory over Japan, was to a significant degree a contest of bilateral and multilateral treaty organizations. No Pacific version of NATO has ever evolved, but strong bilateral relations, particularly between the United States and Australia, Canada, Japan, South Korea—and for a period the Republic of China—confronted a Chinese-Soviet alliance.

Both traditional and nontraditional threats on the seas currently are prevalent; counterterrorism and counterpiracy operations by Asian navies are under way. More traditional maritime missions, such as defense of the homeland, certainly remain prominent among any nation's prioritized list of national security concerns, but maritime Asia today offers only one even possible example—the refusal of China not to threaten military action against Taiwan under certain circumstances. Another traditional naval mission high on national security concerns in Asia is securing the region's SLOCs. Underlying all maritime concerns and missions is the relatively recent United Nations Convention on the Law of the Sea. This treaty's assigned rights and responsibilities are, to a significant degree, geographically delineated and provide a useful focus on current disputes in the Asian region.

Maritime disputes of varying degrees of seriousness exist throughout Asia; important in their current status and possible future development are the naval strategies, strengths, and weaknesses of the region's major nations, as well as those groups of smaller oceanic states. These were examined in this book, beginning with the post–Cold War search by the United States for an inclusive maritime strategy, a search without satisfactory result. Instead, the navy continues to shrink in numbers in the face of more than a decade of continental wars and diffuse, nontraditional national security threats.

The United States remains the dominant naval power in Asia but is embracing multinational maritime paradigms as an attractive way to leverage shrinking naval forces. This is one leg in the U.S. maritime "rebalancing" to Asia and is being pursued, but with as yet unproven effectiveness. The second major leg in American maritime strategy in Asia is the series of mutual defense treaties with South Korea, Japan, the Philippines, and Australia.

A third leg is the body of special relationships between Washington and Taiwan, New Zealand, Singapore, Malaysia, Thailand, India, and an emerging state, Myanmar. Farther west, the United States has significant relationships with Pakistan, Saudi Arabia, and Iraq and other Persian Gulf states, as well as with Djibouti. Additionally, since the terrorist attacks of September 2001, Washington has established logistical arrangements with Central Asian nations. Although removed from maritime Asia, these nations form part of an Asia-wide U.S. security presence that is both reassuring to American friends and allies and discomforting to other nations, especially China.

Japan is the U.S. treaty ally in Asia with the strongest maritime power, both navy and merchant marine. It occupies an overwhelmingly maritime strategic position in North Asia. The modernizing Japan Maritime

Self-Defense Force supports a dramatically shifting strategic focus, from Cold War concern with the Soviet Union to the north, toward current concern with China to the southwest. Coloring Tokyo's strategic calculations are continuing domestic economic and political situations, both somewhat at sea during the past two decades.

While the JMSDF remains on a day-to-day basis the most capable naval force in Asia, Tokyo's revised strategy continues to rely on the mutual defense treaty with the United States. That strategy has been published and modified, as events dictate and in conjunction with U.S. intentions.

The relationship contains at least two significant rocks and shoals, however: the uncertainty of Okinawa's role and U.S. willingness to back Japan's claims in the East China Sea. Tokyo and Beijing dispute both the sovereignty of the Diaoyu/Senkaku Islands and the limits of the two nations' respective continental shelves, which in turn delineate the ownership of seabed energy reserves. Washington has promulgated the interesting, not to say contradictory, position that while not taking sides as to whether Japan or China holds sovereignty over Diaoyus/Senkakus, their defense is covered by the mutual defense treaty with Japan.

Japan's strategic seascape may be described as "North Asia," discussion of which includes reviews of the maritime situations and strategies of Canada, Russia, and the two Koreas. Canada, like the United States, is both a Pacific and Atlantic nation and a member of the North Atlantic Treaty Organization. Canada deploys a small but capable, modern navy and offers a strong strategic maritime presence in the Arctic and in northern Pacific waters. It has published a short, but, as noted, remarkably coherent and complete, maritime strategy.

Russia has not been a major Pacific maritime power since its navy was largely destroyed by Japan in 1905. Despite periodic announcements of a "return" to the Asia-Pacific, Moscow has been unable to find the resources and national security interests to rebuild a major naval presence in Asian waters. One exception was the presence of a seaborne strategic nuclear deterrence represented by fleet ballistic-missile submarines in the Sea of Okhotsk "bastion" during the Cold War, a presence that continues to a much lesser degree. Most recent, and typical, were reports from Moscow that the Russian navy was seeking to resume stationing warships overseas; bases in Cuba, Vietnam, and Seychelles were specifically mentioned. These reports were followed almost immediately by denials from Vietnam and from Russia's navy commander.[4]

North Korea deploys a navy of small submarines and surface craft, a fleet best described as a maritime terror force. It is capable of striking disruptive blows, as witnessed in the sinking of the South Korean corvette, but is a strategic force only in the sense of causing political unrest in the volatile northeast Asian arena. The Republic of South Korea Navy, on the other hand, is already a capable force and is modernizing at a rate that may raise it to the level of the JMSDF in terms of technology.

The ROKN maritime strategy is focused on the North Korean threat in the short term, but national security priorities also place attention on Japanese and Chinese maritime intentions. The former has a very bad history with Korea that engenders suspicion and even hatred; the latter is so much the "big guy on the block" that Seoul must pay serious attention to Beijing's policies, intentions, and maritime force. Nonetheless, apparent ROKN concern with the JMSDF and the PLAN seems overdrawn.[5]

China clearly is the dominant Asian continental power, but Beijing has been modernizing its navy at a consistent, moderate pace since the late 1980s. It may be on course for a precedent-setting strategic conversion of itself from a major continental power to one that is also a major maritime power. The Chinese merchant fleet and civilian ship construction infrastructure are already among of the world's top two; the navy does not yet match that status but no doubt has aspirations to increase its capability to the point of effective defense of China's national security interests, as defined in Beijing.[6]

Historically, only the United States, having no major continental threats, has achieved both continental and maritime major-power status, and that episodically. Even today, U.S. ground forces have demonstrated the capability to fight two limited wars simultaneously for more than a decade, albeit at a cost of trillions of dollars spent on a professional military. But while the U.S. Navy remains the world's strongest, there is almost no U.S. merchant fleet. Other nations that have aspired to dual-power status—such as Spain in the sixteenth century, France in the eighteenth and nineteenth centuries, Germany in the late nineteenth and twentieth centuries, and the Soviet Union in the twentieth century—have failed to achieve that goal in a lasting fashion.

If Beijing maintains its current pace of naval modernization, expanding that process to include aviation and surface warfare communities, the PLAN will fulfill Adm. Liu Huaqing's long-range ambitions, which include a navy capable by midcentury of deploying global naval power. That eventuality may well mean a tectonic shift in the maritime world, if the U.S. Navy continues to decline in numbers and China supplants the United States as chief guarantor of the maritime commons in Asia.

The 2050 goal may loom larger in the eyes of other nations than it does for China, however, since Beijing has yet to develop a maritime strategy consistent with global naval expansion. Furthermore, the dominance of domestic issues is almost certain to continue driving basic Chinese security actions, with Taiwan remaining the only maritime issue Beijing categorizes as a "core" interest.

China's interpretations of certain UNCLOS provisions are of particular interest to Asia generally. Beijing has expressed contradictory interpretations of the UNCLOS when condemning the actions of other claimants to South China Sea land features, while defending its own similar actions in East China Sea waters contested with Japan.

Southeast Asia contains one of Asia's most important maritime arenas. All of the maritime nations in the region—Australia, Brunei, Indonesia, Malaysia, New Zealand, the Philippines, Singapore, Taiwan, Thailand, and Vietnam—are striving to improve their naval power, with submarines the most popular platform for doing so.

Taiwan's status remains the most volatile issue in the region, but South China Sea issues are central to most of this region's maritime concerns. Sovereignty claims in that sea are troublesome and occasionally violent. Clashes not infrequently occur over fisheries, marine surveying, and intelligence gathering. Attempts at resolution of claims consistently fail due to the intransigence of the claimants, but as long as significant energy reserves are not discovered in the central South China Sea, the issues there should not lead to major armed conflict.

Australia and New Zealand have published respectable maritime strategic documents. Their location on Southeast Asia's maritime perimeter at least symbolically limits their participation in regional issues, but their links to the United States and Great Britain empower their navies with certain allies. Australia and New Zealand both are members of the Five-Power Defense Arrangement, which means strong maritime relations with Singapore and Malaysia, in addition to Great Britain. Australia also joins the United States in a mutual defense treaty; recent closer military relations with Washington have ameliorated the effects of New Zealand's suspension from the ANZUS pact.

Taiwan has a unique relationship with the United States, codified in the U.S. Taiwan Relations Act. This 1979 legislation does not obligate the United States to defend Taiwan against possible Chinese military attack, but that is the message it sends to Beijing, Taipei, and even the U.S. Congress. This places Washington in direct opposition to Beijing's most cherished national security objective: the reunification of Taiwan with mainland China.

Other Southeast Asian nations have special relationships with the United States. Singapore provides significant logistical support to U.S. naval forces, including hosting the Seventh Fleet's logistics command. Singapore also provides port facilities to U.S. naval forces, including the forthcoming homeporting of four littoral combat ships. Finally, Singapore at its own expense built at Changi a huge pier capable of servicing U.S. nuclear-powered aircraft carriers.

Malaysia has since the late 1980s welcomed U.S. naval vessels to its logistics base at Lumut. Thailand has defense and diplomatic agreements with the United States that in total approach a defense treaty. Washington is also establishing closer relationships with Vietnam. Additionally, U.S. naval forces conduct exercises at sea with almost all the region's nations, including Indonesia and Brunei.

The 2007 maritime strategy published by New Delhi is long and repetitive but reflects the Indian navy's determination to fulfill New Delhi's maritime security objectives. That ambition is constrained by two bureaucratic obstacles. First is the military's understandable focus on Pakistan as the most important national security concern. Second is the national government's reluctance to overspend on the military, especially the navy, in the face of very serious domestic economic, social, and political problems.

The navy faces a steep uphill battle to obtain the budget resources it needs to attain its goal of three aircraft carriers, escorting destroyers, and a force of nuclear-powered submarines. Perhaps more realistic than the published maritime strategy are the Look West and Look East policies. The former consists of increased Indian interest in the Persian Gulf and western African areas from which India acquires much of its petroleum. The latter is more enterprising for India and more portentous for Asia.

The Look East policy has already included a strengthening of India's naval forces homeported on its east coast and the organization of a new naval command based on the Andaman-Nicobar Islands with responsibility for the easternmost Indian Ocean, leading to the Malacca and Singapore Straits. The Indian navy has also conducted several deployments east of those straits, with port calls and naval exchanges with Vietnam, China, Japan, and South Korea. This obvious attempt to extend Indian maritime power to the Pacific Ocean is likely viewed by Beijing as a direct challenge and by other East Asian nations as a possible counterweight to expanding Chinese naval power.

The IN also has expanded its exercise program. It now includes participation by both Asian and Western navies, including U.S. and Australian units. Although not seeking an alliance relationship, New Delhi clearly seeks stronger relations with the United States to counter China's perceived goal of becoming a major Indian Ocean presence. New Delhi's position on several UNCLOS provisions is close to Beijing's interpretations, however, which could prove troublesome in the long term for the United States.

Otherwise, India faces only smaller South and Southwest Asian nations, including Bangladesh, Sri Lanka, Seychelles, Maldives, and Pakistan. On this maritime front, New Delhi has no maritime challenger other than Pakistan. Analysts' oft-voiced concerns about Chinese naval penetration into the Indian Ocean have not come to fruition and are unlikely to do so.

The Persian Gulf states also lie in the Indian Ocean region, but except for Iran, they possess only minor maritime forces. Of all the IOR states, only Pakistan and Iran deploy significant naval forces—although Saudi Arabia, Oman, Iraq, Kuwait, and the UAE all have purchased new, capable surface combatants and aircraft. The IOR island nations possess only coast guards but do play roles in counterpiracy operations.

None of the Gulf States have maritime strategies other than in reaction to their fears of Iranian dominance. They all to a degree rely on the United States and other Western supporters to counter Tehran's threats, especially about closing the Strait of Hormuz.

Iran actually deploys two "navies." The Islamic Republic of Iran Navy is a relatively modern force including submarines and cruise-missile-equipped surface combatants. It has a primary mission of operating outside the Persian Gulf. The Gulf waters are usually, however, the responsibility of the radicalized Iranian Revolutionary Guard Corps Navy, a force more under religious than secular government control in Tehran—and hence more dangerous to international peace and the safety of the SLOCs in the area.

CONFLICT SCENARIOS

The North Korean and Iranian regimes not only mark the extreme boundaries of maritime Asia but pose the most danger to peace and stability in that great oceanic expanse. The former does not represent a primarily maritime issue, and the Six-Party Talks, long in hiatus, may still provide the venue for constraining Pyongyang's aggression. Peaceful resolution on the peninsula will require Beijing to modify North Korean intransigence.

Iran's determination to control events in the Persian Gulf relies in significant part on the maritime balance of power in the region. Currently, Iranian ambitions are constrained almost solely by American and other Western militaries. This places China, a primary customer of Iranian energy resources, in political opposition to the United States but ironically also in the position of a friendly power at sea, with both engaging in counterpiracy operations in the region.

Hostile situations with the potential for major-power clashes make up a relatively short list—in fact, Taiwan arguably is the only issue important enough to draw these two nuclear powers into armed conflict. Peaceful resolution of the Taiwan issue has since 2008 appeared to be on a promising trajectory.

The East China Sea issues between Japan and China pose economic and nationalistic issues; neither the Diaoyu/Senkaku Islands nor seabed resources appear important enough to lead to military conflict, as opposed to the ongoing diplomatic and public vitriol. Similarly, the Korean-Japanese dispute over Dokdo/Takeshima draws more on historical enmity than on economic importance to either nation.

The South China Sea offers much more complex and contentious issues. China, Vietnam, the Philippines, Brunei, Indonesia, and Malaysia all have sovereignty claims in the area, while Taiwan agrees with China's claims. The regional reaction to the 1995 Mischief Reef incident, the 2002 code of conduct, the 2004–5 exploration agreements with the Philippines and Vietnam, and the 2005 joint patrolling agreement with the latter have all impressed upon Beijing the dangers attendant to its episodically assertive behavior in the South China Sea.

The American "rebalancing" signaled by Secretary of State Clinton's July 2010 speech at the ARF meeting in Hanoi has further colored China's views. The South China Sea situation offers opportunities both for conflict and cooperation, but resolution of that choice will depend on the easing of hitherto consistent intransigence on the part of all the claimants.

COOPERATION SCENARIOS

The majority of these scenarios fall under the rubric of SLOC security. This is an unobjectionable, important issue for all maritime nations. The United States has long assumed the role of guaranteeing SLOC security throughout Indo-Pacific waters, but other Asian nations now are participating actively in securing the sea-lanes. This in part reflects doubts about the durability of the U.S. presence, in view of the post–Cold War diffusion of Washington's interests and drawdown in naval numbers, the 2008 economic downturn, the apparent impotence of Congress, and the U.S. commitment to wars of choice in Southwest Asia for more than a decade.

The most obvious instances of maritime cooperation in Asia are the counterterrorism and counterpiracy operations in the South China and Andaman Seas and those in the northwest Indian Ocean, particularly the Gulf of Aden. The former operations began in 2004 and continue under the aegis of Indonesia, Singapore, and Malaysia, with assistance from Japan, Australia, and others.

The Gulf of Aden operations involve a great many maritime nations, from Norway to Japan. They are more notable as a model of international maritime cooperation than as an effective means of combatting piracy. Other cooperative measures and agreements in maritime Asia address fisheries, search and rescue, safety at sea, port security, seamen safety, environmental preservation, and support of humanitarian operations ashore.

All navies have to deal with certain verities. First—simply because the future is unknown—naval planning is hampered from the beginning by having to anticipate and prepare for a wide range of eventualities. Second, navies, especially in the twenty-first century, face a bifurcated, most basic decision—how to balance preparations for traditional missions, focused on war at sea, and nontraditional missions, focused on transnational and other threats arising from globalization. These latter threats include terrorism, crime at sea, human and material trafficking, environmental disaster, and support for humanitarian relief ashore.

Third, navies face the challenges of new and emerging technologies. These may represent the next stage in development of a known technology, such as cruise missiles, or a revolutionary new development, such as efficient directed-energy weapons. Fourth is the problematic, sometimes arcane nature of international law. A survey of the statements made by signatories of the UNCLOS, for example, reveals a fairly wide span of interpretations of what they thought they were signing.

Fifth are problems with strategic identity. Will Washington always be convinced, for instance, that U.S. strategy should be based on serving as a "city upon a hill" or as a sort of global policeman? And how seriously does the concept of the "Middle Kingdom" serve China's strategic culture?[7]

Sixth, the economics of sea power are as important in twenty-first-century Washington as they were in eighteenth-century London or in the sixteenth-century Ming court. As will be discussed below, the cost of navies is rapidly becoming so heavy a burden even to the world's richest economy as to be casting doubt on centuries-old concepts of the necessary size, capabilities, and missions of naval forces.

Seventh, and finally, is a subtle but real decline in the independence of naval forces. The advent of radio communications first made itself felt at the 1905 battle of Tsushima. In less than a century, navies progressed to (or became burdened by) computerization, satellites, and the Internet. No longer will a Comm. Matthew G. Perry be dispatched on a two-year voyage with only the most general orders to deal with a little-known Japan.

These seven precepts form a common denominator with which any maritime strategy must deal. They also are tied inextricably to the strictures and freedoms of globalization.[8] This includes unprecedented public knowledge of naval movements and recognition of the sometimes remarkable flexibility of maritime strategic tenets.

BUDGET ISSUES

This book has indirectly dealt with the question of Asia surpassing the West economically and militarily, to include in maritime affairs. While there is no doubting the past half century's remarkable economic progress in East Asia generally or the past quarter century's growth in China and India specifically, the preeminence of the per-capita wealth and performance of the West, led by the United States and the European countries, is far from at its end. Globalization has blurred considerably the ability to make such judgments, and lineal projections of continued Chinese economic growth are problematic to a degree; consider Japan's fall from the late 1980s "Japan Number One" view.[9]

Almost all the Asian nations are spending significant amounts of money trying to acquire more capable naval forces. Clearly, resources are being invested in a way that reflects lack of certainty about the future peace of the large, maritime Indo-Pacific region.

The most common concern today is submarine warfare—the potential threat posed by China's dramatic increase in its submarine force. In response, Japan, South Korea, Vietnam, Australia, Singapore, Malaysia, and India are all modernizing their undersea forces. Taiwan continues talking about modernizing its antiquated submarine force. Even Philippine naval officers talk of acquiring submarines—if rather wistfully.[10]

Pakistan and Iran deploy capable submarines, although not with China in mind. The former is concerned primarily with India as a threat, while the latter operates from justifiable fear that the international community may curtail its threatening behavior.

All the Asian nations recognize the simple fact that sea power, in the form of both navies and merchant fleets, is getting more expensive. South Korea, China, and Japan are the world's three largest shipbuilders, but in 2013 they face a static market. This results in part both from overbuilding and from a financial downturn for shipping lines.[11]

Merchant fleets clearly form an important element in global maritime power. The internationalization of that industry, from keel laying to deck manning, greatly increases the complexity of analyzing its impact on national power. The United States, for instance, possesses one of the world's smallest shipbuilding infrastructures. In 2000, 95 percent of American foreign trade was carried in non–U.S. flag ships. Only 2 percent of world merchant tonnage is owned by the United States;[12] that shipping, in turn, is crewed and commanded overwhelmingly by non–U.S. citizens.

Despite those data, the United States remains the world's strongest naval power. However, the U.S. Navy confronts a financially challenging shipbuilding plan based on multi-billion-dollar destroyers and submarines and a class of aircraft carriers each costing more than $13 billion—not including its aircraft wing. Even the world's richest country will not be able to afford such costs indefinitely.

DETERRENCE

Navies in Asia have entered what might be called the second nuclear age. The Cold War offered an essentially bipolar strategic venue, with the United States and the Soviet Union possessing nuclear arsenals capable of mutually assured destruction (MAD). MAD remains in the hands of those two powers, but in Asia, the nations of China, India, and Pakistan now deploy nuclear weapons; North Korea also has joined the nuclear club; and rumblings about possessing these weapons have been heard from South Korea, Japan, Taiwan, and Myanmar during the past few decades.

All nations possessing nuclear weapons regard them as deterrence against an existential threat. This is usually for deterring other nuclear powers, but in North Korea's case, at least, conventional deterrence may also be rationale for acquiring nuclear weapons.[13] Nuclear deterrence is a naval mission for the United States and Russia; China intends deploying nuclear-armed ICBMs in its new Jin-class submarine. If Beijing follows a Soviet-style bastion strategy, stationing its SSBNs in the South China Sea, it will place that sea in a new strategic position.[14] India also plans for that mission, probably with the scheduled deployment in 2016 of the *Arihant*-class submarine.

Navies also provide vehicles for conventional deterrence, of course. Naval forces are particularly well suited for conventional deterrence, given their inherent mobility and ability to project power without needing to occupy or even visit other nations. This may be accomplished through engagement with regional friends and allies, by means of port visits, exercises, staff talks, and just the presence of naval forces.

MULTILATERALISM

Multilateral organizations are important in securing the maritime arena. The United Nations remains the overarching treaty structure in Asia and is being supplemented by an increasing number of multilateral organizations. These are increasingly prized as a means of balancing China, as is the hoped-for continued U.S. presence. Asia apparently is too diverse and marked by too high a degree of historical distrust for a multilateral structure such as NATO to emerge, but other arrangements are growing.

ASEAN is the most important Asian multilateral organization. It includes all ten Southeast Asian nations, with China, South Korea, and Japan serving as close observers. Australia, India, New Zealand, and the United States have also become frequent attendees at ASEAN meetings.

The ASEAN Regional Forum is an important subsidiary organization, formed to provide a platform where member states' defense organizations can interact. ASEAN's ten Southeast Asian members attend ARF meetings, as do seventeen other states, including Australia, China, Taiwan, Japan, Russia, and the United States.

At a less formal level is the Six-Party Talks; at yet another level are organizations linked to ASEAN, such as the ARF, ASEAN+3, and the ADMM+. Dialogues and cooperative agreements also exist among several Asian nations, some of them dealing with humanitarian affairs and other transnational issues.[15]

The Five-Power Defense Arrangement is another little-noticed Asian multilateral defense treaty. The FPDA was formed in 1971 by Great Britain, Australia, New Zealand, Singapore, and Malaysia as a consultative framework for the defense of the latter two countries. Member-nation defense ministers meet periodically; the FPDA also conducts periodic military exercises.[16]

One other multilateral forum has recently come into some prominence, primarily because of the attendance of the American president. The East Asia Summit has met six times, with President Barack Obama attending the most recent meeting, in Bali, Indonesia, in November 2011. The EAS may not lead to a permanent security infrastructure, but it has signaled strengthened U.S. interest in maritime Asia and intention to remain a strategic participant.

Several maritime cooperative programs are already in place. These include the Container Security Initiative, counterpiracy operations, joint participation in the North Pacific Coast Guard Forum, cooperative research-and-rescue activities, and ongoing Military Maritime Consultative Agreement (MMCA) talks. The PLAN's new hospital ship, first large amphibious ships, and first aircraft carrier now enable China to more actively participate in international humanitarian-relief operations, in company, if not jointly, with U.S. naval forces.

This includes the Trans-Pacific Partnership Agreement, a proposed trade agreement currently in negotiation among nine countries, including Australia, Brunei, Canada, Japan, Malaysia, New Zealand, Singapore, Vietnam, and the United States. Chile, Mexico, and Peru have also announced their intention to join the TPP. This is an ambitious plan that if completed will cover a market area almost half again as big as the European Union, heretofore the world's richest economic zone.[17]

The general international situation in Asia and the region's views of the United States, China, Japan, and India will have the most significant influence on the dynamics of regional security. This does not, however, lessen the importance of other individual nations; the Koreas' futures, for instance, are at least as undetermined as any other eventuality in Asia. Additionally, many lesser possible maritime conflicts not involving major states form a low noise level of disagreement among the region's nations.

UNITED STATES

While it may be argued that during and since the end of the Cold War the United States has furnished the defensive bulwark for Asia both to prosper economically and achieve general international stability, the Asian nations are advancing and Washington may be falling into a reactive position.

This is not a zero-sum situation but one that has changed Asia's international order. A new balance of power may be emerging in Asia, in which straightforward U.S. dominance will no longer prevail.

The United States remains the dominant maritime power in Asia and is moving to include multilateral support for its already substantial bilateral relationships. The U.S. plan in the 1930s for war with Japan, discussed in chapter 1, was based on the assumption that conflict would break out between the two countries, neither of which would have allies in the fight, because of "Japan's quest for national greatness by attempting to dominate the land, people, and resources of the Far East," which would require its navy to "expunge American power from its sea flank by depriving it of bases in the Philippine Islands and Guam." The United States, however, "regarded itself as the guardian of Western influence [favoring] self-determination of peoples and open international trade."[18]

This description of geopolitical assumptions in East Asia might well be applied to the current situation between China and the United States. It may not be accurate, and the conflict it preordains is certainly is not inevitable, but the assumption of its political and economic apposition exists in naval circles in both countries. It is a body of assumptions that must be overcome by more accurate perceptions of national interests and national security concerns in Washington and Beijing.

CHINA

China's economic and military rise has been the most significant post–Cold War change in Asia's maritime strategic picture. The PLAN seems roughly on schedule for its stated goal of deploying a state-of-the-art navy fully capable of open-ocean operations by 2050.[19] However, present PLAN platforms may accurately be described as no more than 50 percent "modern," a figure admittedly subjective but still useful.[20] This has been marked by dramatic increases in that country's navy and merchant fleet that are causing perturbations among the regions' other nations.

Some Chinese analysts are classifying India's Look East policy as "interference" in the South China Sea and associated issues, however, and as representing Indian strategic links with the United States and Japan. Hence, India's move to establish a presence east of Malacca is a "negative influence on the implementation of China's strategy of peaceful rise" and will "inescapably produce new uncertainties for solutions to the South China Sea issue."[21]

China by the end of the first decade of the twenty-first century had overcome thousands of years of relative insularity, resulting from its consistently continentalist security perspective. Even the early fifteenth-century voyages of Zheng He were an aberration; almost no Chinese emperor felt the need to extend China's power beyond its coastlines. When Great Britain's first envoy to imperial China, Lord McCartney, arrived in 1793, Emperor Qianlong replied to his appeal for trade dismissively, declaring, "We possess all things [and] have no use for your manufactures."[22]

Contrary to opinions that are too widespread in the United States, Chinese military modernization during the past quarter century has been relatively moderate. Naval modernization, in particular, has not exceeded the pace expected of a country with an economy growing as fast as has China's during that period.

The one exception has been the increase in conventionally powered submarines, a factor tied to a Taiwan scenario as the highest priority for the navy's operational readiness. These boats are designed primarily for regional operations, not the long-range cruising required for maintaining a constant presence in distant waters. That is the mission of nuclear-powered submarines, and China's remain noisy and few in number.

The PLAN has become a capable maritime force, and one buttressed by the increasingly numerous and capable coast guard–type organizations deployed by Beijing. But China is far from being a global or even extraregional naval power of significance. In fact, it is not clear that Beijing has made a decision to build such a navy.[23]

U.S.-Chinese Relations

A primary question for the future of maritime Asia—with 2025 offering a useful reference point in time and with Japan and India particularly important adjuncts to the calculus—is the relationship between the United States and China. Some basic assumptions will almost certainly underlie that future; these include economic growth, military modernization progress, domestic political tranquility, and national pride in each of the states.

Beijing still complains about the "century of humiliation," a period now more obviously than ever an aberration in China's very long history. Washington, meanwhile, is still recovering both from the end of the Cold War and the "war on terrorism" inappropriately declared in 2001. The first, although a victory, came at huge economic cost to the United States, while the latter wrought societal changes with still unknown effects.

Continued constructive peace, stability, and economic growth in the region will depend on whether Beijing and Washington reach a modus vivendi about their own and each other's roles on the region's waters. Cooperative steps are under way. The MMCA discussions have occurred regularly since 1998 but have produced little except recognition of the basic interpretative differences between Beijing and Washington regarding their purpose. However, the United States and China have signed an Agreement Concerning Maritime Search and Rescue Cooperation between the Bureau of Harbor Superintendency of the People's Republic of China and the United States Coast Guard.

The two nations have also established a U.S.-China Joint Liaison Group on Law Enforcement Cooperation, which administers an agreement "concerning cooperation in maritime immigration law enforcement," signed in 1999. This pact cites both the 1967 Status of Refugees protocol and the 1974 International Convention for the Safety of Life at Sea, as well as other international agreements, in cooperating "in combatting illicit traffic" of persons.[24]

PROSPECTS

While geography very rarely changes physically, a significant conceptual change by 2025 will be continuing development of the "Indo-Pacific" as the focus of maritime discussion and concerns in oceanic Asia. Consideration of vital national interests is unlikely to change, even if—as may safely be assumed—no rogue nation emerges capable of dominating the maritime commons or using them for aggressive purposes. These interests will include and even focus upon maintaining the security of the sea lines of communication—coastal, regional, and international. This will in turn ensure the development of navies capable of safeguarding the sea-lanes.

The relationship between China and the United States will remain the key determinant of international peace in Asian waters. A peaceful, constructive future is in both nations' interests, but neither may be willing to cede primacy to the other. That is, economic interests may well be overcome by national hubris. Conflict is not inevitable, but cooperation will be difficult to achieve.

Beijing will have to adjust to global power responsibilities, while Washington will have, finally, to adjust to the post–Cold War world without bipolarity or MAD. Neither of these adjustments seems in 2012 to be progressing at a rapid pace; the national security communities in both countries appear to suffer from bureaucratic inertia that is inhibiting change. Failure to adjust will significantly heighten the adversarial character of the relationship between China and the United States.

China continues to modernize its military, especially its navy. So have and are Japan, India, Australia, and almost every maritime nation in Asia. This modernization does not yet add up to a significant naval arms race, despite the attraction to submarines by several nations who appear to lack a strategic rationale for acquiring the boats.

A military power shift is yet to occur in Asia. The Western naval powers of Australia, Canada, New Zealand, the United Kingdom, and the United States (AUSCANNZUKUS) remain dominant in the Indo-Pacific when operating together. This grouping focuses on improving naval command, control, communications, and computer interoperability. It emphasizes joint and combined operations.

More to the point is a statement by then–Secretary of Defense Leon Panetta at the June 2012 Shangri La Dialogue in Singapore. His explanation of the U.S. rebalancing toward Asia was clear and direct: "Make no mistake—in a steady, deliberate, and sustainable way the United States military is rebalancing and bringing an enhanced capability development to this vital region." When it comes to the question of sustaining this capability, he noted, "We were there then, we are here now, and we will be here for the future."[25]

The PLA remains neither quantitatively nor qualitatively capable of seriously challenging the United States, or perhaps even Japan, now or in the near term. U.S. naval and economic power remains unmatched, as does its political and social attraction throughout the region.

One Australian commentator has spelled out three possible future U.S. strategies in the face of China's rise to global power. First, Washington can "resist China's challenge and try to preserve the status quo in Asia." Second, Washington "can step back from its dominant role in Asia, leaving China to attempt to establish hegemony." Third, the United States might accede to a larger role for China while "maintaining a strong presence of its own."[26] These are simplistic options but not without portent. The third option may well be the most viable for future peace and security in Asia, but it would require a degree of Sino-American cooperation and mutual respect perhaps novel in the histories of the two nations.

The current naval developments in the region evince elements of a naval arms race but lack the coherent maritime strategies that would make them dangerous to regional peace and security. Most telling will be whether American power and focus remain on the region and adjust themselves to continued Chinese maritime power in a way acceptable to both nations.

Notes

Introduction

1. The epigraph is from Amru bin al-'As, the Arab conqueror of Egypt, quoted by James Taylor, "Traditional Arab Sailing Ships" (lecture to the British-Yemeni Society, August 2003), *Al-Bab: An Open Door to the Arab World*, www.al-bab.com/bys/articles/taylor03.htm (accessed 29 June 2012).

2. "Maritime commons" is used to denote the world's oceans, without regard to specific bodies of water or national maritime territory. SLOCs, or sea lines of communication—sometimes called sea lanes of communication—refer to standard paths of ship movements on the world's oceans. For instance, a ship proceeding from San Francisco to Tokyo to Singapore to Umm Qasr is going to follow well-known, standard routes (SLOCs) across the seas.

3. Niall Ferguson, "The Decade the World Tilted East," *Financial Times*, 27 December 2009, www.ft.com/intl/cms/s/0/ac26eb9a-f30a-11de-a888–00144feab49a.html#axzz1v7gFpsHN (accessed 17 May 2012).

4. For instance, bad weather was nearly as serious a threat to merchant ships as were German U-boats in the North Atlantic during World War II (author's discussion with noted British naval historian Hedley P. Willmott, in 1994).

5. The best work on Zheng He is Edward L. Dreyer, *Zheng He: China and the Oceans in the Early Ming Dynasty, 1405–1433* (London: Longman, 2006).

6. Halford John Mackinder, *Democratic Ideals and Reality* (London: Constable, 1919); Nicholas Spykman, *America's Strategy in World Politics: The United States and the Balance of Power* (New York: Harcourt, Brace, 1942).

7. This massive energy project is discussed in Bernard D. Cole, *Sea Lanes and Pipelines: Energy Security in Asia* (Westport, Conn.: Praeger, 2008), 27–30.

8. See Victor Cha, *The Sinking of the* Cheonan (Washington, D.C.: Center for Strategic and International Studies [hereafter CSIS], 22 April 2010).

9. Data is from Sam Bateman, Joshua Ho, and Jane Chan, *Good Order at Sea in Southeast Asia* (Singapore: Rajaratnam School of International Studies [hereafter RSIS], April 2009), 9.

10. Distances may be found in U.S. National Imagery and Mapping Agency, *Distances between Ports,* Pub. 151, 10th ed. (Bethesda, Md., 1999).

11. "World Oil Transit Chokepoints," *U.S. Energy Information Administration (EIA),* 30 December 2011.

12. Henry Luce, "The American Century," editorial, *Life,* 17 February 1941.

13. Alfred Thayer Mahan, *The Influence of Sea Power upon History, 1660–1783* (repr., New York: Dover, 1987), is a modern edition of Mahan's original book, published in 1890 in Boston by Little, Brown. This discussion of Mahan's theories draws on the best modern Mahan scholar, Jon Tetsuro Sumida. See his *Inventing Strategy and Teaching Command: The Classic Works of Alfred Thayer Mahan Reconsidered* (Washington, D.C.: Woodrow Wilson Center Press, 1997). Sumida (page 1) quotes Paul M. Kennedy, *The Rise and Fall of British Naval Mastery* (London: A. Lane, 1976).

14. Sumida, *Inventing Strategy and Teaching Command,* 27.

15. Mahan, *The Influence of Sea Power upon the French Revolution and Empire, 1793–1812* (Boston: Little, Brown, 1892), 141.

16. The 1805 battle of Trafalgar and that of Midway in 1942 may be the two most momentous sea battles in modern history, but France fought on for ten years after Trafalgar and Japan for more than three years after Midway.

17. Corbett's major work is *Some Principles of Maritime Strategy* (London: Longmans, Green, 1911; Annapolis, Md.: Naval Institute Press, 1988).

18. Ibid., 336, in the modern edition.

19. J. S. Wylie, *Military Strategy* (New Brunswick, N.J.: Rutgers University Press, 1967; Annapolis, Md.: Naval Institute Press, 1989), 125. Also see p. xxvi in the introduction, by John B. Hattendorf, citing Wylie's "idea that the purpose of sea power is to project control over the land."

20. See Clay Blair, *Silent Victory: The U.S. Submarine War against Japan* (New York: J. B. Lippincott, 1975), and *Hitler's U-Boat War: The Hunters, 1939–1942* (New York: Random House, 1996).

21. Donald C. Evans and Mark R. Peattie, *Kaigun: Strategy, Tactics, and Technology in the Imperial Japanese Navy, 1887–1941* (Annapolis, Md.: Naval Institute Press, 1997), is the most complete book on its subject; losses to U.S. submarines are discussed on 496.

22. Karl von Clausewitz, *On War,* ed. and trans. Michael Howard and Peter Paret (Princeton, N.J.: Princeton University Press, 1976), ignores the maritime arena, but its principles are so immutable as to define the tenets of warfare in all elements.

23. Corbett, *Some Principles of Maritime Strategy,* xvii, 11. As Sumida, *Inventing Strategy and Teaching Command,* 44, points out, Mahan did not advocate battle for battle's sake, however, insisting that a battle should be fought only for an important strategic objective.

24. Mahan, *Influence of Seapower upon the French Revolution and Empire*, i, v.
25. Burke is quoted in David Alan Rosenberg, "Process: The Realities of Formulating Modern Naval Strategy," in *Mahan Is Not Enough: The Proceedings of a Conference on the Works of Sir Julian Corbett and Admiral Sir Herbert Richmond*, ed. James Goldrick and John B. Hattendorf (Newport, R.I.: Naval War College Press, 1993), 144. The second quotation is by Rosenberg himself, who also provides, 150–72, a list of seventeen "kinds of information" needed to "understand the modern naval strategy-making process." As individual attributes these are beyond the scope of this book, emphasizing personnel, financial, administrative, organizational, and political factors.
26. Geoffrey Till, *Asia Rising and the Maritime Decline of the West: A Review of the Issues*, RSIS Working Paper 205 (Singapore: RSIS, 29 July 2010), 5.
27. Identifying aircraft generations is somewhat subjective. Commonly accepted fourth-generation aircraft include the U.S. F-15, Russian Su-27, and Chinese J-11. The U.S. F-22 is a fifth-generation aircraft as is, arguably, the Chinese J-20.

Chapter 1. Setting the Scene

1. Edward L. Dreyer, "The Poyang Campaign 1363: Inland Naval Warfare in the Founding of the Ming Dynasty," in *Chinese Ways of Warfare*, ed. Frank A. Kierman Jr. and John K. Fairbank (Cambridge, Mass.: Harvard University Press, 1974).
2. Zheng He did not, however, discover America, as British author and retired Royal Navy officer Gavin Menzies asserts in his book, *1421: The Year China Discovered the World* (2002), which is fanciful speculation, not history.
3. Dreyer, "Poyang Campaign 1363,"186.
4. Quoted in "The Chinese Revolution and the Chinese Communist Party," in *Selected Works of Mao Tse-tung* (Beijing, 1970 ed.), 51.
5. Immanuel C. Y. Hsu, *The Rise of Modern China* (New York: Oxford University Press, 1970), 405.
6. This paragraph draws on Evans and Peattie, *Kaigun*, epilogue.
7. Sadao Asada, *From Mahan to Pearl Harbor: The Imperial Japanese Navy and the United States* (Annapolis, Md.: Naval Institute Press, 2006), 287.
8. The definitive work on this war plan is Edward S. Miller, *War Plan Orange: The U.S. Strategy to Defeat Japan* (Annapolis, Md.: Naval Institute Press, 1991). Nimitz's opinion about the completeness of War Plan Orange is, curiously, split between pages 2 and 356. Other "color plans" were developed for Germany (Black), Mexico (Green), and Great Britain (Red).
9. Wayne Hughes, "Naval Operations: A Close Look at the Operational Level of War at Sea," *Naval War College Review* 65, no. 3 (Summer 2012): 25.
10. The best biography of Lejeune is Merrill Bartlett, *Lejeune: A Marine's Life, 1867–1942* (Annapolis, Md.: Naval Institute Press, 1996). The advanced-bases concept is discussed on p. 194.

11. See Brian M. Linn, *Guardians of Empire: The U.S. Army and the Pacific, 1902–1940* (Chapel Hill: University of North Carolina Press, 1999) The fact that Gen. (Field Marshal, in the Philippine army) Douglas MacArthur, commander of U.S. and Philippine forces, allowed his forces to be surprised by the Japanese attack, nine hours after that on Pearl Harbor, was a worse disgrace than the 7 December attack, but his political stature enabled him to escape the fate of the Pearl Harbor commanders, Adm. Husband E. Kimmel and Gen. Walter C. Short.

12. The political-military situation in Japan is discussed in Robert J. C. Butow, *Tojo and the Coming of the War* (1969), and his *Japan's Decision to Surrender* (1954), both Palo Alto, Calif.: Stanford University Press.

13. Data in this section are from United Nations, *Review of Maritime Transport: 2011*, Conference on Trade and Development Report, UNCTAD/RMT/2011 (New York, 2011). The report for 2012 reports that in 2011 the merchant fleet expanded by 10 percent in tonnage, while world trade expanded 4 percent; Alaric Nightingale, "Shipping Bears Ascendant," *Bloomberg*, 25 June 2012.

14. Vice Adm. Ray Griggs, "The Navy's Role in the Maritime Century" (address to the Lowy Institute, Sydney, Australia, 17 August 2012), www.lowyinstitute .org/events/distinguished-apekers-series-navy-maritime-century-vice-admiral-griggs (accessed 22 August 2012)

15. Anna Bowden and Shikha Basnet, *Economic Cost of Somali Piracy 2011*, Working Paper (n.p.: One Earth Future Foundation, 2012).

Chapter 2. The United States

1. Article 1, section 8, www.usconstitution.net/xconst_A1Sec8.html (accessed 15 April 2012).

2. See Craig Symonds, *The Civil War at Sea: Reflections on the Civil War Era* (Santa Barbara, Calif.: ABC Clio, 2009).

3. The best description of this process is in Miller, *War Plan Orange*. The U.S. Navy conducted over three hundred war games at Newport between 1919 and 1940. It also carried out a series of exercises—"fleet problems"—during the 1920s and 1930s that were pathbreaking events, both strategically and operationally; see Albert A. Nofi, *To Train the Fleet for War: The U.S. Navy Fleet Problems, 1923–1940* (Newport, R.I.: Naval War College Press, 2010).

4. The most complete discussions of the development of this strategy are John B. Hattendorf, *The Evolution of the U.S. Navy's Maritime Strategy, 1977–1986*, Newport Paper 19 (Newport, R.I.: Naval War College Press, 2004), and Hattendorf and Peter Swartz, *U.S. Naval Strategy in the 1980s: Selected Documents*, Newport Paper 33 (Newport, R.I.: Naval War College Press, 2008).

5. Available at www.fas.org/man/docs/nssr-98.pdf (accessed 7 March 2012).

6. This document may be found at www.defense.gov/news/Defense_Strategic_ Guidance.pdf (accessed 25 August 2012).

7. See, for instance, Stewart M. Patrick, "Obama's Plan for America's Pacific Century," *Atlantic Online,* 11 November 2011. Clinton is quoted in Mike O'Sullivan, "Clinton: 21st Century Will Focus on Asia-Pacific," *VOA News,* 9 November 2011; and Tom Donilon, "America Is Back in the Pacific and Will Uphold the Rules," *Financial Times,* 27 November 2011, 9.

8. *Sustaining U.S. Global Leadership: Priorities for 21st Century Defense* (Washington, D.C., January 2012), 4. Panetta spoke at a press conference on 26 January 2012; see www.defense.gov/Transcripts/Transcript.aspx? TranscriptID=4962 (accessed 7 March 2012).

9. Samuel P. Huntington, "National Policy and the Transoceanic Navy," Naval Institute *Proceedings* 80, no. 5 (May 1954).

10. Stansfield Turner, "Missions of the U.S. Navy," *Naval War College Review* 26, no. 5 (March/April 1974): 2–17.

11. The 1986 Maritime Strategy was published as a Naval Institute *Proceedings* supplement in January 1986, 41–47.

12. *From the Sea* is at www.dtic.mil/jv2010/navy/b014.pdf (accessed 7 March 2012).

13. *Forward . . . from the Sea* is at www.dtic.mil/jv2010/navy/b014.pdf (accessed 11 November 2011).

14. Clark describes "Seapower 21" in his "Seapower 21: Projecting Decisive Joint Capabilities," Naval Institute *Proceedings* (October 2002), www .navy.mil/navydata/cno/Proceedings.html (accessed 11 November 2011).

15. Speech at *Government Executive Magazine* Leadership Breakfast, Washington, D.C., 1 May 2007, at www.navy.mil/navydata/leadership/ quotes.asp?q=11&c=2 (accessed 8 April 2012). Mullen later stated, "We will be prepared to support and defend our freedom of navigation and access to the global commons. Our partners and allies are our greatest strategic asset." (Quoted in Stephanie Hszieh, George Galdorisi, Terry McKearney, and Darren Sutton, "Networking the Global Maritime Partnership," *Naval War College Review* 65, no. 2 [Spring 2012]: 11–29.)

16. Speech to the World Affairs Council, Pittsburgh (19 May 2006), www .navy.mil/navydata/leadership/quotes.asp?q=11&c=2 (accessed 8 April 2012).

17. The 2005 National Strategy for Maritime Security is at *U.S. Department of Homeland Security,* www.dhs.gov/. Also see "Aircraft Carriers: Expanding America's Reach," Navy Office of Information *Rhumb Lines,* 16 November 2010.

18. The 2007 Cooperative Strategy is described at "Cooperative Strategy for 2007," www.navy.mil/. The Commandant of the Marine Corps became a member of the Joint Chiefs of Staff in 1978.

19. John B. Hattendorf, "The United States Navy in the Twenty-First Century: Thoughts on Naval Theory, Strategic Constraints, and Opportunities," *Mariner's Mirror* 97, no. 1 (February 2011): 289.

20. Discussed in *Maritime Stability Operations,* MCIP 3-33.-2/NWP 3-07/ COMDTINST M3120.11 (Washington, D.C.: Department of the Navy and U.S. Coast Guard, 2011).

21. Gary Roughead, "CNO Guidance for 2011," www.navy.mil, October 2010. Also, senior U.S. naval officer, interview with author, September 2011; this is a lower number than the 17,000 reported in December 2009 in the author's conversation with a senior U.S. naval officer.

22. Explained in Mark A. Campbell, John Krempasky, and Michael Bosworth, "A Persistent, Effective, and Affordable Global Fleet Station Concept," American Society of Naval Engineers *Naval Engineers Journal,* no. 4. (2012): 51–66.

23. "Pacific Partnership 2010 Accomplishments," *Rhumb Lines,* 6 October 2010; U.S. Navy Office of Information, "USS *Preble* Conducts Fisheries Patrol," NNS110307–08, 3 July 2011, www.uscarriers.net/ddg88history .htm (accessed 7 March 2010).

24. Cited in Jeremy Black, *Naval Power* (London: Palgrave, 2009), 204.

25. Ronald O'Rourke, *Navy Ford (CVN-78) Class Aircraft Carrier Program: Background and Issues for Congress* RS-20643 (Washington, D.C.: Congressionsl Research Service, 10 December 2012). Tony Capaccio, "Navy Delays Carrier's Combat Tests," *Business Week,* 9 August 2012, gives $14.13 billion as the carrier's cost.

26. Ronald O'Rourke, *Navy Force Structure and Shipbuilding Plans: Background and Issues for Congress,* RL 2665 (Washington, D.C.: Congressional Research Service, 17 August 2010), reports on the insufficiency of the SCN (shipbuilding) fund by even the Navy's own estimates to achieve the 313-ship level. Also see the critique *An Analysis of the Navy's Fiscal Year 2013 Shipbuilding Plan* (Washington, D.C.: Congressional Budget Office July 2011) and the summary in O'Rourke's most recent CRS report, *Navy Force Structure and Shipbuilding Plans: Background and Issues for Congress* (Washington, D.C.: Congressional Research Service, 21 June 2012). The link of increased cost and the "pivot" to Asia is discussed in Michael C. Horowitz, *How Defense Austerity Will Test U.S. Strategy in Asia,* NBR Analysis Brief (Seattle, Wash.: National Bureau of Asian Research, 7 August 2012).

27. Jonathan Greenert, *U.S. Navy Program Guide 2012: Meeting Today's Challenges and Preparing for the Future* (Washington, D.C.: Department of the Navy, 2012). Greenert then issued a "CNO's Navigation Plan, 2012–2017," in which he provides a succinct but detailed and comprehensive list of his goals and objectives for his tour as CNO, under the headings "warfighting first, operate forward, and be ready."

28. Eric C. Jones and Joseph E. Vorbach III, "The Maritime Domain Awareness Conundrum," U.S. Naval Institute *Proceedings* 137/10/1,304 (October 2011): 29.

29. "Multi-Service Office to Advance Air-Sea Battle Concept," U.S. Department of Defense News Release 943–11, 9 November 2011. Author's discussion with USN flag officer and USN and USAF 0-6 (captain and colonel) officers.

30. Author's discussion with a senior U.S. Navy officer.

31. Quoted in "Release of the Joint Operational Concept (JOAC)," U.S. Department of Defense News Release, 17 January 2012.

32. Quoted in Donna Miles, "Locklear: Pacom's Priorities Reflect New Strategic Guidance," American Forces Press Service, 18 May 2012.

33. See Ronald Reagan, "Statement on United States Oceans Policy," 10 March 1983, in *Public Papers of Ronald Reagan,* American Reference Library, AN: 9FVPPRWR030254; and Will Rogers, *Security at Sea: The Case for Ratifying the Law of the Sea Convention,* Policy Brief (Washington, D.C.: Center for a New American Security, April 2012).

34. Linda Bentley, "Law of the Sea Treaty Dead in the Water," *Phoenix Examiner,* 19 July 2012, www.examiner.com/article/law-of-the-sea-treaty-dead-the-water (accessed 2 August 2012). The arguments against the United States ratifying the UNCLOS are presented in Daniel Blumenthal and Michael Mazza, "Why to Forget UNCLOS," *Diplomat,* 17 February 2012.

35. Ray Mabus, "Remarks" ("Week of Valor" Veterans Job Fair Luncheon, Jacksonville, Fla., 28 February 2012).

36. Greenert, *U.S. Navy Program Guide 2012,* 3–4.

37. Statement of Admiral Jonathan Greenert Before the Congress on FY2013 Department of Navy Posture (March 2012), at: http://www.navy.mil/cno/120316_PS.pdf (accessed 10 May 2013).

38. Chua Chin Hon, "US Reaffirms Commitment to Asia-Pacific," *Straits-Times* (Singapore), 5 April 2012, reports the ships being homeported in Singapore. Also see "US to Deploy LCS in Singapore in 2012," *Xinhua,* 3 June 2012, news.xinhuanet.com/english/world/2012-06/02/c_131627418.htm (accessed 3 March 2013), which is more cautious, quoting the Singapore defense minister as declaring that his government "agrees in principle" with the LCS homeporting "on a rotational basis." The Australian training facility is reported in Anna Murline, "US Training Base in Australia Is All about the Rise of China," *Christian Science Monitor,* 16 November 2011, but like almost all reports, her article errs in calling the proposed training facility a "base." Phil Stewart and Paul Eckert, "No Big U.S. Naval Buildup in Asia, Top Officer Says," Reuters, 10 January 2012.

39. Christopher P. Cavas, "8 LCSs Could Be Based in Gulf, Says U.S. Navy Undersecretary," *Defense News,* 21 May 2012. A comprehensive examination of possible future U.S. Navy strength in Asia is provided in *U.S. Force Posture Strategy in the Asia Pacific Region: An Independent Assessment* (Washington, D.C.: Center for Strategic and International Studies, July 2012).

Chapter 3. Japan

1. Japan's military is designated as comprising "self-defense forces," as a result of its 1950 peace treaty. The Japanese Ministry of Defense achieved cabinet status only in 2007; attempts by the services to resume more traditional titles—such as navy, army (instead of the Japan Ground Self-Defense Force, or JGSDF), and air force (Japan Air Self-Defense Force, or JASDF) have been

unsuccessful. The Japan Coast Guard is not a Defense Ministry organization but reports to the Ministry of Land, Infrastructure, Transport, and Tourism.

2. See Hisani Misaki, "Japanese Shipbuilders Worry about Dwindling Backlog," *Journal of Commerce*, 20 January 2012. Japan lost its position as the world's leading builder of commercial ships to South Korea in 2004; since then, China has surpassed both nations. The United States and European Union countries remain the world leaders in building military vessels, but China is making significant strides in this area.

3. Fourth-generation war is discussed in T. X. Hammes, *The Sling and the Stone: War in the 21st Century* (St. Paul, Minn.: Zenith, 2006).

4. Found at *Ministry of Defense*, www.mod.go.jp/e/d_act/d_policy/dp02.html (accessed 4 May 2012).

5. This historical discussion draws on the excellent Bhubhindar Singh and Philip Shetler-Jones, *Japan's New Security Imperative: The Function of Globalization*, RSIS Working Paper 209 (Singapore: RSIS, 11 October 2010).

6. The Nixon Doctrine may be found at John G. Keilers, "The Nixon Doctrine and Vietnamization," Army.mil, 29 June 2007, www.army.mil/article/3867/nixon-doctrine-and-vietnamization/ (accessed 30 April 2012). The Nixon-Sato communiqué is at *Archive*, www.niraikanai.wwma.net/pages/archive/sato69.html (accessed 30 April 2012).

7. "The Japan-U.S. Joint Declaration on Security, 1996," may be found at *Ministry of Foreign Affairs of Japan*, www.mofa.go.jp/region/n-america/us/security/security.html (accessed 30 April 2012).

8. One subsidiary effect of repeated use of this phrase is that it leads many analysts and government officials in Taipei to the conclusion that Japan and the United States both would come to Taiwan's assistance in the event that China used military force against the island. I frequently have heard references to "our American and Japanese allies" from senior civilian and military officials in Taiwan over the past decade.

9. See various U.S. and Japanese statements at the website of the Japanese embassy in the United States, *Embassy of Japan: Washington, D.C.*, www.us.emb-japan.go.jp/english/html/japanus/japanusoverview.htm (accessed 30 April 2012).

10. My conversation with a senior USN officer. Also see Jung Nam-ku, Park Byung-soo, and Ha Eo-young, "Japan to Send Destroyers to China's Doorstep," *Hankoryeh*, 31 May 2012, english.hani.co.kr/arti/english_edition/e_international/535484.html (accessed 7 June 2012).

11. Ken Jimbo, *Japan Should Build ASEAN's Security Capacity*, Japan Institute of International Affairs Commentary 150 (n.p., 29 May 2012). Richard J. Samuels, "New Fighting Power?" *International Security* 32, no. 3 (Winter 2007/08), is the definitive excellent article in English on the JCG.

12. My conversation with the responsible USN and JMSDF officers, 1987. The point at which the thousand nautical miles was to be measured was not stipulated in the formal agreement, but the naval officers who first reached agreement measured from the joint naval base at Yokosuka, which means the thousand nautical miles ended just short of the Luzon Strait, between Taiwan and the Philippines.

13. Naolo Sajima and Kyoichi Tachikawa, *Japanese Sea Power: A Maritime Nation's Struggle for Identity* (Canberra, ACT, Australia: Sea Power Centre, 2009): 83.

14. A useful, if pro–United States, discussion of JMSDF refueling data is at *Information Dissemination,* 6 October 2007, www.information dissemination.net/2007/10/jmsdf-refueling-mission-debate.html (accessed 27 April 2012). The Japanese Ministry of Defense position in favor of continuing these deployments (21 April 2006) is at, "Japan Decides to Continue to Dispatch JMSDF Vessels to the Indian Ocean in Order to Support International Efforts to Fight against Terrorism (Extension of the Basic Plan of the Anti-Terrorism Special Measures Law," at *Ministry of Foreign Affairs of Japan,* www.mofa.go.jp/policy/terrorism/measure0604.html (accessed 27 April 2012). The end of the refueling mission was announced in January 2010; see Japan Orders End of Refueling Mission in Indian Ocean," *China View,* 15 January 2010.

15. "SDF Readies Overseas Base in Djibouti: 1st Outpost Abroad to Fight Piracy," *Yomiuri Shimbun,* 29 May 2011.

16. *NIDS China Security Report 2011* (Tokyo: National Institute for Defense Studies, n.d.): executive summary, 1.

17. Ibid., 4. Also see Chico Harlan, "New Japanese Defense Plan Emphasizes Threat of China," *Washington Post,* 12 December 2010, www.washington post.com/wp-dyn/content/article/2010/12/12/AR2010121203790.html (accessed 29 April 2012).

18. For the guidelines, Masako Toki, "Japanese Defense Guidelines: New Conventional Strategy, Same Old Nuclear Dilemma," *NTI,* 1 March 2011, www.nti.org/analysis/articles/japans-defense-guidelines/ (accessed 29 April 2010). Also see Yoji, Koda. "A New Carrier Race? Strategy, Force Planning, and JS *Hyuga,*" *Naval War College Review* 64, no. 3 (Summer 2011): 33.

19. Yuka Hayashi, "Japan to Boost Defense in Pacific, Minister Says," *Wall Street Journal,* 26 June 2012, A11; my interview with senior JMSDF officer, September 2011. Also see U.S. Department of State, *Joint Statement of the Security Consultative Committee* (Washington, D.C., 26 April 2012).

20. "Japan, U.S., Australia to Strengthen Unity with Pacific Island Nations with Eye on Rising China," *Yomiuri,* 25 May 2012: 2. China is not mentioned, however, in the official report of this meeting, "The Sixth Pacific Islands Leaders Meeting (PALM 6) Okinawa 'Kizuna' Declaration," n.d., *Ministry of Foreign Affairs of Japan,* www.mofa.go.jp/region/asia-paci/palm/palm6/kizuna_en.html (accessed 31 May 2012).

21. Korean-Japanese discussions were ongoing in June 2012 about a possible military treaty between the two countries. Choe Hang-Hun, "South Korea to Sign Military Pact with Japan," *New York Times,* 29 June 2012, www .nytimes.com/2012/06/29/world/asia/south-korea-to-sign-historic-military-pact-with-japan.html (accessed 29 June 2012); my discussions with retired and active-duty JMSDF officers, 2002–2011.

22. See Ernest Z. Bower and Michael J. Green, *U.S.-Japan-ASEAN Trilateral Strategic Dialogue* (Maui, Hawaii: Center for Strategic and International Studies, 7 January 2011).

23. Takashi Oshima and Koichi Furuya, "Japan Dives into South China Sea Flap with China," *Asahi Shimbun,* 6 November 2011.

24. Cited in "Japan, Vietnam Sign Memo on Defense Cooperation Enhancement," *Mainichi,* 25 October 2011; Nane Kurashiga, "Japan, Vietnam Agree on Defense Cooperation," *Asahi Shimbun,* 25 October 2011. Also see "Changing World 2012: Japan and East Asia/Nations Face Off beneath the Waves," *Yomiuri Shimbun,* 24 January 2012, for a report of possible Japanese-Vietnamese naval cooperation; "China's Brooding 'Dragons' Complicate Standoffs at Sea," *Japan Times,* 12 June 2012.

25. "The Signing of the Japan-Australia Acquisition and Cross-Servicing Agreement," *Ministry of Foreign Affairs of Japan,* 19 May 2010, www .mofa.go.jp/announce/announce/2010/5/0519_02.html (accessed 2 August 2012).

26. Subhash Kapila, *Japan-Australia Defense Agreement: Perspectives,* South Asia Analysis Group Paper 2191 (Noida, India, 4 February 2007), calls the 2007 agreement "a Mutual Security Pact for all practical purposes" and "a strategic landmark." The 2010 meeting is reported in Malcolm Cook and Thomas S. Wilkins, *Australia and Japan: Allies in Partnership,* Asia Pacific Bulletin 101 (Honolulu: East-West Center, 17 March 2011).

27. For a discussion of this disaster, see www.iaea.org/newscenter/news/tsunami update01.html (accessed 4 May 2012).

28. The home islands are Kyushu, Shikoku, Honshu, and Hokkaido.

29. See the discussion in Cook and Wilkins, *Australia and Japan.*

30. Kyle Mizokami, *ASDF Intercepts vs. China at Five Year High* (n.p.: Japan Security Watch: New Pacific Institute, 28 December 2010).

31. "Japan Warns of China's Growing Naval Muscle," Agence France-Presse, 2 August 2011.

32. See "Japan Plans Okinawa Base to Keep Watch on China," WantChinaTimes kl, 22 August 2011, and Jonathan Manthorpe, "Japan Boosts Defense of Outer Islands to Deter China," *Vancouver Sun,* 26 April 2012. Satoshi Morimoto, "Japan Must Make Efforts to Defend Itself in Line with Air-Sea Battle," *Sankei Shimbun,* 7 December 2011, offers a particularly strong view of a threatening China that "is attempting to spread out its area denial capabilities beyond the first island chain to the second island chain" while conducting "aggressive [military] activities."

33. James F. Giblin, "National Strategies and Japan's Northern Territories," *Naval War College Review* 40, no. 4 (Winter 1987): 53–68, remains a useful description of this dispute. A more recent account is Kazuhiko Togo, *Japan's Territorial Problem* (Seattle, Wash.: National Bureau of Asian Research, 8 May 2012).

34. Tetsuo Kotani, *Freedom of Navigation and the US-Japan Alliance: Addressing the Threat of Legal Warfare*, U.S.-Japan Papers (Tokyo: Japan Center for International Exchange, December 2011): 2. Kotani continues that "the security of this maritime lifeline is a primary mission of the Japan Maritime Self-Defense Force."

35. See Timothy Walton, *China's Three Warfares*, Delex Special Report 3 (Herndon, Va.: Delex Systems, Inc., 18 January 2012). Iran is also perceived as pursuing "legal warfare" in attempting to impose national claims over international waters.

36. Cited in Samuels, "New Fighting Power?," 86.

37. Ibid., 88.

38. Ibid., 96. This incident occurred roughly equidistant between Japan and China but elicited a relatively mild protest from Beijing.

39. JDC spokesman, December 2005, quoted in ibid., 101.

40. Euan Graham, *Japan's Sea Lane Security, 1940–2004* (New York: Routledge, 2006): 150.

41. Ibid., 154; Elliot Brennan, "Rising Tide of Conflict in the South China Sea," *Asia Times*, 3 March 2012.

42. *Defense Budget and Programs of Japan: Overview of FY2012 Budget* (Tokyo: Ministry of Defense, n.d.), www.mod.go.jp/e/d_budget/pdf/240301 .pdf (accessed 12 August 2012).

43. "MSDF 16-Sub Fleet to Get Six More to Up Presence," *Japan Times Online*, 21 October 2010. The number of submarines is likely to end up at sixteen, since Japan's plan apparently is to decommission older boats as new ones join the fleet; interview with senior U.S. submariner.

44. Zhang Haizhou and Zhang Chunyan, "Japan Joins Elite Aircraft Carrier Club," *China Daily*, 9 March 2011, points out that Japan, a leader in maritime aviation in the early twentieth century, is deploying carriers for the first time since 1945.

45. Mari Yamaguchi, "Japan to Continue Paying $2 Billion for US Troops," *Washington Post*, 14 December 2010.

46. Quoted in "Government Defines Emergencies in Surrounding Areas," *Yomiuri Shimbun*, 27 April 1998. Also see "Lower House Passes Guideline Bills," Foreign Press Center–Japan, 7 May 1999. More recently, the JMSDF commander noted that this force's previously exclusive defensive missions had been "adapted . . . to the changing global security environment," with an emphasis on "effective deterrence and response." See Adm. Katsutoshi Kawano, "Japan Maritime Self-Defense Force," in "The Commanders Respond," U.S. Naval Institute *Proceedings* 139/3/1,321 (March 2013), 22–23.

47. JCG officers apparently consider their service to be Japan's first line of defense and express disdain for their JMSDF counterparts; my interviews with senior JCG and JMSDF officers, 2005, 2009.

48. I am indebted to Paul Giarra for this observation.

Chapter 4. North Asia

1. Used by P. T. Etherton, *The Cockpit of Asia* (New York: Frederick A. Stokes, 1932), to describe the imbroglio in Manchuria.

2. *Adjusting Course: A Naval Strategy for Canada* (Ottawa: Canada Communications Group, 1997); Royal Canadian Navy, *Leadmark: The Navy's Strategy for 2020,* Ottawa, 6 August 2002.

3. See the short but interesting article, "Canada Integrating Maritime Capabilities," United Press International, 30 March 2011.

4. Erin McCracen, "HMCS *Victoria* Returns to Sea," *Victoria News,* 19 April 2011), and Andrew Vaughan, "Canada's Stuck with Second-Hand Subs until 2030, Navy Says," *Canadian Press,* 27 February 2012. Future fleet composition is discussed by the navy commander, Vice Adm. Paul Maddison, "The Commanders Respond," U.S. Naval Institute *Proceedings* 139/3/1,321 (March 2013): 18.

5. "Canada Deploys HMCS *Charlottetown* to Arabian Sea Region," *Defence Professionals,* 26 April 2012, www.defpro.com/news/details/34704/ (accessed 25 May 2012).

6. Paul Richardson, *Russia in the Asia-Pacific: Between Integration and Geopolitics,* Asia Pacific Bulletin 150 (Washington, D.C.: East-West Center, 16 February 2012).

7. Cited in Rens Lee, "The Far East between Russia, China, and America," *FPRI E-Notes,* July 2012.

8. Gorshkov wrote two important books: *Red Star Rising at Sea* and *The Seapower of the State.*

9. Central Intelligence Agency, *Soviet Naval Strategy and Programs through the 1990s,* National Intelligence Estimate 11–15–82 (Washington, D.C., March 1983), 5.

10. V. Dotsenko, "Soviet Art of Naval Warfare in the Postwar Period," *Morskoy Sbornik,* no. 7 (1989): 26.

11. *Military Doctrine of the Russian Federation* (Moscow, 5 February 2010). See "Russia to Send New Anti-Piracy Force to Gulf of Aden," RIA Novosti, 28 March 2012, which notes the latest in a series of deployments that began in 2008.

12. This discussion is based on the eighteen-page *Maritime Doctrine of Russian Federation 2020,* Pr-1387, approved by President of the Russian Federation Vladimir Putin (Moscow, 27 July 2001), 2ff.

13. Alexander Muraviev, *Russian Naval Power in the Pacific: Today and Tomorrow,* Working Paper 15 (Canberra, ACT, Australia Sea Power Center, 2003), 4–5.

14. This discussion draws on Thomas R. Fedyszyn, "Renaissance of the Russian Navy?" U.S. Naval Institute *Proceedings* 138/3/1,309 (March 2012): 30–35.

15. Miles Yu, "Inside China: China, Russia to Hold Drill near Korea," *Washington Times*, 18 April 2012. Other reports lower Russian participation to three or four ships; see "Sino-Russian Drills Enter Live-Fire Stage," Xinhua, 26 April 2012. Despite these exercises, Moscow has dramatically reduced arms sales to China, making no significant transaction since November 2007; see, for instance, "Russia Scales Back Arms Sales to China," WantChinaTimes .com 17 January 2012, which lists "the top five buyers of Russian weapons systems" as India, Venezuela, Algeria, Vietnam, and Syria.

16. "Russian Naval Developments in the Far East" (paper presented at Conference on Asian Navies, Center for Naval Analyses, Alexandria, Virginia, 9 August 2012).

17. Muraviev, *Russian Naval Power in the Pacific*, 47.

18. Dmitri Trenin, *True Partners? How Russia and China See Each Other* (London: Center for European Reform, February 2012), 3. For additional unfulfilled Russian naval ambitions, see Ilya Kramnik, "The Russian Navy Participates in Vostok-2010 Military Exercises," RIA Novosti, 7 July 2010.

19. Thomas Nilsen, "Russia to More than Double Number of New SSBNs," *Barents Observer*, 20 September 2011; Nilsen, "New Subs Made of Old Spare Parts," *Barents Observer*, 27 October 2011; Nilsen, "Dozens of Major Flaws on Newest Submarine," *Barents Observer*, 9 November 2011 (which shows a very disturbed-looking Vladimir Putin poking a finger into the chest of a shipyard official). Another report noted that a sister ship of *Kursk*, the Oscar II–class boat that sank in 2001, was in a yard more than five years "for emergency repairs" and to recore its nuclear reactors; Nilsen, "*Kursk*'s Sister Ship Returns to Service," *Barents Observer*, 7 November 2011.

20. See, for instance, Vladimir Radyuhin, "Russia Sets Up Arctic Forces," *Hindu*, 1 July 2011; Alexey Druzhinin, "Russia to Build Up Submarine Task Force along Northern Sea Route," RIA Novosti, 11 August 2011, en.ria .ru/russia/20111108/168513774.html; and Trude Pettersen, "Russia Sets Up New Arctic Border Posts," *Barents Observer*, 16 April 2012.

21. Aleksy Kudenko, "State-of-the-Art Re-armament for Kuril Islands," RIA Novosti, 12 October 2011, gives 2015 as the completion date for this modernization. Also see "Russia to Deploy Cruise Missiles on Kuril Islands," Xinhua, 2 March 2011, and "Japan Slams Russian Military Build-Up on Islands," Agency France-Presse, 2 March 2011. One interesting sidelight is provided by "Japan Protests over Korean Builders on Kuril Islands," *Chosun Ibo*, 1 June 2012, english.chosun.com/site/data/html_ dir/2012/06/01/2012060101228.html (accessed 06 June 2012).

22. For instance, Vladimir Petrov, "Medvedev Orders Construction of Aircraft Carriers for Russian Navy," *Jane's Defense Weekly*, 14 October 2008, but also see "No New Russian Aircraft Carriers until 2020," Xinhua, 18 November 2011), and "Russia Halts Aircraft Carriers Building," United Press International, 10 December 2010, www.upi.com/Business_News/

Security-Industry/2010/12/10/Russia-halts-aircraft-carriers-building/UPI-38401292018235/ (accessed 27 May 2012).

23. Katerzinya Zisk, "Russia's Naval Ambitions: Driving Forces and Constraints," in *Twenty-First Century Seapower: Cooperation and Conflict at Sea,* ed. Peter Dutton, Robert Ross, and Oystein Tusnjo, (London: Routledge, 2012), 212, 215.

24. Hazel Smith, *North Korean Shipping: A Potential for WMD Proliferation?* Analysis from the East-West Center 87 (Honolulu, February 2009).

25. Chris Buckley, "China's Li Prods North Korea on Improving Regional Ties," Reuter's, 23 October 2010.

26. "Annual Defense Report for 2011," *Jane's Defense Weekly,* 14 December 2011, 39.

27. Nack Hoon Han, *South Korea's Defense Reforms: Impact on the Navy,* RSIS Commentary 183/2011 (Singapore: RSIS, 12 December 2011).

28. "Korea Must Get Tough on Illegal Chinese Fishing," *Chosun Ilbo,* 18 November 2011.

29. Euan Graham, *South Korea's Maritime Challenges: Between a Rock and a Hard Base,* RSIS Commentary 063/2012 (Singapore: RSIS, 11 April 2012).

30. Mingi Hyun, "South Korea's Blue-Water Ambitions," *Diplomat,* 18 November 2011.

31. "KSS-II: Korea Orders Six More U-214 AIP Submarines," *Defense Industry Daily,* 28 July 2010.

32. Dong-Joon Park and Danielle Chubb, "Why Dokdo Matters to Korea," *Diplomat,* 17 August 2011, describes Dokdo as the symbol of Korean "national identity" and anti-Japanese feeling. This "in your face" ship-naming attitude was also demonstrated in the 2011 launch of the first in a twenty-ship class of frigates named *Incheon,* which is the municipality controlling five islands controlled by Seoul but claimed by Pyongyang; "Navy Gets 2,300-Ton Frigate," *Korea Herald,* 29 April 2011.

33. The Universal Declaration of Human Rights may be found at *United Nations,* www.un.org/.

34. Craig Scanlan, "Socotora Rock (Ieodo, Suyan) Tensions Continue to Increase as Regional Naval Powers Continue to Grow," New Pacific Institute *Asia Security Watch,* 15 March 2012.

Chapter 5. China

1. See, for instance, Fei Shiting and Chen Xiaojing, "Enrich and Strengthen the Nation through Maritime Development: PLA Deputies to the NPC Call for Introducing a Maritime Strategy," *Jiefangjun Bao,* 9 March 2012, 7; Rear Adm. Yin Zhou's statement in "China's Maritime Strategy Being Tested amid South China Sea Disputes," *Bejing Caijing,* 24 October 2011; Maj. Gen. Luo Yuan, quoted in Russell Hsiao, "Military Delegates Call for National Maritime Strategy to Protect Expanding Interests," Jamestown Foundation

China Brief 11, no. 4 (10 March 2011). The degree of policy-making incoherence in Beijing was indicated in a July 2011 speech by Maj. Gen. Zhu Chenghu, reported at opinion.huanqiu.com/roll/2011–07/1792964.html (no longer available online), who called for a South China Sea strategy "where the lead agency is the State Oceanic Administration with input from the PLA, MOFA, PSB, MoCom, Ministries of Agriculture, Transportation, Defense, Customs, and coastal provinces."

2. An old document that still seems accurate in describing China's current maritime policies is Information Office of the State Council of China, *National Ocean Policy of China*, Beijing, May 1998. But also see "China Issues Plan for Maritime Development," *Xinhua*, 26 April 2012.

3. "Marine" and "maritime" are used interchangeably in this book, except when Marine Corps personnel are discussed.

4. *National Ocean Policy of China*, 76–78. Also see Liu Shuguang, "China's Marine Economy," *East Asia Forum*, 17 November 2011, which reports that "national-level marine economic-development zones" have been established by Guangdong, Shandong, and Zhejiang Provinces.

5. "Sailing on a Harmonious Sea: A Chinese Perspective," *Global Asia* 5, no. 4 (Winter 2010). A well-written exposition of China's view of maritime issues is Senior Capt. (Dr.) Ren Xiaofeng, "China's Maritime Security Policy Making and Maritime Confidence Building Measures," in *Twenty-First Century Seapower: Cooperation and Conflict at Sea*, ed. Peter Dutton, Robert Ross, and Øystein Tunsjø(London: Taylor & Francis, 2012).

6. My interview with senior Ministry of Foreign Affairs (MOFA) official, Beijing, 2011. Also see Lyle Goldstein, *Five Dragons Stirring Up the Sea: Challenge and Opportunity in China's Improving Maritime Enforcement Capabilities*, China Maritime Study 5 (Newport, R.I.: Naval War College Press, 2005), the most authoritative description of this situation. But in fact there are at least nine and possibly eleven organizations in China responsible for aspects of the "coast guard" missions, not including the PLAN itself. Also see Wu Jiao and Xin Dingding, "Adviser Says Coast Guard Needed for Maritime Disputes," *China Daily*, 6 March 2012.

7. "Twelfth Five-Year Plan on National Economic and Social Development," *Xinhua*, 16 March 2011; "Twelfth Five-Year Plan on Guangxi's Ocean Economic Development Approved," *Guangxi Daily*, 14 November 2011; "Twelfth Five-Year Plan on Guangdong's Economic Development Principally Approved by Provincial Government," *China Ocean News*, 17 January 2012; "12th Five-Year Plan on Hainan's Economic and Social Development," *Hainan Daily*, 3 March 2012.

8. China's defense white papers may be found at china.org.cn/.

9. "China Evacuates 12,000 from Libya, Sends Frigate to Help," *Xinhua*, 25 February 2011; "Chinese Navy Frigate Arrives Waters off Libya," *Xinhua*, 1 March 2011, english.peopledaily.com.cn/90001/90776/90883/7305215.html (accessed 12 February 2012).

10. See Cortez Cooper, "The PLA Navy's New Historic Missions," *RAND Corporation*, June 2009, at www.rand.org/pubs/testimonies/2009/RAND_CT332.pdf (accessed 3 March 2013).

11. Discussed in James Mulvenon, "Chairman Hu and the PLA's 'New Historic Mission,'" *China Leadership Monitor*, no. 27 (9 January 2009).

12. A useful summary is in Ni Eryan, "Putting Weapons Down to Achieve Peace: The Calmness of PLA Diplomacy," *Feng Huang Chou Kan*, no. 378 (15 October 2010): 42–43, OSC-CPP20101018787005. Also see K. K. Agnohotri, "Military Operations Other than War: PLA's Role in 'Peaceful Development' of China," *India Military Review* (November 2011).

13. These data are from "Sailing on a Harmonious Sea."

14. This final thought is mine; indeed, given the positive trend of relations between Beijing and Taipei under the Ma Ying-jeou administrations and Beijing's continental grasp on Tibet and Xinjiang, China's "core interests" seem relatively secure in 2012. The core-interests issue is discussed in Michael Swaine, *China's Assertive Behavior* (Washington, D.C.: Carnegie Endowment for International Peace, n.d.).

15. See Bernard D. Cole, "Drawing Lines at Sea," U.S. Naval Institute *Proceedings* 137/11/1, no. 305 (November 2011).

16. I am indebted to Dennis Blasko for these brief paragraphs describing Liu Huaqing's island-chain theory, which previously most U.S. observers, including myself, have misinterpreted. Blasko provided extensive translated excerpts of writings by Chinese strategists, including Liu himself, in justifying this new understanding.

17. My discussion with a very senior PLA officer, May 1996. One of the carriers, USS *Independence*, was already under way, operating from its home port at Yokosuka, Japan; the second, USS *Nimitz*, was en route to the Pacific, following a deployment in the Persian Gulf.

18. My conversation with senior PLA officers in Beijing, May 1996.

19. This theory is discussed in June Teufel Dreyer, "Why Taiwan Matters" (Philadelphia: Foreign Policy Research Institute, 18 July 2011), and at length in Alan Wachman, *Why Taiwan? Geostrategic Rationales for China's Territorial Integrity* (Palo Alto, Calif.: Stanford University Press, 2007). Also see J. Michael Cole, "PLA Sorties Threaten Encirclement," *Taipei Times*, 9 February 2012.

20. Hai Tao is the nongovernmental analyst who wrote this article: "The Chinese Navy Has a Long Way to Go to Get to the Far Seas," *Guoji Xianqu Daobao* (Beijing), 6 January 2012, OSC-CPP20120109671003 (accessed 9 February 2012). On *Varyag*, Norman Friedman, "A Long Wait," U.S. Naval Institute *Proceedings* 137/10/1,304 (October 2011): 88–89, provides an excellent analysis of this ship's history and problematic future, noting that it had been under construction since the early 1980s. An indigenously built carrier is discussed in Kathrin Hille, "China Reveals Aircraft Carrier Plans," *Financial Times*, 17 December 2010; Lin Liyao, "Ex-*Varyag* Carrier May Join PLA Navy in 2012," China.org.cn, 10 March 2012.

21. See the excellent work by Christopher Yung and Ross Rustici, with Isaac Kardon and Joshua Wiseman, *China's Out of Area Naval Operations: Case Studies, Trajectories, Obstacles, and Potential Solutions,* China Strategic Perspectives 3 (Washington, D.C.: National Defense University Press, 2012).

22. Hu's speech was routine for its occasion; see M. Taylor Fravel, "Did Hu Jintao Call for War?," *M. Taylor Fravel,* 11 December 2011. Hu is quoted in "Chinese President Meets Deputies for Military Meetings," Xinhua, 7 December 2011.

23. See Thomas M. Skypek, *China's Sea-Based Nuclear Deterrent in 2020: Four Alternative Futures for China's SSBN Fleet,* Collection of Papers from the 2010 Nuclear Scholars' Initiative (Washington, D.C.: Center for Strategic and International Studies, 2010).

24. An account of the ships assigned to these deployments is in Blasko, e-mail to author, with data gathered from www.bjreview.com.cn/rint/txt/2010–04/19content_264350_4.htm; eng.chinamil.com.cn/special-reports/2008hjdj hd/node_21074.htm;andeng.chinamil.com.cn/news-channels/china-military-news/2010–01/06/content_4762058.htm.

25. Status of this ship is described in Song Taisheng and Dong Yongjun, "China's Aircraft Carrier Returns from Sixth Sea Trial Lasting a Total of Nine Days," *Zhongguo Xinwen She Online,* 15 May 2012. Also see "China's Aircraft Carrier Finishes 9th Sea Trial," Xinhua, 31 July 2012, news.xinhuanet.com/english/photo/2012–07/31/c_131749394.htm (accessed 25 August 2012).

26. Leah Averitt, "China's Growing Maritime HA/DR," Jamestown Foundation *China Brief* 10, no. 12 (11 June 2010).

27. U.S. Department of Defense, *A Report to Congress Pursuant to the National Defense Authorization Act for Fiscal Year 2000* (Washington, D.C.: Office of the Secretary of Defense, 2011): 43.

28. Numbers are from "China to Strengthen Maritime Forces amid Disputes," *People's Daily,* 17 June 2011. A more general report about five other "coast guard" organizations' plans is in Chen Guan Gwen, "China's Maritime Security Forces," *Bangui Shish,* 1 May–30 June 2009. *People's Daily* also reported that unmanned air vehicles were being used to "monitor maritime territory"; Up Yang, "Air Drones Scan China's Seas," *People's Daily,* 1 December 2011.

29. My conversation with senior U.S. analyst. Also see James C. Buster, "Parsing China's Fourth Fleet," *Signal Online* (November 2011).

30. See, for instance, Ma Hauling, "China Needs to Break Through the Encirclement of First Island Chain," *Ta Kung Palo,* 21 February 2009.

31. Andrew S. Erickson, "Ballistic Trajectory: China Develops New Anti-Ship Missile," *Jane's China Watch,* 4 January 2010, discusses the Sam's strategic effects.

32. Liu Yen, "The US Military Reveals Secret Tactics That Take Aim at China," *Beijing China Radio,* 18 November 2011; Yang Yi, "Chinese Officials for the First Time Make Public Criticism of the United States' Air Sea Battle," Xinhua, 12 December 2011, in *A Translation of Yang Yi's Xinhua Article*

on *Air Sea Battle,* ed. and trans. Timothy A. Walton and Bryan McGrath, Delex Special Report 2 (Herndon, Va.: Delex Systems, 15 December 2011). Also see Greg Torode, "Beijing Wary as New US Military Strategy Emerges: PLA Officer Warns of Response to Pentagon Plan to Integrate Forces," *South China Morning Post,* 25 April 2011.

33. My discussions with senior Chinese officials and PLA officers, 2011.

34. Identified in Oystein Tensor, *Security and Profits in China's Energy Policy: Hedging against Risk* (New York: Columbia University Press, forthcoming).

35. David Shamaugh, *Modernizing China's Military* (Berkeley: University of California Press, 2004), 189.

36. This section draws on Dennis J. Blasko, "An Analysis of China's 2011 Defense Budget and Total Military Spending: The Great Unknown," Jamestown Foundation *China Brief* 11, no. 4 (10 March 2011).

37. [Chinese Ministry of Defense spokesman], "China's Defense Budget to Grow 11.2 Pct in 2012," *People's Daily,* 4 March 2012, english.peopledaily.com .cn/102775/204254/204390/7747223.html (accessed 22 July 2012).

38. Shamaugh, *Modernizing China's Military* (Berkeley: University of California Press, 2004), 189. Also see Jane Perlez, "China Increases Military Spending More than 11 Percent," *New York Times,* 4 March 2012, www .nytimes.com/2012/03/05/world/asia/china-boosts-military-spending-more-than-11-percent.html (accessed 3 March 2013).

39. China's 2010 defense white paper; Wu Zhong, "PLA Fires Budget Guns," *Asia Times,* 9 March 2011.

40. My discussion with Dennis J. Blasko.

41. My conversations with senior PLAN officers, 2010–11. Also see Shen Shu and Qin Ruoyun, "PLA Navy Opens First Training Class for Escort Mission," *PLA Daily,* 15 February 201.

42. Statement is at the Ministry of Foreign Affairs website, www.mfa.gov.cn/ chngxh/tyb/fyrbt/jzhsl/t714888.htm (accessed 22 December 2011).

43. Antiaccess/area denial apparently is not discussed, per se, in Chinese literature, although Shi Xiaoqin, "The Boundaries and Directions of China's Sea Power," in *Twenty-First Century Seapower: Cooperation and Conflict at Sea,* ed. Peter Dutton, Robert Ross, and Øystein Tunsjø (London: Taylor & Francis, 2012), 137, argues that the PLAN should develop "the capacity to deny access to the [U.S.] navy to China's sea territory." The PLA's "Active Strategic Counterattacks on Exterior Lines" (ASCEL) approximates that operational policy and is discussed in Anton Lee Wishik, "An Anti-Access Approximation: The PLA's Active Strategic Counterattacks on Exterior Lines," *China Security,* no. 19 (2011): 37–48. Maj. Gen. Peng Guangqian, *Research on China Military Strategy Issues* (Beijing: PLA Press, 2006), 248, quoted in Wishik, "Anti-Access Approximation," 3, and in Michael A. McDevitt, "The PLA Navy Anti-Access Role in a Taiwan Contingency" (paper prepared for the 2010 Pacific Symposium on "China's Naval Modernization: Cause for Storm Warnings," National Defense University, Washington D.C., 10 June 2010), 3.

44. "Campaign Battlefield," *Science of Campaigns* (Beijng: AMS, n.d.), excerpt furnished by Blasko (2006): 52, 577–79.

45. See, for instance, James R. Holmes and Yoshi Toshihara, *Red Star over the Pacific: China's Rise and the Challenge to U.S. Maritime Strategy* (Annapolis, Md.: Naval Institute Press, 2010).

46. My conversations with Capt. Bernard Moreland, USCGR (Ret.), and Capt. George Vance, USCG (Ret.), both former U.S. Coast Guard representatives in Beijing; my conversation with the director of MOFA's Bureau of Boundary and Maritime Affairs (Beijing, December 2011). For a useful explanation of China's coast-guard organizations, see Goldstein, *Five Dragons Stirring Up the Sea*. Nine such organizations are noted in Fei Shiting and Chen Xiaojing, "Enrich and Strengthen the Nation through Maritime Development."

47. I am indebted to Dr. Nan Li, of the Navy War College's China Maritime Studies Institute, and to Dr. Thomas Bickford, of the Center for Naval Analyses, for this discussion.

48. Statement is at www.mfa.gov.cn/chngxh/tyb/fyrbt/jzhsl/t714888.htm (accessed 22 December 2011).

49. See Andrew Erickson and Gabe Collins, "Near Seas 'Anti-Navy' Capabilities, Not Nascent Blue Water Fleet, Constitute China's Core Challenge to U.S. and Regional Militaries," *ChinaSignPost,* 7 March 2012, for an informed explanation of this concept.

50. China's use of excessive straight baselines is described in C. M. Legrand, "Chinese Straight Baseline Declaration," Memorandum for Undersecretary of Defense for Policy, 21 May 1996, copy in possession of author. China's excessive views of its rights within the EEZ are exhaustively examined in Raul Pedrozo, "China's Maritime Claims: Exceeding the Limits of International Law," *University of New South Wales,* and his "Preserving Navigational Rights and Freedoms: The Right to Conduct Military Activities in China's EEZ," *Chinese Journal of International Law* 9, no. 1 (2010), 9–29.

51. Jonathan G. Odom, "The True 'Lies' of the *Impeccable* Incident: What Really Happened, Who Disregarded International Law, and Why Every Nation (Outside of China) Should Be Concerned," *Michigan State University College of Law Journal of International Law* 18, no. 3, 2010 (1 April 2010).

52. Stuart Kaye, *Freedom of Navigation in the Indo-Pacific Region,* Papers in Australian Maritime Affairs, no. 22 (Canberra, ACT, Australia: Sea Power Centre, 2008), 1. The best argument for China's position may be Wu Jilu and Zhang Haiwen, "Freedom of the Seas and the Law of the Sea: A Chinese Perspective," in *Twenty-First Century Seapower: Cooperation and Conflict at Sea,* ed. Peter Dutton, Robert Ross, and Øystein Tunsjø (London: Taylor & Francis, 2012). Also see Zhang Haiwen, "Is It Safeguarding the Navigation or Maritime Hegemony of the United States?," *Chinese Journal of International Law* (2010): 31–47.

53. This law is found at *United Nations,* www.un.org/Depts/los/LEGISLA TIONANDTREATIES/PDFFILES/CHN_1992_Law.pdf (accessed 25 May 2012).

54. My discussion with a senior official in China's Ministry of Foreign Affairs, Beijing, December 2011. Nations apparently agreeing with some or all of China's reservations include India and Brazil.

55. See, for instance, the discussion and satellite photographs in Gregory Poling, *Arguing over Blocks: Do China and the Philippines Both Have a Claim?* (Washington, D.C.: Center for Strategic and International Studies, 16 April 2012).

56. See, for instance, Chris Buckley, "China Issues Guidelines to Ease South China Sea Disputes," Reuters, 2 August 2011; "China 'Constructive' on South China Sea Rows, Says US," *BBC News,* 19 November 2011; Xia Wenhui, "Maintaining 'Safety Valve' in South China Sea Vital," Xinhua, 13 January 2012; and as a summary, Lyle Goldstein, "Chinese Naval Strategy in the South China Sea: An Abundance of Noise and Smoke, but Little Fire," *Contemporary Southeast Asia* 33, no. 3 (2011): 320–47.

57. "China, U.S. Start Megaports Initiative Pilot Project to Boost Cargo Security," Xinhua, 7 December 2012.

58. A useful summary is Li Ming Jiang, "China and Maritime Cooperation in East Asia: Recent Developments and Future Prospects," *Journal of Contemporary China* 19, no. 64 (March 2010): 291–310. The CSI program is discussed in Melanie Lee, "China, US Launch Radiation Detection System at Shanghai Port to Check for Nuclear Materials," Reuters, 7 December 2011.

59. Quotes are from Ma Xiaojun, "Recognition of China's National Territorial Sovereignty: Complete, United, and Secure," *Shijie Zhishi,* 16 July 2012, 14–21.

60. Dai Bingguo, "Persisting with Taking the Path of Peaceful Development," Ministry of Foreign Affairs statement, Beijing, 15 September 2011. The latter quote is from Han Xudong, "Peaceful Development Also Requires Military Support," *Liaowang,* no. 27 (4–10 July 2011), 68, www.9abc.net/index .php/archives/5711 (accessed 13 May 2012).

61. Several Chinese analysts are cited in Mathieu Duchatel, "The PLA Navy in the Indian Ocean," in *China's Sea Power, Reaching Out to the Blue Waters* (London: Asia Centre of the European Council on Foreign Relations, 2011), 3–5, and other essays in that document. Also see Chris Buckley, "Analysis: China Looks across Asia and Sees New Threats," Reuters, 14 November 2011.

62. Shi Xiaoqin, "Boundaries and Directions of China's Sea Power," 125.

63. See Gong Jinahua, "Sea Dispute a Real Test for China," *China Daily,* 8 June 2011. Historically, only the United States has been able to exercise both continental and maritime power; Moscow's attempt to do so in the 1970s and 1980s contributed to the Soviet Union's downfall.

64. Quoted in Yoichi Kato, "U.S. Commander Says China Aims to Be a 'Global Military' Power," *Asahi Shimbun,* 28 December 2010.

65. See, for instance, John J. Mersheimer, "China's Unpeaceful Rise," *Current History* 105, no. 690 (April 2006): 160–62; Robert S. Ross, "China's Naval

Nationalism: Sources, Prospects, and the U.S. Response," *International Security* 34, no. 2 (Fall 2009): 46–81. On the Chinese side, see Yang Yi, "China Must Have Strong Navy," Xinhua, 5 December 2011, www .chinadaily.com.cn/opinion/2011–12/02/content_14200571.htm (accessed 14 May 2012), and statements by Maj. Gen. Luo Yuan, quoted by in HJ et al., *Nan Fang Du Shi Bao,* 4 November 2010. A more questioning position is offered in Bernard D. Cole, *The Great Wall at Sea: China's Navy in the Twenty-First Century,* 2nd ed. (Annapolis, Md.: Naval Institute Press, 2010), and in Liu Zhongmin, "Some Thoughts on the Issue of Sea Power and Rise of Great Nations," *World Economy and Politics,* no. 12 (2007), 22, n. 24.

66. This term is found in Theodore Ropp, *The Development of a Modern Navy: French Naval Policy, 1871–1904* (Annapolis, Md.: Naval Institute Press, 1987), 6–7.

67. Jeffrey Engstrom, "PLA's Growing Force Projection Capabilities," Jamestown Foundation *China Brief* 10, no. 25 (17 December 2010).

68. Linda Jakobson and Dean Knox, *New Foreign Policy Actors in China,* SIPRI Policy Paper 26 (Solna, Swed.: Stockholm International Peace Research Institute, September 2010), notes the PLA's reputation as "hard-line" on issues such as Taiwan's status but concludes that PLA influence on national policy making remains "difficult to assess."

69. Glada Lahn, *Trends in Asian National Oil Company Investment Abroad: An Update,* Chatham House Working Paper (London: International Institute for Strategic Studies, November 2007).

70. See Song Yann-Huei and Zou Keyuan, "Maritime Legislation of Mainland China and Taiwan: Developments, Comparison, Implications, and Potential Challenges for the United States," *Ocean Development & International Law* 31, no. 4 (October 2000): 303–34. The white paper on ocean policy may be found at *Japanese Oceanographic Data Center,* www.jodc.go.jp/info/ioc_doc/Technical/158387e.pdf (accessed 28 February 2012).

71. See Erickson and Collins, "Near Seas 'Anti-Navy' Capabilities."

Chapter 6. Southeast Asia

1. Nick Owen, "Oil Disputes in the South China Sea in Context," in *Maritime Energy Resources in Asia: Energy and Geopolitics,* ed. Clive Schofield, NBR Special Report 35 (Seattle, Wash.: National Bureau of Asian Research, December 2011).

2. The "plus" countries joining the ASEAN members are Australia, China, India, Japan, New Zealand, Russia, South Korea, and the United States.

3. "The 2nd ASEAN Maritime Forum," *Maritime Institute of Malaysia,* 11–14 August 2011, www.mima.gov.my/index.php?option=com_content& view=article&id=390:the-2nd-asean-maritime-forum&catid=79:general-annoucement; "ASEAN Defense Ministers Meet in Cambodia to Strengthen Security Cooperation," Xinhua (Phnom Penh), 29 May 2012, news.xinhua net.com/english/world/2012–05/29c_131617759.htm; "ASEAN Defense

Ministers Sign Joint Declaration," *Channel News Asia,* 29 May 2012, www.channelnewsasia.com/stories/singaporelocalnews/view/1204326/1/ .html (all accessed 5 June 2012).

4. A short summary of these programs is in Leithen Francis, "SE Asian Nations Seek Improved ASW, AEW," *Aviation Week,* 1 February 2012.

5. Australian Department of Defense, *Defending Australia in the Asia-Pacific Century: Force 2030* (Canberra, 2009), 52–55 addresses the RAN's missions. Also see Iskander Rehman, *From Down Under to Top Center: Australia, the United States, and This Century's Special Relationship,* Transatlantic Academy Paper Series (Washington, D.C., May 2011).

6. "ANZAC" referred in World War I to the Australia–New Zealand Army Corps but has come to stand for any cooperative endeavor between the two nations' militaries. The defense agreement with the United States is called the ANZUS Treaty.

7. "Australia Creates Vast Marine Conservation Zone," *Financial Times,* 14 June 2012, www.ft.com/cms/s/0/ca23dcb0-b5eb-11e1-a14a-00144feabdc0 .html#axzz1z7fUn9X0 (accessed 28 June 2012).

8. Australian Department of Defense, "Projects of Concern-Update," *Australian Government: Department of Defense,* 28 November 2011, www.minister .defence.gov.au/2011/11/28/minister-for-defence-and-minister-for-defence-materiel-projects-of-concern-update-2/ (accessed 31 May 2012)." Also see Dan Oakes, "Rusty Ships, Boats That Don't Fit Leave Minister All at Sea," *Australian Strategic Policy Institute,* 2 February 2011.

9. Brendan Nicholson, "New Landing Ship Out of Action," *Australian,* 20 June 2012, www.theaustralian.com.au/national-affairs/defence/new-landing-ship-out-of-action/story-e6frg8yo-1226401689269 (accessed 28 June 2012); Mark Dodd, "Navy's Rescue Ships Out of Action in Dry Dock," *Australian,* 3 February 2011, www.theaustralian.com.au/news/nation/navys-rescue-ships-out-of-action-in-dry-dock/story-e6frg6nf-1225999037966 (accessed 1 June 2012).

10. Eddie Walsh, *Australia's Military Capabilities Up in the Air,* ISN Insights (Zurich, Switz.: International Relations and Security Network, 19 September 2011); comment by a U.S. Marine Corps aviator at the U.S. Naval Institute Press Annual Meeting in San Diego, January 2012, describing the F-35 as "one pilot, one bomb, one pilot." The aircraft's original operational date of 2008 has slipped to 2013, and its cost has risen dramatically.

11. "Submarines Decision Not Due until 2013/2014," *AEDT,* 30 April 2011, news.ninemsn.com.au/national/8459547/subamarines-decision-not-due-until-2015 (accessed 1 June 2012); Hamish McDonald, "Navy Eyeing Off New Japanese Submarines," *Sydney Morning Herald,* 9 July 2012, www .smh.com.au/national/navy-eyeing-off-new-japanese-submarines-2012 0708-21pgb.html (accessed 26 August 2012).

12. Sam Bateman, *Looking West: Australian Defense Force Posture Review,* RSIS Commentary 110/2011 (Singapore: RSIS, 25 July 2011); Brahma Chellaney, "New Australia-India Security Accord: Asia's New Strategic

Partners," *Japan Times,* 10 December 2009), chellaney.spaces.live.com/blog/cns!4913C7C8A2EA4A30!1138.entry (both accessed 1 June 2012).

13. "Australia–United States Ministerial Consultations (AUSMIN) 2011 Joint Communique," Media Note PRN: 2011/1511, *U.S. Department of State,* 15 September 2011, www.state.gov/r/pa/prs/ps/2011/09/172517.htm (accessed 1 June 2012).

14. Quoted in "Speech to the AsiaLink and Asia Society Lunch, Melbourne," *Prime Minister of Australia,* 28 September 2011, www.pm.gov.au/press-office/speech-asialink-and-asia-society-lunch-melbourne (accessed 1 June 2012).

15. Quoted in Ray Griggs, "The Commanders Respond," U.S. Naval Institute *Proceedings* 137/3/1,297 (March 2012): 17–18.

16. Somjade Kongrawd, "Thailand and Cambodia Maritime Disputes," *Royal Thai Navy,* n.d., discusses the Memorandum of Understanding for Joint Development in 2001 between Thailand and Cambodia regarding their overlapping maritime claims to the continental shelf, signed on 18 June 2001, www.navy.mi.th/judge/Files/Thailand%Cambodia.pdf (accessed 21 March 2012).

17. Ristian Atriandi Supriyanto, *"Armada Jaya XXX/11" Naval Exercise: Indonesia's Naval Strategy,* RSIS Commentary 176/2011 (Singapore: RSIS, 29 November 2011).

18. Ristian Atriandi Supriyanto, *Indonesia's Naval Modernization: A Sea Change?* RSIS Commentary 020/2012 (Washington, D.C.: East-West Center, 27 January 2012).

19. Stuart Kaye, *Freedom of Navigation in the Indo-Pacific Region,* Papers in Australian Maritime Affairs, no. 22 (Canberra, ACT, Australia: Sea Power Centre, 2008), 10.

20. I Made Andi Arsana, "Is China a Neighbor to Indonesia?," *Jakarta Post,* 8 August 2011. Also see Ristian Atriandi Supriyanto, *Indonesia's South Sea Dilemma between Neutrality and Self-Interest,* RSIS Commentary 126/2012 (Singapore: RSIS, 12 July 2012).

21. Sourabh Gupta, *India and Indonesia: Renewing Asia's Collective Destiny,* Asia Pacific Bulletin 99 (Washington, D.C.: East-West Center, 11 March 2011).

22. Adm. Dato' Dri Abdul Aziz bin Haji Jaafar, in "The Commanders Respond," U.S. Naval Institute *Proceedings* 137/3/1,297 (March 2011), 32.

23. Qiu Renjie, "ASEAN Demonstrates Spirit of Unity in Inaugural Brunei Fleet Review," *China Press,* 13 July 2011; "Navy Plan to Buy More Submarines," *New Strait Times,* 26 April 2012, www.nst.com.my/latest/navy-plan-to-buy-more-submarines-1.77968 (accessed 1 June 2012).

24. Kaye, *Freedom of Navigation in the Indo-Pacific Region,* 11.

25. "Two Chinese Frigates for Myanmar," *Maritime Propulsion,* 13 March 2012, rusnavy.com/news/othernavies/index.php?ELEMENT_ID=14516 (accessed 7 June 2012), reports the delivery of two old *Jianghu*-class ships.

26. Wellington Declaration, signed by New Zealand and the United States (November 2010), which notes "the U.S.-New Zealand strategic partnership," with a "new focus on practical cooperation"; "Statement by Trade Minister Phil Goff," *New Zealand Ministry of Foreign Affairs and Trade,* 23 September 2008), www.mfat.govt.nz/downloads/trade-agreement/transpacific/Phil-goff-welcomes-FTA.pdf (accessed 30 May 2012).

27. I was director of plans, programs, and special projects on the Pacific Fleet staff when this decision was made.

28. The New Zealand 2010 defense white paper is available at *The New Zealand Ministry of Defence,* www.defence.govt.nz/reports-publications/defence-white-paper-2010/contents.html (accessed 5 June 2012).

29. Discussion of the 2010 white paper and Wellington Declaration relies on Sam Bateman, *Coming Back to the US Fold: New Zealand Defense and Security Policies,* RSIS Commentary 146/2010 (Singapore: RSIS, 10 November 2011).

30. Found at the New Zealand navy website, *Navy,* www.navy.mil.nz/visit-the-fleet/(accessed 21 March 2012).

31. The Hukbong Bayan Laban sa mga Hapon (or Hukbalahap) was the military arm of the Philippine Communist Party and fought an insurgency against Manila from 1946 to 1954, until defeated by Gen. Ramon Magsaysay, with the advice of U.S. Air Force major Edward Lansdale, who instituted a land-reform program that eventually isolated the Huks from the population.

32. My conversation with the commandant of the Philippine Marine Corps, 2003.

33. While Philippine officials believe that the treaty obligates the United States to defend the Philippine claims in the South China Sea, article IV of the treaty states, "Each Party recognizes that an armed attack in the Pacific Area on either of the Parties would be dangerous to its own peace and safety and declares that it would act to meet the common dangers in accordance with its constitutional processes," while article V notes that "for the purpose of Article IV, an armed attack on either of the Parties is deemed to include an armed attack on the metropolitan territory of either of the Parties, or on the island territories under its jurisdiction in the Pacific or on its armed forces, public vessels or aircraft in the Pacific." See "Manila: The US Obliged to Defend Filipinos in Spratlys," *Seattle Times,* 22 June 2011, seattletimes.nwsource.com/html/nationworld/2015389170_apassouthchinaseadispute.html (accessed 1 June 2012).

34. "The U.S.-Philippines: Fact Sheet," PRN: 2012/667, *U.S. Department of State,* 30 April 2012, iipdigital.usembassy.gov/st/english/texttrans/2012/04/201204304823.html#axzz1wZc7mjGs (accessed 1 June 2012); Matikas Santos, "6,000 US Troops to Arrive in PH for Balikatan 2012," *Inquirer,* 7 March 2012, globalnation.inquirer.net/27471/6000-us-troops-to-arrive-in-ph-for-balikatan-2012 (accessed 7 June 2012). Also see "U.S., Philippine Navies Join for 17th CARAT Exercise in Palawan," *NavyNews,*

NNS110628–04, 28 June 2011, www.navy.mil/search/display.asp?story_ id=61298 (accessed 1 June 2012).

35. Quoted in Jaime Laude, "US Troops Can Use Clark, Subic Bases," *Philippine Star,* 6 June 2012.

36. Hrvoje Hranjski, "U.S. Okays Transfer of Second Warship," *Asian Journal,* 10 February 2012; Mritunjoy Mazumdar and Jon Rosamond, "Philippines Eyes US Cutter amid Wider Buying Plan," *Jane's Defense Weekly,* 11 May 2011, 15. The typically sad state of the Philippine navy is addressed in Swee Lean Collin Koh, "The Philippines' Navy Challenge," *Diplomat,* 27 December 2011.

37. My discussions with Australian representative and Philippine coast guard officers, Manila, May 2003; Adam Westlake, "Philippine Coast Guard Gets 12 New Patrol Boats from Japan," *Japan Daily Press,* 30 July 2012, japandailypress.com/philippine-coast-guard-gets-12-new-patrol-boats-from-japan-307728 (accessed 26 August 2012).

38. Norman Bodadora, "Aquino Warns of Arms Race," *Philippine Daily Inquirer,* 25 May 2011, www.google.com/hostednews/afp/article/ALeqM5h4 RURjalFM4o2MmWLLO5dCGKJHFQ?docId=CNG.1fb9aa96b31956ee9 261462a61ec573e.1e1#sthash.oQQ77eV1.dpuf; "Philippines Ups Spending to Guard South China Sea," Agence France-Press, 7 September 2011, www .defensenews.com/article/20110907/DEFSECT04/109070309/Philippines-Ups-Spending-Guard-South-China-Sea (both accessed 3 March 2013); Michela P. Del Callar, "China Claims Two New Areas Close to Palawan," *Daily Tribune,* 14 November 2011, www.tribune.net.ph/ (accessed 3 March 2013).

39. "Military Expenditure Data Base," 2011, *Stockholm International Peace Research Institute,* milexdata.sipri.org.

40. Voltaire Gazmin, quoted in "Philippine Defense Chief Says Military Too Weak," *Honolulu Star Adviser,* 24 May 2011.

41. See, for instance, Bernie Cahiles-Magkilat, "RP-China Joint Exploration Okayed," *Manila Bulletin,* 26 August 2011, and "Joint Statement of the People's Republic of China and the Republic of the Philippines," *Official Gazette,* 1 September 2011, www.gov.ph/2011/09/01/joint-statement-of-the-philippines-and-the-peoples-republic-of-china-september-1–2011/ (both accessed 1 June 2012).

42. See, for instance, "Joint Statement of the U.S.-Republic of Singapore Meeting at Shangri-La," *Defpro.news,* 4 June 2012, www.defpro.com/news/details/3 6023/?SID=5cf3231dd12265b1f279727c430a0548 (accessed 5 June 2012).

43. "Singapore: Annual Security Outlook 2003," *ASEAN Regional Forum,* www.aseansec.org/14988.htm (accessed 1 June 2012).

44. Discussed in Weichong Ong, *Singapore's Total Defense: Shaping the Pillars,* RSIS Commentary 25/2011 (Singapore: RSIS, 21 February 2011).

45. "Minister for Defense Commissions RSS *Archer,*" *Singapore Ministry of Defense,* 2 December 2011, www.mindef.gov.sg/imindef/news_and_events/

nr/2011/dec/02dec11_nr.html (accessed 2 June 2012), reports that the second boat was undergoing sea trials.

46. For instance, see Christine Gargan, "Republic of Singapore Navy Trains with U.S. Navy," *NavyNews,* NNS110121–01, 21 January 2011; Wendell Minnick, "Brunei and Singapore Conduct Pelican Exercises," *Defense News,* 13 July2011; and "Singapore Armed Forces Conduct Readiness Exercise," *Asian Military Review Online,* 20 September 2011, www.channelnewsasia. com/stories/singaporelocalnews/view/1144551/1/.htm (all accessed 2 June 2012).

47. My conversation with Ma Ying-jeuo, 2008; Meg Chang, "President Ma Reiterates Three Lines of Defense to Safeguard Taiwan," *Taiwan Today,* 2 June 2011, taiwantoday.tw/ct.asp?xItem=166439&CtNode=452 (accessed 2 June 2012). Taiwan's 2000 defense reorganization included working toward an all-volunteer military. Progress has been unsatisfactory, but the administration is persisting; see "Taiwan to Reduce Length of Military Service," *Channel News Asia,* 14 December 2011, www.channelnewsasia .com/stories/afp_asiapacific/view/1171274/1/.html.

48. "Taiwan Sets Up Airborne Unit For Spratlys," Agence France-Press, 1 May 2012, www.straitstimes.com/BreakingNews/Asia/Story/STIStory_794662 .html (accessed 3 June 2012). Taiwan has manned Pratas and Itu Aba with coast guard personnel, who replaced marines. Also see Bernard D. Cole, *Taiwan's Security: History and Prospects* (New York: Routledge, 2006), 76–77.

49. May Tan-Mullins, "Implications of Seabed Energy Resource Development," in *Maritime Energy Resources in Asia: Energy and Geopolitics,* ed. Clive Schofield, NBR Special Report 35 (Seattle, Wash.: National Bureau of Asian Research, December 2011).

50. "Thai Navy Base Joins Anti-Pirate Joint Patrol," *Phuket Gazette,* 23 February 2012, www.phuketgazette.net/archives/articles/2012/article12399. html (accessed 2 June 2012). The new support ship, HTMS *Ang Thong,* displaces just 7,600 tons; "Navy Officially Welcomes HTMS *Ang Thong* to Fleet," *Bangkok Post,* 20 April 2012, www.bangkokpost.com/news/ local/289551/navy-officially-welcomes-htms-ang-thong-to-fleet (accessed 05 June 2012).

51. Cherdchinda Chotiyaputta, "Marine Policy and Management in Thailand" (paper presented at the International Workshop on Cooperation and Development in the South China Sea, Beijing, 30–31 August 2011).

52. An example of the belligerent side of Hanoi's policy is reported in Sajbal Dasgupta, "Vietnamese Threat to China, from the Sea?," *Times of India,* 12 June 2011. Also see Lucio Blanco Pitlo, *Vietnam's Exploration and Production Contracts: Using Energy Interests to Strengthen Maritime Claims,* RSIS Commentary 106/2012 (Singapore: RSIS, 21 June 2012).

53. "Vietnam, China Look to Sign Agreement on Resolving Sea Disputes," *Thanh Nien News,* 13 May 2011, www.thanhniennews.com/2010/pages/ 20110513171316.aspx; "Vietnam Affirms Sovereignty over Hoang Sa,

Truong Sa," *Vietnam News Agency,* 23 February 2012, english.vietnamnet .vn/en//vn/politics/19214/vn-affirms-sovereignty-over-hoang-sa-truong-sa .html. The two nations have resolved maritime boundary disputes in the Gulf of Tonkin/Beibu Gulf; see "Vietnam, China Hold Joint Naval Patrol Despite Ongoing Spat over Disputed Territory," *Washington Post,* 20 June 2011, www.washingtonpost.com/blogs/checkpoint-washington/post/ in-south-china-sea-every-side-has-its-say/2011/06/20/AGhGRIdH_blog .html?wprss=checkpoint-washington (all accessed 2 June 2012).

54. Kaye, *Freedom of Navigation in the Indo-Pacific Region,* 36; Mark J. Valencia and Jon M. Van Dyke, "Vietnam's National Interests and the Law of the Sea," *Ocean Development and International Law* 25, no. 2 (1994): 219–29, discusses Vietnam's positions on the UNCLOS and its conflicts with neighbors.

55. "Maritime Security and Vietnamese Perspective" (paper presented by a Vietnamese representative at the SCA Join-Project Workshop on Ocean Security in Asia, Hanoi, Vietnam, May 2005), www.scj.go.jp/en/sca/pdf/ 5thsecuritythao.pdf (accessed 7 June 2012).

56. Viet Long, "China's Strategy of Widening Disputed Areas in East Sea," *Quan Doi Nhan Dan Online,* 18 June 2011, in OSC-SEP20110708178001.

57. For instance, see Juan Pinalez, "Vietnam Representatives Visit USS *George Washington,*" *Navy News Service,* NNS110309–12, 9 March 2011; Patrick Barta, "U.S., Vietnam in Exercises amid Tensions with China," *Wall Street Journal,* 16 July 2011; "India, Vietnam: Testing China's Patience," *IRGA,* 26 September 2011, www.irgamag.com/?page=Stories_26092011; and Donald Kirk, "Seoul and Hanoi Eye a Glowing Partnership," *Asia Times Online,* 10 November 2011.

58. "Maritime Strategy Calls for Concerted Effort: Officials," *VietNamNet Bridge,* 27 June 2011, vietnamnews.vnagency.com.vn/Economy/212718/ maritime-strategy-calls-for-concerted-effort-officials.html (accessed 7 June 2012).

59. Le Dinh Tinh, *Vietnam: New Thinking, New Risks, New Opportunities,* PacNet 15 (Honolulu: Center for Strategic and International Studies, 6 March 2012).

60. My conversation with senior U.S. Navy officer.

61. See David Pilling, "Asia's Quiet Anger with 'Big, Bad' China," *Financial Times,* 1 June 2011.

Chapter 7. India

1. Figures are from A. R. Tandon, "India and the Indian Ocean," in *Maritime India,* ed. K. K. Nayar (New Delhi: National Maritime Foundation, 2005): 22–77.

2. The ISA is an international organization headquartered in Kingston, Jamaica, established under the UNCLOS as a platform for regulating and managing seabed mineral deposits recovery; see its website, www.isa.org.jm/en/home (accessed 2 August 2012).

3. See, for instance, "India, China Square Off for Sea Fight," *MaritimeSecurity. Asia*, 18 September 2011.

4. Mihir Roy, *Maritime Security in South West Asia* (New Delhi: Society for Indian Ocean Studies, 2002).

5. India's statements upon ratification of the UNCLOS are at *United Nations,* www.un.org/Depts/los/convention_agreements/convention_declarations .htm#India%20Declaration%20made%20upon%20ratification (accessed 5 June 2012).

6. Discussion of past and present Indian maritime strategy is based on *Freedom to Use the Seas: India's Maritime Military Strategy* (New Delhi: Ministry of Defense, 2007).

7. Rahul Roy-Chaudhury, quoted in James Goldrick, "India's Expeditionary Journey," U.S. Naval Institute *Proceedings* 139/3/1,321 (March 2013): 31.

8. See the discussion by Arun Prakash, "Rise of the East: The Maritime Dimension," *Maritime Affairs* 7, no. 2 (Winter 2011): 1–13; also see Prakash, "China's Maritime Challenge in the Indian Ocean," *Maritime Affairs* 7, no. 1 (Summer 2011): 31.

9. Prakash, "China's Maritime Challenge," 37. Also see *Indian Maritime Doctrine Revisited* (New Delhi: India Defense Consultants, 10 April 2005).

10. Expeditionary operations as a specific mission are discussed in Manu Pubby, "12th Defense Plan: Focus on Navy's 'Expeditionary' Ops," *Indian Express,* 4 May 2012.

11. See Ashok Sawhney, *Indian Naval Effectiveness for National Growth,* RSIS Working Paper 197 (Singapore: RSIS, 7 May 2010), ii.

12. These numbers are based on Stephen Saunders, ed., *Jane's Fighting Ships, 2011–2012* (Coulsden, Surrey: Jane's Information Group, 2011), and on my discussions with senior Indian naval officers, March 2012. The figure of five nuclear-powered submarines is reported in "Navy Plans to Operate 5 Nuke Submarines by End of the Decade," *Economic Times,* 5 April 2012. The delay in delivery of the six Scorpène-class submarines is reported in a statement by Indian Minister of Defense Antony mentioned in "IANS Report: Scorpenes Delayed by 3 Years," *India Strategy* 7, no. 4 (April 2012): 43.

13. Sawhney, *Indian Naval Effectiveness for National Growth,* describes (p. 27) the budget process as "ad-hoc, without much heed to long-term planning." For a report by the Indian Space Research Organization discussing planned launches of navigation and surveillance satellites that will support IN missions, see the ISRO website, isro.org/ (accessed 4 December 2012).

14. Rajat Pandit, "India Is Now 6th Nation to Have a Nuclear Sub," *Times of India,* 24 January 2012. Missile testing is reported in Andrew MacAskill, "India Plans Test of Missile Capable of Reaching China," *Bloomberg,* 17 April 2012.

15. *Vikramaditya* began sea trials in the White Sea in June 2012, six years behind schedule and after a modernization five times as expensive as originally estimated. "Indian Carrier Begins Sea Trials," *Defense News,* 8 June 2012.

In fact, the IN received the smallest share of the 2013–14 defense-budget increase of 14 percent; the army reportedly received approximately 73 percent, the air force 16 percent, and the navy just 10 percent of the defense budget. See P. Chidambaram, "Budget 2013: India Hikes Military Spending 14 Percent," zeenews.com, 28 February 2013 (accessed 3 March 2013).

16. Rahul Datta, "Govt Nod for Two More Arihants," *Pioneer,* 28 February 2012.

17. Quoted in Thomas A. Bowditch, et al., *A U.S. Navy–Indian Navy Partnership for the Future,* CRM D0023588.A2/Final (Arlington, Va.: Center for Naval Analyses, November 2010), 33. I am grateful to Ms. Catherine Lea and Ms. Nilanthi Samaranayake for bringing this study to my attention.

18. Reported in "India's Navy Boosts Spending 74 Percent," *Defense News,* 26 March 2012. Also see Joshy M. Paul, "Emerging Security Architecture in the Indian Ocean Region: Policy Options for India," *Maritime Affairs* 7, no. 1 (Summer 2011): 41.

19. My discussions with Indian navy officers, March 2012. See C. M. Sane, "Functioning of the Aviation Arm of the Indian Navy," *Comptroller and Auditor General of India,* 2010.

20. K. K. Agnihotri and Sunil Kumar Agarwal, "Legal Aspects of Marine Scientific Research in Exclusive Economic Zones: Implications of the *Impeccable* Incident," National Maritime Foundation (New Delhi) *Maritime Affairs,* 5 July 2010, 140. Vijay Sakhuja, "Maritime Multilateralism: China's Strategy for the Indian Ocean," Jamestown Foundation *China Brief* 9, no. 22 (4 November 2010), provides a different but no less accusatory picture of China's plans for the Indian Ocean.

21. See Paul, "Emerging Security Architecture in the Indian Ocean Region," 34. Analysts of Booz, Allen, Hamilton conducted the study, which remains classified; one of its primary authors told me of the Office of the Secretary of Defense involvement. Also see Andrew Selth, *Chinese Military Bases in Burma: The Explosion of a Myth,* Griffith Asia Institute Regional Outlook Paper 10 (Nathan, Qld., Australia: 2007), for a detailed look at China's military presence in Myanmar. Sittwe is often mentioned as the site of Chinese-assisted construction, but that port is actually the site of an Indian construction project, as discussed in Nilanthi Samaranayke, *The Long Littoral Project: Bay of Bengal—A Maritime Perspective on Indo-Pacific Security,* CNA Report IRP-2012-U-002319-Final (Alexandria, Va.: Center for Naval Analyses, 2012).

22. "Major warships" include destroyers, cruisers, aircraft carriers, and replenishment-at-sea ships.

23. My discussion with Adm. (retired) Arun Prakash, April 2012; the admiral is also quoted in Patrick Bratton, "The Creation of Indian Integrated Commands: Organizational Learning and the Andaman and Nicobar Command," *Strategic Analysis* 36, no. 3 (May-June 2012): 447. One new base opening is reported in "India Gets Hawk Eye over Strait of Malacca,"

Indo-Asian News Service, 30 July 2012, www.ndtv.com/article/india/india-gets-hawk-eye-over-strait-of-malacca-249214 (accessed 26 August 2012).

24. "Annual Defense Report 2011," *Jane's Defense Weekly,* 14 December 2011, 38.

25. Sruthi Gottipati, "India Reaches Out to Myanmar," *New York Times,* 29 May 2012.

26. "Naval Fleet to Sail Through S. China Sea," *Oman Tribune/Press Trust of India,* 5 May 2012; "Indian Warships Visit Shanghai," *PLA Daily,* 15 June 2012.

27. P. Vijian, "India-Thailand Ties Shift Gear on Republic Day," *Bernama,* 26 January 2012.

28. See, for instance, Manu Pubby, "India Activates First Listening Post on Foreign Soil: Radars in Madagascar," *Indian Express,* 18 July 2007, www.indianexpress.com/news/india-activates-first-listening-post-on-foreign-soil-radars-in-madagascar/205416 (accessed 4 December 2012).

29. My conversations with senior Indian naval officers, 2012. Sawhney dismisses Pakistan's navy "as no match for the" Indian navy but accuses that country of sending terrorist groups against India "for the last twenty years."

30. "IONS Meeting in South Africa," *IAS 100,* 23 April 2012. Also see Nitin Gokhale, "India, China and the Pirates," *Diplomat,* 6 March 2012.

31. The Agni V has been successfully tested; the longer-range Agni VI is scheduled for a 2014 introduction to the fleet; "Agni-VI to Be Ready by Mid-2014," *IBN,* 23 May 2012.

32. My conversation with senior Indian naval officers, 2012.

33. Ibid.

34. Reported in Ninan Koshy, "India: Lynchpin of Asia Pivot?," *Albany Tribune,* 22 September 2012, www.albanytribune.com/22092012-india-linchpin-of-asia-pivot-analysis/ (accessed 4 December 2012).

35. Admiral Sureesh Mehta, *Freedom to Use the Sea: India's Maritime Strategy* (New Delhi: Ministry of Defense [Navy], 2007): 31.

36. Ibid., 35.

37. My discussions with senior Indian naval officers, 2012.

38. Goldrick, "India's Expeditionary Journey," 33.

39. My discussions with senior Indian naval officers, 2012.

40. *Maritime Strategy,* 44–45.

41. Ibid., 47.

42. Ibid., 52.

43. "Navy to Host 14-Nation 'Milan' Exercise from Feb 1," *Times of India,* 31 January 2012.

44. Paul, "Emerging Security Architecture in the Indian Ocean Region," 38–39. The meeting was reported in "The Indian Ocean Naval Symposium," *3rd Indian Ocean Naval Symposium,* www.navy.mil.za/IONS_2011/index.html (accessed 11 May 2012). China was refused entry to the symposium; the United States has sent junior officers as observers to IONS meetings.

45. Robert Kaplan, *Monsoon: The Indian Ocean and the Future of American Power* (New York: Random House, 2010): 296, is a well-written travelogue about the Indian Ocean and its socio-political-economic characteristics, placed within a historical framework.

46. For a modern justification for an Indian navy centered on aircraft carriers, see Gurpreet S. Khurana, "Aircraft Carriers and India's Naval Doctrine," *Journal of Defense Studies* 2, no. 1 (Summer 2008).

47. See Suvi Dogra, *India and Japan Strengthen Ties* (London: International Institute for Strategic Studies, 2 May 2012), describes a planned exercise between the two navies that will take place in the "same waters" where a Sino-Russian naval exercise was conducted in April 2012. The exercise was reported in "Indo-Japan First Joint Naval Exercise Today," *Top News Today,* 9 June 2012, and K. J. M. Varma, "Indian Warships to Dock at Chinese Port after 6 Yrs' Gap," *Indian Express,* 12 June 2012.

48. A useful summary of IN activities and composition is in Nirmal Verma, "Farewell Press Conference [as IN Commander]," *Indian Navy,* 7 August 2012, indiannavy.nic.in/cns-speeches/farewell-press-conference-outgoing-cns (accessed 26 August 2012). The next day Verma emphasized that the Indian Ocean, not the South China Sea, was the IN's number-one concern; Ajai Shukla, "Navy Chief Says Indian Ocean Is Priority," *Business Standard,* New Delhi, 8 August 2012, www.business-standard.com/india/news/navy-chief-says-indian-ocean-is-priority-not-south-china-sea/482661/ (accessed 26 August 2012).

Chapter 8. South Asia

1. See Alan Villiers on the ubiquity of piracy, cited by Kaplan, *Monsoon,* 298ff. O'Brian's quote is in *H.M.S. Surprise* (London: William Collins, 1973), 51. In his *The Thirteen Gun Salute* (London: William Collins, 1989), 267, the lead character says of piracy (although talking about the South China Sea) that "by all accounts, the rule is to take anything you can overcome and avoid or trade with anything you cannot."

2. This discussion is based on Joshua C. Himes, *Iran's Maritime Evolution* (Washington, D.C.: CSIS, July 2011).

3. Quoted in Robin Pomeroy, "Iran Tests West with Plans for More War Games in Strait of Hormuz," *National Post,* 6 January 2012.

4. Cited in ibid., 2.

5. One example of antipiracy operations is reported in "Iran Navy Thwarts Somali Pirate Attack," *PressTV,* 18 May 2011.

6. "Iran Adds Two New Subs to Navy Fleet," UPI.com, 10 February 2012.

7. Expressed as a statement at the time of signing the UNCLOS; see www.un.org/Depts/los/convention_agreements/convention_declarations.htm#Pakistan Upon ratification.

8. "Fourth F-22P Frigate of Pakistan Navy Launched," *Free Republic,* 17 June 2011. Also see Zhang Haizhou, "China-Made Frigate Ready to Set Sail

for Pakistan," *China Daily,* 5 April 2008; L. Dickerson, "Pakistan Eying Chinese Torpedoes, Missiles for Submarines," *ForecastInternational,* 9 March 2011; "Pakistani Navy Launches New Fast Attack Missile Ship," *Naval Technology,* 22 September 2011; and especially Daniel Byman and Roger Cliff, *China's Arms Sales: Motivations and Implications* (Santa Monica, Calif.: RAND, 1999): 52.

9. Cao Xiaoguang, "Pakistan's Mehran Naval Air Base," *Naval & Merchant Ships,* July 2011), 40–42.

10. Jason Webb, ed., "Pakistan Hands Management of Strategic Gwadar Port to China," Reuters, 18 February 2013, news.yahoo.com/pakistan-hands-management-strategic-gwadar-port-china-164350339.html (accessed 3 March 2013).

11. Christophe Jaffrelot, "Gwadar and Chabahar Display Chinese-Indian Rivalry in the Arabian Sea," *YaleGlobal,* 7 January 2011. Also see Urmila Venugopalan, "Pakistan's Black Pearl," *Foreign Policy,* 3 June 2011. Management of the port did shift to a Chinese company in mid-2012, according to Syed Fazi-e-Haider, "China Set to Run Gwadar Port as Singapore Quits," *Asia Times,* 5 September 2012, http://atimes.com/atimes/China_Business/N105Cb01.html (accessed 4 December 2012).

12. Trista Talton, "Pakistani Marines Tour East Coast Bases," *Marine Corps Times,* 19 May 2007, www.marinecorpstimes.com/news/2007/05/marine_pakistan_delegation_070519/ (accessed 5 August 2012).

13. "Navy Receives US Surveillance Aircraft," *Dawn,* 21 February 2012.

14. See, for instance, "China Keen on Military Aid," *Daily Star,* 12 November 2010.

15. Bangladesh and Myanmar did submit their disputed EEZ boundary to the International Tribunal for the Law of the Sea (ITLOS) in 2010; the court's 2012 decision may be found at the tribunal's website, www.itlos.org/fileadmin/itlos/documents/press_releases_english/pr_175_engf.pdf (accessed 4 December 2012).

16. This paragraph draws on Abu Rushd, "A Sea of Capability," *Defense Management Journal,* no. 56, n.d. Bangladesh's claims under the UNCLOS are discussed in Kaye, *Freedom of Navigation in the Indo-Pacific Region,* 8.

17. *Bangladesh Navy,* www.bangladeshnavy.org.html (accessed 11 March 2012).

18. See ibid. Information about the coast guard is found at its website, www.coastguard.gov.bd/index.html (accessed 4 December 2012).

19. An extreme Chinese view of a close relationship is provided in "China, Myanmar Forge Strategic Partnership, Ink Deals," *Global Times,* 28 May 2011.

20. Some of these issues are addressed in Jared Bissinger, "The Maritime Boundary Dispute between Bangladesh and Myanmar: Motivations, Potential Solutions, and Implications," *Asia Policy,* no. 10 (July 2010): 103–42.

21. Bernhard Teuteberg, "Africa's Strategy for Maritime Security: ASA Navy Perspective" (presentation, 25 March 2012), www.slideserve.com/rock/africa-s-strategy-for-maritime-security-a-sa-navy-perspective (accessed 26 August 2012).

22. Declaration at time of signing the UNCLOS; see www.un.org/Depts/los/convention_agreements/convention_declarations.htm#South Africa Upon ratification.

23. "Strategy 2017: Creating Our Nation's Wealth Together," *Seychelles Government Portal*.

24. Michael Rosette, Seychelles Coast Guard, cited in "The Commanders Respond," Naval Institute *Proceedings* 137/3/1,297 (March 2011): 37. Chinese interest in the Seychelles is reported in Mandip Singh, *Proposed PLAN Naval Base in Seychelles and India's Options*, IDSA Comment (New Delhi: Institute for Defence Studies and Analyses, 15 December 2011); "Seychelles Invites China to Set Up Anti-Piracy Presence," Agence France-Presse, 2 December 2011; and Raseeh Rahman, "Chinese Plans in Seychelles Revive Indian Fears of Encirclement," *Guardian,* 22 March 2012.

25. Described at the *Maldives Coast Guard,* maldivescoastguard.com/.

26. Thisara Samarasinghe, a Sri Lankan navy commander, provides that service's perspective in Sergei Desilva-Ranasinghe, "Separatist Insurgency," *SP's Naval Forces* 5, no. 6 (December 2010-January 2011), www.spsnavalforces .net/ebook/18062010.pdf (accessed 26 August 2012).

27. See the Sri Lankan navy website. These missions are addressed by the navy's commander, Vice Adm. Jayanath Colombage, in "Sri Lanka Navy," in "The Commanders Respond," U.S. Naval Institute *Proceedings* 139/3/1,321 (March 2013): 27.

28. "SLPA to Fast Track Construction of New Deepwater Berth in Colombo Port's South Harbor," *Port Technology International,* 12 December 2011. Also see "Sri Lanka Port and Infrastructure Improvements Continue with Support from China," U.S. Army Asian Studies Detachment OSIR: ASD11F08093, 8 August 2011.

29. My discussion with Sri Lankan analyst; Sri Lanka Ports Authority website.

30. This and the following paragraphs rely on the excellent analysis provided by Nilanthi Samaranayake, "Are Sri Lanka's Relations with China Deepening? An Analysis of Economic, Military, and Diplomatic Data," *Asian Security* 7, no. 2 (2011): 119–46.

31. These organizations are discussed in Mustapha Alani, "Toward a Comprehensive Maritime Security Arrangement in the Gulf," in *The Indian Ocean: Resource and Governance Challenges,* ed. Ellen Laipson and Amit Pandya (Washington, D.C.: Stimson Center, 2009), 46–48.

32. Mahan supposedly wrote in 1902, "Whoever controls the Indian ocean dominates Asia. This Ocean is the key to the seven seas. In the twenty first century, the destiny of the world will be decided in its waters." He is so quoted, perhaps erroneously, in Geoffrey Till, *Seapower: A Guide for the*

Twenty-First Century (London: Taylor & Francis, 2009), 333; similar opinion offered in Henry Kissinger, "Power Shifts and Security" (keynote address, Eighth IISS Global Strategic Review, Geneva, 10 September 2010).

Chapter 9. Conflict and Cooperation

1. Hugh Griffiths and Michael Jenks, *Maritime Transport and Destabilizing Commodity Flows,* SIPRI Policy Paper 2 (Solna, Swed.: Stockholm International Peace Research Institute, January 2012), 1, 47.

2. A good explanation of this dispute is Ralf Emmers, *Japan-Korea Relations and Todko/Takeshima Dispute: The Interplay of Nationalism and Natural Resources,* RSIS Working Paper 212 (Singapore: RSIS, 10 November 2010).

3. The CLSC is explained at *United Nations,* www.un.org/depts/los/clcs_new/clcs_home.htm (accessed 23 December 2011). South Korea is also a claimant to the continental shelf in the East China Sea. In all such cases, Taiwan agrees with China.

4. Lee Tae-hoon, "Seoul to Summon Chinese Diplomats over Ieodo Remarks," *Korea Times,* 11 March 2012; "China Boosts Naval Presence near Korean Peninsula," *Chosun Ilbo,* 12 March 2012.

5. The UNCLOS, article 121, states that "an island is a naturally formed area of land, surrounded by water, which is above water at high tide" and is entitled to all the UNCLOS zones, including an EEZ and continental shelf. "Rocks," however, "which cannot sustain human habitation or economic life of their own" are not so entitled. See *Admiralty & Maritime Law Guide,* www.admiraltylawguide.com/conven/unclosparts8–10.html (accessed 12 August 2012).

6. Hai Tao, "China Breaks Through Japan's Diaoyu Islands Defense Line," *Guoji Xianqu Daobao,* 12 December 2008.

7. "23 Remote Isles Put under State Ownership," *Yomiuri Shimbun,* 8 March 2012; "China Protests Japan's Island Naming Plan," Agence France-Presse, 30 January 2012; "China Releases Standard Names of Diaoyu Islands," Xinhua, 3 March 2012. The Takeshima/Dokdo incident is reported in "Japan PM Rejects S. Korea's Call to Withdraw Dokdo Remarks," *KBS World,* 27 January 2012.

8. "China to Intensify Maritime Territory Patrols," Xinhua, 19 March 2012; "Coast Guard to Get Power to Make Arrests on Uninhabited Islands," *Asahi Shimbun,* 22 February 2012.

9. "U.N. Approves Japan's Claim on Wider Seas," *Yomiuri Shimbun,* 29 April 2012. Japan's submission to the CLCS is at *United Nations,* www.un.org/Depts/los/clcs_new/submissions_files/submission_jpn.htm (accessed 3 June 2012). China's submission is not listed by the CLCS as of 12 April 2012, but Beijing disagreed with Japan's submission, in a *note verbale* to the UN Secretary General in April 2012.

10. Submission to the CLCS at *United Nations,* www.un.org/Depts/los/clcs_new/commission_submissions.htm (accessed 10 February 2012).

11. Shin Hyon-hee, "Korea, China Agree on Joint Maritime Claim against Japan," *Korea Herald,* 8 July 2012, view.koreaherald.com/kh/view .php?ud=20120708000284&cpv=0 (accessed 20 August 2012).

12. Timor-Leste's counter is at *United Nations,* www.un.org/Depts/los/clcs_new/ submissions_files/aus04/clcs_03_2004_los_tls.pdf (accessed 10 February 2012).

13. Gong Yingchun, *The Development and Current Status of Maritime Disputes in the East China Sea,* NBR Special Report 35 (Seattle, Wash.: National Bureau of Asian Research, December 2011). Also see Zhang Tuosheng, "East Asian Territorial and Maritime Rights Disputes and Their Political and Economic Implications," *Modern International Relations,* 27 February 2011, 120–27 (translated for me by Anton Wishik, of NBR); Yoichi Kato, "China's Naval Expansion in the Western Pacific," *Global Asia 5,* no. 4 (Winter 2010); and "Japan, China to Begin High-Level Maritime Talks," *Mainichi Japan,* 5 April 2012.

14. My discussion with senior MOFA official, Beijing, 2011; "PRC Calls Senkaku Islands Beijing's 'Core Interest,'" Kyodo World Service, 21 January 2012; "China Now Calls Senkakus Core Interest," *Asahi News,* 4 February 2012; "Chinese Marine Survey Vessel Spotted near Senkaku Islands," *Kyodo,* 15 November 2011; Jun Ando, "Chinese Official Says Enhanced Patrols near Senkakus Aimed at 'Breaking' Japan's Effective Control," *Tokyo Shimbun,* 22 March 2012; J. Michael Cole, "Chinese Navy Vessels Spotted Close to Japanese Coast," *Jane's Defense Weekly,* 15 May 2012.

15. See the excellent Nancy Bernkopf Tucker and Bonnie Glaser, "Should the United States Abandon Taiwan?" *Washington Quarterly* 34, no. 4 (Fall 2011): 23–37.

16. "South China Sea," *U.S. Energy Information Administration (EIA),* 1994, www.eia.gov (accessed 17 June 2012).

17. See Carlyle A. Thayer, "Code of Conduct in the South China Sea Undermined by ASEAN Disarray," News.USNI.org, 19 July 2012, news.usni.org/news-analysis/news/code-conduct-south-china-sea-undermined-asean-disarray (accessed 5 August 2012).

18. See, for instance, "Chinese Might," *Manila Times,* 8 March 2011; "PHL Asks China to Explain Ships near Reed Bank," *GMA News,* 1 June 2011; Simone Orendain, "Philippines Seeks Answers about Latest South China Sea Incident," Reuters, 1 June 2011; "China Demands Manila Hands Back Seized Fishing Boats," "Philippines: No Immediate Return of Chinese Boats," and "China Paper Warns of 'Sound of Cannons' in Sea Disputes," all Reuters, 20–25 October 2011; "Philippines Rejects New Chinese Territorial Claim," Associated Press, 14 November 2011; "China to Step Up Maritime Patrols in Spratlys," *Philippine Star,* 21 March 2012; and "Huangyan Crisis Hints Long-Term Tensions," *Global Times,* 21 April 2012, www.globaltimes.cn/ NEWS/tabid/99/ID/705942/Huangyan-crisis-hints-long-term-tensions.aspx (accessed 4 March 2013).

19. Philip C. Tabeza and T. J. Burgonio, "China Ropes Off Scarborough Shoal," *Philippine Daily Inquirer,* 3 August 2012, globalnation.inquirer.net/46289/china-ropes-off-panatag-shoal.

20. "PRC's Xi Jinping Said Warning Vietnam to Keep Distance from US on SCS Issue," *Kyodo,* 20 January 2012; "China and Vietnam to Ease Maritime Tensions," *Al Jazeera,* 26 June 2011; "Apparent Text of Agreement on the Basic Principles for Guiding the Settlement of Maritime Issues between the PRC and the SRV," Xinhua, 11 October 2011; Zhang Haiwen and Liu Qing, "Sincerity Needed to Solve South China Sea Dispute," *People's Daily,* 23 October 2011; Huynh Phan, "Vietnam-China Relations in the Eye of a Senior Diplomat," *VietNamNet,* 26 January 2012. Also see Amitav Acharya, "ASEAN's Dilemma: Courting Washington without Hurting Beijing," *Asia Pacific Center Bulletin* 133 (18 October 2011).

21. Quoted in Marcus Weisgerber, "Panetta: Partnerships, Training Focus of U.S. Pacific Strategy," *Defense News,* 11 June 2012. Also see Jennifer Hlad, "Panetta: US Strategy Aims to Build Peace, Stability in Pacific," *Stars and Stripes,* 31 May 2012.

22. Michael Wines, "Dispute between Vietnam and China Escalates over Competing Claims in South China Sea," *New York Times,* 10 June 2011; Tran Truong Thuy, "New Round of Tension," *VietNamNet Bridge,* 30 July 2011; "Vietnam Slams China Sea Survey in Disputed Area," Agence France-Presse, 9 August 2011; "Researchers Suggest Solutions to Reclaim Hoang Sea [South China Sea]," *Tuoi Tre,* 29 November 2011.

23. M. Taylor Fravel, "China's Behavior in Its Territorial Disputes and Assertiveness in the South China Sea" (paper presented at the CSIS, Washington, D.C., October 2011). See Zakir Hussain, "Asean Nations Welcome US Pivot," *Straits Times,* 27 November 2011, 28; "ASEAN Foreign Ministers Affirm Common Stance on the East Sea," *Vietnam.net Bridge,* 11 January 2012, quoting Vietnamese foreign minister Pham Binh Minh; "China, ASEAN Countries Hold Meeting on South China Sea," Xinhua, 15 January 2012. Also see Zhong Sheng, "Hold Firm to the Main Trend in China-ASEAN Relations," *Renmin Ribao Online,* 5 April 2012.

24. Donald E. Weatherbee, *China, the Philippines, and the US Security Guarantee,* PacNet 28 (Honolulu: CSIS, 26 April 2012); U.S. Department of State, "Signing of the Manila Declaration on Board the USS *Fitzgerald* in Manila Bay, Manila, Philippines," *U.S. Department of State,* 16 November 2011; Manuel Mogato and Rosemarie Francisco, "Manila Offers U.S. Wider Military Access, Seeks Weapons," Reuters, 29 March 2012. Also see Chris Buckley, "China Military Warns of Confrontation over Seas," Reuters, 21 April 2012; "Don't Play with Fire," *China Daily,* 12 April 2012; Yuan Peng, "Reminds US Not to Be Deranged in Intervening in Maritime Dispute," *Renmin Ribao,* 27 July 2012, 1, in OSC-CPP20120727787001; and Li Xiaokun, "US 'Using Islands Dispute to Muddy Waters," *China Daily,* 6 August 2012, usa.chinadaily

.com.cn/china/2012–08/06/content_15645778.htm (both accessed 20 August 2012).

25. "Scarborough Shoal Issue Reaches UN," *Sun Star,* 5 May 2012; Floyd Whaley, "Clinton Reaffirms Military Ties with the Philippines," *New York Times,* 17 November 2011, www.nytimes.com/2011/11/17/world/asia/clinton-reaffirms-military-ties-with-the-philippines.html (accessed 17 August 2012); Eric Bellman and Cris Larano, "Clinton: South China Sea Dispute Must Be Resolved Peacefully," *Wall Street Journal,* 16 November 2011.

26. Patrick Ventrell, "Press Statement: South China Sea," *U.S. Department of State,* 3 August 2012, www.state.gov/r/pa/prs/ps/2012/08/196022.htm. China's response is in "Statement by Spokesperson Qin Gang of the Ministry of Foreign Affairs of China on the US State Department Issuing a So-Called Press Statement on the South China Sea," *Ministry of Foreign Affairs,* 4 August 2012, www.fmprc.gov.cn/eng/xwfw/s2510/t958226.htm (both accessed 5 August 2012).

27. Zhang Yunbi, "U.S. Military Swings to Asia-Pacific Region," *China Daily,* 6 August 2012, www.chinadaily.com.cn/cndy/2012–08/06/content_15645903.htm (accessed 22 August 2012). See Sam Bateman, *Increasing Competition in the South China Sea,* RSIS Commentary 157/2012 (Singapore: RSIS, 21 August 2012).

28. Note Verbale, Permanent Mission of the PRC to the UN, CML/8/2011, 14 April 2011. China's claims in the South China Sea are comprehensively discussed in Peter Dutton, "Three Disputes and Three Objectives: China and the South China Sea," *Naval War College Review* 64, no. 4 (Autumn 2011): 42.

29. Ibid., 62.

30. Mark Landler, "Offering to Aid Talks, U.S. Challenges China on Disputed Islands," *New York Times,* 23 July 2012. The 1995 statement is in "U.S. Policy on Spratly Islands and South China Sea," *Department of State Daily Press Briefings,* 10 May 1995.

31. Jeffrey A. Bader, *Obama and China's Rise: An Insider's Account of America's Asia Strategy* (Washington, D.C.: Brookings, 2012), 105. The first two quotations are Bader's; he then quotes Yang.

32. Dina Indrasafitri, "Defense Chiefs Push for South China Sea Rules," *Jakarta Post,* 20 May 2011; "ASEAN Countries to Increase Defense Industry Cooperation," *Nation,* 19 May 2011; Tan Seng Chye, *ADMM+8: Adding Flesh to a New Regional Architecture,* RSIS Commentary 131/2010 (Singapore: RSIS, 15 October 2010).

33. Rudolfo Soverino, "Toward a Code of Conduct in the South China Sea," *East Asia Forum,* 11 August 2012.

34. *Broader Horizons* (New Delhi: Institute for Defence Studies and Analyses, April 2012). Also see Chamal Weerakkaody, "Embassy Takes Custody of Chinese Fishing Crew," *Sri Lanka Times,* 11 August 2012, www.sundaytimes.lk/120812/news/embassy-takes-custody-of-chinese-fishing-crew-8564.html

(accessed 19 August 2012); "Russian Coast Guard Fires on Chinese Boats in Sea of Japan," WantChinaTimes.com, 18 July 2012, www.wantchinatimes .com/news-subclass-cnt.aspx?id=20120718000081&cid=1101 (accessed 26 August 2012).

35. Frank E. Loy, "Doherty Lecture," University of Virginia, Charlottesville, Va., 11 Mary 1999, 2. This section on fisheries crime draws on Euan Graham's concise but inclusive *Transnational Crime in the Fisheries Industry: Asia's Problem?* RSIS Commentary 62/2011 (Singapore: RSIS, 25 April 2011).

36. Conflicts, sometimes violent and armed, are reported almost daily in the Asian press—for instance, Zhou Wa, "Chinese Fishermen Face Arrest by ROK," *China Daily,* 2 May 2012. See also Nguyen Dang Thang, *China's Fishing Ban in the South China Sea: Implications for Territorial Disputes,* PacNet 35A (Honolulu: CSIS, 20 July 2011).

37. The degradation of South China Sea fish stocks is discussed in Pakjuta Khemakorn, *Suitable Management of Pelagic Fisheries in the South China Sea Region* (New York: United Nations, November 2006). China's efforts are discussed in David Rosenberg, "Managing the Resources of the China Seas: China's Bilateral Fisheries Agreements with Japan, South Korea, and Vietnam," *Asia-Pacific Journal: Japan Focus,* 30 June 2005.

38. This section on fisheries crime draws on Graham, *Transnational Crime in the Fisheries Industry.*

39. See Sam Bateman, *Saving Lives at Sea: Everyone's Responsibility,* RSIS Commentary 148/2012 (Singapore: RSIS, 10 August 2012); "Economies of Bangladesh, Philippines, Myanmar, India, Viet Nam at Highest Risk from Natural Hazards: Risk Atlas," *Maplecroft,* 15 August 2012, maplecroft. com/about/news/nha_2012.html (accessed 26 August 2012).

40. Discussed in Robert B. Killebrew, "Crime & War," U.S. Naval Institute *Proceedings* 137/10/1,304 (October 2011): 22–26.

41. Quoted in Martin N. Murphy, *Contemporary Piracy and Maritime Terrorism: The Threat to International Security,* Adelphi Paper 388 (London: International Institute for Strategic Studies, 2007), 85.

42. Charles Emmerson and Paul Stevens, *Maritime Choke Points and the Global Energy System: Charting a Way Forward,* Chatham House Briefing Paper (London: International Institute for Strategic Studies, January 2012).

43. Joshua Ho, *Piracy in the South China Sea,* RSIS Commentary 47/2011 (Singapore: RSIS, 24 March 2011).

44. Catherine Zara Raymond, "Countering Piracy and Armed Robbery in Asia: A Study of Two Areas," in *Emerging Naval Powers,* ed. Robert Ross, Peter Dutton, and Øystein Tunsjø (London: Routledge, 2012), 319–33, offers a concise summary of the South China Sea piracy situation. Also "New System to Help Vessels in Malacca Strait," *Jakarta Post,* 8 June 2012.

45. See collection of articles at *EU NavFor Somalia,* www.eunavfor.eu/ (accessed 2 August 2012).

46. Raymond, "Countering Piracy and Armed Robbery in Asia," 333; "Remarks by General Chen Bingde" (National Defense University, Washington, D.C., 18 May 2011), notes in author's possession; also reported www.ndu.edu/press/lib/pdf/books/chinese-navy.pdf; author's discussion with senior U.S. naval officer, October 2011.

47. "India Proposes Norms for Indian Ocean Anti-Piracy Patrols," *IANS,* 13 April 2012; Vice Adm. Ding Yiping, quoted in Zhao Shengnan, "PLA Navy Calls for More Cooperation against Piracy," *China Daily,* 24 February 2012. Also see Reshma Patil, "China Wants Talks on Indian Ocean," *Hindustan Times,* 11 August 2011.

48. The 2010–11 comparison is in "Pirate Attacks at Sea Getting Bigger and Bolder," *ICC Commercial Crime Services,* 14 July 2011; "Piracy and Armed Robbery News and Figures," *IMB,* 30 August 2012; my discussion with shipping line security director. The eighteen-knot figure is from the Stockholm International Peace Research Institute; also see "Ships Increasingly Turning to Armed Guards to Combat Piracy," [U.S.] *Homeland Security Newswire–Maritime Security,* 19 May 2011.

49. Raymond, "Countering Piracy and Armed Robbery in Asia," 340.

50. Discussed in Sam Bateman, "Regional Responses to Enhance Maritime Security in East Asia," *Korean Journal of Defense Analysis* 18, no. 2 (Summer 2006): 26–31. Also see Sam Bateman and Michael Richardson, *A Time Bomb for Global Trade: Maritime-Related Terrorism in an Age of Weapons of Mass Destruction* (Singapore: Institute of Southeast Asian Studies, 2004).

51. "Philippines Ratifies Australia Military Pact," *Defense News,* 24 July 2012, www.defensenews.com/article/20120724/DEFREG03/307240001/Philippines-Ratifies-Australia-Military-Pact; Vivek Raghuvanshi, "India to Continue Training of Singapore Troops," *Defense News,* 12 July 2012, www.defensenews.com/article/20120712/DEFREG03/307120005/India-Continue-Training-Singapore-Troops (accessed 26 August 2012); and Koh Swee Lean Collin, *Indonesia-Singapore Submarine Rescue Pact,* RSIS Commentary 134/2012 (Singapore: RSIS, 24 July 2012).

52. My conversations with senior civilian and military officials in Beijing, Oslo, and New Delhi, 2009–12.

53. Vladimir Radyuhin, "Russia Sets Up Arctic Forces," *Hindu,* 1 July 2011; Trude Pettersen, "Russia Sets Up New Arctic Border Posts," *Barents Observer,* 16 April 2012; Alexey Druzhinin, "Russia to Build Up Submarine Task Force along Northern Sea Route," RIA Novosti, 11 August 2011.

54. My discussions with Chinese academics and senior PLA officers, 2009–11. Wen Jiabao is quoted in Allison Jackson, "Chinese Premier Wen Jiaobao Signs Agreements on Energy, Arctic during Iceland Visit," *Global Post,* 20 April 2012. China's icebreaker construction is discussed in Wang Qian, "New Ship to Boost Arctic Expeditions," *China Daily,* 24 February 2012; and in Joseph Spears, "The Snow Dragon Moves into the Arctic Ocean Basin," Jamestown

Foundation *China Brief* 11, no. 2 (28 January 2012). Also see Anne Marie Brady, "Polar Stakes: China's Polar Activities as a Benchmark for Intentions," Jamestown Foundation *China Brief* 12, no. 14 (19 July 2012).

55. See, for instance, P. K. Gautam, *The Arctic as a Global Common,* IDSA Issue Brief (New Delhi: Institute for Defence Studies and Analyses, 2 September 2011).

56. Jeremy Torobin, "Military Plans a Show of Force in the Arctic," *Globe and Mail* (Ottawa), 11 July 2012, www.theglobeandmail.com/news/politics/military-plans-a-show-of-force-in-high-arctic/article586436/ (accessed 30 August 2012).

57. This argument is ably made by M. Taylor Fravel, "China's Response to a Rising India," interview by Erin Fried, NBR, 4 October 2011.

58. U.S. Navy Dept., *A Cooperative Strategy for 21st Century Seapower* (Washington, D.C., October 2007), discussed in chap. 2.

59. Halford John Mackinder, "The Geographical Pivot of History," *Geographical Journal* 23, no. 4 (April 1904): 421–37.

60. See Li Jinming, "Nansha Indisputable Territory," *China Daily* (15 June 2011), www.chinadaily.com.cn/opinion/2011–06/15/content_12698262.htm (accessed 16 June 2012); Douglas Paal, *South China Sea: Plenty of Hazards for All,* Asia Pacific Brief (Washington, D.C.: Carnegie Endowment for International Peace, 7 July 2011).

61. See description of the different national claims in Greg Austin, *China's Ocean Frontier: International Law, Military Force, and National Development* (Sydney, Australia: Allen & Unwin, 1998).

62. My discussions at the Ministry of Foreign Affairs and Ministry of Defense, Beijing, 2011. Also see Selig S. Harrison, *Stirring Up the South China Sea,* Asia Report 223 (Brussels: International Crisis Group, 23 April 2012), 7, 8, 19.

63. "China's Foreign Ministry Spokesperson Hong Lei's Regular Press Conference," *Foreign Ministry of the People's Republic of China,* 29 February 2012. Even this statement lacks complete clarity, however, since it fails to address Beijing's position about claimed EEZs for the various land features.

64. A good summary of China's activities in the South China Sea is M. Taylor Fravel, "China's Strategy in the South China Sea," *Contemporary Southeast Asia* 33, no. 3 (December 2011): 292–319.

Conclusion

1. Hughes, "Naval Operations," 39.

2. Gen. Chen Bingde, quoted in Agence France-Presse, "General: China Never Intends to Challenge U.S.," *Defense News,* 18 May 2011, www.defensenews.com/story.php?i=6548219&c=ASI&s=POL; Yang Yi, "For Strategic China-US Ties," *China Daily,* 16 February 2011; Yuan Peng, "Awaiting the Handshake: China-US Relations Are the Key to Stability in Northeast Asia," *Global Asia* 6, no. 2 (Summer 2011).

3. For instance, more merchant ships were lost to bad weather than to German U-boats in the North Atlantic during World War II. Willmott

4. See, for example, "Russian Navy Looks to Expand Bases Abroad, Goes Hunting in Southeast Asia, India Ocean and Caribbean," *International Business Times*, 27 July 2012, www.ibtimes.com/articles/367754/20120727/ russia-navy-cuba-seychelles-vietnam.htm; "Vietnam Ready to Host Russian Maritime Base," *Ria Novosti*, 27 July 2012, en.rian.ru/world/20120727/ 174804220.html. Denials are at Li Meng, "Vietnam Declines to Give Russia Exclusive Rights to Naval Base," Xinhua, 27 July 2012, news.xinhuanet .com/english/world/2012-07/31/c_131750785.htm; "Russia Denies Reports of Opening Overseas Naval Bases in Vietnam, Cuba," *RussiaNews.Net*, 28 July 2012, www.defensenews.com/article/20120728/DEFREG01/ 307280003/Russia-Denies-8217-s-Pursuing-Naval-Bases-Abroad?od yssey=mod|newswell|text|FRONTPAGE|swww.russianews.net/index .php?sid/207796703/scat/723971d98160d438; "Russia Denies It's Pursuing Naval Bases Abroad," *Defense News*, 28 July 2012, www.defensenews .com/article/20120728/DEFREG01/307280003/Russia-Denies-8217-s- Pursuing-Naval-Bases-Abroad?odyssey=mod|newswell|text|FRONTPAGE|s (all accessed 5 August 2012).

5. My discussions with senior Korean naval analysts, 2012.

6. The 2005 statement by then–U.S. secretary of defense Donald Rumsfeld was both supercilious and irrelevant: "Since no nation threatens China, one must wonder: Why this growing investment? Why these continuing large and expanding arms purchases? Why these continuing robust deployments?" *DefenseTalk*, 27 June 2005, www.defencetalk.com/rumsfeld-questions- chinas-military-buildup-2994/#ixzz22cigNUiz (accessed 4 August 2012).

7. The "city upon a hill" comment is commonly attributed to John Winthrop, written while he crossed the Atlantic in 1630 en route to the new Massachusetts Bay colony: "We shall be as a city upon a hill." "Middle kingdom" is a translation of the Mandarin name for China: "zhongguo".

8. I am indebted to Geoffrey Till, one of our most distinguished naval historians and strategic thinkers, for these points.

9. Ezra Vogel, *Japan as Number One: Lessons for America* (Cambridge, Mass.: Harvard College, 1979); Till, *Asia Rising and the Maritime Decline of the West*.

10. Jon Grevatt, "Philippines Eyes Submarine Acquisition by 2020," *IHS Jane's*, 18 May 2011, www.janes.com/products/janes/defence-security-report.aspx? id=1065929630; Jaime Laude, "After New Patrol Ship, Navy Mulls Getting Submarines," *Philippine Star*, 13 May 2011, www.philstar.com/nation/ article.aspx?publicationsubcategoryid=65&articleid=685453 (both accessed 5 August 2012).

11. Zhou Siyu, "Boomtime Buys Lead to Bust," *China Daily*, 14 December 2011.

12. "U.S. Merchant Marine/U.S. Merchant Fleet," *Global Security*, 20 July 2007. The 2 percent figure is in "Modern Merchant Marine," *American Maritime Congress* (2011).

13. The deterrent perception is addressed in Christopher P. Twomey, "Asia's Complex Strategic Environment: Nuclear Multipolarity and Other Dangers," *Asia Policy,* no. 11 (January 2011): 68.

14. The missile intended for the *Jin*—the JuLang-2 (JL-2), or "giant wave," CSS-NX-4 in NATO parlance—remains in testing and does not possess the range to reach the continental United States from a South China Sea firing position; hence, a Chinese bastion strategy would require a new ICBM for the *Jin.*

15. See, for instance, Karl F. Inderfurth and S. Amer Latif, "The Elephant Engages Asia at Its Own Pace," *U.S.-India Insight* 1, no. 6 (9 September 2011); and M. Taylor Fravel, "Japan-China Maritime Step," *Diplomat,* 18 May 2012.

16. Peter Ho, *FPDA at 40: Still Effective and Relevant,* RSIS Commentary 179/2011 (Singapore: RSIS, 5 December 2011).

17. Deborah Elms and C. L. Lim, *The Trans-Pacific Partnership Agreement (TPP) Negotiations: Overview and Prospects,* RSIS Working Paper 232 (Singapore: RSIS, 21 February 2012); H.T., "Opening Up the Pacific," *Economist,* 12 November 2011. The EU comparison was made before the current, very serious problems with Greece and other members.

18. Miller, *War Plan Orange,* 3.

19. The goal of Adm. Liu Huaqing, who promulgated China's first modern maritime strategy, as discussed in "China's Military Rise: The Dragon's New Teeth," *Economist,* 7 April 2012.

20. Conversations with senior PLAN officers and tours of approximately twelve PLAN combatants, 1994–2012. Also see U.S. Department of Defense, *PLA Modernization Areas, 2000–2010: Annual Report to Congress—Military and Security Developments Involving the PRC* (Washington, D.C.: 2010), 43.

21. Wang Chuanjian, "India's South China Sea Policy: Intentions, Impact," *Waijiao Pinglun* (Beijing), 25 June 2010, 107–22.

22. Quoted in Ezra Vogel, *Deng Xiaoping and the Transformation of China* (Cambridge, Mass.: Harvard University Press, 2011), 695.

23. See the excellent Christopher Yung and Ross Rustici, with Isaac Kardon and Joshua Wiseman, *China's Out of Area Naval Operations: Case Studies, Trajectories, Obstacles, and Potential Solutions,* China Strategic Perspectives 3 (Washington, D.C.: National Defense University Press, 2012).

24. The first treaty, signed in January 1987, may be found at treaties.un.org/ (accessed 4 March 2013). The second agreement is discussed in Peter Dutton, "Charting a Course: US-China Cooperation at Sea," *China Security* 5, no. 1 (Winter 2009): 11–26.

25. Quoted in Ralph A. Cossa, *U.S. 1, China 0,* PacNet 35 (Honolulu: CSIS, 6 June 2012).

26. Hugh White, *The China Choice: Why America Should Share Power* (Collingwood, Australia: Black, 2011). Quotes are in "Extract from the 'China Choice: Why America Should Share Power,'" Sydney, www.lowyinstitute.org (accessed 4 March 2013).

Bibliography

"23 Remote Isles Put under State Ownership." *Yomiuri Shimbun,* 8 March 2012. http://www.yomiuri.co.jp/dy/national/T120307006853.htm.

Acharya, Amitav. "ASEAN's Dilemma: Courting Washington without Hurting Beijing." *Asia Pacific Center Bulletin* 133 (18 October 2011). http://www.east westcenter.org/publications/aseans-dilemma-courting-washington-without-hurting-beijing (accessed 17 June 2012).

Adjusting Course: A Naval Strategy for Canada. Ottawa: Canada Communications Group, 1997.

"Agni-VI to Be Ready by Mid-2014." *IBN,* 23 May 2010. http://ibnlive.in.com/news/agnivi-to-be-ready-by-mid-2014/260489-60-117.html.

Agnihotri, K. K. "Military Operations Other than War: PLA's Role in 'Peaceful Development' of China." *India Military Review* (November 2011). http://maritimeindia.org/article/military-operations-other-war-pla-navys-role-peaceful-development-china (accessed 14 May 2012).

Agnihotri, K. K., and Sunil Kumar Agarwal. "Legal Aspects of Marine Scientific Research in Exclusive Economic Zones: Implications of the *Impeccable* Incident." National Maritime Foundation (New Delhi) *Maritime Affairs,* 5 July 2010. http://academic.research.microsoft.com/Author/28353984/k-k-agnihotri (accessed 8 September 2012).

"Aircraft Carriers: Expanding America's Reach." Navy Office of Information *Rhumb Lines,* 16 November 2010. http://www.navy.mil/navco/pages/rhumb_lines.html.

Alani, Mustapha. "Toward a Comprehensive Maritime Security Arrangement in the Gulf." In *The Indian Ocean: Resource and Governance Challenges,* edited by Ellen Laipson and Amit Pandya, 46–48. Washington, D.C.: Stimson Center, 2009.

An Analysis of the Navy's Fiscal Year 2013 Shipbuilding Plan. Washington, D.C.: Congressional Budget Office, July 2011.

Ando Jun. "Chinese Official Says Enhanced Patrols near Senkakus Aimed at 'Breaking' Japan's Effective Control." *Tokyo Shimbun,* 22 March 2012. http://www.china-defense-mashup.com/china-sends-more-patrol-ships-to-break-japans-control-over-senkaku.html.

"Annual Defense Report for 2011." *Jane's Defense Weekly,* 14 December 2011. http://jdw.janes.com/public/jdw/warfare.shtml.

"Apparent Text of Agreement on the Basic Principles for Guiding the Settlement of Maritime Issues between the PRC and the SRV." Xinhua, 11 October 2011. http://www.google.com/search?client=safari&rls=en&q=apparent+text +of+Agreement+on+the+Basic+Principles+for+Guiding+the+Settlement+of+ Maritime+Issues+Between+the+People's+Republic+of+China+and+the+Soci alist+Republic+of+Vietnam&ie=UTF-8&oe=UTF-8.

Arsana, I Made Andi. "Is China a Neighbor to Indonesia?" *Jakarta Post,* 8 August 2011. http://www.thejakartapost.com/news/2011/08/08/is-china-a-neighbor-indonesia.html.

Asada, Sadao. *From Mahan to Pearl Harbor: The Imperial Japanese Navy and the United States.* Annapolis, Md.: Naval Institute Press, 2006.

"ASEAN Countries to Increase Defense Industry Cooperation." *Nation,* 19 May 2011. http://www.nationmultimedia.com/home/Asean-countries-agree-to-increase-defence-industry-30155719.html.

"ASEAN Foreign Ministers Affirm Common Stance on the East Sea." *Vietnam .net Bridge,* 11 January 2012. http://english.vietnamnet.vn/en/politics/17708/ asean-foreign-ministers-affirm-common-stance-on-the-east-sea.html.

Austin, Greg. *China's Ocean Frontier: International Law, Military Force, and National Development.* Sydney, Australia: Allen & Unwin, 1998.

Australian Department of Defense. *Defending Australia in the Asia-Pacific Century: Force 2030.* Canberra, 2009. http://www.defence.gov.au/white paper/docs/defence_white_paper_2009.pdf (accessed 26 December 2011).

Averitt, Leah. "China's Growing Maritime HA/DR." Jamestown Foundation *China Brief* 10, no. 12 (11 June 2010). http://www.jamestown.org/ programs/chinabrief/single/?tx_ttnews%5Btt_news%5D=36476&tx_ ttnews%5BbackPid%5D=414&no_cache=1 (accessed 7 June 2012).

Bader, Jeffrey A. *Obama and China's Rise: An Insider's Account of America's Asia Strategy.* Washington, D.C.: Brookings, 2012.

Bangladesh Navy, http://www.bangladeshnavy.org.html.

Barta, Patrick. "U.S., Vietnam in Exercises amid Tensions with China." *Wall Street Journal,* 16 July 2011. http://online.wsj.com/article/SB10001424052 702304223804576447412748465574.html.

Bartlett, Merrill. *Lejeune: A Marine's Life, 1867–1942.* Annapolis, Md.: Naval Institute Press, 1996.

Bateman, Sam. *Coming Back to the US Fold: New Zealand Defense and Security Policies.* RSIS Commentary 146/2010. Singapore: Rajaratnam School of International Studies, 10 November 2011. http://www.rsis.edu.sg/ publications/Perspective/RSIS1462010.pdf (accessed 1 June 2012).

————. *Increasing Competition in the South China Sea*. RSIS Commentary 157/2012. Singapore: Rajaratnam School of International Studies, 21 August 2012. http://www.rsis.edu.sg/publications/commentaries.html (accessed 8 September 2012).

————. *Looking West: Australian Defense Force Posture Review*. RSIS Commentary 110/2011. Singapore: Rajaratnam School of International Studies, 25 July 2011. http://dr.ntu.edu.sg/bitstream/handle/10220/8000/RSIS1102011.pdf?sequence=1 (accessed 1 June 2012).

————. "Regional Responses to Enhance Maritime Security in East Asia." *Korean Journal of Defense Analysis* 18, no. 2 (Summer 2006): 26–31.

————. *Saving Lives at Sea: Everyone's Responsibility*. RSIS Commentary 148/2012. Singapore: Rajaratnam School of International Studies, 10 August 2012. http://www.eurasiareview.com/17082012-saving-lives-at-sea-everyones-responsibility-analysis/ (accessed 26 August 2012).

Bateman, Sam, Joshua Ho, and Jane Chan. *Good Order at Sea in Southeast Asia*. Singapore: Rajaratnam School of International Studies, April 2009. http://www.rsis.edu.sg/publications/policy_papers/RSIS_Policy%20Paper%20-%20Good%20Order%20at%20Sea_270409.pdf (accessed 5 September 2012).

Bateman, Sam, and Michael Richardson. *A Time Bomb for Global Trade: Maritime-Related Terrorism in an Age of Weapons of Mass Destruction*. Singapore: Institute of Southeast Asian Studies, 2004.

Bellman, Eric, and Cris Larano. "Clinton: South China Sea Dispute Must Be Resolved Peacefully." *Wall Street Journal*, 16 November 2011. http://online.wsj.com/article/SB10001424052970204190504577041213482505688.html.

Bingde, Chen. "Remarks." National Defense University. Washington, D.C., May 2011.

Bissinger, Jared. "The Maritime Boundary Dispute between Bangladesh and Myanmar: Motivations, Potential Solutions, and Implications." *Asia Policy*, no. 10 (July 2010): 103–42. http://nbr.org/publications/issue.aspx?id=203 (accessed 9 April 2012).

Black, Jeremy. *Naval Power*. London: Palgrave, 2009.

Blair, Clay. *Hitler's U-Boat War: The Hunters, 1939–1942*. New York: Random House, 1996.

————. *Silent Victory: The U.S. Submarine War against Japan*. New York: J. B. Lippincott, 1975.

Blasko, Dennis J. "An Analysis of China's 2011 Defense Budget and Total Military Spending: The Great Unknown." Jamestown Foundation *China Brief* 11, no. 4 (10 March 2011). http://www.jamestown.org/programs/chinabrief/single/?tx_ttnews%5Btt_news%5D=37631&tx_ttnews%5BbackPid%5D=25&cHash=962dd98d4000505226b122227911ea48 (accessed 30 January 2012).

———. E-mail to author, 18 July 2012, with data gathered from http://www.bj review.com.cn/rint/txt/2010–04/19content_264350_4.htm; http://eng.china mil.com.cn/special-reports/2008hjdjhd/node_21074.htm; http://eng.china mil.com.cn/news-channels/china-military-news/2010–01/06/content_4762058 .htm.

Blumenthal, Daniel, and Michael Mazza. "Why to Forget UNCLOS." *Diplomat,* 17 February 2012. http://www.aei.org/article/foreign-and-defense-policy/ why-to-forget-unclos/ (accessed 28 June 2012).

Bodadora, Norman. "Aquino Warns of Arms Race." *Philippine Daily Inquirer,* 25 May 2012. http://newsinfo.inquirer.net/8968/aquino-warns-of-arms-race.

Bowden, Anna, and Shikha Basnet. *Economic Cost of Somali Piracy 2011.* Working Paper. N.p.: One Earth Future Foundation, 2012. http://www.oceans beyondpiracy.org (accessed 13 February 2012).

Bowditch, Thomas A., et al. *A U.S. Navy-Indian Navy Partnership for the Future.* CRM D0023588.A2/Final. Arlington, Va.: Center for Naval Analyses, November 2010.

Bower, Ernest Z., and Michael J. Green. *U.S.-Japan-ASEAN Trilateral Strategic Dialogue.* Maui, Hawaii: Center for Strategic and International Studies, 7 January 2011. http://csis.org/publication/us-japan-asean-trilateral-strategic-dialogue (accessed 8 September 2012).

Brady, Anne Marie. "Polar Stakes: China's Polar Activities as a Benchmark for Intentions." Jamestown Foundation *China Brief* 12, no. 14 (19 July 2012). http://www.jamestown.org/single/?no_cache=1&tx_ttnews%5Btt_ news%5D=39647&tx_ttnews%5BbackPid%5D=7&cHash=99f7e4c63e50 4c25e7be08acfda148db (accessed 26 August 2012).

Bratton, Patrick. "The Creation of Indian Integrated Commands: Organizational Learning and the Andaman and Nicobar Command." *Strategic Analysis* 36, no. 3 (May–June 2012): 440–60. http://www.idsa.in/strategicanalysis/36_3/ TheCreationofIndianIntegratedCommands_PatrickBratton (accessed 8 September 2012).

Brennan, Elliot. "Rising Tide of Conflict in the South China Sea." *Asia Times,* 3 March 2012. http://www.atimes.com/atimes/China/NC03Ad01.html.

Broader Horizons. New Delhi: Institute for Defence Studies and Analyses, April 2012. http://www.rsis.edu.sg/research/maritime/BroaderHorizons1204.pdf.

Buckley, Chris. "Analysis: China Looks across Asia and Sees New Threats." Reuters, 14 November 2011. http://www.reuters.com/article/2011/11/10/us-china-asia-idUSTRE7A91CY20111110.

———. "China Issues Guidelines to Ease South China Sea Disputes." Reuters, 2 August 2011. http://af.reuters.com/article/worldNews/idAFTRE7710 OT20110802.

———. "China Military Warns of Confrontation over Seas," Reuters, 21 April 2012. http://www.reuters.com/article/2012/04/21/us-china-usa-philippines-idUSBRE83K08D20120421.

———. "China's Li Prods North Korea on Improving Regional Ties." Reuters, 23 October 2010. http://in.reuters.com/article/2011/10/23/idIN India-60072520111023.

———. "PLA Research Says U.S. Aims to Encircle China," Reuters, 28 November 2011. http://www.reuters.com/article/2011/11/28/us-china-usa-pla-idustre7AR07QI0111128 (accessed 2 March 2013).

Buster, James C. "Parsing China's Fourth Fleet." *Signal Online* (November 2011). http://www.afcea.org/signal/articles/templates/SIGNAL_Article_Template .asp?articleid=2774&zoneid=7 (accessed 16 May 2012).

Butow, Robert J. C. *Japan's Decision to Surrender*. Palo Alto, Calif.: Stanford University Press, 1954.

———. *Tojo and the Coming of the War*. Palo Alto, Calif.: Stanford University Press, 1969.

Byman, Daniel, and Roger Cliff. *China's Arms Sales: Motivations and Implications*. Santa Monica, Calif.: RAND, 1999.

Cahiles-Magkilat, Bernie. "RP-China Joint Exploration Okayed." *Manila Bulletin* (26 August 2011). http://www.mb.com.ph/artcles/332229/rpchina-joint-exploration-okayed.

"Campaign Battlefield," *Science of Campaigns* (Beijng: AMS, n.d.). Excerpt furnished by Blasko (2006): 52, 577–79.

Campbell, Mark A., John Krempasky, and Michael Bosworth. "A Persistent, Effective, and Affordable Global Fleet Station Concept." American Society of Naval Engineers *Naval Engineers Journal*, no. 4. (2012): 51–66.

"Canada Integrating Maritime Capabilities." United Press International, 30 March 2011. http://www.upi.com/Business_News/Security-Industry/2011/03/30/Canada-integrating-maritime-capabilities/UPI-30671301487863/.

Cao, Xiaoguang. "Pakistan's Mehran Naval Air Base." *Naval & Merchant Ships* (July 2011): 40–42.

Capaccio, Tony. "Navy Delays Carrier's Combat Tests." *Business Week*, 9 August 2012. http://www.businessweek.com/news/2012–08–09/navy-delays-carrier-s-combat-tests-weapons-tester-says (accessed 19 August 2012).

Cavas, Christopher P. "8 LCSs Could Be Based in Gulf, Says U.S. Navy Undersecretary." *Defense News*, 21 May 2012. http://www.defensenews.com/article/20120521/DEFREG02/305210015/8-LCSs-Could-Be-Based-In-Gulf.

Central Intelligence Agency. *Soviet Naval Strategy and Programs through the 1990s*. National Intelligence Estimate 11–15–82. Washington, D.C., March 1983. Declassified by CIA Historical-Review Program.

Cha, Victor. *The Sinking of the* Cheonan. Washington, D.C., Center for Strategic and International Studies, 22 April 2010. http://csis.org/publication/sinking-cheonan (accessed 29 January 2012).

"Changing World 2012: Japan and East Asia/Nations Face Off beneath the Waves." *Yomiuri Shimbun*, 24 January 2012. http://www.yomiuri.co.jp/dy/world/T120123004718.htm.

Chellaney, Brahma. "New Australia-India Security Accord: Asia's New Strategic Partners." *Japan Times*, 10 December 2009. http://chellaney.spaces.live.com/blog/cns!4913C7C8A2EA4A30!1138.entry.

Chen, Guan Gwen. "China's Maritime Security Forces." *Bangui Zhishi*, 1 May–30 June 2009. OSC-CPP20090610678001.

Chidambaram, P. "Budget 2013: India Hikes Military Spending 14 Percent." zeenews.com. 28 February 2013.

"China and Vietnam to Ease Maritime Tensions." *Al Jazeera*, 26 June 2011. http://www.aljazeera.com/news/asia-pacific/2011/06/201162610193480905.html.

"China, ASEAN Countries Hold Meeting on South China Sea." Xinhua, 15 January 2012. http://www.fmprc.gov.cn/chn/gxh/tyb/wjbxw/t895779.htm.

"China Boosts Naval Presence near Korean Peninsula." *Chosun Ilbo*, 12 March 2012. http://english.chosun.com/site/data/html_dir/2012/03/12/2012031201520.html.

"China 'Constructive' on South China Sea Rows, Says US." *BBC News*, 19 November 2011. http://www.bbc.co.uk/news/world-asia-15802063.

"China Demands Manila Hands Back Seized Fishing Boats." Reuters, 20–25 October 2011. http://in.reuters.com/article/2011/10/20/idINIndia-60014520111020.

"China Evacuates 12,000 from Libya, Sends Frigate to Help." Xinhua, 25 February 2011. http://www.chinadaily.com.cn/china/2011–02/25/content_12075249.htm.

"China Issues Plan for Maritime Development." Xinhua, 26 April 2012. http://news.xinhuanet.com/english/china/2012–04/25/c_131551501.htm.

"China Keen on Military Aid." *Daily Star*, 12 November 2010. http://www.thedailystar.net.

"China Must Have Strong Navy." Xinhua, 5 December 2011. http://www.chinadaily.com.cn/opinion/2011–12/02/content_14200571.htm.

"China, Myanmar Forge Strategic Partnership, Ink Deals." *Global Times*, 28 May 2011. http://world.globaltimes.cn/asia-pacific/2011–05/659824.html.

"China Never Intends to Challenge U.S." *AFP* in *Defense News*, 18 May 2011. http://chinadigitaltimes.net/2011/05/china-never-intends-to-challenge-us-top-general/.

"China Now Calls Senkakus Core Interest." *Asahi News*, 4 February 2012. http://article.wn.com/view/2012/02/04/China_now_calls_Senkaku_Islands_core_interest/.

"China Protests Japan's Island Naming Plan." Agence France-Presse, 30 January 2012. http://www.news.yahoo.com/china-protests-japans-island-naming-plan.

"China Releases Standard Names of Diaoyu Islands." Xinhua, 3 March 2012. http://www.china.org.cn/china/2012–03/03/content_24790180.htm.

"China to Intensify Maritime Territory Patrols." Xinhua, 19 March 2012. http://news.xinhuanet.com/english/china/2012–03/19/c_131476187.htm.

"China to Step Up Maritime Patrols in Spratlys." *Philippine Star,* 21 March 2012. http://www.philstar.com/Article.aspx?articleId=789302&publicationSubCategoryId=63.

"China to Strengthen Maritime Forces amid Disputes." *People's Daily,* 17 June 2011. http://english.people.com.cn/90001/90776/90883/7412388.html.

"China, U.S. Start Megaports Initiative Pilot Project to Boost Cargo Security." Xinhua, 7 December 2012. http://news.xinhuanet.com/english/china/2011–12/07/c_131293615.htm.

"China's Brooding 'Dragons' Complicate Standoffs at Sea." *Japan Times,* 12 June 2012. http://www.japantimes.co.jp/text/eo20120612a1.html.

"China's Foreign Ministry Spokesperson Hong Lei's Regular Press Conference." *Foreign Ministry of the People's Republic of China,* 29 February 2012. http://www.fmprc.gov.cn/eng/xwfw/s2510/t910855.htm.

"China's Maritime Strategy Being Tested amid South China Sea Disputes." *Bejing Caijing,* 24 October 2011. http://english.caijing.com.cn/2011–10–24/110914257.html.

"China's Military Rise: The Dragon's New Teeth." *Economist,* 7 April 2012. http://www.economist.com/node/21552193.

China's White Paper on Ocean Policy. http://www.jodc.go.jp/info/ioc_doc/Technical/158387e.pdf.

"Chinese Marine Survey Vessel Spotted near Senkaku Islands." *Kyodo,* 15 November 2011. http://www.reuters.com/article/2011/08/24/us-japan-china-disputes-idUSTRE77N0R620110824.

"Chinese Might." *Manila Times,* 8 March 2011. No longer online.

"Chinese Navy Frigate Arrives Waters off Libya." Xinhua, 1 March 2011. http://english.peopledaily.com.cn/90001/90776/90883/7305215.html.

"Chinese President Meets Deputies for Military Meetings." Xinhua, 7 December 2011. http://news.xinhuanet.com/english/china/2011–12/06/c_131291648.htm.

Choe, Hang-Hun. "South Korea to Sign Military Pact with Japan." *New York Times,* 29 June 2012. http://www.nytimes.com/2012/06/29/world/asia/south-korea-to-sign-historic-military-pact-with-japan.html.

Chotiyaputta, Cherdchinda. "Marine Policy and Management in Thailand." Paper presented at the International Workshop on Cooperation and Development in the South China Sea, Beijing, 30–31 August 2011. http://km.dmcr.go.th/attachments/267_Cherdchinda-MarinePolicyandMangement inThailand.pdf.

Chua, Chin Hon. "US Reaffirms Commitment to Asia-Pacific." *Straits Times* (Singapore), 5 April 2012. http://www.straitstimes.com/BreakingNews/Singapore/Story/STIStory_785555.html.

Clausewitz, Karl von. *On War,* edited and translated by Michael Howard and Peter Paret. Princeton, N.J.: Princeton University Press, 1976.

"Coast Guard to Get Power to Make Arrests on Uninhabited Islands." *Asahi Shimbun,* 22 February 2012. http://ajw.asahi.com/article/behind_news/politics/AJ201202220047.

Cole, Bernard D. "Drawing Lines at Sea." U.S. Naval Institute *Proceedings* 137/11/1, no. 305 (November 2011). http://www.usnavyoilers.com/Proceedings/Drawing_Lines_at_Sea.html (accessed 16 May 2012).

———. *The Great Wall at Sea: China's Navy in the Twenty-First Century*. 2nd ed. Annapolis, Md.: Naval Institute Press, 2010.

———. *Sea Lanes and Pipelines: Energy Security in Asia*. Santa Barbara, Calif.: Praeger, 2008.

———. *Taiwan's Security: History and Prospects*. New York: Routledge, 2006.

Cole, J. Michael. "Chinese Navy Vessels Spotted Close to Japanese Coast." *Jane's Defense Weekly,* 15 May 2012. http://www.janes.com/products/janes/defence-security-report.aspx?id=1065967528 (accessed 3 June 2012).

———. "PLA Sorties Threaten Encirclement." *Taipei Times,* 9 February 2012. http://www.taipeitimes.com/News/front/archives/2012/02/09/2003525025.

Colombage, Jayanath. "Sri Lanka Navy" in "The Commanders Respond." U.S. Naval Institute *Proceedings* 139/3/1,321 (March 2012): 27.

"The Commanders Respond." U.S. Naval Institute *Proceedings* 137/3/1,297 (March 2011): 12. http://www.usni.org/magazines/proceedings/2011–03/commanders-respond-lieutenant-colonel-michael-rosette-seychelles-coast (accessed 8 September 2012).

"The Commanders Respond." U.S. Naval Institute *Proceedings* 137/3/1,297 (March 2011). http://www.usni.org/magazines/proceedings/2011–03/commanders-respond-admiral-nirmal-verma-indian-navy.

"Cooperative Strategy for 2007." http://www.navy.mil/maritime/display.asp?page=strglance.html (accessed 25 February 2013).

Cook, Malcolm, and Thomas S. Wilkins. *Australia and Japan: Allies in Partnership*. Asia Pacific Bulletin 101. Honolulu: East-West Center, 17 March 2011. http://www.eastwestcenter.org/publications/australia-and-japan-allies-partnership (accessed 11 May 2012).

Cooper, Cortez. "The PLA Navy's New Historic Missions." Santa Monica, Calif.: RAND Corporation. June 2009. http://www.rand.org/pubs/testimonies/2009/RAND_CT332.pdf (accessed 3 March 2013).

Corbett, Julian F. *Some Principles of Maritime Strategy*. London: Longmans, Green. 1911; Annapolis, Md.: Naval Institute Press, 1988.

Cossa, Ralph A. *U.S. 1, China 0*. PacNet 35. Honolulu: Center for Strategic and International Studies, 6 June 2012. http://csis.org/publication/pacnet-35-us-1-china-0 (accessed 7 June 2012).

Dai, Bingguo. "Persisting with Taking the Path of Peaceful Development." Ministry of Foreign Affairs statement, Beijing, 15 September 2011. http://www.fmprc.gov.cn/eng/zxxx/t860218.htm.

Dasgupta, Sajbal. "Vietnamese Threat to China, from the Sea?" *Times of India,* 12 June 2011. http://articles.timesofindia.indiatimes.com/2011–06–12/china/29649924_1_south-china-sea-chinese-fishermen-ammunition-drill.

Datta, Rahul. "Govt Nod for Two More *Arihant*s." *Pioneer,* 28 February 2012. http://dailypioneer.com/nation/46122-govt-nod-for-two-more-arihants-.html.

Defense White Papers, China. http://www.china.org.cn/e-white/; http://china .org.cn/government/whitepaper/node_7114675.htm.

Del Callar, Michela P. "Nay to Seek US Reassurance of Support in Spratlys Conflict." *Daily Tribune,* 14 November 2011. http://www.tribuneonline .org/headlines/20111114hed5.html.

Dickerson, L. "Pakistan Eying Chinese Torpedoes, Missiles for Submarines." *ForecastInternational,* 9 March 2011. http://www.forecastinternational .com.

Dodd, Mark. "Navy's Rescue Ships out of Action in Dry Dock." *Australian,* 3 February 2011. http://www.theaustralian.com.au/news/nation/navys-rescue-ships-out-of-action-in-dry-dock/story-e6frg6nf-1225999037966.

Dogra, Suvi. *India and Japan Strengthen Ties.* London: International Institute for Strategic Studies, 2 May 2012. http://iissvoicesblog.wordpress. com/2012/05/02/india-and-japan-strengthen-ties/.

Donilon, Tom. "America Is Back in the Pacific and Will Uphold the Rules." *Financial Times,* 27 November 2011, 9. http://www.ft.com/intl/cms/ s/0/4f3febac-1761–11e1-b00e-00144feabdc0.htmlaxzz1v7gFpsHN.

"Don't Play with Fire." *China Daily,* 12 April 2012. http://www.chinadaily.com .cn/cndy/2012–04/12/content_15027794.htm.

Dotsenko, V. "Soviet Art of Naval Warfare in the Postwar Period." *Morskoy Sbornik,* no. 7 (1989): 22–38.

Dreyer, Edward L. "The Poyang Campaign 1363: Inland Naval Warfare in the Founding of the Ming Dynasty." In *Chinese Ways of Warfare,* edited by Frank A. Kierman Jr. and John K. Fairbank. Cambridge, Mass.: Harvard University Press, 1974.

———. *Zheng He: China and the Oceans in the Early Ming Dynasty, 1405–1433.* London: Longman, 2006.

Dreyer, June Teufel. "Why Taiwan Matters." Philadelphia: Foreign Policy Research Institute, 18 July 2011. http://www.fpri.org/enotes/2011/201107 .dreyer.taiwan.html (accessed 30 January 2012).

Druzhinin, Alexey. "Russia to Build Up Submarine Task Force along Northern Sea Route." RIA Novosti, 11 August 2011. http://en.ria.ru/ russia/20111108/168513774.html.

Duchatel, Mathieu. "The PLA Navy in the Indian Ocean." In *China's Sea Power, Reaching Out to the Blue Waters,* 3–5. London: Asia Centre of the European Council on Foreign Relations, 2011. http://www.centreasia.eu/.

Dutton, Peter. "Charting a Course: US-China Cooperation at Sea." *China Security 5,* no. 1 (Winter 2009): 11–26. http://www.chinasecurity.us/index. php?option=com_content&view=article&id=220 (accessed 18 January 2012).

———. "Three Disputes and Three Objectives: China and the South China Sea." *Naval War College Review 64,* no. 4 (Autumn 2011): 42–62.

Elms, Deborah, and C. L. Lim. *The Trans-Pacific Partnership Agreement (TPP) Negotiations: Overview and Prospects.* RSIS Working Paper 232. Singapore:

Rajaratnam School of International Studies, 21 February 2012. http://www
.rsis.edu.sg/publications/WorkingPapers/WP232.pdf (accessed 17 June 2012).

Emmers, Ralf. *Japan-Korea Relations and Todko/Takeshima Dispute: The Interplay of Nationalism and Natural Resources.* RSIS Working Paper 212. Singapore: Rajaratnam School of International Studies, 10 November 2010. http://www.rsis.edu.sg/publications/WorkingPapers/WP212.pdf (accessed 3 June 2012).

Emmerson, Charles, and Paul Stevens. *Maritime Choke Points and the Global Energy System: Charting a Way Forward.* Chatham House Briefing Paper. London: International Institute for Strategic Studies, January 2012. http://www.chathamhouse.org (accessed 22 February 2012).

Engstrom, Jeffrey. "PLA's Growing Force Projection Capabilities." Jamestown Foundation *China Brief* 10, no. 25 (17 December 2010). http://www.jamestown.org/programs/chinabrief/single/?tx_ttnews%5Btt_news%5D=37295&cHash=06626d6bb4 (accessed 31 May 2012).

Erickson, Andrew S. "Ballistic Trajectory: China Develops New Anti-Ship Missile." *Jane's China Watch,* 4 January 2010. http://www.janes.com/products/janes/defence-security-report.aspx?id=1065926157 (accessed 16 May 2012).

Erickson, Andrew, and Gabe Collins. "Near Seas 'Anti-Navy' Capabilities, Not Nascent Blue Water Fleet, Constitute China's Core Challenge to U.S. and Regional Militaries." *ChinaSignPost,* 7 March 2012. http://www.chinasignpost.com/2012/03/near-seas-"anti-navy"-capabilities-not-nascent-blue-water-fleet-constitute-china's-core-challenge-to-u-s-and-regional-militaries/ (accessed 11 July 2012).

Etherton, P. T. *The Cockpit of Asia.* New York: Frederick A. Stokes, 1932.

Evans, Donald C., and Mark R. Peattie. *Kaigun: Strategy, Tactics, and Technology in the Imperial Japanese Navy, 1887–1941.* Annapolis, Md.: Naval Institute Press, 1997.

Fedyszyn, Thomas R. "Renaissance of the Russian Navy?" U.S. Naval Institute *Proceedings* 138/3/1,309 (March 2012): 30–35.

Fei Shiting and Chen Xiaojing. "Enrich and Strengthen the Nation through Maritime Development: PLA Deputies to the NPC Call for Introducing a Maritime Strategy." *Jiefangjun Bao,* 9 March 2012, 7. OSC-CPP 20120309787007.

Ferguson, Niall. "The Decade the World Tilted East." *Financial Times,* 27 December 2009.

"Forward, from the Sea." http://ww.dtic.mil/jv2010/navy/b014.pdf.

"Fourth F-22P Frigate of Pakistan Navy Launched." *Free Republic,* 17 June 2011. http://www.freerepublic.com/focus/f-news/2736423/posts 2012.

Francis, Leithen. "SE Asian Nations Seek Improved ASW, AEW." *Aviation Week,* 1 February 2012. http://www.aviationweek.com/Article.aspx?id=/article-xml/DT_02_01_2012_p28–414011.xml (accessed 22 February 2012).

Fravel, M. Taylor. "China's Behavior in Its Territorial Disputes and Assertiveness in the South China Sea." Paper presented at the Center for Strategic and International Studies, Washington, D.C., October 2011.

———. "China's Response to a Rising India." Interview by Erin Fried, NBR, 4 October 2011. http://www.nbr.org/research/activity.aspx?id=177.

———. "China's Strategy in the South China Sea." *Contemporary Southeast Asia* 33, no. 3 (December 2011): 292–319.

———. "Did Hu Jintao Call for War?" 11 December 2011. taylorfravel.com/2011/12/did-hu-jintao-call-for-war/ (accessed 22 July 2012).

———. "Japan-China Maritime Step." *Diplomat*, 18 May 2012. http://taylorfravel.com/2012/05/japan-chinas-maritime-step/ (accessed 17 June 2012).

———."Why 'Non-Combat' PLA Operations Are Vital for China's Regime Stability." *Global Asia* 6, no. 2 (June 2011). http://www.globalasia.org/V6N2_Summer_2011/M_Taylor_Fravel.html.

Freedom to Use the Seas: India's Maritime Military Strategy. New Delhi: Ministry of Defense, 2007. http://indiannavy.nic.in/maritime_strat.pdf.

Friedman, Norman. "A Long Wait." U.S. Naval Institute *Proceedings* 137/10/1,304 (October 2011): 88–89.

"From the Sea." http:// www.dtic.mil/jv2010/navy/b014.pdf.

Gargan, Christine. "Republic of Singapore Navy Trains with U.S. Navy." *NavyNews*, NNS110121–01, 21 January 2011. http://www.cpf.navy.mil/media/news/articles/2011/jan/jan20_USN_RSN.shtml.

Gautam, P. K. *The Arctic as a Global Common*. IDSA Issue Brief. New Delhi: Institute for Defence Studies and Analyses, 2 September 2011. http://www.idsa.in/issuebrief/TheArcticasaGlobalCommon.

"General: China Never Intends to Challenge U.S.", Agence France-Presse, 18 November 2011. http://www.defensenews.com/story.php?i=6548219&c=ASI&s=POL (accessed 2 March 2013).

Giblin, James F. "National Strategies and Japan's Northern Territories." *Naval War College Review* 40, no. 4 (Winter 1987): 53–68.

Gokhale, Nitin. "India, China and the Pirates." *Diplomat*, 6 March 2012. http://the-diplomat.com/2012/03/06/india-china-and-the-pirates/?all=true (accessed 17 May 2012).

Goldrick, James. "India's Expeditionary Journey." U.S. Naval Institute *Proceedings* 139/3/1,321 (March 2013): 30–35.

Goldstein, Lyle. "Chinese Naval Strategy in the South China Sea: An Abundance of Noise and Smoke, but Little Fire." *Contemporary Southeast Asia* 33, no. 3 (2011): 320–47.

———. *Five Dragons Stirring Up the Sea: Challenge and Opportunity in China's Improving Maritime Enforcement Capabilities*. China Maritime Study 5. Newport, R.I.: Naval War College Press, 2005.

Gong Jinahua. "Sea Dispute a Real Test for China." *China Daily*, 8 June 2011. http://usa.chinadaily.com.cn/opinion/2011/06/08/content_12656288.htm.

Gong Yingchun. *The Development and Current Status of Maritime Disputes in the East China Sea.* NBR Special Report 35. Seattle, Wash.: National Bureau of Asian Research, December 2011. http://www.nbr.org/publications/element.aspx?id=562 (accessed 17 June 2012).

Gorshkov, Sergei. *Red Star Rising at Sea.* Annapolis, Md.: Naval Institute Press, 1978.

———. *The Seapower of the State.* Annapolis, Md.: Naval Institute Press, 1983.

Gottipati, Sruthi. "India Reaches Out to Myanmar." *New York Times,* 29 May 2012. http://india.blogs.nytimes.com/2012/05/29/india-reaches-out-to-myanmar/.

"Government Defines Emergencies in Surrounding Areas." *Yomiuri Shimbun,* 27 April 1998. FBIS-EAS-98–117.

Graham, Euan. *Japan's Sea Lane Security, 1940–2004.* New York: Routledge, 2006.

———. *South Korea's Maritime Challenges: Between a Rock and a Hard Base.* RSIS Commentary 063/2012. Singapore: Rajaratnam School of International Studies, 11 April 2012. http://www.rsis.edu.sg/publications/Perspective/RSIS0632012.pdf (accessed 26 May 2012).

———. *Transnational Crime in the Fisheries Industry: Asia's Problem?* RSIS Commentary 62/2011. Singapore: Rajaratnam School of International Studies, 25 April 2011. http://pk2pm.wordpress.com/2011/04/13/transnational-organized-crime-in-the-fishing-industry/.

Greenert, Jonathan. "CNO's Navigation Plan, 2012–2017." http://www.navy.mil/cno/Navplan2012–2017-V-Final.pdf.

———. *U.S. Navy Program Guide 2012: Meeting Today's Challenges and Preparing for the Future.* Washington, D.C.: Department of the Navy, 2012. http://www.navy.mil/navydata/policy/seapower/npg12/top-npg12.pdf.

Griffiths, Hugh, and Michael Jenks. *Maritime Transport and Destabilizing Commodity Flows.* SIPRI Policy Paper 2. Solna, Swed.: Stockholm International Peace Research Institute, January 2012.

Griggs, Ray. "The Commanders Respond." U.S. Naval Institute *Proceedings* 137/3/1,297 (March 2011).

Gupta, Sourabh. *India and Indonesia: Renewing Asia's Collective Destiny.* Asia Pacific Bulletin 99. Washington, D.C.: East-West Center, 11 March 2011. http://www.eastwestcenter.org/publications/india-and-indonesia-renewing-asias-collective-destiny (accessed 1 June 2012).

Hai Tao. "China Breaks Through Japan's Diaoyu Islands Defense Line." *Guoji Xianqu Daobao,* 12 December 2008. OSC-CPP20081215005001.

———. "The Chinese Navy Has a Long Way to Go to Get to the Far Seas." *Guoji Xianqu Daobao.* 9 January 2010, OSC-CPP20120109671003.

Hammes, T. X. *The Sling and the Stone: War in the 21st Century.* St. Paul, Minn.: Zenith, 2006.

Han, Nack Hoon. *South Korea's Defense Reforms: Impact on the Navy.* RSIS Commentary 183/2011. Singapore: Rajaratnam School of International Studies, 12 December 2011. http://www.eurasiareview.com/14122011-south-korea's-defence-reforms-impact-on-the-navy-analysis/ (accessed 26 May 2012).

Han, Xudong. "Peaceful Development Also Requires Military Support." *Liaowang*, no. 27 (4–10 July 2011). http://www.9abc.net/index.php/archives/5711.

Harlan, Chico. "New Japanese Defense Plan Emphasizes Threat of China." *Washington Post*, 12 December 2010. http://www.washingtonpost.com/wp-dyn/content/article/2010/12/12/AR2010121203790.html.

Harrison, Selig S. *China, Oil, and Asia: Conflict Ahead?* New York: Columbia University Press, 1977.

———. *Stirring Up the South China Sea.* Asia Report 223. Brussels: International Crisis Group, 23 April 2012.

Hattendorf, John B. *The Evolution of the U.S. Navy's Maritime Strategy, 1977–1986.* Newport Paper 19. Newport, R.I.: Naval War College Press, 2004.

———. "The United States Navy in the Twenty-First Century: Thoughts on Naval Theory, Strategic Constraints, and Opportunities." *Mariner's Mirror* 97, no. 1 (February 2011): 285–97.

Hattendorf, John B., and Peter Swartz. *U.S. Naval Strategy in the 1980s: Selected Documents.* Newport Paper 33. Newport, R.I.: Naval War College Press, 2008.

Hayashi, Yuka. "Japan to Boost Defense in Pacific, Minister Says." *Wall Street Journal*, 26 June 2012, A11.

Hille, Kathrin. "China Reveals Aircraft Carrier Plans." *Financial Times*, 17 December 2010. http://www.ft.com/cms/s/O/fa7f5e6a-09cc-11e0–8b29–00144feabdc0.html?ftcamp=rssaxzz18NkTvXM6.

Himes, Joshua C. *Iran's Maritime Evolution.* Washington, D.C.: Center for Strategic and International Studies, July 2011. http://csis.org/publication/gulf-analysis-paper-irans-maritime-evolution (accessed 9 April 2012).

Hlad, Jennifer. "Panetta: US Strategy Aims to Build Peace, Stability in Pacific." *Stars and Stripes*, 31 May 2012. http://www.stripes.com/news/panetta-us-strategy-aims-to-build-peace-stability-in-pacific-1.179256.

Ho, Joshua. *Piracy in the South China Sea.* RSIS Commentary 47/2011. Singapore: Rajaratnam School of International Studies, 24 March 2011. http://www.rsis.edu.sg/publications/Perspective/RSIS0472011.pdf (accessed 16 June 2012).

Ho, Peter. *FPDA at 40: Still Effective and Relevant.* RSIS Commentary 179/2011. Singapore: Rajaratnam School of International Studies, 5 December 2011. http://dr.ntu.edu.sg/handle/10220/8043 (accessed 17 June 2012).

Holmes, James R., and Yoshi Toshihara. *Red Star over the Pacific: China's Rise and the Challenge to U.S. Maritime Strategy.* Annapolis, Md.: Naval Institute Press, 2010.

Horowitz, Michael. *How Defense Austerity Will Test U.S. Strategy in Asia.* NBR Analysis Brief. Seattle, Wash.: National Bureau of Asian Research, 7 August 2012. http://www.nbr.org/publications/analysis/pdf/Brief/080712_ Horowitz_DefenseAusterity.pdf (accessed 19 August 2012).

Hranjski, Hrvoje. "U.S. Okays Transfer of Second Warship." *Asian Journal,* 10 February 2012. http://asianjournal.com/dateline-philippines/headlines/ 14831-us-oks-transfer-of-2nd-warship-to-philippines-.html.

Hsiao, Russell. "Military Delegates Call for National Maritime Strategy to Protect Expanding Interests." Jamestown Foundation *China Brief* 11, no. 4 (10 March 2011). http://www.jamestown.org/single/?no_cache=1&tx_ ttnews%5Btt_news%5D=37629&tx_ttnews%5BbackPid%5D=7&cHash= 79f56b556ae0003e6afc755934e1fa54 (accessed 14 May 2012).

Hsu, Immanuel C. Y. *The Rise of Modern China.* New York: Oxford University Press, 1970.

Hszieh, Stephanie, George Galdorisi, Terry McKearney, and Darren Sutton. "Networking the Global Maritime Partnership." *Naval War College Review* 65, no. 2 (Spring 2012): 11–29. http://www.usnwc.edu/ getattachment/493473de-ac4b-4f0a-b1b3–3671efdbd0af/Networking-the-Global-Maritime-Partnership (accessed 1 July 2012).

H.T. "Opening Up the Pacific." *Economist,* 12 November 2011. http://www. economist.com/blogs/banyan/2011/11/free-trade-agreements (accessed 17 June 2012).

"Huangyan Crisis Hints at Long-Term Tensions." *People's Daily,* 3 May 2012. http://english.people.com.cn/102774/7806679.html.

Hughes, Wayne. "Naval Operations: A Close Look at the Operational Level of War at Sea." *Naval War College Review* 65, no. 3 (Summer 2012): 23–46.

Huntington, Samuel P. "National Policy and the Transoceanic Navy." U.S. Naval Institute *Proceedings* 80, no. 5 (May 1954).

Hyun, Mingi. "South Korea's Blue-Water Ambitions." *Diplomat,* 18 November 2011. http://the-diplomat.com/2010/11/18/south-koreas-blue-water-ambitions/ (accessed 26 May 2012).

"IANS Report: Scorpenes Delayed by 3 Years." *India Strategy* 7, no. 4 (April 2012): 43.

Inderfurth, Karl F., and S. Amer Latif. "The Elephant Engages Asia at Its Own Pace." *U.S.-India Insight* 1, no. 6 (9 September 2011). http://csis.org/ publication/elephant-engages-asia-its-own-pace (accessed 17 June 2012).

"India, China Square Off for Sea Fight." *MaritimeSecurity.Asia,* 18 September 2011. http://maritimesecurity.asia/free-2/south-china-sea-2/india-china-square-off-for-sea-fight/.

"India Proposes Norms for Indian Ocean Anti-Piracy Patrols." *IANS,* 13 April 2012. http://news.taaza.com/news/927130-india-proposes-norms-for-indian-ocean-anti-piracy-patrols.html.

"Indian Carrier Begins Sea Trials." *Defense News,* 8 June 2012. http://www .defnesenews.com/fdcp/?unique=1339758275976.

Indian Maritime Doctrine Revisited. New Delhi: India Defense Consultants, 10 April 2005. http://www.indiadefence.com/indoctrine.htm.

"Indian Ocean Naval Symposium." Navy.mil. http://www.navy.mil.za/IONS_2011/index.html.

"Indian Warships Visit Shanghai." *PLA Daily*, 15 June 2012. http://english.people daily.com.cn/90786/7847433.html.

"India's Navy Boosts Spending 74 Percent." *Defense News*, 26 March 2012. http://www.defensenews.com/article/20120326/DEFREG03/303260003/India-8217-s-Navy.

"Indo-Japan First Joint Naval Exercise Today." *Top News Today*, 9 June 2012. http://home.topnewstoday.org/home/article/2484101/.

Indrasafitri, Dina. "Defense Chiefs Push for South China Sea Rules." *Jakarta Post*, 20 May 2011. http://www.thejakartapost.com/news/2011/05/20/defense-chiefs-push-south-china-sea-rules.html.

Information Office of the State Council of China. *National Ocean Policy of China.* Beijing, May 1998. http://www.jodc.go.jp/info/ioc_doc/Technical/158387e.pdf.

"IONS Meeting in South Africa." *IAS 100*, 23 April 2012. http://www.ias100.in/news_details.php?id=841.

"Iran Adds Two New Subs to Navy Fleet." UPI.com, 10 February 2012. http://www.upi.com/Top_News/World-News/2012/02/10/Iran-adds-two-news-subs-to-navy-fleet/UPI-28061328902395/?rel=39921334940331.

"Iran Navy Thwarts Somali Pirate Attack." *PressTV*, 18 May 2011. http://www.presstv.ir/detail/180498.html.

Jaafar, Adm. Dato' Dri Abdul Aziz bin Haji. In "The Commanders Respond." U.S. Naval Institute *Proceedings* 137/3/1,297 (March 2011): 32.

Jackson, Allison. "Chinese Premier Wen Jiaobao Signs Agreements on Energy, Arctic during Iceland Visit." *Global Post*, 20 April 2012. http://mobile.globalpost.com/dispatch/news/regions/europe/120420/chinese-premier-wen-jiabao-signs-agreements-energy-arctic-during.

Jaffrelot, Christophe. "Gwadar and Chabahar Display Chinese-Indian Rivalry in the Arabian Sea." *YaleGlobal*, 7 January 2011. http://yaleglobal.yale.edu/sites/default/files/images/2011/01/gwadrar1.jpg. Replaced by http://yaleglobal.yale.edu/content/tale-two-ports.

Jakobson, Linda, and Dean Knox. *New Foreign Policy Actors in China.* SIPRI Policy Paper 26. Solna, Swed.: Stockholm International Peace Research Institute, September 2010.

"Japan, China to Begin High-Level Maritime Talks." *Mainichi Japan*, 5 April 2012. http://www.japantimes.co.jp/text/nn20120405a8.html.T94iYI5uHFI.

"Japan Decides to Continue to Dispatch JMSDF Vessels to the Indian Ocean in Order to Support International Efforts to Fight against Terrorism." *Ministry of Foreign Affairs of Japan*, 21 April 2006. http://www.mofa.go.jp/policy/terrorism/measure0604.html.

"Japan Orders End of Refueling Mission in Indian Ocean." *China View,* 15 January 2010. http://news.xinhuanet.com/english/2010–01/15/content_12813652.htm.

"Japan Plans Okinawa Base to Keep Watch on China." WantChinaTimes.com, 22 August 2011. http://www.wantchinatimes.com/news-print-cnt.aspx?id=2 0110822000090&cid=1101.

"Japan PM Rejects S. Korea's Call to Withdraw Dokdo Remarks." *KBS World,* 27 January 2012. http://world.kbs.co.kr/english/news/news_In_detail.htm?la ng=e&id=In&No=87778&current_page=.

"Japan Protests over Korean Builders on Kuril Islands." *Chosun Ibo,* 1 June 2012. http://english.chosun.com/site/data/html_dir/2012/06/01/2012060101228 .html.

"Japan Slams Russian Military Build-Up on Islands." Agence France-Presse, 2 March 2011. http://www.google.com/hostednews/afp/article/ALeqM5hAgX 5TuePAuLAwoBiFvQB6zNnbhw?docId=CNG.6f16a0d80ca69b0ceb3b801 f55d1d760.301.

"Japan-U.S. Joint Declaration on Security, 1996." *Ministry of Foreign Affairs of Japan.* http:// www.mofa.go.jp/region/n-america/us/security/security.html.

"Japan, U.S., Australia to Strengthen Unity with Pacific Island Nations with Eye on Rising China." *Yomiuri,* 25 May 2012, 2.

"Japan, Vietnam Sign Memo on Defense Cooperation Enhancement." *Mainichi,* 25 October 2011. http://mdn.mainichi.jp/mdnnews/news/20111025p2g 00m0dm013000c.html.

"Japan Warns of China's Growing Naval Muscle." *Agence France-Presse,* 2 August 2011. http://www.defensenews.com/article/20110802/DEFSECT03/ 108020307/Japan-Warns-of-China-s-Growing-Naval-Muscle.

Japanese submission to the CLCS, 12 November 2008. http://www.un.org/Depts/ los/clcs_new/submissions_files/submission_jpn.htm.

Jones, Eric C., and Joseph E. Vorbach III. "The Maritime Domain Awareness Conundrum." U.S. Naval Institute *Proceedings* 137/10/1,304 (October 2011): 29.

Jung, Nam-ku, Park Byung-soo, and Ha Eo-young. "Japan to Send Destroyers to China's Doorstep." *Hankoryeh,* 31 May 2012. http://english.hani.co.kr/arti/ english_edition/e_international/535484.html.

Kapila, Subhash. *Japan-Australia Defense Agreement: Perspectives.* South Asia Analysis Group Paper 2191. Noida, India, 4 February 2007. http://www .southasiaanalysis.org/%5Cpapers22%5Cpaper2191.html.

Kaplan, Robert. *Monsoon: The Indian Ocean and the Future of American Power.* New York: Random House, 2010.

———. "U.S. Commander Says China Aims to Be a 'Global Military' Power." *Asahi Shimbun,* 28 December 2010. http://www.asahi.com/english/ TKY201201270279.html.

Kato, Yoichi. "China's Naval Expansion in the Western Pacific." *Global Asia 5,* no. 4 (Winter 2010). http://www.globalasia.org/V5N4_Winter_2010/Yoichi_

Kato.html?PHPSESSID=d096d516f3d35a8bf0742b070f8c1b3e (accessed 17 June 2012).

Kawano, Katsutoshi. "Japan Maritime Self-Defense Force," in "The Commanders Respond." U.S. Naval Institute *Proceedings* 139/3/1,321 (March 2013): 22–23.

Kaye, Stuart. *Freedom of Navigation in the Indo-Pacific Region*. Papers in Australian Maritime Affairs, no. 22. Canberra, ACT, Australia: Sea Power Centre, 2008.

Killebrew, Robert B. "Crime & War." U.S. Naval Institute *Proceedings* 137/10/1,304 (October 2011): 22–26.

Ken, Jimbo. *Japan Should Build ASEAN's Security Capacity*. Japan Institute of International Affairs Commentary 150. N.p., 29 May 2012. http://www.jiia .or.jp/en_commentary/201205/30–1.html (accessed 7 June 2012).

Kennedy, Paul M. *The Rise and Fall of British Naval Mastery*. London: A. Lane, 1976.

Khurana, Gurpreet S. "Aircraft Carriers and India's Naval Doctrine." *Journal of Defense Studies* 2, no. 1 (Summer 2008). http://www.idsa.in/jds/2_1_2008_ AircraftCarriersandIndiaNavalDoctrine_GSKhurana (accessed 6 April 2012).

Khemakorn, Pakjuta. *Suitable Management of Pelagic Fisheries in the South China Sea Region*. New York: United Nations, November 2006. http:// www.un.org/depts/los/nippon/unnff_programme_home/fellows_pages/ fellows_papers/khemakorn_0607_thailand.pdf (accessed 8 September 2012).

Kirk, Donald. "Seoul and Hanoi Eye a Glowing Partnership," *Asia Times Online*, 10 November 2011. http://www.atimes.com/atimes/korea/mk10dg01.html.

Kissinger, Henry. "Power Shifts and Security." Keynote address, eighth IISS Global Strategic Review, Geneva, 10 September 2010. http://www.iiss.org/ conferences/global-strategic-review/global-strategic-review-2010/plenary- sessions-and-speeches-2010/keynote-address/henry-kissinger/.

Koda, Yoji. "A New Carrier Race? Strategy, Force Planning, and JS *Hyuga*." *Naval War College Review* 64, no. 3 (Summer 2011): 31–60.

Koh, Swee Lean Collin. *Indonesia-Singapore Submarine Rescue Pact*. RSIS Commentary 134/2012. Singapore: Rajaratnam School of International Studies, 24 July 2012. http://www.rsis.edu.sg/publications/Perspective/ RSIS1342012.pdf (accessed 26 August 2012).

———. "The Philippines' Navy Challenge." *Diplomat*, 27 December 2011. http://the-diplomat.com/flashpoints-blog/2011/12/27/the-philippines'-navy- challenge/ (accessed 7 June 2012).

Kongrawd, Somjade. "Thailand and Cambodia Maritime Disputes." *Royal Thai Navy*, n.d. http://www.navy.mi.th/judge/Files/Thailand%Cambodia.pdf.

"Korea Must Get Tough on Illegal Chinese Fishing." *Chosun Ilbo*, 18 November 2011. http://english.chosun.com/site/data/html_dir/2011/11/18/ 2011111801200.html.

Kotani, Tetsuo. *Freedom of Navigation and the US-Japan Alliance: Addressing the Threat of Legal Warfare*. U.S.-Japan Papers. Tokyo: Japan Center for

International Exchange, December 2011. http://www.jcie.org/researchpdfs/USJapanPapers/Kotani.pdf.

Kramnik, Ilya. "The Russian Navy Participates in Vostok-2010 Military Exercises." RIA Novosti, 7 July 2010. http://en.rian.ru/analysis/20100707/159728960.html.

"KSS-II: Korea Orders Six More U-214 AIP Submarines." *Defense Industry Daily*, 28 July 2010. http://www.defenseindustrydaily.com/KSS-II-South-Korea-Orders-6-More-U-214-AIP-Submarines-05242/.

Kudenko, Aleksy. "State-of-the-Art Re-armament for Kuril Islands." RIA Novosti, 12 October 2011. http://rt.com/politics/kuril-islands-defense-tanks-663/.

Kurashiga, Nane. "Japan, Vietnam Agree on Defense Cooperation." *Asahi Shimbun*, 25 October 2011. http://ajw.asahi.com/article/behind_news/AJ2011102515718.

Lahn, Glada. *Trends in Asian National Oil Company Investment Abroad: An Update*. Chatham House Working Paper. London: International Institute for Strategic Studies, November 2007. http://www.google.com/search?client=safari&rls=en&q=chatham+house+report,+2007,+on+china's+energy+investments&ie=UTF-8&oe=UTF-8 (accessed 1 July 2012).

Lai, David, and Mark Miller. "Introduction." In *Beyond the Strait: PLA Missions Other than Taiwan*, edited by Roy Kamphausen and David Lai. Carlisle, Penn.: U.S. Army Strategic Studies Institute, 2008.

Landler, Mark. "Offering to Aid Talks, U.S. Challenges China on Disputed Islands." *New York Times*, 23 July 2012. http://www.nytimes.com/2010/07/24/world/asia/24diplo.html.

Laude, Jaime. "US Troops Can Use Clark, Subic Bases." *Philippine Star*, 6 June 2012. http://www.philstar.com/Article.aspx?articleId=814442&publicationSubCategoryId=63.

Le Dinh Tinh. *Vietnam: New Thinking, New Risks, New Opportunities*. PacNet 15. Honolulu: Center for Strategic and International Studies, 6 March 2012. http://csis.org/publication/vietnam-new-thinking-new-risks-new-opportunities (accessed 7 June 2012).

Lee, Melanie. "China, US Launch Radiation Detection System at Shanghai Port to Check for Nuclear Materials." Reuters, 7 December 2011. http://www.reuters.com/article/2011/12/07/us-china-us-nuclear-idUSTRE7B60EK20111207.

Lee, Rens. "The Far East between Russia, China, and America." *FPRI E-Notes*, July 2012. http://www.fpri.org/enotes/2012/201207.lee.fareast.pdf (accessed 19 August 2012).

Lee, Tae-hoon. "Seoul to Summon Chinese Diplomats over Leodo Remarks." *Korea Times*, 11 March 2012. http://110.45.173.105/www/news/special/2012/03/116_106688.html.

Lee-Brago, Pia. "China Seeks Discussion of South China Sea Issue with Phl: Says U.S. Not 'Party to Anything.'" *Manila Philippine Star*, 6 April 2011. http://www.philstar.com/Article.aspx?articleId=673464&publicationSubCategoryId=63.

Legrand, C. M. "Chinese Straight Baseline Declaration." Memorandum for Under Secretary of Defense for Policy, 21 May 1996. Copy in possession of author.

Li Hongmei, "South China Sea Matters Not a Whit to Philippines, U.S." Xinhua, 21 November 2011. http://news.xinhuanet.com/english2010/indepth/2011–11/21/c_131259724.htm.

Li, Jinming. "Nansha Indisputable Territory." *China Daily,* 15 June 2011. http://www.chinadaily.com.cn/opinion/2011–06/15/content_12698262.htm (accessed 14 May 2012).

Li Ming Jiang. "China and Maritime Cooperation in East Asia: Recent Developments and Future Prospects." *Journal of Contemporary China* 19, no. 64 (March 2010): 291–310 http://dx.doi.org/10.1080/10670560903444249 (accessed 8 September 2012).

Lin, Liyao. "Ex-*Varyag* Carrier May Join PLA Navy in 2012." China.org .cn, 10 March 2012. http://www.china.org.cn/china/NPC_CPPCC_2012/2012–03/10/content_24860546.htm.

Linn, Brian M. *Guardians of Empire: The U.S. Army and the Pacific, 1902–1940.* Chapel Hill: University of North Carolina Press, 1999.

Liu Shuguang. "China's Marine Economy." *East Asia Forum,* 17 November 2011. http://www.eastasiaforum.org/2011/11/17/china-s-marine-economy/ (accessed 16 May 2012).

Liu Yan. "The US Military Reveals Secret Tactics That Take Aim at China." *Beijing China Radio,* 18 November 2011. http://gb.cri.cn.

Liu Zhongmin. "Some Thoughts on the Issue of Sea Power and Rise of Great Nations." *World Economy and Politics,* no. 12 (2007).

"Lower House Passes Guideline Bills." Foreign Press Center–Japan, 7 May 1999. http://www.fas.org/news/japan/j9907.htm.

Luce, Henry. "The American Century." Editorial. *Life,* 17 February 1941.

Ma Haoliang. "China Needs to Break Through the Encirclement of First Island Chain." *Ta Kung Pao,* 21 February 2009. OSC-CPP20090221708020.

Ma Xiaojun. "Recognition of China's National Territorial Sovereignty: Complete, United, and Secure." *Shijie Zhishi,* 16 July 2012: 14–21. OSC-CPP20101021671007.

Mabus, Ray. "Remarks." "Week of Valor" Veterans Job Fair Luncheon, Jacksonville, Fla., 28 February 2012. http://www.navy.mil/navydata/people/secnav/Mabus/Speech/JacksonvilleJobFairLuncheon.pdf.

MacAskill, Andrew. "India Plans Test of Missile Capable of Reaching China." *Bloomberg,* 17 April 2012. http://www.bloomberg.com/news/2012–04–16/india-plans-test-of-missile-capable-of-reaching-northern-china.html?ftcamp-crm/email/2012417/nbe/beyondbricsNewYork/product.

Mackinder, Halford John. *Democratic Ideals and Reality.* London: Constable, 1919.

———. "The Geographical Pivot of History." *Geographical Journal* 23, no. 4 (April 1904): 421–37.

Maddison, Paul. "The Commanders Respond," U.S. Naval Institute *Proceedings,* 139/3/1,321 (March 2013): 18.

Mahan, Alfred Thayer. *The Influence of Sea Power upon History, 1660–1783.* Boston: Little, Brown, 1890; New York: Dover, 1987.

———. *The Influence of Sea Power upon the French Revolution and Empire, 1793–1812.* Boston: Little, Brown, 1892.

Maldives Coast Guard, http://maldivescoastguard.com/.

Manthorpe, Jonathan. "Japan Boosts Defense of Outer Islands to Deter China." *Vancouver Sun,* 26 April 2012. http://www.vancouversun.com/opinion/editorials/Manthorpe+Japan+boosts+defence+outer+islands+deter+China/6526629/story.html.

Mao Zedong. "The Chinese Revolution and the Chinese Communist Party." In *Selected Works of Mao Tse-tung.* Beijing, n.d. http://www.marxists.org/reference/archive/mao/selected-works/volume-2/mswv2_23.htm (accessed 21 August 2012).

Maritime Doctrine of Russian Federation 2020. Pr-1387. Approved by President of the Russian Federation Vladimir Putin. Moscow, 27 July 2001. http://www.scribd.com/doc/49589025/Russian-Maritime-Policy-2020.

Maritime Stability Operations. MCIP 3–33.-2/NWP 3–07/COMDTINST M3120.11. Washington, D.C.: Department of the Navy and U.S. Coast Guard, 2011. http://www.marines.mil/news/publications/Documents/MCIP%203–33_02.pdf.

"Maritime Strategy, 1986." U.S. Naval Institute *Proceedings.* Supplement (January 1986): 41–47.

Mazumdar, Mritunjoy, and Jon Rosamond. "Philippines Eyes US Cutter amid Wider Buying Plan." *Jane's Defense Weekly,* 11 May 2011: 15.

McCracen, Erin. "HMCS *Victoria* Returns to Sea." *Victoria News,* 19 April 2011. http://www.saanichnews.com/news/120218204.html.

McDevitt, Michael A. "The PLA Navy Anti-Access Role in a Taiwan Contingency." Paper prepared for the 2010 Pacific Symposium on "China's Naval Modernization: Cause for Storm Warnings," National Defense University, Washington D.C., 10 June 2010.

Mehta, Admiral Sureesh. *Freedom to Use the Sea: India's Maritime Strategy.* New Delhi: Ministry of Defense (Navy), 2007.

Menzies, Gavin. *1421: The Year China Discovered the World.* London: Transworld, 2002.

Mersheimer, John J. "China's Unpeaceful Rise." *Current History* 105, no. 690 (April 2006): 160–62.

Miles, Donna. "Locklear: Pacom's Priorities Reflect New Strategic Guidance." American Forces Press Service, 18 May 2012. http://www.defense.gov/news/newsarticle.aspx?id=116397.

Military Doctrine of the Russian Federation. Moscow, 5 February 2010. http://www.sras.org/military_doctrine_russian_federation_2010.

Miller, Edward S. *War Plan Orange: The U.S. Strategy to Defeat Japan.* Annapolis, Md.: Naval Institute Press, 1991.

Minnick, Wendell. "Brunei and Singapore Conduct Pelican Exercises." *Defense News,* 13 July 2011. http://www.defensenews.com/article/20110713/DEF SECT03/107130306/Brunei-Singapore-Conduct-Pelican-Exercises.

Misaki, Hisani. "Japanese Shipbuilders Worry about Dwindling Backlog." *Journal of Commerce,* 20 January 2012. http://www.joc.com/infrastructure/ japanese-shipbuilders-worry-over-backlog-after-poor-year (accessed 11 May 2012).

Mizokami, Kyle. *ASDF Intercepts vs. China at Five Year High.* N.p.: Japan Security Watch: New Pacific Institute, 28 December 2010. http://jsw .newpacificinstitute.org/?m=201012.

"Modern Merchant Marine." *American Maritime Congress* (2011). http://www .americanmaritime.org/merchant/.

Mogato, Manuel, and Rosemarie Francisco. "Manila Offers U.S. Wider Military Access, Seeks Weapons." Reuters, 29 March 2012. http://www.reuters.com/ article/2012/03/29/us-philippines-us-idUSBRE82S0LD20120329.

Morimoto, Satoshi. "Japan Must Make Efforts to Defend Itself in Line with Air-Sea Battle." *Sankei Shimbun,* 7 December 2011. No longer online.

"MSDF 16-Sub Fleet to Get Six More to Up Presence." *Japan Times,* 21 October 2010. http://www.japantimes.co.jp/text/nn20101021a1.html.

"Multi-Service Office to Advance Air-Sea Battle Concept." U.S. Department of Defense News Release 943–11, 9 November 2011. http://defensenewsstand .com/NewsStand-General/The-INSIDER-Free-Article/pentagon-poised-to-announce-new-multiservice-airsea-battle-office/menu-id-720.html.

Mulvenon, James. "Chairman Hu and the PLA's 'New Historic Mission.'" *China Leadership Monitor,* no. 27 (9 January 2009). http://www.fnvaworld.org/ download/tibet-related-doc/Hu-PLAs-missions-2008.pdf.

Muraviev, Alexander. *Russian Naval Power in the Pacific: Today and Tomorrow.* Working Paper 15. Canberra, ACT, Australia: Sea Power Center, 2003. http:// www.navy.gov.au/w/images/Working_Paper_15.pdf.

———. *The Russian Pacific Fleet from the Crimean War to Perestroika.* Papers in Australian Maritime Affairs, no. 20. Canberra, ACT, Australia: Sea Power Centre, 2007.

Murline, Anna. "US Training Base in Australia Is All about the Rise of China." *Christian Science Monitor,* 16 November 2011. http://www.csmonitor.com/ USA/Military/2011/1116/New-US-training-base-in-Australia-is-all-about-the-rise-of-China.

Murphy, Martin N. *Contemporary Piracy and Maritime Terrorism: The Threat to International Security.* Adelphi Paper 388. London: International Institute for Strategic Studies, 2007.

"National Strategy for Maritime Security." *U.S. Department of Homeland Security.* http://www.dhs.gov/ . . . /assets/HSPD13_MaritimeSecurityStrategy. pdf.

"Naval Fleet to Sail Through S. China Sea." *Oman Tribune/Press Trust of India,* 5 May 2012. http://www.indiandefence.com/forums/indian-air-force/17700-naval-fleet-sail-through-s-china-sea%3B-chinese-ship-call-kochi.html.

"Navy Gets 2,300-Ton Frigate." *Korea Herald,* 29 April 2011. http://view.koreaherald.com/kh/view.php?ud=20110429000700&cpv=0.

"Navy to Host 14-Nation 'Milan' Exercise from Feb 1." *Times of India,* 31 January 2012. http://articles.timesofindia.indiatimes.com/2012–01–31/india/31008894_1_indian-navy-routes-and-energy-lifelines-maritime-terrorism.

"Navy Receives US Surveillance Aircraft." *Dawn,* 21 February 2012. http://dawn.com/2012/02/21/navy-receives-us-surveillance-aircraft/.

"Navy to Operate 5 Nuke Submarines by End of the Decade." *Economic Times,* 5 April 2012. http://articles.economictimes.indiatimes.com/2012–04–05/news/31294337_1_nuclear-submarine-arihant-class-ins-chakra.

"New System to Help Vessels in Malacca Strait." *Jakarta Post,* 8 June 2012. http://www.thejakartapost.com/news/2012/06/08/new-system-help-vessels-malacca-strait.html.

Nguyen Dang Thang. *China's Fishing Ban in the South China Sea: Implications for Territorial Disputes.* PacNet 35A. Honolulu: Center for Strategic and International Studies, 20 July 2011. http://csis.org/publication/pacnet-35a-chinas-fishing-ban-south-china-sea-implications-territorial-disputes (accessed 16 June 2012).

Ni, Eryan. "Putting Weapons Down to Achieve Peace: The Calmness of PLA Diplomacy." *Feng Huang Chou Kan,* no. 378 (15 October 2010): 42–43. OSC-CPP20101018787005.

Nicholson, Brendan. "New Landing Ship out of Action." *Australian,* 20 June 2012. http://www.theaustralian.com.au/national-affairs/defence/new-landing-ship-out-of-action/story-e6frg8yo-1226401689269.

NIDS China Security Report 2011. Tokyo: National Institute for Defense Studies, n.d. http://www.nids.go.jp/english/publication/chinareport/index.html.

Nightingale, Alaric. "Shipping Bears Ascendant." *Bloomberg,* 25 June 2012. www.bloomberg.com/news/2012–06–25/shipping-bears-ascendant-as-fleet-growth-swamps-cargoes-freight.html (accessed 26 August 2012).

Nilsen, Thomas. "Dozens of Major Flaws on Newest Submarine." *Barents Observer,* 9 November 2011. http://barentsobserver.com/en/security/new-subs-made-old-spare-parts.

———. "*Kursk*'s Sister Ship Returns to Service." *Barents Observer,* 7 November 2011. http://barentsobserver.com/en/security/kursks-sister-ship-returns-service.

———. "New Subs Made of Old Spare Parts." *Barents Observer,* 27 October 2011. http://barentsobserver.com/en/security/new-subs-made-old-spare-parts.

———. "Russia to More than Double Number of New SSBNs." *Barents Observer,* 20 September 2011. http://barentsobserver.com/en/security/russia-more-double-number-new-ssbns.

"Nixon Doctrine." Army.mil. http://www.army.mil/article/3867/nixon-doctrine-and-vietnamization/.

"Nixon-Sato Communique." *Ryukyu-Okinawa History & Culture Website.* http://www.niraikanai.wwma.net/pages/archive/sato69.html.

"No New Russian Aircraft Carriers until 2020." Xinhua, 18 November 2011. http://www.english.news.cn.

Nofi, Albert A. *To Train the Fleet for War: The U.S. Navy Fleet Problems, 1923–1940.* Newport, R.I.: Naval War College Press, 2010.

Note Verbale. Permanent Mission of the PRC to the UN, CML/8/2011, 14 April 2011. Copy in author's possession.

Oakes, Dan. "Rusty Ships, Boats That Don't Fit Leave Minister All at Sea." *Australian Strategic Policy Institute,* 2 February 2011. http://www.smh.com.au/national/rusty-ships-boats-that-dont-fit-leave-minister-all-at-sea-20110201–1acgx.html (accessed 1 June 2012).

O'Brian, Patrick. *H.M.S.* Surprise. London: William Collins, 1973.

———. *The Thirteen Gun Salute.* London: William Collins, 1989.

Odom, Jonathan G. "The True 'Lies' of the *Impeccable* Incident: What Really Happened, Who Disregarded International Law, and Why Every Nation (Outside of China) Should Be Concerned." *Michigan State University College of Law Journal of International Law* 18, no. 3, 2010 (1 April 2010). http://papers.ssrn.com/sol3/papers.cfm?abstract_id=1622943 (accessed 1 July 2012).

Ong, Weichong. *Singapore's Total Defense: Shaping the Pillars.* RSIS Commentary 25/2011. Singapore: Rajaratnam School of International Studies, 21 February 2011. http://www.rsis.edu.sg/publications/Perspective/RSIS025 2011.pdf (accessed 2 June 2012).

Orendain, Simone. "Philippines Seeks Answers about Latest South China Sea Incident." Reuters, 1 June 2011. http://www.voanews.com/content/philippines-seeks-answers-about-latest-south-china-sea-incident-12293 6653/140180.html.

O'Rourke, Ronald. *Navy Force Structure and Shipbuilding Plans: Background and Issues for Congress.* RL 2665. Washington, D.C.: Congressional Research Service, 17 August 2010.

———. *Navy Force Structure and Shipbuilding Plans: Background and Issues for Congress.* Washington, D.C.: Congressional Research Service, 21 June 2012.

———. *Navy Ford (CVN-78) Class Aircraft Carrier Program: Background and Issues for Congress.* RS-20643.Washington, D.C.: Congressional Research Service, 10 December 2012.

Oshima, Takashi, and Koichi Furuya. "Japan Dives into South China Sea Flap with China." *Asahi Shimbun,* 6 November 2011. http://ajw.asahi.com/article/behind_news/politics/AJ2011110616738.

O'Sullivan, Mike. "Clinton: 21st Century Will Focus on Asia-Pacific." *VOA News,* 9 November 2011. http://www.voanews.com/articleprintview/168193.html.

Owen, Nick. "Disputed South China Sea Oil in Context." In *Maritime Energy Resources in Asia: Energy and Geopolitics,* edited by Clive Schofield. NBR Special Report 35. Seattle, Wash.: National Bureau of Asian Research, December 2011.

Paal, Douglas. *South China Sea: Plenty of Hazards for All.* Asia Pacific Brief. Washington, D.C.: Carnegie Endowment for International Peace, 7 July 2011. http://carnegieendowment.org/2011/07/07/south-china-sea-plenty-of-hazards-for-all/2w68 (accessed 16 June 2012).

"Pacific Partnership 2010 Accomplishments." *Rhumb Lines,* 6 October 2010. http://www.navy.mil/navco/pages/rhumb_lines.html.

"Pakistani Navy Launches New Fast Attack Missile Ship." *Naval Technology,* 22 September 2011. http:// www.naval-technology.com/news/news130516. html.

Pandit, Rajat. "India Is Now 6th Nation to Have a Nuclear Sub." *Times of India,* 24 January 2012. http://www.articles.timesofindia.indiatimes.com.

Park, Dong-Joon, and Danielle Chubb. "Why Dokdo Matters to Korea." *Diplomat,* 17 August 2011. http://thediplomat.com/new-leaders-forum/2011/08/17/why-dokdo-matters-to-korea/ (accessed 17 August 2012).

Patrick, Stewart M. "Obama's Plan for America's Pacific Century." *Atlantic Online,* 11 November 2011. http://www.theatlantic.com/international/archive/2011/11/obamas-plan-for-americas-pacific-century/249045/ (accessed 17 May 2012).

Paul, Joshy M. "Emerging Security Architecture in the Indian Ocean Region: Policy Options for India." *Maritime Affairs* 7, no. 1 (Summer 2011). http://www.theatlantic.com/international/archive/2011/11/obamas-plan-for-americas-pacific-century/249045/.

Pedrozo, Raul. "China's Maritime Claims: Exceeding the Limits of International Law." *University of New South Wales.* http://www.Unsworks.unsw.edu.au/fapi/datastream/unsworks:3198/SOURCE06.

———. "Preserving Navigational Rights and Freedoms: The Right to Conduct Military Activities in China's EEZ." *Chinese Journal of International Law* 9, no. 1 (2010): 9–29.

Perlez, Jane. "China Increases Military Spending More than 11 Percent." *New York Times,* 4 March 2012. http://www.nytimes.com/2012/03/05/world/asia/china-boosts-military-spending-more-than-11-percent.html.

Petrov, Vladimir. "Medvedev Orders Construction of Aircraft Carriers for Russian Navy." *Jane's Defense Weekly,* 14 October 2008. http://articles.janes.com/articles/Janes-Defence-Weekly-2008/Medvedev-orders-construction-of-aircraft-carriers-for-Russian-Navy.html.

Pettersen, Trude. "Russia Sets Up New Arctic Border Posts." *Barents Observer,* 16 April 2012. http://barentsobserver.com/en/security/russia-sets-new-arctic-border-posts.

Phan, Huynh. "Vietnam-China Relations in the Eye of a Senior Diplomat." *VietNamNet,* 26 January 2012. http://english.vietnamnet.vn/en/special-report/17459/vietnam-china-relations-in-the-eye-of-a-senior-diplomat.html.

"Philippine Defense Chief Says Military Too Weak." *Honolulu Star Adviser,* 24 May 2011. http://www.staradvertiser.com/news/breaking/122506473.html ?id=122506473.

"Philippines Rejects New Chinese Territorial Claim." Associated Press, 14 November 2011. http://globalnation.inquirer.net/18039/philippines-rejects-new-chinese-territorial-claim.

"PHL Asks China to Explain Ships near Reed Bank." *GMA News,* 1 June 2011. http://www.gmanetwork.com/news/story/222246/news/nation/phl-asks-china-to-explain-ships-near-reed-bank.

"PHL Seeks ASEAN Support for Possible China Meet on Spratly Row." *GMA News,* 15 January 2012. http://www.gmanetwork.com/news/story/244658/news/nation/phl-seeks-asean-support-for-possible-china-meet-on-spratly-row.

Pilling, David. "Asia's Quiet Anger with 'Big, Bad' China." *Financial Times,* 1 June 2011. http://www.ft.com/intl/cms/s/0/da3396b6–8c81–11e0–883f-00144feab49a.htmlaxzz1zPMRz4ta.

Pinalez, Juan. "Vietnam Representatives Visit USS *George Washington.*" Navy News Service, NNS110309–12, 9 March 2011. http://www.navy.mil/search/display.asp?story_id=58986.

Pitlo, Lucio Blanco. *Vietnam's Exploration and Production Contracts: Using Energy Interests to Strengthen Maritime Claims.* RSIS Commentary 106/2012. Singapore: Rajaratnam School of International Studies, 21 June 2012. http://www.rsis.edu.sg/publications/Perspective/RSIS1062012.pdf (accessed 1 July 2012).

Poling, Gregory. *Arguing over Blocks: Do China and the Philippines Both Have a Claim?* Washington, D.C.: Center for Strategic and International Studies, 16 April 2012. http://csis.org/publication/arguing-over-blocks-do-china-and-philippines-both-have-claim.

Pomeroy, Robin. "Iran Tests West with Plans for More War Games in Strait of Hormuz." *National Post,* 6 January 2012. http://news.nationalpost.com/2012/01/06/iran-tests-west-with-plans-for-more-war-games-in-strait-of-hormuz/.

Prakash, Arun. "China's Maritime Challenge in the Indian Ocean." *Maritime Affairs* 7, no. 1 (Summer 2011): 20–31.

———. "Rise of the East: The Maritime Dimension." *Maritime Affairs* 7, no. 2 (Winter 2011): 1–13.

"PRC Calls Senkaku Islands Beijing's 'Core Interest.'" Kyodo World Service, 21 January 2012. OSC-JPP20121969029.

"PRC's Xi Jinping Said Warning Vietnam to Keep Distance from US on SCS Issue." *Kyodo,* 20 January 2012. OSC-JPP20120120969109.

Pubby, Manu. "12th Defense Plan: Focus on Navy's 'Expeditionary' Ops." *Indian Express,* 4 May 2012. http://www.indianexpress.com/news/12th-defence-plan-focus-on-navys-expeditionary-ops/945283.

Qiu, Renjie, "ASEAN Demonstrates Spirit of Unity in Inaugural Brunei Fleet Review." *China Press*, 13 July 2011. OSC-SEP20110715166003.

Radyuhin, Vladimir. "Russia Sets Up Arctic Forces." *Hindu*, 1 July 2011. http://www.thehindu.com/news/international/article2151197.ece.

Rahman, Raseeh. "Chinese Plans in Seychelles Revive Indian Fears of Encirclement." *Guardian*, 22 March 2012. http://www.guardian.co.uk/world/2012/mar/22/china-seychelles-indian-fears-encirclement.

Raymond, Catherine Zara. "Countering Piracy and Armed Robbery in Asia: A Study of Two Areas," 319–33. In *Emerging Naval Powers*, edited by Robert Ross, Peter Dutton, and Øystein Tunsjø. London: Routledge, 2012.

Reagan, Ronald. "Statement on United States Oceans Policy," 10 March 1983. In *Public Papers of Ronald Reagan*, American Reference Library, AN: 9FVPPRWR030254. http://www.gc.noaa.gov/documents/031083-reagan_ocean_policy.pdf.

Rehman, Iskander. *From Down Under to Top Center: Australia, the United States, and This Century's Special Relationship*. Transatlantic Academy Paper Series. Washington, D.C.: May 2011. http://www.transatlanticacademy.org/publications/down-under-top-center (accessed 31 May 2012).

"Release of the Joint Operational Concept (JOAC)." U.S. Department of Defense News Release, 17 January 2012. http://www.dodlive.mil/index.php/2012/01/release-of-the-joint-operational-access-concept-joac/.

Ren Xiaofeng. "China's Maritime Security Policy Making and Maritime Confidence Building Measures." In *Twenty-First Century Seapower: Cooperation and Conflict at Sea*, edited by Peter Dutton, Robert Ross, and Øystein Tunsjø, chap. 12. London: Taylor & Francis, 2012.

"Researchers Suggest Solutions to Reclaim Hoang Sea [South China Sea]." *Tuoi Tre*, 29 November 2011. http://tuoitrenews.vn/cmlink/tuoitrenews/society/researchers-suggest-solutions-to-reclaim-hoang-sa-1.52877.

Patil, Reshma. "China Wants Talks on Indian Ocean." *Hindustan Times*, 11 August 2011. http://www.hindustantimes.com/world-news/RestOfAsia/China-wants-talks-on-Indian-Ocean/Article1-731930.aspx.

"Piracy and Armed Robbery News and Figures." *IMB*, 30 August 2012. http://www.icc-ccs.org/piracy-reporting-centre/piracynewsafigures.

"Pirate Attacks at Sea Getting Bigger and Bolder." *ICC Commercial Crime Services*, 14 July 2011. http://www.icc-ccs.org/news/450-pirate-attacks-at-sea-getting-bigger-and-bolder-says-imb-report.

Richardson, Paul. *Russia in the Asia-Pacific: Between Integration and Geopolitics*. Asia Pacific Bulletin 150. Washington, D.C.: East-West Center, 16 February 2012. http://www.eastwestcenter.org/publications/russia-asia-pacific-between-integration-and-geopolitics (accessed 26 May 2012).

Rogers, Will. *Security at Sea: The Case for Ratifying the Law of the Sea Convention*. Policy Brief. Washington, D.C.: Center for a New American Security, April 2012. http://www.cnas.org/blogs/naturalsecurity/2012/04/security-sea-case-ratifying-law-sea-convention.html (accessed 17 May 2012).

Ropp, Theodore. *The Development of a Modern Navy: French Naval Policy, 1871–1904*. Annapolis, Md.: Naval Institute Press, 1987.

Rosenberg, David. "Managing the Resources of the China Seas: China's Bilateral Fisheries Agreements with Japan, South Korea, and Vietnam." *Asia-Pacific Journal: Japan Focus* (30 June 2005). http://www.japanfocus.org/-David-Rosenberg/1789 (accessed 17 June 2012).

———. "Process: The Realities of Formulating Modern Naval Strategy." In *Mahan Is Not Enough: The Proceedings of a Conference on the Works of Sir Julian Corbett and Admiral Sir Herbert Richmond*, edited by James Goldrick and John B. Hattendorf. Newport, R.I.: Naval War College Press, 1993.

Ross, Robert S. "China's Naval Nationalism: Sources, Prospects, and the U.S. Response." *International Security* 34, no. 2 (Fall 2009): 46–81.

Roughead, Gary. "CNO Guidance for 2011." Navy.mil, October 2010. http://www.navy.mil/features/CNOG%202011.pdf.

Roy, Mihir. *Maritime Security in South West Asia*. New Delhi: Society for Indian Ocean Studies, 2002. http://www.iips.org/Roy-paper.pdf (accessed 19 March 2012).

Royal Canadian Navy. *Leadmark: The Navy's Strategy for 2020*. Ottawa, 6 August 2002. http://www.navy.dnd.ca/leadmark/doc/part1_e.asp.

Rushd, Abu. "A Sea of Capability." *Defense Management Journal*, no. 56. http://www.defencemanagement.com (accessed 20 March 2012).

"Russia Halts Aircraft Carrier Building." UPI, 10 December 2010. http://www.upi.com/Business_News/Security-Industry/2010/12/10/Russia-halts-aircraft-carriers-building/UPI-38401292018235/.

"Russia Scales Back Arms Sales to China." WantChinaTimes.com 17 January 2012. http://bbs.chinadaily.com.cn/thread-728283-1-1.html.

"Russia to Deploy Cruise Missiles on Kuril Islands." Xinhua, 2 March 2011. http://news.xinhuanet.com/english2010/world/2011–03/02/c_13757988.htm.

"Russia to Send New Anti-Piracy Force to Gulf of Aden." RIA Novosti, 28 March 2012. http://en.rian.ru/mlitary_news/20120327/172427290.html.

"Sailing on a Harmonious Sea: A Chinese Perspective." *Global Asia* 5, no. 4 (Winter 2010). http://www.globalasia.org/V5N4_Winter_2010/Yang_Mingjie.html?PHPSESSID=85334648f6085f2a1b817371decea408.

Sajima, Naolo, and Kyoichi Tachikawa. *Japanese Sea Power: A Maritime Nation's Struggle for Identity*. Canberra, ACT, Australia: Sea Power Centre, 2009.

Sakhuja, Vijay. "Maritime Multilateralism: China's Strategy for the Indian Ocean." Jamestown Foundation *China Brief* 9, no. 22 (4 November 2010). http://www.jamestown.org/programs/chinabrief/single/?tx_ttnews%5Btt_news%5D=3569 (accessed 12 May 2012).

Samaranayake, Nilanthi. "Are Sri Lanka's Relations with China Deepening? An Analysis of Economic, Military, and Diplomatic Data." *Asian Security* 7, no. 2 (2011): 119–46.

———. *The Long Littoral Project: Bay of Bengal—A Maritime Perspective on Indo-Pacific Security.* CNA Report IRP-2012-U-002319-Final. Alexandria, Va.: Center for Naval Analyses, 2012.

Samuels, Richard J. "New Fighting Power?" *International Security* 32, no. 3 (Winter 2007/08). http://belfercenter.ksg.harvard.edu/publication/17970/new_fighting_power_japans_growing_maritime_capabilities_and_east_asian_security.html.

Sane, C. M. "Functioning of the Aviation Arm of the Indian Navy." *Comptroller and Auditor General of India*, 2010. http://www.cag.gov.in/html/reports/defence/2010–11_7AFN-PA/chap2.pdf (accessed 13 May 2012).

Saunders, Stephen, ed. *Jane's Fighting Ships, 2011–2012.* Coulsden, Surrey: Jane's Information Group, 2011.

Sawhney, Ashok. *Indian Naval Effectiveness for National Growth.* RSIS Working Paper 197. Singapore: Rajaratnam School of International Studies, 7 May 2010.

Scanlan, Craig. "Socotora Rock (Ieodo, Suyan) Tensions Continue to Increase as Regional Naval Powers Continue to Grow." New Pacific Institute *Asia Security Watch*, 15 March 2012. http://asw.newpacificinstitute.org/?attachment_id=10615 (accessed 2 August 2012).

"Scarborough Shoal Issue Reaches UN." *Sun Star,* 5 May 2012. http://www.sunstar.com.ph/manila/local-news/2012/05/05/scarborough-shoal-issue-reaches-un-219938.

"SDF Readies Overseas Base in Djibouti: 1st Outpost Abroad to Fight Piracy." *Yomiuri Shimbun,* 29 May 2011. http://www.yomiuri.co.jp/dy/national/T110528002667.htm.

"Seapower 21." Navy.mil. http://www.navy.mil/navydata/cno/Proceedings.html.

Selth, Andrew. *Chinese Military Bases in Burma: The Explosion of a Myth.* Griffith Asia Institute Regional Outlook Paper 10. Nathan, Qld., Australia, 2007. http://www.griffith.edu.au/__data/assets/pdf_file/0018/18225/regional-outlook-andrew-selth.pdf (accessed 6 May 2012).

"Seychelles Invites China to Set Up Anti-Piracy Presence." Agence France-Press, 2 December 2011. http://www.google.com/hostednews/afp/article/ALeqM5hzLeEjtGSSVemRHFDVibF9PygyrQ?docId=CNG.b29b9b135996dff1204f4d15809adf61.611.

Shambaugh, David. *Modernizing China's Military.* Berkeley: University of California Press, 2004.

Shen Shu and Qin Ruoyun. "PLA Navy Opens First Training Class for Escort Mission." *PLA Daily,* 15 February 2012. http://eng.mod.gov.cn/DefenseNews/index.htm.

Shi Xiaoqin. "The Boundaries and Directions of China's Sea Power." In *Twenty-First Century Seapower: Cooperation and Conflict at Sea,* edited by Peter Dutton, Robert Ross, and Oysteign Tunsjo, chap. 23. London: Taylor & Francis, 2012.

"Ships Increasingly Turning to Armed Guards to Combat Piracy." [U.S.] *Homeland Security Newswire–Maritime Security,* 19 May 2011. http://www.homelandsecuritynewswire.com/ships-increasingly-turning-armed-guards-combat-piracy.

Singh, Bhubhindar, and Philip Shetler-Jones. *Japan's New Security Imperative: The Function of Globalization.* RSIS Working Paper 209. Singapore: Rajaratnam School of International Studies, 11 October 2010. http://www.rsis.edu.sg/publications/WorkingPapers/WP209.pdf.

Singh, Mandip. *Proposed PLAN Naval Base in Seychelles and India's Options.* IDSA Comment. New Delhi: Institute for Defence Studies and Analyses, 15 December 2011. http://www.idsa.in/idsacomments/TheProposedPLANavalBaseinSeychellesandIndiasOptions_msingh_151211 (accessed 3 June 2012).

"Sino-Russian Drills Enter Live-Fire Stage." Xinhua, 26 April 2012. http://news.xinhuanet.com/english/china/2012–04/25/c_131549771.htm.

"Sixth Pacific Islands Leaders Meeting (PALM 6) Okinawa 'Kizuna' Declaration." *Ministry of Foreign Affairs of Japan,* n.d. http://www.mofa.go.jp/region/asia-paci/palm/palm6/kizuna_en.html.

Skypek, Thomas M. *China's Sea-Based Nuclear Deterrent in 2020: Four Alternative Futures for China's SSBN Fleet.* A Collection of Papers from the 2010 Nuclear Scholars' Initiative. Washington, D.C.: Center for Strategic and International Studies, 2010. http://csis.org/files/publication/110916_Skypek.pdf (accessed 16 May 2012).

"SLPA to Fast Track Construction of New Deepwater Berth in Colombo Port's South Harbor." *Port Technology International,* 12 December 2011. http://www.porttechnology.org/news/slpa_to_fast_track_construction_of_new_deepwater_berth_in_colombo_ports_south.

Smith, Hazel. *North Korean Shipping: A Potential for WMD Proliferation?* Analysis from the East-West Center 87. Honolulu, February 2009. http://www.eastwestcenter.org/sites/default/files/private/api087.pdf (accessed 26 May 2012).

Song Taisheng and Dong Yongjun. "China's Aircraft Carrier Returns from Sixth Sea Trial Lasting a Total of Nine Days." *Zhongguo Xinwen She Online,* 15 May 2012. OSC- CPP20120515503003.

Song Yann-Huei and Zou Keyuan. "Maritime Legislation of Mainland China and Taiwan: Developments, Comparison, Implications, and Potential Challenges for the United States." *Ocean Development & International Law* 31, no. 4 (October 2000): 303–34.

Soverino, Rudolph. "Toward a Code of Conduct in the South China Sea." *East Asia Forum,* 11 August 2012. http://www.eastasiaforum.org/2012/08/11/toward-a-code-of-conduct-for-the-south-china-sea/ (accessed 30 August 2012).

Spears, Joseph. "The Snow Dragon Moves into the Arctic Ocean Basin." Jamestown Foundation *China Brief* 11, no. 2 (28 January 2012). http://www.jamestown.org/programs/chinabrief/single/?tx_ttnews%5Btt_

news%5D=37429&tx_ttnews%5BbackPid%5D=25&cHash=ed639f4996 (accessed 6 June 2012).

Spykman, Nicholas. *America's Strategy in World Politics: The United States and the Balance of Power.* New York: Harcourt, Brace, 1942.

Sri Lanka Navy. http://www.navy.lk/.

"Sri Lanka Port and Infrastructure Improvements Continue with Support from China." U.S. Army Asian Studies Detachment OSIR: ASD11F08093, 8 August 2011. No longer available online.

Sri Lanka Ports Authority. http://www.slpa.lk/port_hambantota.asp?chk=4.

Stephens, David. *A Critical Vulnerability: The Impact of the Submarine Threat on Australia's Maritime Defense 1915–54.* Paper in Australian Maritime Affairs, no. 15. Canberra, ACT: Australia Sea Power Center. 2003.

Stewart, Phil, and Paul Eckert. "No Big U.S. Naval Buildup in Asia, Top Officer Says." Reuters, 10 January 2012. http://www.reuters.com/article/2012/01/10/us-usa-asia-military-idUSTRE8092CG20120110.

Storry, Richard. *Double Patriots: A Study of Japanese Nationalism.* London: Chatto and Windus, 1957.

"Strategy 2017: Creating Our Nation's Wealth Together." *Seychelles Government Portal.* http://www.egov.sc/documents/strategy2017.pdf.

Sumida, Jon Tetsuro. *Inventing Strategy and Teaching Command: The Classic Works of Alfred Thayer Mahan Reconsidered.* Washington, D.C.: Woodrow Wilson Center Press, 1997.

Supriyanto, Ristian Atriandi. *"Armada Jaya XXX/11" Naval Exercise: Indonesia's Naval Strategy.* RSIS Commentary 176/2011. Singapore: Rajaratnam School of International Studies, 29 November 2011. http://www.eurasiareview.com/01122011-armada-jaya-xxx11-naval-exercise-indonesia's-naval-strategy-analysis/ (accessed 1 June 2012).

———. *Indonesia's Naval Modernization: A Sea Change?* RSIS Commentary 020/2012. Washington, D.C.: East-West Center, 27 January 2012. http://www.rsis.edu.sg/publications/Perspective/RSIS0202012.pdf (accessed 2 March 2013).

———. *Indonesia's South Sea Dilemma between Neutrality and Self-Interest.* RSIS Commentary 126/2012. Singapore: Rajaratnam School of International Studies, 12 July 2012. http://www.rsis.edu.sg/publications/Perspective/RSIS1262012.pdf (accessed 26 August 2012).

Sustaining U.S. Global Leadership: Priorities for 21st Century Defense. Washington, D.C., January 2012. www.defense.gov/news/Defense_Strategic_Guidance.pdf (accessed 7 March 2012).

Swaine, Michael. *China's Assertive Behavior.* Washington, D.C.: Carnegie Endowment for International Peace, n.d. http://carnegieendowment.org/files/CLM34MS_FINAL.pdf.

Symonds, Craig. *The Civil War at Sea: Reflections on the Civil War Era.* Santa Barbara, Calif.: ABC Clio, 2009.

Tan-Mullins, May. *The Implications of Seabed Energy Resource Development: The Gulf of Thailand Case.* NBR Special Report 35. Seattle, Wash.: National Bureau of Asian Research, December 2011. http://nbr.org/publications/element.aspx?id=561 (accessed 2 June 2012).

Tan Seng Chye. *ADMM+8: Adding Flesh to a New Regional Architecture.* RSIS Commentary 131/2010. Singapore: Rajaratnam School of International Studies, 15 October 2010. http://www.rsis.edu.sg/publications/Perspective/RSIS1312010.pdf (accessed 17 June 2012).

Tandon, A. R. "India and the Indian Ocean." In *Maritime India,* edited by K. K. Nayar, 22–77. New Delhi: National Maritime Foundation, 2005.

Till, Geoffrey. *Asia Rising and the Maritime Decline of the West: A Review of the Issues.* RSIS Working Paper 205. Singapore: Rajaratnam School of International Studies, 29 July 2010. http://www.rsis.edu.sg/publications/WorkingPapers/WP205.pdf (accessed 13 July 2012).

———. *Seapower: A Guide for the Twenty-First Century.* London: Taylor & Francis, 2009.

Togo, Kazuhiko. *Japan's Territorial Problem.* Seattle, Wash.: National Bureau of Asian Research, 8 May 2012. http://www.nbr.org/research/activity.aspx?id=247 (accessed 17 May 2012).

Torode, Greg. "Beijing Wary as New US Military Strategy Emerges: PLA Officer Warns of Response to Pentagon Plan to Integrate Forces." *South China Morning Post,* 25 April 2011. http://guanyu9.blogspot.com/2011/05/beijing-wary-as-new-us-military.html.

Tran Truong Thuy. "New Round of Tension." *VietNamNet Bridge,* 30 July 2011. http://english.vietnamnet.vn/en/special-report/11076/new-round-of-tension.html.

Trenin, Dmitri. *True Partners? How Russia and China See Each Other.* London: Center for European Reform, February 2012. http://www.cer.org.uk/publications/archive/report/2012/true-partners-how-russia-and-china-see-each-other.

Tucker, Nancy Bernkopf, and Bonnie Glaser. "Should the United States Abandon Taiwan?" *Washington Quarterly* 34, no. 4 (Fall 2011): 23–37.

Tunsjø, Øystein. *Security and Profits in China's Energy Policy: Hedging against Risk.* New York: Columbia University Press, forthcoming.

Turner, Stansfield. "Missions of the U.S. Navy." *Naval War College Review* 26, no. 5 (March/April 1974): 2–17.

"Twelfth Five-Year Plan on Guangdong's Economic Development Principally Approved by Provincial Government." *China Ocean News,* 17 January 2012. http://www.newsgd.com/specials/12thFive-Year/default.htm.

"Twelfth Five-Year Plan on Guangxi's Ocean Economic Development Approved." *Guangxi Daily,* 14 November 2011. http://eastasia.makeoffer.mobi/category/guangxi-beibu-bay-economic-zone-development-plan.

"12th Five-Year Plan on Hainan's Economic and Social Development." *Hainan Daily,* 3 March 2012. No longer online.

"Twelfth Five-Year Plan on National Economic and Social Development."
Xinhua, 16 March 2011. http://news.xinhuanet.com/english/china/2012–
03/16/c_131471892.htm.

Twomey, Christopher P. "Asia's Complex Strategic Environment: Nuclear
Multipolarity and Other Dangers," *Asia Policy,* no. 11 (January 2011):
51–78.

"U.N. Approves Japan's Claim on Wider Seas." *Yomiuri Shimbun,* 29 April
2012. http://www.yomiuri.co.jp/dy/national/T120428003634.htm.

United Nations. *Review of Maritime Transport: 2011.* Conference on Trade
and Development Report, UNCTAD/RMT/2011. New York, 2011. http://
unctad.org/en/docs/rmt2011_en.pdf.

———. "Universal Declaration of Human Rights." *United Nations.* http://www
.un.org/en/documents/udhr/.

U.S. Department of Defense. *PLA Modernization Areas, 2000–2010: Annual
Report to Congress—Military and Security Developments Involving the
PRC.* Washington, D.C., 2010. http://www.defense.gov/pubs/pdfs/2010_
CMPR_Final.pdf.

———. U.S. Defense Dept., *A Report to Congress Pursuant to the National
Defense Authorization Act for Fiscal Year 2000.* Washington, D.C.: Office
of the Secretary of Defense, 2011.

———. *Sustaining U.S. Global Leadership: Priorities for 21st Century Defense.*
Washington, D.C., January 2012. http://www.defense.gov/news/Defense_
Strategic_Guidance.pdf.

U.S. Department of State. *Joint Statement of the Security Consultative
Committee.* Washington, D.C., 26 April 2012. http://www.state.gov/r/pa/
prs/ps/2012/04/188586.htm.

———. "Signing of the Manila Declaration on Board the USS *Fitzgerald* in
Manila Bay, Manila, Philippines." *U.S. Department of State,* 16 November
2011. http://www.state.gov/r/pa/prs/ps/2011/11/177226.htm.

U.S. Energy Information Administration. *South China Sea.* Washington, D.C.,
1994. http://www.eia.gov.

———. *World Oil Transit Chokepoints.* Washington, D.C., 30 December 2011.
http://www.eia.doe.gov.

*U.S. Force Posture Strategy in the Asia Pacific Region: An Independent
Assessment.* Washington, D.C.: Center for Strategic and International
Studies, July 2012. csis.org/files/publication/120814_FINAL_PACOM_
optimized.pdf (accessed 22 August 2012).

U.S.-Japan-India Strategic Dialogue. Washington, D.C.: Center for Strategic and
International Studies, 18 October 2011. http://csis.org/publication/us-japan-
india-strategic-dialogue-2011.

"U.S. Merchant Marine/U.S. Merchant Fleet." *Global Security,* 20 July 2007.
http://www.globalsecurity.org/military/systems/ship/merchant-marine.htm.

U.S. National Imagery and Mapping Agency. *Distances between Ports.* Pub. 151.
10th ed. Bethesda, Md., 1999.

"U.S. Policy on Spratly Islands and South China Sea." *Department of State Daily Press Briefings,* 10 May 1995. http://dosfan.lib.uic.edu/ERC/briefing/daily_briefings/1995/9505/950510db.htm.

"US to Deploy LCS in Singapore in 2012," Xinhua, 3 June 2012. http://news.xinhuanet.com/english/world/2012-06/02/c_131627418.htm.

Valencia, Mark J., and Jon M. Van Dyke. "Vietnam's National Interests and the Law of the Sea." *Ocean Development and International Law* 25, no. 2 (1994): 219–29.

Varma, K. J. M. "Indian Warships to Dock at Chinese Port after 6 Yrs' Gap." *Indian Express,* 12 June 2012. http://www.indianexpress.com/news/indian-warships-to-dock-at-chinese-port-after-6-yrs-gap/961018/.

Vaughan, Andrew. "Canada's Stuck with Second-Hand Subs until 2030, Navy Says." *Canadian Press,* 27 February 2012. http://www.cbc.ca/news/canada/story/2012/02/27/submarines-2030.html.

Venugopalan, Urmila. "Pakistan's Black Pearl." *Foreign Policy,* 3 June 2011. http://search.yahoo.com/search?ei=utf-8&fr=aaplw&p=pakistan's+black+pearl (accessed 9 April 2012).

"Vietnam Slams China Sea Survey in Disputed Area." Agence France-Presse, 9 August 2011. http://www.google.com/hostednews/afp/article/ALeqM5hibGCagATLfYsp6dYFFQjt57PQpw?docId=CNG.b67300196a0d906b8819cbbadd1aeba1.81.

Vijian, P. "India-Thailand Ties Shift Gear on Republic Day." *Bernama,* 26 January 2012. http://www.bernama.com/bernama/v6/newsgeneral.php?id=642309.

Vogel, Ezra. *Deng Xiaoping and the Transformation of China.* Cambridge, Mass.: Harvard University Press, 2011.

———. *Japan as Number One: Lessons for America.* Cambridge, Mass.: Harvard College, 1979.

Von Clausewitz. *On War.* Edited and translated by Michael Howard and Peter Paret. Princeton, N.J.: Princeton University Press, 1989.

Wachman, Alan. *Why Taiwan? Geostrategic Rationales for China's Territorial Integrity.* Palo Alto, Calif.: Stanford University Press, 2007.

Walsh, Eddie. *Australia's Military Capabilities Up in the Air.* ISN Insights. Zurich, Switz.: International Relations and Security Network, 19 September 2011. http://www.africanewsanalysis.com/2011/09/20/australia's-military-capabilities-up-in-the-air-by-eddie-walsh-for-isn-insights/.

Walton, Timothy. *China's Three Warfares.* Delex Special Report 3. Herndon, Va.: Delex Systems, 18 January 2012. http://www.delex.com/pub/dsr/Three%20Warfares.pdf.

Wang Chuanjian. "India's South China Sea Policy: Intentions, Impact." *Waijiao Pinglun* (Beijing), 25 June 2010: 107–22. OSC-CPP20110324671004.

Wang Qian. "New Ship to Boost Arctic Expeditions." *China Daily,* 24 February 2012. http://www.chinadaily.com.cn/cndy/2012-02/24/content_14681412.htm.

Weatherbee, Donald E. *China, the Philippines, and the US Security Guarantee.* PacNet 28. Honolulu: Center for Strategic and International Studies, 26

April 2012. http://csis.org/publication/pacnet-28-china-philippines-and-us-security-guarantee (accessed 8 September 2012).

Webb, Jason, ed. "Pakistan Hands Management of Strategic Gwadar Port to China." Reuters, 18 February 2013. http://news.yahoo.com/pakistan-hands-management-strategic-gwadar-port-china-164350339.html.

Weisgerber, Marcus. "Panetta: Partnerships, Training Focus of U.S. Pacific Strategy." *Stars and Stripes*, 11 June 2012. http://www.stripes.com/news/panetta-us-strategy-aims-to-build-peace-stability-in-pacific-1.179256.

White, Hugh. *The China Choice: Why America Should Share Power.* Collingwood, Australia: Black, 2011.

Willmott, Hedley P. *The Great Crusade.* London: Reed, 1990.

Wines, Michael. "Dispute between Vietnam and China Escalates over Competing Claims in South China Sea." *New York Times*, 10 June 2011. http://www.nytimes.com/2011/06/11/world/asia/11vietnam.html.

Wishik, Anton Lee. "An Anti-Access Approximation: The PLA's Active Strategic Counterattacks on Exterior Lines." *China Security*, no. 19 (2011): 37–48. http://www.chinasecurity.us/index.php?option=com_content&view=article&id=48 (accessed 14 May 2012).

"World Oil Transit Chokepoints." *U.S. Energy Information Administration (EIA)*, 30 December 2011. http://www.eia.doe.gov (accessed 8 March 2012).

Wu Jiao and Xin Dingding. "Adviser Says Coast Guard Needed for Maritime Disputes." *China Daily*, 6 March 2012. http://www.chinadaily.com.cn/cndy/2012–03/06/content_14763060.htm.

Wu Jilu and Zhang Haiwen. "Freedom of the Seas and the Law of the Sea: A Chinese Perspective." In *Twenty-First Century Seapower: Cooperation and Conflict at Sea,* edited by Peter Dutton, Robert Ross, and Øystein Tunsjø, chap. 16. London: Taylor & Francis, 2012.

Wu Zhong. "PLA Fires Budget Guns." *Asia Times*, 9 March 2011. http://www.atimes.com/atimes/China/MC09Ad01.html.

Wylie, J. S. *Military Strategy.* New Brunswick, N.J.: Rutgers University Press, 1967; Annapolis, Md.: Naval Institute Press, 1989.

Xia Wenhui. "Maintaining 'Safety Valve' in South China Sea Vital." Xinhua, 13 January 2012. http://www.philstar.com/article.aspx?articleid=767655&publicationsubcategoryid=200.

Xu Yang. "Air Drones Scan China's Seas." *People's Daily*, 1 December 2011. http://english.peopledaily.com.cn/90786/7662461.html.

Yamaguchi, Mari. "Japan to Continue Paying $2 Billion for US Troops." *Washington Post*, 14 December 2010. http://www.washingtonpost.com/wp-dyn/content/article/2010/12/14/AR2010121401711_pf.html.

Yang Yi. "Chinese Officials for the First Time Make Public Criticism of the United States' Air Sea Battle." Xinhua, 12 December 2011. In *A Translation of Yang Yi's Xinhua Article on Air Sea Battle,* edited and translated by Timothy A. Walton and Bryan McGrath. Delex Special Report 2. Herndon, Va.: Delex

Systems, 15 December 2011. http://www.delex.com/pub/dsr/Delex%20CSA-Translation%20of%20Yang%20Yi%20Article%20on%20AirSea%20Battle.pdf.

———. "For Strategic China-US Ties." *China Daily*, 16 February 2011. http://www.chinadaily.com.cn/opinion/2011–02/16/content_12022458.htm.

Yu, Miles. "Inside China: China, Russia to Hold Drill near Korea." *Washington Times*, 18 April 2012. http://www.washingtontimes.com/news/2012/apr/18/inside-china-china-russia-to-hold-drill-near-korea/.

Yuan Peng. "Awaiting the Handshake: China-US Relations Are the Key to Stability in Northeast Asia." *Global Asia* 6, no. 2 (Summer 2011). http://www.globalasia.org/V6N2_Summer_2011/Yuan_Peng.html.

Yung, Christopher, and Ross Rustici, with Isaac Kardon and Joshua Wiseman. *China's Out of Area Naval Operations: Case Studies, Trajectories, Obstacles, and Potential Solutions*. China Strategic Perspectives 3. Washington, D.C.: National Defense University Press, 2012. http://www.ndu.edu/inss/docuploaded/ChinaStrategicPerspectives3.pdf (accessed 7 September 2012).

Zakir, Hussain. "Asean Nations Welcome US Pivot." *Straits Times*, 27 November 2011, 28. http://www.asean-society.org/asean/special-report-asean-nations-welcome-us-pivot-maritimesecurity/.

Zhang Haiwen. "Is It Safeguarding the Navigation or Maritime Hegemony of the United States?" *Chinese Journal of International Law* (2010): 31–47.

Zhang Haiwen and Liu Qing. "Sincerity Needed to Solve South China Sea Dispute." *People's Daily*, 23 October 2011. http://english.peopledaily.com.cn/90780/7619141.html.

Zhang Haizhou. "China-Made Frigate Ready to Set Sail for Pakistan." *China Daily*, 5 April 2008. http://www.chinadaily.com.cn/china/2008–04/05/content_6593319.htm.

Zhang Haizhou and Zhang Chunyan. "Japan Joins Elite Aircraft Carrier Club." *China Daily*, 9 March 2011. http://www.cdeclips.com/en/world/fullstory.html?id=61929.

Zhang Tuosheng. "East Asian Territorial and Maritime Rights Disputes and Their Political and Economic Implications." *Modern International Relations* (27 February 2011): 120–27. Translated by Anton Wishik.

Zhao Shengnan. "PLA Navy Calls for More Cooperation against Piracy." *China Daily*, 24 February 2012. http://www.chinadaily.com.cn/china/2012–02/24/content_14680613.htm.

Zhong Sheng. "Hold Firm to the Main Trend in China-ASEAN Relations." *Renmin Ribao Online*, 5 April 2012. OSC-CPP20120405702001.

Zhou Siyu. "Boomtime Buys Lead to Bust." *China Daily*, 14 December 2011. http://www.chinadaily.com.cn/business/2011–12/14/content_14263475.htm.

Zhou Wa. "Chinese Fishermen Face Arrest by ROK." *China Daily*, 2 May 2012. http://news.xinhuanet.com/english/china/2012–05/02/c_131562909.htm.

Zhu Chenghu. "Speech," July 2011. http://opinion.huanqiu.com/roll/2011–07/1792964.html.

Zisk, Katerzinya. "Russia's Naval Ambitions: Driving Forces and Constraints." In *Twenty-First Century Seapower: Cooperation and Conflict at Sea*, edited by Peter Dutton, Robert Ross, and Øystein Tusnjø, chap 7. London: Routledge, 2012.

Index

regional security missions, 62–63,
65–73, 75–77, 206, 220n8;
Russia, naval war between, 24,
76, 78, 167, 193, 195; sea and
SLOCs, importance of, 61, 71,
76, 223n34; shipbuilding industry,
61, 203, 220n2; shipping and
commerce interests, 73, 76–77;
SLOC protection by, 64–65, 66, 73,
221n12; South Korea, relationship
with, 77, 88, 196, 226n32;
strategic position and importance
of, 194–95; technology use by,
196; territory and sovereignty
disputes, 33, 68, 70–71, 195;
UNCLOS provisions, interpretation
of, 71–72; US, relationship with,
66–67, 69, 74, 77, 90–91; Vietnam,
relationship with, 67; World War II
and expansionist policies of, 78–79;
World War II and treatment of
POW and civilian populations, 90;
World War II strategy against, 3,
18, 25–28, 40, 193, 207

Korean War, 43, 64
Kuril Islands, 6, 7, 14, 71, 84, 89, 167
Kuwait, 12, 163, 199

land power, sea power to control, 5,
17, 214n19
Laos, 111, 191
law enforcement, 209, 254n24
Lehman, John, 43–44
littoral law enforcement, 191
Liu Huaqing, 96–99, 113, 197,
254n19

Mahan, Alfred Thayer, 15–16, 18, 39,
165, 181, 192, 214n23, 245–46n32
Malacca Strait, 10–11, 114, 121, 128,
140, 182, 199, 207–8
Malaysia: ASEAN participation, 111,
123; commons, dependence on, 5;
counterterrorism activities, 201;
economic growth and power, 2, 4;

Five-Power Defense Arrangement,
197–98, 205; geography of, 9, 10,
123; Indian naval exercise program,
participation in, 149; maritime
strategies and policies, 123; naval
power and modernization, 20, 37,
123, 197, 203; South China Sea,
sovereignty claims in, 14, 201;
UNCLOS provisions and EEZ
claims and disputes, 33, 123, 131,
171; US, relationship with, 57–58,
194; US naval port facilities in, 198
Maldives: geography of, 12; India,
relationship with, 149, 199;
maritime strategies and policies,
160–61
maritime power: basis for strong,
16; Chinese power status, 5,
37, 191, 197, 207–8, 210, 211,
254n19; commerce, trade, and
shipping and, 16, 204; continental
and maritime power status, 17,
114, 196, 232n62; economics,
economic power, and, 16, 39, 191,
202, 203–4; European maritime
power in Asia, 3, 192; naval power
compared to, 16, 17; sea power
compared to, 16; US power status,
5–6, 37, 190–91, 206–7, 210–11
maritime strategies and policies:
application of, 193; defense-budget
realities and, 20, 190; definition
and schools of thought on, 15–20,
39, 192; development and adoption
of, 19–20, 193, 215n25; effective
and successful strategy, 19, 20, 28;
examples of, 23–29; flexibility of,
19; future strategies for region,
209–11; geopolitical status of
Asia and application of, 3, 193,
207; globalization and, 202–3;
independence of naval forces and,
202; major strategy, 19; national
interests and, 190; national security
and defense interests and, 1–2;
naval planning, 202; naval strategy